TARS

Also by Tim Clayton

FINEST HOUR

END OF THE BEGINNING

TRAFALGAR: the Men, the Battle, the Storm
(all with Phil Craig)

From the author of *Finest Hour* and *Trafalgar*

TARS

THE MEN WHO MADE BRITAIN
RULE THE WAVES

TIM CLAYTON

HODDER &
STOUGHTON

Copyright © 2007 by Tim Clayton

First published in Great Britain in 2007 by Hodder & Stoughton
A division of Hodder Headline

A Hodder & Stoughton book

1

A CIP catalogue record for this title is available from the British Library

ISBN 978 0 340 89802 4

Typeset in Bembo by Hewer Text UK Ltd, Edinburgh
Printed and bound by Clays Ltd, St Ives plc

Hodder Headline's policy is to use papers that are natural, renewable
and recyclable products and made from wood grown in sustainable
forests. The logging and manufacturing processes are expected to
conform to the environmental regulations of the country of origin.

Hodder & Stoughton Ltd
A division of Hodder Headline
338 Euston Road
London NW1 3BH

Contents

Author's Note

The Seven Years War (1756–63) was the war from which Britain emerged as the world's major power – its first global power. In fighting it, Britain's most powerful weapon was the Royal Navy. This is the story of the overlapping crews of two ships in that war, *Monmouth* and *Dragon* – a story that illustrates 'that remarkable superiority British seamen have over others, on all important occasions' and reveals some of the reasons why those British tars were so very proficient.

The incomprehensible language spoken by seamen was a commonplace of Georgian humour. It remains extremely difficult to avoid naval solecisms while trying to describe sea-fights and voyages in a way that can be understood by those who are not familiar with sea-terms and maritime jargon. I hope that genuine seamen will be charitable with this land-lubber's effort to describe life at sea to other landsmen. For those who fall foul of unfamiliar terminology, the glossary and the *dramatis personae* or list of ship's companies should provide some bearings.

Manuscripts have been transcribed exactly, as far as possible, without the use of *sic*, except that superscript has been regularised and all ship names italicised. Documents transcribed from printed collections, however, have sometimes already been modernised by their editors.

Where commonly understood British versions of foreign place names exist I have used them. So Belle-Île is Belle Isle, Livorno is Leghorn, Ouessant is Ushant.

At this date the pound sterling comprised twenty shillings of twelve pence. A guinea was one pound and one shilling.

Tim Clayton, April 2007

I

A Question of Honour

What they remembered most clearly about Captain Gardiner that day was his grim determination. From the instant he saw the signal for a general chase displayed by the flagship in the grey first light, Gardiner was intent on pursuit. He had the fastest ship in the Royal Navy. At his command topmen raced up the shrouds and edged along the lowered yard seventy feet above the deck, with their feet on the rope beneath. Untying the reefknots in the lines that held the sail to the yard, they shook two reefs out of the topsails. On deck they hauled the yards back up while the topmen saw them clear of any snags. With this spread of canvas the *Monmouth* surged forward on the light northerly breeze. The next order rapped out, 'Up topgallant yards', and expectant hands responded instantly. Gardiner knew how speedily his men could do these routine tasks. His attention was fixed on the two fleeing ships ahead of him.

It was the last, cold, misty dawn of February 1758. Off Cartagena in south-eastern Spain the fourteen vessels of Admiral Henry Osborn's Mediterranean squadron strung out according to their relative speed. *Monmouth* soon drew clear. Lieutenant James Baron recorded in his log that 'we gave chace steering for the headmost as we now plainly perceiv'd em to be french men of war'.

Britain had been at war with France since 1756. Tension in America had caused the struggle, and it was there that Britain aimed to resolve it with a powerful attack on the French stronghold of Louisbourg. Since early December 1757 a French squadron had been lying at Cartagena awaiting a reinforcement of four ships from Toulon, before breaking through the Strait of Gibraltar to reinforce

New France, now Canada, the French province in America. Britain aimed to conquer New France and to achieve this it was imperative to stop French reinforcements getting there. With this heavy responsibility weighing on his mind, Admiral Osborn had been guarding the Strait, fearful of missing the enemy in more open water. But two days ago, with a strong westerly wind behind him and a report that the French were at sea, he had risked sailing in search of them. The wind had turned northerly, but, finding the French were not in Almeria Bay where he had expected them to be, Osborn stood on and rounded Cabo de Gata, where the coast of Spain turns north and the Mediterranean opens out.

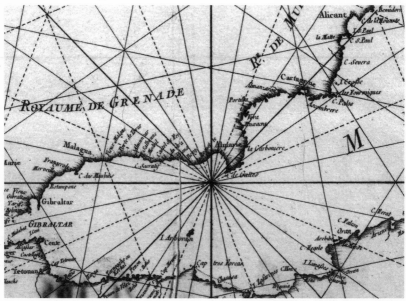

French chart showing the coastline from Gibraltar to Cartagena.

The British squadron reached a position west of the cape and south of Cartagena under cover of darkness. The wind dropped away. Before dawn they discovered the unfamiliar sails. Once the light was clear it was not long before those eager British officers who owned telescopes made out four French men-of-war – unmistakable, despite the cross of the Knights of Malta flown by one of them as a disguise – and quite possibly the anticipated reinforcement from

Toulon. The French ships had been trying to get in to Cartagena but had been driven south and scattered by the strong northerly of the previous day.

If this was the squadron from Toulon, Gardiner reasoned, then *Monmouth*'s 'chase' was the famous *Foudroyant*. She was now the flagship of Ange Duquesne, whose expansive policies while he was Governor of New France had sparked off this conflict which would come to be known as the Seven Years War. She was 185 feet long, twelve feet longer than the largest British battleship, and at fifty feet almost as wide. The captain of a privateer that *Monmouth* had seized six weeks ago had boasted that the *Foudroyant* was the finest vessel afloat – 'she was not to be taken: she would fight, he said, to-day, and tomorrow, and next-day, but never could be taken.' She was alarmingly bigger than the 151-foot *Monmouth* and far more powerful, having eighty guns to *Monmouth*'s sixty-four. But would she be faster? Although *Monmouth* had never yet been beaten in a race, *Foudroyant* had a very long lead. She was steering a course parallel with the shore, as close to Cartagena as the northerly allowed. *Monmouth* was gaining on her, but the breeze, gradually shifting westerly, was ever feebler. The last day of February was short. Darkness might well frustrate them. So might Admiral la Clue's larger squadron, should he choose to come out of Cartagena.

Far away to the south, Captain Augustus Hervey was assessing his options. He had set off after one Frenchman, which he could now tell was a sixty-four-gun ship like his own *Hampton Court*, but to his frustration he had been overtaken by the faster *Revenge* and *Berwick*, even though he 'had every sail set and were getting up fast with my chase'. That slow-sailing French ship was hugging the wind, steering straight for the safety of Cartagena. Two more British ships were chasing another Frenchman, who ran for the coast and eventually took shelter under the castle at Águilas; Hervey reckoned the greater danger lay with Gardiner, his friend and former shipmate. 'Perceiving the *Monmouth* after the largest', he noted in his journal, 'I bore away after her to assist her, as I saw the *Swiftsure* a great way from the *Monmouth*.'

Judging the detached ships sufficient to beat the French if they caught them, Admiral Osborn gathered the rest of his fleet in a body to follow up slowly towards Cartagena in case the French Admiral chose to come out and fight. He signalled *Hampton Court* to rejoin. Hervey, however, 'kept pursuing this chace, which I then was certain was Monsieur du Quesne in the *Foudroyant*' and ignored Osborn's order 'as I thought he could not distinguish, as I could, the force of the ship and the superiority of it to the *Monmouth*'.

By four o'clock the main body of the fleet was out of Gardiner's sight. The French frigate made sail off to the eastward to make good her escape to the open sea, reckoning the *Foudroyant* could handle the *Monmouth* alone. *Monmouth*'s officers could see that they were now 'coming up wth: the chase very fast'. *Revenge* and *Berwick* were in sight chasing the sixty-four, 'the *Swiftsure* & *Hampton Court* in chase wth: us but at a great Distce:'. The only thing deterring *Foudroyant* from blasting *Monmouth* was that if she turned to fight she might end up fighting those two ships as well. That was what Gardiner must make Duquesne do. His duty was clear. Lieutenant John Campbell of Whitmore's Regiment was the officer commanding a detachment of soldiers put aboard to reinforce *Monmouth*'s marines. He recalled that, as they drew closer to the *Foudroyant* and a fight became more certain, Gardiner remarked to him, 'Whatever becomes of you and I, this ship will go into Gibraltar.'

Arthur Gardiner had come close to the *Foudroyant* before, and the fact that they had not fought then was the root cause of his present misery. On that occasion, nearly two years ago off Minorca, he had been captain of his patron Admiral Byng's flagship. *Foudroyant* had been the enemy flagship. After an inconclusive battle, Byng had withdrawn his fleet and the important British Mediterranean base at Minorca had surrendered to the French. It was a catastrophic beginning to the present war at sea. Admiral Byng had been recalled to London for trial by court martial and Gardiner had gone with him as a witness. The complaint was that Byng had not done his utmost to destroy the enemy. Under oath, Gardiner was asked whether all sail had been set and he answered that it had not. Asked whether he had urged the admiral to attack, he replied that 'he advised the admiral to bear down, but that he objected thereto'. These answers were damaging evidence against Byng. The court martial found him guilty and sentenced him to death, but recommended mercy. King George II insisted that the admiral be shot.

Captain Gardiner felt doubly guilty. In the eyes of the Admiral's enemies he was a favourite of Byng and deeply involved in his disgrace. In the eyes of his friends, in giving evidence that worked against Byng he had betrayed his shipmate and patron. Gardiner was a tall, sensitive Irishman from County Wicklow and he felt both accusations bitterly. It was observed that a settled melancholy had affected him since the trial.

The war had continued to go badly with repeated defeats on land. In America the scalps of British officers decorated the lodges of Indians allied with the French; in Germany British forces were driven from King George II's beloved homeland Hanover. The press had begun to make fun of Britain's armed forces. The *London Evening Post* published a spoof petition from the women of Kent who begged to be made eligible to serve as generals and admirals since the men were failing so miserably. Gardiner took such slurs personally. He had heard rumours that First Lord Anson himself had insinuated that he was a coward. An officer of the *Volunteer* privateer reported that Gardiner had revealed his steely unhappiness to an army colonel and a merchant at Gibraltar:

> Captain Gardiner, two days before he left this port with great anguish of soul told them, that my lord Anson had reflected on him, and told him that he was one of the men that had brought disgrace upon the nation, that it touched him excessively, but that it ran strongly in his mind, that he should have an opportunity shortly to convince his lordship, how much he had the honour of the nation at heart, and that he was not culpable.

Now, if the *Foudroyant* was to go into Gibraltar as an English prize, *Monmouth* had to sacrifice herself. The British officers knew that an eighty-gun ship, armed with 42-, 24- and 12-pounders should smash to matchwood a sixty-four-gun ship armed with 24-, 12- and 6-pounders. Their respective broadsides – the weight of iron they could hurl against each other – were, in British measures, 1,212 against 504 pounds. The French ship carried 880 men (863 on the day). *Monmouth*'s 466 men and boys had been reinforced with thirty soldiers, but they still numbered few more than half the French. But if the *Monmouth* could delay the *Foudroyant* by forcing her to fight, it would enable the *Swiftsure* and *Hampton Court* to catch up. Those two ships together should overwhelm the Frenchman, even if *Monmouth* could no longer help them.

By then it was quite possible that *Monmouth* would be in no condition to help them. By then she might well be a litter of smashed wood and corpses wallowing in the calm sea. There was a high likelihood that many of her people would be killed.

The Monmouths had made their wager with death when they came aboard. Lives were lost at sea routinely, most commonly without a battle. Many seamen, perhaps even most, had made wills. They did so at the start of any campaign abroad, 'considering the perils and dangers of the seas and other uncertainties of this Transitory Life', as the formula ran. Robert Spencer, quartermaster of the starboard watch, had made his will nearly ten years earlier when he had first joined the ship in August 1748, just after the birth of his daughter Temperance. Now he was 'at the conn', watching how the sails caught the wind and shouting instructions to the men at the wheel to get the course perfect. Spencer was thirty-seven years old and had rejoined *Monmouth* as soon as she commissioned in 1755. Since then he had been promoted, rated first midshipman, then quartermaster.

Spencer was one of many Monmouths who came from the peninsula that jutted out to sea opposite Plymouth on the Cornish side of the Hamoaze. Men often joined ships commanded by their local gentry, and two former captains lived there – Henry Harrison at Torpoint and George Edgcumbe at Mount Edgcumbe. William Vallack, one of the team setting the forward studding sails, had been christened at Maker Church, the prominent sea mark for Plymouth sound, serving a parish that included the villages of Cawsand, notorious for smuggling, and neighbouring Kingsand, with their twisting lanes, cobbled yards, and red-brick Elizabethan pilchard cellars.

Edward Salmon came from Maker too, though he had practically grown up in the *Monmouth*. He had joined her as a boy – Captain Harrison's servant – in 1743 and was rated ordinary seaman when he reached eighteen. When Harrison took his old ship to sea in 1755 he volunteered again and was made a midshipman, the rank of a potential officer. The following year he married a local girl. Now twenty-seven, he would celebrate his second wedding anniversary in April if he lived.

As they followed the French ship all through the long day these men had tedious hours in which to contemplate duty and the possibility of imminent death. Death was a lottery. Some would die and others would get promoted into their places. Disaster for some resulted in happiness for others. That was a fact of sea life. Casualties in sea fights were normally light, but a fight with the *Foudroyant* was likely to be a more bloody affair than normal.

One grade above Salmon was James Powell. As senior master's mate he was supervising Spencer on the quarterdeck and watching the Frenchman through his spy glass. Powell had been promoted from able seaman in autumn 1755 while the ship was at Plymouth. The promotion had required him to obtain clothes that were fit for the quarterdeck, and either that or his growing family – a wife and three children in Antony, the parish next to Maker – had caused him to be imprisoned briefly for debt the following February. The next step up for Powell was either a lieutenant's commission or a master's warrant. Whereas master's mate was just a rating that a captain might change on a whim, a commission or a warrant provided security for a family man. If Powell performed bravely in the coming fight, an accident to one of the lieutenants might just get him a permanent place as a naval officer.

A third-rate ship such as *Monmouth* had four lieutenants and

Monmouth's had been hardened by many years at sea. Only one had enjoyed the fast-track route to promotion of a gentleman's son with patronage behind him. That was James Baron, the third lieutenant. He was twenty-two and had been a lieutenant for a year and a quarter. His father was vicar of Lostwithiel, an important man in a borough controlled by the Edgcumbe family. Captain Edgcumbe had brought young James into the navy as a twelve-year-old captain's servant in 1747. A year later Baron had joined *Monmouth* when Edgcumbe took over from Harrison. After three years he had followed Edgcumbe into the *Deptford*, a ship that played a supporting role in Byng's battle of Mahon. In August 1756 he had passed for lieutenant and three months later got his first post, back in the *Monmouth*.

The other three were more experienced and had been promoted chiefly on merit. This was one of the distinctive features of this ship. In most of Europe it was usual for officers to be noblemen. In the *Monmouth* they were professionals: middling men hoping to rise through good work.

The first lieutenant, Robert Carkett, was slightly older than the captain. He had served in the navy all his adult life, rising from able seaman to midshipman, and making lieutenant in 1747. Whereas Gardiner was *Monmouth*'s third captain since she had raised her crew to wartime strength in 1755, Carkett had been first lieutenant all that time. Consequently, he knew *Monmouth*'s people very well. It was he who drew up the quarter bills displayed under the forecastle that determined where the men were stationed for their different duties. In the coming battle, he would be Gardiner's deputy, stationed near him on the quarterdeck. If they won, he had an outside chance of promotion to command his own ship.

Second lieutenant Stephen Hammick, born near Plymouth, was forty-five, two years older than the captain. He had been at sea for more than twenty years and had risen through the ratings, able to quarter-gunner to midshipman to master's mate and lieutenant in 1746. He had seen two fleet actions in *Princess Louisa* in 1747, winning £1000 or so in prize money from the capture of a French convoy after the first battle. Once again, if they beat the *Foudroyant* and he lived, there was a prospect of profit.

The junior lieutenant David Winzar was a relative foreigner, born in Dorchester and living in Weymouth. He was thirty-five. He shared with midshipman Salmon, who had joined the same day, the status of having served in *Monmouth* for longer than any other member of the crew. He had come as a midshipman with Captain Harrison and had fought as master's mate in the two victorious fleet actions against the French off Cape Finisterre in 1747. The first had brought him about £500 in prize money (about ten years' wages), the second the glory of a hard fight in which *Monmouth* took heavy casualties. When Harrison manned her again in 1755 Winzar joined immediately. In 1757 Gardiner gave him his commission. He was a thorough seaman.

The bulk of the original crew of 1755 were from Plymouth, Devon and north Cornwall, but Winzar belonged to a knot of Monmouths from Weymouth and neighbouring Melcombe Regis. Like Winzar, Richard Tizard was rated midshipman when he joined, Marmaduke Johns quartermaster and William Coffen was a quarter gunner.

Men trickled in subsequently, like Jabus Yelverton who said he was from London, but only two distinct groups had been added to the original people. The first was a haul of about fifty pressed men and volunteers produced by a recruiting drive in 1756 along the north-west coast. Among the better finds here was William Corrin, a Manxman in his mid-thirties, rated quartergunner. Some of them bore Scottish names: Walter McFarlane, Archibald Macmillan, Daniel McColl.

The second smaller group of about a dozen comprised the survivors of a troop recruited in Ireland in December 1756. The men who arrived in *Monmouth* were volunteers, but landsmen with no experience of the sea. Among them were Edward Dunn, Thomas Lawler, and Peter Hanlon, who had been taken in hired press tenders to the *Ludlow Castle* receiving ship in January 1757. There they had been deloused and given new clothes before they joined the *Monmouth* in March. (*Monmouth*'s surgeon rejected several of them as unfit for duty and sent them to hospital, never to return.) They had seen action already in their first year at sea, but the action that was coming would be of an intensity that few ships ever faced.

At present these men were deployed in the roles they always took when the ship was chasing. By sheer chance we know what some of their roles were. Quarter bills are extremely rare because they were generally thrown away, but Carkett used one of his as a cover for the journal that he submitted to the admiralty, and for that reason it has survived.

Marmaduke Johns, the Weymouth quartermaster, was on the quarterdeck 'to attend the braces'. The braces were the ropes that turned the yards on which the sails hung so as to catch the wind. They were also turned when running the yards up or down to let out reefs, for instance. His fellow townsman, able seaman William Crossman, was also on the quarterdeck – one of the team Johns directed in bracing the yards.

A similar group under the captain of the forecastle James Scott and midshipman Edward Lund went to the fore tacks – the ropes attached to the bottom corners of the fore course to keep it fixed in the right position for the wind. Lund was also responsible for making sure that the jib and staysail remained unentangled. During the chase, Gardiner gradually increased the amount of sail *Monmouth* was carrying and other men came into play. A group of quarter-gunners undertook the precarious task of mounting the studding sail booms into the boom irons to extend the yards. This meant manoeuvring cumbersome spars of wood, way out to the side of the ship, over the sea, and slipping them into place. Quarter-gunners each had charge of four of the ship's guns, for which they were responsible to the gunner. But in many ships, including *Monmouth*, they were elite seamen, chosen from the highly skilled. These quarter gunners then supervised the setting of the studding sails, the larboard ones at 'noon', the starboard ones at 'three', when *Foudroyant* altered course slightly to run almost before the wind.

Each mast had a boatswain's mate enforcing swift action and piping orders with his shrill whistle or 'boatswain's call'. The foretopmen set the foresails, usually the most important in pressing the ship forward. The chase team included John Trevillick, Richard Damerel, Anthony Stephens and William Vallack as well as a man who claimed to be a Greek, Marco Nicholas. The topmen were young, agile men who lived, much of the time, way up in the air with only ropes to trust to. A seaman wrote that the job 'not only requires alertness but courage, to ascend in a manner sky high when stormy winds do blow . . . the youngest of the topmen generally go highest.' Up the taller mainmast climbed the maintopmen, among them Archibald Macmillan.

For most of that Tuesday the more active preparations had been going on down below. Carpenter Robert Narramore, his Welsh mate David Edwards, their crew and their helpers had taken down all the partitions that made cabins on the gun decks. All furniture and unnecessary wood that might splinter rapidly disappeared. Then Narramore went down to his store in the bows of the orlop deck to prepare shot plugs of various sizes to stop up dangerous holes that might be made and to get out the spare ironwork to repair the pumps, should they sustain damage.

Further aft on the orlop deck, surgeon Robert Smith and his mates were turning what dimly lit space was available into an operating theatre. He laid out his tools, bandages and medicines, checking the sharpness of knives and saws.

Busiest of all was old gunner Jeffreys, who hurried about the semi-darkness of the lower regions of his cavernous, oaken construction, imposing order on potential chaos. He had lived in the *Monmouth* for ten years and he knew every last nook and crevice in her. He had started as a seaman, interested in cannon. He had got his gunner's warrant in 1741 and progressed, as warrant officers did, from small ships to important ones. He had moved from the *Mortar* bomb vessel to the fifth-rate *Torrington*, the fourth-rate *Hampshire*, and the third-rate *Monmouth*. He would never be the gunner of a three-decker of second or first rate because he was now very nearly eligible for his pension, needing only a few months more to reach the necessary sixteen years of service. As a standing officer he stayed with his ship in peace and war. It was his home. He was fifty-seven years old.

Jeffreys' responsibilities lay below decks, close to or below the water level, a dim realm of passages and ladders lit by lamplight. He looked after magazines, powder, cartridges, shot, guns and their carriages. He lived and slept in the gun room at the end of the two rows of his largest guns, the twenty-six 24-pounders, among stacks of arms chests containing muskets, pistols, cutlasses and pikes. This was on the lower deck, a few feet above the water. A ladder led down to the orlop deck and another shorter one to the filling room of the main magazine well below the water level. A second, smaller, hanging magazine at the same level in the stern of the ship served the aftermost guns. In these two very dry sealed chambers he kept 274 barrels of gunpowder weighing more than twelve tons. In his storeroom next to Narramore's in the bows on the orlop deck he kept the accessories required to fire the guns. Below even the magazines, acting partly as ballast, was his store of shot, mostly round shot for the 24- 12- and 6-pounders, but also grape and double-headed shot and little shot for the swivels. He kept a log, and also kept accounts of how much powder and shot was expended in practice.

Section of a First Rate Man of War. Monmouth *had only two gun decks instead of the three shown here.*

He was also head of a team. He had two mates, William Pattey and David Scott, and two yeomen of the powder room, John Lee and Richard Viney, each responsible for the handling room next to a magazine. Subordinate to him were armourer Luke Scardefield and his mate John Sympson, who were responsible for the small arms, muskets, pistols, cutlasses and pikes. They were the ship's blacksmiths, forging ironwork and repairing any broken metal parts. To fetch and carry, he had two servants, Robert Axworthy and William Vine, who were his apprentices, learning his trade. All of them were 'idlers', which meant that they worked during the day and slept at night, whereas most seamen stood watches of four hours on and four hours off.

With an engagement looming, the gunner's team could not afford a mistake. First Jeffreys unlocked the magazines. Yeomen Lee and Viney each took charge of a powder room. Their two great fears were fire and water. If the powder became damp, the guns would not fire. On the other hand, a single spark in the magazine might blow up the whole ship. Powder barrels were hooped with copper or wood, because iron hoops might spark. Before anybody could go into a powder room they had to remove anything at all that might create a spark. In the powder rooms there were 'ready-use' cartridges with charges of appropriate weight for the ship's various guns already made up and stored on racks. Since many more would be needed, new barrels of powder were taken from the magazine and opened. The yeomen supervised the filling of more cartridges, with copper scoops to measure the quantity of powder. Meanwhile, woollen screens were fixed to the doors and dampened, and the passages leading to the magazines were also wetted, in case any powder was spilled, to prevent flame reaching the magazine. The powder rooms were lit from adjacent light rooms screened with glass and copper grills to stop a lighted candle falling in if the glass broke.

When the call came for the crew to take up their quarters for action, Tom Cook, the cook, stood guard in the light room, making sure that no flame got near the powder. One of Jeffreys's mates, either Pattey or Scott, was responsible for the transfer of extra shot of appropriate weight and type from the hold to the various gun decks. Some shot was always kept close to the guns, but if insufficient was shifted up before the battle, transferred to each of the decks through a pre-determined chain of hands, there might be an appalling period when the ship received fire without being able to return it.

The other mate supervised the distribution of equipment for the guns. Coffen, Curtis and all the other gun captains formed a queue in the dark passage to the gunner's storeroom to collect their powder horn, three-foot linstock, slow match, priming wire, vent reamer, a salt box to carry two cartridges, and a pouch containing quill firing tubes. The gun captains also collected a lantern to light the gun because they would probably be fighting after dark. Crewmen carried up stacks of junk wads to be rammed between and after charges and balls to hang in nets or pile near guns.

Armourer Scardefield's mate John Sympson issued chests containing muskets, pistols and cutlasses to each gun crew, and pikes as well as the other weapons were sent up for the designated boarding party.

As the afternoon drew on, *Monmouth*'s sailing master John Wilson recorded that the wind veered west north-west and the *Foudroyant* was steering north-east by east. Just about every scrap of sail had been set that might urge them forward without taking the wind from a more important sail, and the gap between them was closing. The boatswain reinforced all the yards with chains to stop them falling on the deck if the ropes holding them were shot through, and netting was put up to save the people on the deck from falling wood. When all these things had been done there was still plenty of time to get nervous, excited and fearful.

There was no sign of the French leaving Cartagena, though they must have been able to see their own sixty-four fleeing for the port by then. The *Revenge* had left *Berwick* behind in the distance, but she was closing on the French ship. At five o'clock on what was now 1 March on the ship (at sea the day changed at midday, not midnight) came the first distant gunfire: 'we saw the *Revenge* & her chase firing there bow & stern chase at Each other'. *Revenge* and *Monmouth* were 'called the twin sisters being of the same size and model'. *Revenge*'s French quarry was racing for the shelter of Cartagena harbour, and even though *Revenge* was within gunshot she would be hard put to stop her. They had not been watching the distant engagement for very long when ahead of them *Foudroyant* also raised her French ensign, the lily-white flag of the Bourbon kings, as the rules of war demanded she must do before engaging. There was a red flash and a puff of smoke from her stern. With a splash the ball from this first range-finding shot fell harmlessly into the water well short of *Monmouth*'s prow.

As the two ships sailed slowly on, *Foudroyant* continued to fire occasional ranging shots with her stern chaser. At six o'clock, sailing master Wilson reported, one of them cut through the fore studding sail and struck the bow. She had ranged in on *Monmouth* with impressive accuracy. *Monmouth* replied with her bow chasers and they kept this up for about an hour. With the seas flat it was possible for a skilled gunner with a good cannon to fire quite accurately. Wilson recorded that the wind veered westerly and stayed in that quarter. *Foudroyant* steered east by north, then east, so that both ships were running 'before the wind with everything out', the little black *Monmouth* in the French giant's wake. *Foudroyant*'s best chance of escape now was to fire a shot that disabled *Monmouth*. Anything that slowed her down might help, but if Duquesne brought down a yard or a mast, *Monmouth*'s advantage in speed would disappear and *Foudroyant* would get away. On the other hand a lucky shot from *Monmouth* might end the chase.

It was getting dark. At sunset Gardiner ordered *Monmouth*'s guns to cease firing and the seamen hauled down the studding sails and made all clear for engaging. He was now sure that he could make the Frenchmen fight. John Ayres, the master sailmaker, wetted the fighting sails to stop them catching fire. He had been in charge of canvas for eight years, in three little sloops in peacetime before his appointment to *Monmouth* when hostilities had begun three years ago. *Foudroyant* continued to break the eerie silence with a series of bangs followed by sudden rending crashes or a whirring overhead and the rip of torn canvas. Ayres and his four yeomen made what running repairs they could, but nothing essential had so far carried away. The boatwain's mates Edward May and John Framingham piped the shrill 'all hands!' at every hatchway.

Captain Gardiner called the whole crew together. He stood on the quarterdeck with the setting sun behind him and spoke to them.

'This ship', he said, 'must be taken; she looks to be above our match; but Englishmen are not to mind that, nor will I quit her while this ship can swim, or I have a soul left alive.' His 'honest tars' cheered and 'said they depended upon him for victory, and he might depend upon them'. Then the drums beat and the people went to their quarters.

2

The Music of Great-Guns

Most of the men took up station at their guns. Second lieutenant Stephen Hammick commanded the lower deck, where 143 men and thirteen boys crouched around thirteen 24-pounder cannon, and four or five mates and midshipmen, such as Richard Tizard and Edward Salmon, directed groups of guns. They were crammed into the starboard half of a cleared space about forty yards long and twelve yards wide, with the glass stern window at one end and the tapering bows at the other. All partitions and unnecessary wood had been removed, but it was dark and stuffy as there was barely five foot clearance between decks. James Baron, the twenty-two-year-old from Lostwithiel, was responsible for the thirteen 12-pounders that faced the enemy on the upper deck, each with a crew of eight – 104 men and boys in total, with some midshipmen commanding groups of guns.

Among the sixteen quarter-gunners, who each took charge of four guns, was William Corrin, the thirty-five-year-old Manxman, whom Carkett had promoted to quarter-gunner a year before after nine months rated able. He supervised the placing of crows, handspikes, rammers, sponges, powder-horns, matches and train-tackles in order by the side of each cannon. Junk wads to keep the ball in place were stacked in the netting hanging overhead. Each pair of guns had a captain: as a former quarter-gunner William Coffen probably commanded one crew of twelve. They split into two groups of six if both sides of the ship were firing simultaneously, but that was unlikely today. Several of the gun crew had other duties. Topmen were designated as sail trimmers or boarders and would leave the gun if the ship needed to manoeuvre or repel the enemy. Others would go off to fight fires or pump out water if the ship was holed.

Tizard gave the order to cast loose the lashes binding his guns to the side of the ship. They took the tompion from the mouth of the barrel and the oakum from the vent, opened the red-painted gun ports and ran the cannon out so that their red-painted muzzles protruded. The open ports made a red stripe on the side of the black ship. The barrels were levelled at point blank: they would fire them within the range at which the shot travelled in a straight line. The master-at-arms and his corporals laid the hatches to prevent anybody who deserted his post taking refuge below. Edward Dunn, William Lawler and Peter Hanlon, the Irish landsmen, crouched beside their cannon, waiting apprehensively for whatever might unfold.

The seamen up on the exposed superstructure there were the pick of the crew. They too had guns to prepare against their counterparts on the other ship: five 6-pounders either side of the quarterdeck and two on the forecastle, as well as half-pounder swivels mounted on the sides, but most were preoccupied with other roles. The junior lieutenant, David Winzar, was responsible for training the seamen with small arms and 'his office, in time of battle, is chiefly to direct and attend them'. There were eighty small arms men. The senior mate, in this case James Powell, commanded the forecastle, directing the forward guns. The boatswain, James Everitt, and his mates also took post there. (Captain Gardiner had a low opinion of Everitt, who had been ejected from two previous ships for incompetence, but his mates Edward May and John Framingham were reliable.) They effected the changes of speed and direction that might help *Monmouth* outmanoeuvre the *Foudroyant* so that she could do more damage while receiving less. They also organised running repairs to damaged ropes. In the fore rigging over their heads was James Scott, captain of the forecastle, with a couple of picked men. A similar party was posted in the main rigging and there were also marksmen in the tops with muskets.

On the quarterdeck was the command group consisting of the tall, slim Captain Gardiner, first lieutenant Carkett and John Wilson the master. With them was the signal midshipman, ready to make or read signals, and the captain's aides, who would run messages. George Bernier, the captain's clerk, was taking minutes of all that happened.

There was a quartermaster at the conn and another on the wheel with four helmsmen. Behind and above them on the poop were some sailors for the mizen mast and some of the seventy fit marines, who formed two deep in close order with shouldered arms under their captain, Joseph Austin, and their young lieutenant, George Preston. Nearby John Campbell's thirty soldiers stood to attention, resplendent in their red coats. The remaining marines completed the gun crews.

John Hye, Thomas Nelcoat and James Young sprang to their places as the royal marines formed up. They cut a very different appearance from the soldiers – they had gone native. When they had first arrived on board their uniform coats, hats, caps and white shirts had all been locked up in the marine storeroom, to be worn only to welcome a senior officer or for service ashore. They had bought pursers' slops and now wore sea caps, jackets and checked shirts like the sailors. They could only be distinguished by the military discipline with which they formed ranks.

There had always been soldiers who did sea service and, since the 1660s, regiments that specialised in it, but in 1755 the marine corps had been reformed and placed under the control of the Admiralty as a brand new corps – His Majesty's Marine Forces. With amphibious operations in mind, the navy had acquired amphibious soldiers to train in its own ways. At first most of them had been so seasick they were fit for very little, but once they got their sea legs the sergeants had trained them to fire over the side of the ship in three ranks and two ranks, and taught them how to aim at a mark hung from the furthest extremity of the yard arm. Now, like the seamen, the marines were divided into a starboard watch and a larboard watch, one under Sergeant John Pearson, the other under Sergeant John Harris. They had been at sea for two or three years now and had become hardened sailors, and many of them could and did help competently with the working of the ship. They had long ago mastered the art of firing as the ship rose on the wave, so that their shots did not plunge harmlessly into the sea. But as yet they had seen little serious fighting.

The wind freshened as it grew dark. An arms chest was carried up to the poop and opened. The marines loaded their muskets and corporals Mackrell and Fisher checked that their flints were good. The huge *Foudroyant* loomed directly ahead, at no great distance now.

In the last light, an hour after sunset, Gardiner warned Hammick and Baron to prepare the men to fire the starboard guns. They reloaded them with double-headed shot, aiming to disable. Gardiner hoped to damage the French ship's rigging, or at best, in Master Wilson's words, 'to carry her masts away'.

All the teams gathered on one side. At Gardiner's order, the quartermasters gave the ship a yaw, turning her just far enough off course to bring some guns to bear. As *Monmouth* came round each crew strained to turn its gun forward. Below the elevated marines, on the quarterdeck and in the waist, the 'lanthorn men' belonging to each gun crew held up their black fighting lamps, providing a glimmer of safe light about each gun. Gun captains peered along the barrels of their cannon lining up the notch on the base with the notch on the muzzle ring, aiming high for the rigging. Then, as the ship rose on the wave, they fired all the upper- and lower-deck guns they could bring to bear.

On the *Foudroyant* sails were ripped and torn and key ropes cut away, but she kept going. Having lost some speed thanks to the yaw, it was another hour before *Monmouth* actually overlapped the French ship. Gardiner directed the helmsmen to steer her into an advantageous position across *Foudroyant*'s larboard quarter no more than forty yards away.

Monmouth was to windward of the enemy with her smoke blowing into the eyes of the French. Those marines not serving guns lined the parapet two deep, concentrated on the poop where they were highest up. Behind them one of the marine arms chests was 'lashed upon the Grating abaft the mizen mast to hold Ammunition'. The marines lit their own black lanterns to light the ammunition and spare guns as it was truly dark now, and a few of the best marksmen were given the special duty of firing at port holes. The theory behind this was that 'Two or three expert Men killed at a Gun may silence it for half an Hour'. This was especially true in French ships, where the gun crews relied heavily on the guidance of the specially trained marine artillery-men who pointed each gun. The soldiers, chiefly from the Shropshire regiment, lined up with them. They were at half-musket range, close enough to be as accurate as an eighteenth-century firelock could be. As the ship rose, the front rank fired.

The French replied. The position *Monmouth* had taken up meant that some of the French bow guns could not be trained far enough aft to fire at her, whereas *Monmouth's* full broadside could be directed at the French ship. This reduced *Foudroyant's* power to flash forked lightning and hurl thunderbolts, but not by much. She had 250 small arms men three deep on the spar deck. 130 French soldiers massed on the poop. The French ship was much taller than the *Monmouth* so that they could fire downwards on to the English decks. Moreover, the disadvantage of fighting from the windward was that as the *Monmouth* fell with the wave her decks were exposed to the enemy, while *Foudroyant's* high sides always protected her decks from *Monmouth*. Canister, a cylindrical tin box packed with musket balls, was 'principally used by the French to scour the decks of the enemy'. Soon the air above and around Hye and Nelcoat and Young was filled with bullets whizzing through the air and with bar shot aimed at the masts and rigging. Pieces of wood, detached blocks and sawn ropes fell and were caught by the *sauve-tête* netting suspended over their heads.

Captain Gardiner was hit in the arm almost immediately, but bound the wound and stayed where he was. The marine captain, Joseph Austin, and his young lieutenant, George Preston, strode along the ranks of their men, trying to stop their men trembling or flinching and turning away as they fired, or ducking behind the rows of stuffed hammocks that lined the top of the parapet to soak up enemy fire and prevent splinters. Splintered wood was the main danger – it caused a more savage wound than a clean bullet or ball – and splinters flew off the ship wherever metal struck wood. The men were encouraged to keep up a constant fire, one rank firing while the other loaded. As the manual said, 'nothing can gall an Enemy so much as a constant Fire, which intimidates the common People and often puts it out of an Officer's Power to re-animate them'.

It was up here that most of the casualties would be incurred, and the men knew it. Not only were they exposed and vulnerable without the four feet of solid oak all round them that the gun crews were shielded by below, but the enemy would deliberately target them. The ship's senior officers and the most level-headed of the sailors were the driving force that motivated the machine. Remove enough of them, and the capacity for instant decision-making could disappear, confusion set in, and the will to continue the fight seep away.

It is said that British ships habitually fired roundshot at the enemy ship's hull, but in this case, as John Wilson the master reported, *Monmouth* fired 'all the grap & Duble Headd: shott that is Allowed'. It seems certain that Gardiner exhausted his allowance of these, which were designed to stop the enemy moving, before he started on the roundshot that was designed to destroy the hull and discourage personnel.

Grapeshot was a cluster of small cannonballs packed in a canvas bag and bound with cord, the whole being the same diameter as the iron ball normally used for the gun. The balls of grape used for a 24-pounder each weighed two pounds, and for a 12-pounder, one pound. 'Double-headed' or 'bar' shot' was 'balls cut into two equal parts, and joined together by a kind of iron bar'. They span in the air and were very effective for cutting rigging and damaging sails and masts – the French sometimes used a combustible variety intended to set fire to the enemy sails. The full allowance of double-headed was six rounds for each gun. They had ten rounds of grape for each of Hammick's heavy guns and fourteen each for the lighter cannon. Allowing about three minutes for each round, expending all this shot would have taken rather more than an hour, assuming that all guns were still firing; some were probably knocked out.

In the sealed magazines the shoeless yeomen of the powder room, John Lee and Richard Vinney, steadily passed out pairs of parchment cartridges in salt boxes. The ship's thirty-five boys, aged between thirteen and seventeen, and mostly overexcited, formed chains of hands to pass cartridge boxes to the gun decks where the 'powder monkey' for each gun ran them to the starboard side of the deck opposite the cannon. One such boy, a black servant to a lieutenant, described how in a similar action a year later he 'ran a very great risk for more than half an hour of blowing up the ship. For, when we had taken the cartridges out of the boxes, the bottom of many of them proving rotten, the powder ran all about the deck, near the match tub; we scarcely had water enough at the last to throw on it.' Once on deck the boys might see through flame and choking smoke, but they could hear nothing but thunder and smashing wood.

Even on this March night it soon became hot on the enclosed deck with thirteen large guns firing. William Corrin's gun reared backwards as it fired, restrained by its tackle. Peter Hanlon, rammer, cleaned the barrel with his sponge, withdrawing it with a last twist. Holding its seam downwards, Thomas Lawler, loader, thrust in a new cartridge till his shoulder hit the hot muzzle, pushed wadding in after and rammed both home with two or three firm pushes. Corrin checked that the cartridge was home beneath the touch hole, then they thrust a 24-pound double-header in and rammed in wadding after that. The first broadside or two may even have been double-shotted with bar shot on top of a ball. Protecting the touch hole from water, they ran out the gun till its muzzle protruded from the ship. With crows and handspikes they turned it to bear and levelled the barrel. When Corrin, peering along its length, was satisfied with his aim he pricked the cartridge, primed it with more powder from his horn, bruised the priming, took his match from above the water bucket, blew on it, and made sure his men were well out of the path of the recoil. Then, at what he judged to be the moment before they rose on the wave, he put his smouldering match to the powder and quickly jumped sideways to avoid the recoil. After a few seconds the cannon spoke again. The speed and precision with which all this was done over and over again was likely to govern the outcome of the fight.

Meanwhile, enemy shots crashed against the ship's side. Rarely, one burst through, cutting limbs from men and showering their mates with their blood, while splintered wood sliced ragged wounds wherever it hit. A shot straight through a porthole might demolish a gun, maiming and scattering, perhaps crushing, men beneath the great cannon itself. The dead were pushed through portholes, the wounded carried down to the surgeons on the orlop deck. Any interruption, any break in the rhythm slowed performance and gave an advantage to the other side. If the powder wasn't delivered, if a gun was knocked over, if fire broke out, the crew might become distracted, and with unanswered enemy fire hitting the ship it would become harder to return to idle guns, particularly since, according to one early account, 'at first the enemy's fire was much the quickest'. Some sort of explosion near the magazine probably accounted for wounds to both the master-at-arms and one of the corporals, who were stationed there.

During the night, sixteen shots went right through *Monmouth*'s side, eight between wind and water. Carpenter Robert Narramore was waiting for these. With his mate David Edwards and their crew of eight, he stood in the wings, the cleared passages along the sides of the orlop deck, ready to plug dangerous holes. If water poured in, they threw themselves that way, hammered tarred tarpaulin over a gaping hole or shaped a plug to fit it, and jammed oakum round the edges. Theirs was a constant fight to keep the water out. Narramore checked the well frequently for unseen leaks, but he never had to take men off guns to man the pumps.

The French ship had everything to gain by destroying *Monmouth* quickly and getting away: for them also it was logical to aim first at disabling the enemy, since their object was escape. For the first hour the upper part of the British ship must have been a terrifying place to be as the huge French 42-pounders and the many smaller guns attempted its destruction. Most of *Monmouth*'s casualties were incurred in this opening period when French fire was fierce, and they were concentrated amongst the elite seamen. Master's mate James Powell was carried below seriously wounded. Quartermasters Marmaduke Johns and Robert Spencer, probably still conning the ship, were killed outright and thrown overboard. Quartermaster Philip Hardy was wounded at the wheel. Sailmaker John Ayres was killed with one of his yeomen, and two of the remaining three were wounded, Richard Caswell shot out of the rigging with a broken shoulder blade. It was a dangerous job climbing up shrouds to mend rigging with so much iron flying around and blocks falling from above. Captain of the forecastle James Scott was seriously wounded with two of the topmen of the starboard watch.

But *Monmouth* produced similar carnage on the French deck. Lieutenant Cogolin was cut in half by a cannonball. A musket ball hit flag captain Callian in the arm, but he stayed at his post on the forecastle until a plummeting block smashed his shoulder. On the quarterdeck a single shot produced an explosion of wood: one splinter slashed second captain Fabrègues' cheek, another embedded itself in his thigh. Mezières was hit in the stomach by grapeshot and fell to the deck vomiting blood.

After an hour's fighting Gardiner sent a midshipman to fetch Baron, and 'while in the act of encouraging his people and enquiring what injury had been sustained between decks, he received a second wound'. Carkett reported that 'Capt Gardiner Recd a Mortal Wound in his head which Obliged him to be carryed of the Deck'. Baron, who may have been an eyewitness, noted that he was hit by a grapeshot, which would have done serious damage to his skull. Other accounts speak of a musket ball in the forehead.

Captain Gardiner, conjuring his Lieutenant to Fight the Enemy: 'Before he expired, he sent for his first lieutenant, and told him, the last favour he could ask of him was never to give up the ship.'

Stories soon spread about Gardiner's death:

> Before he expired, he sent for his first lieutenant, and told him, the last favour he could ask of him was never to give up the ship. The lieutenant told him he never would, and instantly went and nailed the flag to the staff, and stood at it with a brace of pistols, declaring he would put any man to death who attempted to come near the colours and strike them, until he was dead:

Gardiner probably did not speak the words 'Never give up the ship'. David Winzar, who was probably at hand, wrote emphatically in his log that the captain expired 'having lain speechless from the minute he was wounded'. Nevertheless, the episode went into the history books. Gardiner's words were remembered for use in future desperate engagements, and 'Don't give up the ship' became the unofficial motto of the American navy.

The wounded captain was carried to 'the cockpit' on the orlop deck at the waterline, where the men were treated in the order that they appeared. There the ship's surgeon, Robert Smith, had created a makeshift operating theatre. He had three mates and several 'loblolly boys' to carry patients and hold them down, together with other non-combatant helpers such as the chaplain, Edward Chicken, and the old purser, Samuel Furzer. Occasionally the wives of warrant and senior petty officers went to sea with their menfolk. They did so unofficially and unrecorded, so there is no evidence of women in *Monmouth* at this time, but if there were any they also helped in the cockpit. Smith had thirty years' experience as a naval surgeon, so he had almost certainly worked during an engagement at some time, and his first mate Nathaniel Herring had started his career in 1747 in the *Vulture* sloop with *Monmouth*'s master, John Wilson, as a shipmate. It is unlikely, however, that anyone in the room had had to deal with the sort of carnage that they dealt with now.

There are very few surviving accounts of what it was like in the cockpit during a savage engagement such as this, but one surgeon's journal, written some years later, describes an action in which ninety wounded were brought down, little different from *Monmouth*'s eighty-six:

The whole cockpit deck, cabins, wing berths and part of the cable tier, together with my platform and my preparations for dressing were covered with them. So that for a time they were laid on each other at the foot of the ladder where they were brought down, and I was obliged to go on deck to the Commanding Officer to state the situation and apply for men to go down the main hatchway and move the foremost of the wounded further forward into the tiers and wings, and thus make room in the cockpit. Numbers, about sixteen, mortally wounded, died after they were brought down, amongst whom was the brave and worthy Captain Burgess, whose corpse could with difficulty be conveyed to the starboard wing berth. Joseph Bonheur had his right thigh taken off by a cannon shot close to the pelvis, so that it was impossible to apply a tourniquet; his right arm was also shot to pieces. The stump of the thigh, which was very fleshy, presented a dreadful and large surface of mangled flesh. In this state he lived near two hours, perfectly sensible and incessantly calling out in a strong voice to me to assist him. The bleeding from the femoral artery, although so high up, must have been very inconsiderable, and I observed it did not bleed as he lay. All the service I could render this unfortunate man was to put dressings over the part and give him drink . . .

Melancholy cries for assistance were addressed to me from every side by wounded and dying, and piteous moans and bewailing from pain and despair. In the midst of these agonising scenes, I was able to preserve myself firm and collected, and embracing in my mind the whole of the situation, to direct my attention where the greatest and most essential services could be performed. Some with wounds, bad indeed and painful, but slight in comparison with the dreadful condition of others, were most vociferous for my assistance. These I was obliged to reprimand with severity, as their voices disturbed the last moments of the dying. I cheered and commended the patient fortitude of others, and sometimes extorted a smile of satisfaction from the mangled sufferers, and succeeded to throw momentary gleams of cheerfulness amidst so many horrors. The man whose leg I had first amputated had not uttered a groan from the time he was brought down, and several, exulting in the news of the victory, declared they regretted not the loss of their limbs.

An explosion of a salt box with several cartridges abreast of the

27

cockpit hatchway filled the hatchway with flame and in a moment 14 or 15 wretches tumbled down upon each other, their faces black as a cinder, their clothes blown to tatters and their hats on fire. A Corporal of Marines lived two hours after the action with all the glutei muscle shot away, so as to excavate the pelvis. Captain Burgess' wound was of this nature, but he fortunately died almost instantly.

After the action ceased, 15 or 16 dead bodies were removed before it was possible to get a platform cleared and come at the materials for operating and dressing, those I had prepared being covered over with bodies and blood, and the store room door blocked up.

First lieutenant Robert Carkett took Captain Gardiner's place and David Winzar came to help him. The loss of their beloved captain merely made the Monmouths more resolute. They were encouraged that the French could not keep up their rate of fire: 'In an hour it slackened, and still got weaker and weaker for the whole action, without any abatement in ours, but rather the contrary.' One reason was that the 42-pound cannonballs fired by the heaviest French guns took some lifting, and their crews tired quickly. Another was that the French had specially trained naval gunners pointing their guns; their loss caused more confusion than the loss of a British gun captain because the remaining Frenchmen were less well qualified to replace them. Beyond that, the British crew was fitter, stronger and more determined.

The guns pounded away, 'Broadside, and Broadside, Great Guns and small without the least Intermission', as Lieutenant Winzar put it, with a hint of a sailor's relish for 'the Music of Great-Guns'. It was a gargantuan effort. They shot off 520 12-pound and 435 24-pound balls, an average of forty rounds for each of Baron's guns and thirty-three for Hammick's. They used up nearly all their ammunition – ships carried sixty to seventy shots per gun – and emptied eighty barrels of powder. The duration of the conflict varies from account to account and it is difficult to judge how its intensity varied over time, but if all his guns were firing constantly, over four or five hours Baron's gunners produced a round every four or five minutes. Fewer guns would have had to fire faster, and some of his guns were almost certainly knocked out. At their best they must have been very fast.

Men climb shrouds to repair damaged rigging as Monmouth *blasts* Foudroyant: *detail from Peter Canot's 1759 engraving.*

Half an hour after midnight, *Monmouth*'s mizenmast was shot away just above the quarterdeck. The French crew cheered, but Winzar soon had men clearing the wreckage and it 'was thrown overboard with all belonging to it'. At one in the morning it was *Monmouth*'s turn to cheer as 'the Enemy's Mizen Mast, Ensign and flying jibb boom went away'. Soon afterwards, Carkett reported, the French ship was 'only firing a lower deck gun now and then'. At half past one the Monmouths cheered resoundingly as *Foudroyant*'s mainmast tottered and fell forwards, smashed the yard and sail from the foretopmast, broke into three pieces, ripped the foresail and crushed the longboat and yawl. Most of the guns were masked with wreckage and French fire petered out altogether. Baron ordered his men to cease firing, 'imagining the enemy had struck'. He could not see whether the

Foudroyant had really 'struck', or lowered her ensign, signifying surrender.

A few guns are still firing when Foudroyant's *mainmast collapses: detail from Peter Canot's 1759 engraving.*

The surviving officers gathered on the quarterdeck. 'We had no Tackle but was shot away,' wrote Lieutenant Winzar, 'otherwise we should [have] hoisted a Boat out and took possession of her.'

Swiftsure had finally caught up. Winzar recalled that 'at this time the *Swiftsure* came under our stern, hailed us and desired we would cease firing, as he was bearing down on the enemy, & was presently alongside her, when the enemy fired two Guns from the upper deck forward, ye *Swiftsure* then gave her a Broadside and soon after took her in tow.'

Hampton Court was ten minutes behind. The moon was high and its captain, Hervey, was struck by the eerie illumination of the now silent scene as he approached: 'I got near enough to see by the light of the moon that the *Monmouth* lay disabled, and her chace dismasted, and both their heads contrary way, but all firing ceased, and I saw the the chace's French colours lying over her taffrail.'

Hervey took *Hampton Court* under *Foudroyant*'s stern 'and gave orders not to fire, as they were calling to us for quarters'. These pleas for mercy and the lowered flag draped over the carved stern rail showed the French had surrendered. Hervey had not bargained for *Swiftsure*'s continued aggression: 'Captain Stanhope too hastily threw in a broadside to the French ship and partly into me'. He hailed Stanhope to tell him that he had sent his boat on board *Foudroyant*, because she had already 'struck to the *Monmouth*, who was disabled and could not get her boat out'. Hervey then went on board the French ship himself, where he met Stanhope's lieutenant, who 'desired that Monsieur du Quesne might be sent on board the *Swiftsure* as the senior officer'. Stanhope outranked Hervey and Gardiner because he had been a captain for longer, and convention dictated that the French captain should surrender to the senior officer present. Hervey agreed that this was right, but remarked that 'without a doubt neither the *Swiftsure* or myself had the least claim to any of the honour which the *Monmouth* acquired by taking such a ship'.

Hervey's barge had just rowed him back to his own ship when the *Monmouth* hailed him with the news that Captain Gardiner had been killed.

3

Dead Men's Clothes

Account of Cloaths sold at the mast belonging to James Powell
* Deceased*
The time when sold: 11 March 1758
507 Edward Lunn To a silver watch, 4 shirts, 2 pairs stockings £4 10s
1084 James Reeves To a sword 7s 6d
1042 James Taylor To 32 shirts & pair Breeches 7s 6d
808 Amos Pitcher To 2 shirts 2 coats 2 waistcoats 10s 6d
770 John Radford To a shirt coat waistcoat breeches & stocking 10s
136 Philip Rowden To a coat waistcoat & breeches £1 2s
603 James Strange To 3 shirts 2 pairs breeches: 2 handkerchiefs 8s
630 Robert Webb To a coat waistcoat hat & lace £1 10s
655 Richard Tizzard To a pair shoes buckles & neck cloth 8s
641 Simon Pengelly To pair shoes pair stockings a pair boots 5s
1018 Barnaby Binnick To a Coat waistcoat Brace of Pistols and a spy
* glass £1 4s*
562 William Langman To a pair of Velvet Breeches & a sheet £1 13s
£12 15s 6d James Dixon attorney to Samuel Furzer

Tucked into the ship's pay book in the National Archives at Kew is
this brief memorandum of the sale of the contents of senior master's
mate, James Powell's sea chest. The auction took place at sea ten days
after the battle and a week after Powell had died of his wounds at half
past two on the morning of 3 March.

The men gathered before the mast. This was the seamen's area,
whereas the officers commanded the quarterdeck and the space
beneath it. Posted on the walls under the forecastle were the articles
of war – the thirty-five commandments of naval life – together with

notices specifying each man's duties and station at the various times when all hands were called to action. These were devised and written on cardboard by Carkett, the first lieutenant.

The disposal of the property of dead men 'at the Mast as is the Custom at Sea' was already traditional at the time the *Monmouth*'s timbers were first cut from oak trees a hundred years before. The present *Monmouth* was already an old ship, having been launched in 1742, but in building her they had reused the oak from the previous *Monmouth*, constructed at Chatham in 1667. Her timber was antique, redolent of a century of naval tradition, present at Solebay, the Texel, Barfleur, Vigo Bay, Gibraltar, Malaga and, more recently, the two battles of Finisterre.

John Wilson, the master, and Samuel Furzer, the purser, were in charge of the sale. Wilson was a sailing master or 'skipper' of fourteen years' standing, and although he had only been in *Monmouth* for a year he was a figure with authority. After the late captain, he was the best paid man in the ship. *Monmouth* was his fifth naval vessel. His first had been the little sloop *Vulture* in which he had scattered some Scottish rebels in 1746. Then the old *Rippon*, a '64' like *Monmouth* until she was broken up in 1751. After that the *Glory*, captured from the French in 1747, and finally the frigate *Dolphin* in which he had cruised the Mediterranean with Captain Richard Howe. Through all these years he had garnered knowledge of navigation in all the places he had sailed. In his notebooks he kept details of seamarks and harbours, tides and dangerous rocks.

Samuel Furzer was about sixty, an experienced businessman with tentacles reaching beyond *Monmouth*, whose purser he had been since the beginning of the war. As purser he acquired and distributed provisions and other supplies. Much had to be done at his own financial risk; pursery was a precarious occupation for a careless or unlucky man, but there was also potential for personal gain. Furzer assessed his present profit from his current account for *Monmouth* at rather more than £1,000, enough to fund a comfortable retirement. From such sound dealing he had acquired a solid, modern brick house in Woolwich, new mahogany furniture, Wilton carpets, a younger wife and four children. He made his profit by being careful with his paperwork and the navy's property and by making 'savings'. Furzer bought supplies in advance and was reinbursed later for what was consumed. He was allowed an eighth of all supplies to compensate for wastage, so he had to keep the loss within that limit or find other ways of recouping a little money. Feeding and selling clothes to dead men was a common form of petty embezzlement. Sailors got very cynical about pursers. They told credulous young boys that the albatrosses that followed ships in southern oceans were the ghosts of pursers, haunting their former ships in an eternal search for savings.

According to the regulations, no seaman was allowed to bid for clothes belonging to a dead officer that were 'above their wear'. Nor were they allowed to bid more than what was, in the judgement of master and purser, the 'real value' of the goods. Nor were they allowed to purchase more than 'the wages due to them can answer'. So with Wilson and Furzer seeing that nobody overstretched their resources, Powell's clothes were put up for sale and his shipmates put in bids.

The seamen crowded before the mast to bid for Powell's clothes or to watch the spectacle wore the classic dress of the eighteenth-century tar – a short jacket and long trousers with a checked shirt and a waistcoat. Many weather-beaten faces were topped with wigs worn over shaved heads. Others kept their own hair, short or pleated in a pigtail, under a hat or Monmouth cap. On a March day, even off southern Spain, some may have wrapped up in tarred woollen 'dreadnoughts' – thick coats for bad weather.

Before a voyage they bought their clothes from specialist 'slop shops', a fixture in any port. Midshipman Richard Tizard's father, a tailor in Weymouth, may well have run a slop shop. Proper outfits were expensive and sailors drew an advance on pay to kit themselves out. Furzer also carried a supply of slops to sea, to be sold to new men without proper clothes or to re-equip others when necessary, setting the cost against their pay. Navy slops were manufactured to specified patterns in specified materials: shirts and drawers were made in blue and white checked linen, jackets were unlined, double-breasted, blue kersey wool in three sizes. Waistcoats were linsey wool, stockings were white worsted, caps were worsted or felt. Calves' leather shoes came in four sizes. Marines got white shirts with red kersey jackets and white turn-ups, together with haversacks of Russia sheeting. So, although there was no prescribed uniform, blue jackets and blue and white checked shirts were common because that was how the navy supplied them.

Sailors' clothes were distinctive in both cut and material. Jackets and coats were short so that long skirts did not get in the way when aloft. Often they wore canvas trousers, a most unusual garment ashore. Canvas, ticking and cotton were rarely worn on land, but common at sea. Materials were selected for their strength and because they dried easily, or kept out water. Many garments were impregnated with tar, giving them a distinctive sea smell. Only the captain's bargemen ever wore a uniform, and then only when rowing the captain on formal occasions. Picture a mass of men in variegated colours, blue predominant, with a smarter group of officers.

Commissioned officers and midshipmen did wear a uniform. For everyday use they had a navy blue coat and white waistcoat, breeches and stockings. Lieutenants' coats were plain; midshipmen were distinguished by white collar-patches. A lieutenant's waistcoat was edged with gold lace. No specific uniform was laid down for master's mates, but the contents of Powell's sea chest suggest that he was equipped to 'appear properly as a quarter deck officer'. He took to sea forty-two shirts; six pairs of breeches, one of them velvet; four pairs of stockings; six coats; six waistcoats; two handkerchiefs and a neckcloth; one hat with lace; two pairs of shoes and a pair of buckles; one pair of boots; a fine bed sheet; a sword; a spy-glass; a brace of pistols, and a silver watch.

Most of the men were young. The ordinary seamen and most of the landsmen were eighteen to twenty-two or so. The bulk of the able seamen and the midshipmen and mates were in their twenties and early thirties. Nevertheless, *Monmouth* had what may have been an above average number of older men, chiefly among the petty officers and idlers. The warrant officers in *Monmouth* were very experienced, even elderly, being in their forties and fifties. Three out of the four lieutenants were mature family men, each married with two children. The mates and midshipmen were mostly in their twenties and at least

five of the sixteen midshipmen were married. 'Snotty' young gentlemen, exercising authority beyond their years, were a rarity in this ship.

When the bidding began, with Furzer playing auctioneer and his
steward David Bowman acting as clerk, midshipmen bought Powell's
more precious belongings. Given the regulations, this was more or less
inevitable. Edward Lund, who was wounded himself, acquired the
silver watch. Lund did not recover and never returned to his wife
Grace at Plymouth Dock; he died at Gibraltar Hospital at the end of
April. James Reeves bought the sword. Barnaby Binnock got the
brace of pistols and the spyglass as well as a coat. Richard Tizard
bought Powell's best shoes, their silver buckles and his neck cloth.
Midshipman Richard Langman, who also had a wife at home, paid £1
13s. for the best velvet breeches and what must have been an
unusually luxurious sheet. Seamen, several of them wounded, bought
suits of clothes and pairs of shoes.

Within the limits allowed by Furzer and Wilson the bids were
generous. Powell's shipmates knew that the proceeds (minus Furzer's
five per cent commission) would be given to Powell's thirty-three-
year-old widow Tabitha, who now had three children to raise on her
own. Tabitha lived in Antony, opposite Plymouth dock, and had
almost certainly become a familiar figure on the ship during the
months *Monmouth* was anchored there in 1756. The midshipmen at
least had probably met five-year-old Charles and three-year-old
Sarah. The youngest daughter, Joanna, had been born in spring
1757, conceived while they were last in port.

On top of the sum raised by this auction, Tabitha was also awarded
a small 'bounty' in compensation for his death in action. £36 12s. 2d.
was sent to her in Devon on 4 October 1760. Another £36 12s. 2d.
was given to Tabitha's relative John Lyne in trust for Charles, Sarah
and Joanna. In August 1758 Tabitha proved his will and claimed the
pay owed to him and his prize money.

Powell's prize money was quite substantial since the swift-sailing
Monmouth had already taken a number of enemy ships during the
course of the war, and the whole value of a captured ship was awarded
to the captors. The money was divided into eighths, of which the
admiral got one, the captain two, and the lieutenants, master and

captain of marines shared a fourth. The warrant officers shared one eighth, the petty officers another and the remainder of the crew split the remaining quarter. Just who counted as a warrant or petty officer was carefully defined. As master's mate Powell shared with the boatswain, carpenter, gunner, purser, surgeon, chaplain, his two fellow mates and the lieutenant of marines. This gave him a tenth share of an eighth of the net value of any prize. A lieutenant got a sixth, a petty officer a forty-ninth, the rest 1/211th of an eighth.

All of the men looked forward to their share in the value of the *Foudroyant*. She was certain to be bought and repaired for use by the Royal Navy, and a huge ship like that was worth a lot, even badly damaged. The Monmouths would have to share her with *Swiftsure* and *Hampton Court* because they were in sight when she was captured, and possibly the whole fleet would claim some share, so they were unlikely to be rewarded as fully as perhaps they should have been. In addition to the prize money for the ship there was also head money, which was awarded at a rate of £5 for each of the 880 men in the French ship, a total of £4,400. Head money went exclusively to those who fought, though even there the unscrupulous *Swiftsure* would claim a half-share on account of her single broadside.

Monmouth's moment of glory, however, was also a moment of crisis. Old friends had been killed or maimed. *Monmouth* had been a happy ship with highly experienced standing officers, a settled crew and a desertion rate of a mere 2.7 per cent. Now many would have to leave the ship injured and things would inevitably change. The battle with the *Foudroyant* had been, in words the Monmouths later used, a 'most bloody engagement'. Of *Monmouth*'s 466 men, one in four was a casualty. Twenty-nine were already dead and another expired two days after the auction. Robert Smith the surgeon and Edward Chicken the chaplain remained busy with the many wounded.

There were empty spaces all over the ship, most obviously in the captain's great cabin at the after end of the quarterdeck behind the wheel. The wardroom beneath it on the main deck had suffered lightly – all the officers who ate and slept there had survived. Separated from the main deck by a light bulkhead, the wardroom had six cabins between the guns which, following the regulation of 1757, were made of canvas so that they could be removed easily before action, the four lieutenants, John Wilson the master and Captain Austin slept there. Carkett's cabin was the aftermost on the larboard side with the keys to the storerooms hanging outside it. Wilson's principal cabin was opposite, although he had a second sleeping berth above, close to the wheel. Custom varied from ship to ship, but it is likely that Furzer the purser, Smith the surgeon, Chicken the chaplain and possibly Marine Lieutenant George Preston joined them for meals.

The chaplain's place on a ship of war was an uncertain one, unless he was a personal friend of the captain. It was not clear how Edward Chicken stood in the pecking order and while some ships allowed him to dine in the wardroom others did not. 'A Sea-Chaplain's Petition to the Lieutenants in the Ward-room, for the Use of the Quarter-Gallery' was published in the *Gentleman's Magazine* in 1758. In this satire the chaplain begged that although the lieutenants excluded him from dining in the wardroom, they might at least allow him to use their toilet over the stern of the ship, rather than the common heads over the bow. He felt they could not refuse him:

> For, sure this answer would be wondrous odd:
> 'Sh—te with the common tars, thou Man of God!'

Edward Chicken had only just joined the *Monmouth*. Warranted in October 1757, he had reached her at Gibraltar towards the end of January 1758. Within a month he found himself comforting dying men and visiting wounded sailors whose faces he can barely have recognised.

Chicken was thirty-one. He was a fluent Latinist, with literary interests inherited from his father, a weaver but also the author of *The Collier's Wedding*, a bawdy, funny, riotous account of the courtship of colliers in his native Newcastle. Chicken had married Elizabeth Legard while he was curate at Hornsea in 1751 and lived in the near ruinous vicarage there, but his curacies (he was also curate at Bridlington) barely provided a living. The couple had a daughter, Elizabeth, and Chicken went to sea in the hope of bettering his condition. He had joined the fifth-rate *Humber* in 1755 and had achieved a promotion into the fourth-rate *Guernsey* late in 1756.

Monmouth, a third-rate with nearly four hundred seamen, was a further promotion, for a chaplain's pay depended on the number that he ministered to. In addition to an ordinary seaman's monthly wage he received fourpence from each member of the crew. The chaplaincy of *Monmouth* therefore brought in just under £100 a year, and Chicken could claim a warrant officer's share of prize money on top. This made the chaplain of a major ship one of the best-rewarded members of the crew. Only the captain and master earned more. But the vagueness of provision for his accommodation encapsulated the implication that he was not quite a proper seaman, less essential than other officers.

In 1677 Samuel Pepys had produced a list of reasons for clerics to join the expanding navy. He tempted them with the prospect of easy duty without expense, undisturbed leisure to study, conversation with the captain, travel without cost and His Majesty's favour for future promotion on proof of serving well at sea. Some chaplains valued the leisure to work. Nicholas Tindal, for instance, completed his translation and continuation of Rapin's *History of England* while serving in the navy. Others might have welcomed the opportunity to join the navy and see the world. However, the last promise must have weighed most heavily for a chaplain like Chicken who lacked an influential patron.

Between his visits to the sick and his formal preaching on Sundays, Chicken courted popularity and fame through his own gift for poetry. Eighteenth-century ships were full of aspiring poets whose verse, sometimes technically competent, and occasionally good, found its way into magazines and newspapers. In the days after the battle the chaplain composed an ode on the *Monmouth* beating the *Foudroyant*.

Gradually Chicken got used to the geography of this ship, the biggest he had ever sailed in. Forward of the wardroom, where he perhaps composed his poem in consultation with the commissioned officers, was the upper gun deck, lined with 12-pounders lashed to she sides. Under the quarterdeck was the capstan, used for raising the anchor, then the mainmast, then the waist, which was open to the sky, with the pump shaft, from which water was pumped when necessary. Under the forecastle was the galley, where Thomas Cook had his huge iron stove, and forward of that a sheltered area for the crew that contained the sick bay and cabins for the carpenter and boatswain. Here, the galley stove provided warmth in bad weather, and the gun ports could be opened to admit light and air when it was fine. Outside over the bows were the heads, the crew's lavatories, which emptied straight into the sea. There were enclosed roundhouses for the senior members and seats in the open air for the rest.

Underneath the sick bay, right forward on the gun deck, was the manger where live animals were kept. At the after end of the gun deck was the gunroom, with the tiller sweeping across it, where the remaining warrant and inferior officers messed. In the corners were two canvas cabins, one of which belonged to Henry Jeffreys the gunner. The mates and midshipmen slept in hammocks slung along the sides. Of sixteen midshipmen, one was killed, one was slowly dying, and two were wounded. One of the three mates was dead, and one of the three surgeon's mates was wounded.

The remaining warrant officers and some petty officers slept on the orlop deck, where surgeon Smith and purser Furzer had cabins. The cable tier, where ropes were stored, was a sleeping place favoured by elite seamen who got to choose their berth. Quartermasters often chose to sleep on the soft manilla ropes. Less important petty officers slept along the sides or in the centre of the gun deck, where they were allowed twenty-eight inches of space, against the private men's fourteen. The bulk of the crew slung their hammocks on the gun deck, where it was relatively warm and dry, but airless when the portholes had to be closed. In most ships the watches slung their hammocks alternately, which meant that that in practice their space allowance was always double since their neighbour of the other watch was on deck when they were sleeping. They slung them according to a pattern devised by the lieutenants so that they knew where to find any man.

The petty officers had suffered heavily in the engagement. Of six quartermasters, three had been killed and one wounded. John Ayres, the sailmaker, was dead. Of his four yeomen one was dead and another badly wounded. One of the gunner's two mates had died of his wounds, and Gardiner's coxwain was too badly wounded to continue in the navy. All in all a quarter of the complement had to be replaced.

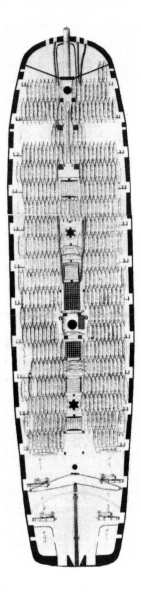

This plan identifies the sleeping positions of more than four hundred men on the gun deck of one of Constantine Phipps's ships. The more spacious berths were for petty officers.

The wounded men might have fared better had they reached Gibraltar earlier, but it was more than three weeks before they got ashore. The mizenmast had been shot away during the battle and the main topmast had fallen over the side during the night. The fore-topmast was so badly damaged that it had to be replaced, along with all the rigging. Lieutenant Edward Hutchins and midshipman Samuel Blow of *Hampton Court* came with twenty men to help set up jury masts (improvised temporary substitutes) and rigging, but even when *Monmouth* could spread sail contrary winds prevented progress.

In the meanwhile surgeon Robert Smith and his mates and assistants did their best to care for the wounded on board, but they must have overflowed from the sick berth, which was not designed to accommodate so many. The cooper made 'necessary buckets' for those who could not walk to the heads, and the carpenter made cradles for those that needed them. Men fished over the side to catch them fresh fish and there may also have been fresh meat and vegetables for them. But they were not comfortable: two days of strong gales shook the wounded about and it soon became stuffy and smelly between decks, even though *Monmouth* was equipped with one of Dr Stephen Hales's new ventilators. This invention for expelling foul and noxious air had been tested in 1750 and distributed to forty ships by 1757. Several men operated a giant bellows, which pumped air to each deck. Wilson noted in his log that they operated the ventilator constantly during the storm that followed the fighting.

The day after Powell's sale, *Monmouth* had rejoined the fleet and learned that *Revenge* and *Berwick* had captured the *Orphée* after a fight that for *Revenge* had been almost as bloody as *Monmouth*'s. A few days later, 150 French prisoners came on board and conditions became much worse. The French were usually worse dressed, less hygiene-conscious and less healthy and the risk of fever grew. Captain Hervey of the *Hampton Court* was the acting chief of staff to Admiral Osborn's squadron, and he gave strict orders that the prisoners should not be robbed or otherwise molested. Of his own ship he wrote, 'I have treated all my Prisoners en Prince – & have taken care that the whole has been so – & I am assured by the Chef D'Escadre, Captains, Officers & seamen to the very boys –

not the least thing of any sort has been taken – which I believe they are more surprized at than anything can be –'

Carkett also set high standards on *Monmouth*, and the arrival of the French brought the first flogging for nine months.

The marines were responsible for guarding the prisoners, with one watch relieving the other. Captain Austin normally appointed sentinels to guard the magazine and key storerooms and to watch various points around the ship. During the night they called out 'All is well' every quarter of an hour in a chain from sentry to sentry. Something of the manner of this can be judged from the journal of Corporal Todd, a soldier who served as a marine corporal in 1757:

> We were Divided into two Watches the Serjeant took the Starboard & I had the Larboard watch Each of us having 15 Men upon Guard. We planted 5 Centrys, 2 upon the Poop, 2 at the forecastle & one at the Gangway and relived them Every 2 Hours. The Watch stood 4 Hours, but at 4 O Clock in the Morning the Dogwatch, so call'd, only stood to 6 O Clock. From 6 to 8 O Clock this watch had the Decks Every Morning to Wash as it caused the Watchs to do it in their turns etc.

To watch over the French prisoners, Austin ordered his sergeants to appoint extra sentinels, some with muskets and some with cutlasses. One of these sentinels was James Young, a twenty-five-year-old Irishman, pressed into the navy in London. He called himself a cabinet-maker, but he had probably been presented to the marines by the London magistrates who liked to dispose of unwanted vagabonds and petty criminals in this way. He was posted by one of the sergeants or corporals, who first checked that his arms were in order. It was his duty to be vigilant, not to sing or smoke tobacco or allow noise around him. He was not to sit down or sleep, but to keep moving about his post.

Every so often a corporal, sergeant or officer toured the posts to check on his sentries, and one of them caught Young 'stealing of cloaths from one of the French prisoners'. By the ninth article of war this was a court-martial offence. The ship's master-at-arms, John Evans, put Young in irons. Evans, recommended to Gardiner as a 'Carefull, Sober Man', had been the ship's policeman ever since

Captain Gardiner had come aboard: Gardiner had had the previous incumbent dismissed for 'letting a man out of Irons who had absented himself from his duty many days' without his permission. Gardiner claimed he was a 'drunken and disobedient person', but he may merely have been following *Monmouth*'s lenient tradition without having first consulted the new captain.

Young's thievery was not something even the lenient Monmouths could condone, especially with a lieutenant acting as captain. On 18 March Evans brought Young before the assembled ship's company and Carkett sentenced him to twelve lashes with the cat-o'-nine-tails, administered by the boatswain's mates, Edward May and John Framingham.

Osborn sent *Monmouth*, *Revenge*, *Foudroyant* and *Orphée* to Gibraltar ahead of the main fleet, and, despite variable and mostly contrary winds, they finally anchored in off the New Mole on 26 March. They came in to a tumultuous welcome, as people saw first that two of the warships were French prizes and then began to recognise the largest of them, 'the very ship the French Admiral Galissonnière was in when he met Byng off Minorca'.

The prisoners and the sad trail of wounded men who staggered or were carried from *Monmouth* to the hospital reinforced the impression that this had been 'the bravest action, by all accounts, that has been known in the memory of man'. People trooped on to the *Foudroyant* to admire her and see the damage. 'I was on board the *Foudroyant* the day she came in,' wrote an officer of the *Volunteer* privateer. 'All that I will say of her is, that she will be the pride of England, and the shame of France.' She towered over the *Monmouth*, tied next to her at the Mole 'like the Monument overlooking a ninepin'. A survey showed that the French ship had more than a hundred shot holes in her starboard side and that several shots had gone right through. Four gun ports had been shot away and many more were damaged.

The triumphant dispatch that Augustus Hervey had penned for Osborn was published in London on 11 April. Next week the letter from 'an officer in Osborn's squadron' (who, it appears from his journal, was also Hervey) was printed in the *London Evening Post*, giving a detailed account of the action. Du Quesne and his officers arrived at Plymouth on 14 April and were sent to Northampton. The French admiral, the *London Evening Post* reported, gave 'a high Encomium on the Bravery and Behaviour of Capt. Gardener and the Officers and Men belonging to the *Monmouth* Man of War'. The accounts of the action were copied for regional newspapers and monthly magazines. When they came home the Monmouths would be famous.

Chicken's ode was printed repeatedly. By 5 May it had reached *Williamson's Liverpool Advertiser and Mercantile Register* to give Monmouth's officers their little fragment of immortality:

> As Lewis sat in regal state
> The Monarch, insolently great,
> Accosts his crouching slaves;
> 'Yon stubborn isle at last must bend;
> For now my Foudroyant I send,
> The terror of the waves.
>
> When once he bursts in dreadful roar,
> And vomits death from shore to shore,
> My glory to maintain,
> Repenting Britons then will see
> Their folly, to dispute with me
> The empire of the main.' . . .
>
> When lo! the heroic Gard'ner fell,
> Whose worth the Muse attempts to tell,
> But finds her efforts vain:
> Some other bard must sing his praise,
> And, bold as fancy's thoughts, must raise
> The sadly mournful strain.

Carket, who well his place supply'd,
The mangling bolts of death defy'd,
Which furious round him rag'd:
While Hammick points his guns with care,
Nor sends one faithless shot in air,
But skilfully engag'd.

Baron and Winzar's conduct show'd,
Their hearts with untam'd courage glow'd,
And manly rage display'd;
Whilst ev'ry seaman firmly stood,
'Midst heaps of limbs and streams of blood,
Undaunted, undismay'd.

Austin and Campbell next the Muse
Thro' fiery deluges pursues,
Serenely calm and great;
With their's the youthful Preston's name Must shine,
Inroll'd in lists of fame,
Above the reach of fate.

Now, haughty Lewis, cease to boast ;
The mighty Foudroyant is lost,
And must be thine no more:
No gasconade will now avail;
Behold he trims the new dress'd sail
To deck Britannia's shore.

If e'er again his voice be heard,
With British thunderbolts prepar'd,
And on thy coast appears:
His dreadful tongue such sounds will send,
As all the neighbouring rocks shall rend,
And shake all France with fears.

4

The New Captain

Hampton Court, 14 March 1758

Capt Gardiner of the Monmouth was killed, & I am going into that ship –
She is the same Rate but the best going Ship in England, & which only of all the
ships outsailed my ship that day – & as mine must soon go home being worn out
. . . let us think of the Foudroyant, Orphée, &c & the Great things we shall
now do this Summer with the Flying <u>*Monmouth*</u>

The Honourable Augustus John Hervey had never liked his ship
Hampton Court, but he liked her crew very much. They were
thorough seamen like the Monmouths, and had been an undisturbed,
settled company until summer 1756 when Admiral Hawke's secretary
had stolen eighty of them for worse-crewed ships. Hervey met
Admiral Osborn and Rear Admiral Saunders in the *Prince* on 13
March and together they discussed replacing the late Captain Gardiner
and choosing commanders for the two newly captured ships, *Foudroyant* and *Orphée*. Hervey asked the admiral for the *Monmouth* and
got his wish. *Monmouth*'s heavy casualties meant that Hervey would be
able to take many of his best men with him. He warmly recommended Carkett for promotion to command the *Foudroyant*. 'I knew
nothing of this gentleman,' he noted later, 'but from his conduct in
this action I thought he deserved it'.

Augustus Hervey was a second son with a private income of £50 a
year. His parents had met when his father, Lord John Hervey, was a
courtier to George, Prince of Wales (the future George II) and Mary,
known as Molly Lepel was reckoned the most attractive of his wife
Princess Caroline's maids of honour. She had little money of her own;
he was the heir to the Earl of Bristol, beautiful, charming and highly

47

cultured, though effeminate in manner. They married for love in 1720, meeting secretly in the garden of Alexander Pope's villa at Twickenham.

The love match did not last. After a few happy years Hervey glued himself to the court, becoming the closest confidant of Caroline, now Queen. She was the only person who could influence the notoriously obstinate, stupid and violent King George II, and Hervey became a vitally important ally to Robert Walpole, who managed the country's affairs. Hervey was a highly intelligent man and a faithful courtier, obsequious, self-abasing, but bitterly aware of the irony of his situation. Although he respected the queen, he disliked and despised the king. His disgust for court life eventually spread to life in general. He seems to have been the father of his eight children, but he had several extramarital affairs and was probably bisexual.

Mary Hervey never liked the Hanoverian court. After the first happy years she spent much of her time at Ickworth, the family's Suffolk estate. Highly intelligent and very well read, Lady Hervey was a great admirer of French culture and a leading proponent of French taste. She was a close friend of Horace Walpole, an acquaintance of Voltaire, and when she was in London cultured people gathered at her salons.

Augustus Hervey went to sea in 1735 at the age of eleven. He was entrusted to his uncle William Hervey, a naval captain 'austere in his disposition, even to a degree of cruelty, [who] became at once an object both of terror and hatred to his people'. Augustus served under his uncle for most of seven years before William Hervey was finally court-martialled and dismissed from the service for his unreasonable harshness. The experience gave the aspiring officer a useful lesson in how not to run a ship. William Hervey's lieutenants quarrelled violently with each other and with the captain, confining each other to their cabins and demanding courts martial at frequent intervals. One of the lieutenants once hit the young Augustus in the course of a savage verbal exchange.

Halfway through this period, in 1739, Britain went to war with Spain, ending a long period of peace. In 1740, while sailing to Spanish America to reinforce the fleet commanded by Admiral

Vernon that had just taken Porto Bello, Augustus Hervey passed for lieutenant. He was sixteen and the minimum legal age for candidates was twenty, although this was a rule that was often waived for privileged youths with talent. Immediately afterwards he came close to losing his life when his uncle's ship lost all three masts in a terrific November gale in the Bay of Biscay. The ship survived, however, and finally reached Jamaica in February 1741. That year Augustus took part in his first night boat attack during the abortive siege of the Spanish stronghold of Carthagena, and in 1742 served for the first time under Captain John Byng. As the son of Admiral Lord Torrington who had won a great victory in 1718, Byng was a useful patron, and the eighteen-year-old Hervey cultivated him as a friend. He also met and befriended Arthur Gardiner, who was at that time Byng's first lieutenant.

Hervey was of medium height, but slim, athletic and good-looking. He enjoyed rowing and fencing and practised at his harpsichord whenever he could. He was charming and intelligent but quick-tempered and highly conscious of his honour and of his station in life. From his diary we know that he was by now already sexually experienced. At Lisbon when he was sixteen the beautiful Italian opera singer Elena Paghetti took him to her bed, and in spring 1743 he had an affair with Mrs Artis, a young lady married to the much older post-master of Great Yarmouth, where Hervey was pressing men for Byng's *Captain*. It is likely that these were not the only girls Augustus knew on shore.

Hervey was at sea when his father died in August 1743, leaving him in shock with very little money and a loss of interest at the Admiralty that was immediately apparent. An offer by the then First Lord to promote him to command a sloop was blocked by the Duke of Newcastle. This would have been the next step up the ladder of promotion. Hervey needed now to get command of his own ship, either as the master and commander of a small sloop, or even better as the post captain of a frigate of twenty guns or more. Once he was made post he would climb up the list of captains by seniority until he eventually became an admiral. Newcastle's intervention was especially untimely from Hervey's point of view, for in March 1744 France declared war on Britain and the prospect of taking prizes and making money became much rosier. Britain was now finally involved in the general European war known as the War of the Austrian Succession, as well as in its own war against Spain.

Hervey was already in funds to the tune of about £1,500 from his lieutenant's share of a good prize taken by his uncle and a much richer one captured by Byng. In May 1744, while his ship refitted at Portsmouth, Lieutenant Hervey went to Winchester races and there encountered the lovely and very sexy Elizabeth Chudleigh, former girlfriend of Lord Pulteney, on the rebound after a fling with the Duke of Hamilton. He was twenty, she twenty-four. Within a month they were secretly married.

The marriage had to be secret because Lord Pulteney had set up his former mistress with a job as maid of honour to Augusta, Princess of Wales, a role that she must surrender when there was some clear public confirmation that she was no longer a maid. Since her £400 per annum was the only significant regular income that the couple had (a lieutenant with his servant earned £84.10s p.a.), their marriage remained secret. After a few days of wedded bliss, Hervey rejoined his ship and sailed to the West Indies in the flagship of Admiral Davers to defend Jamaica against the combined forces of Spain and France.

Hervey hoped and expected to be made a post captain by Davers, a neighbour of his grandfather Lord Bristol in Suffolk. Promotion almost always came first to the lieutenants of the flagship, but Davers kept the *Cornwall* in Port Royal in miserable inactivity. Davers fell out with the Governor of Jamaica over island politics and Hervey, who found Davers both incompetent and corrupt, supported Governor Trelawney. He resigned his commission in *Cornwall* and returned home without promotion, without a ship and without money, bitter at having fallen behind many rivals in naval seniority.

He was met with the news that his wife had renewed her acquaintance with the Duke of Hamilton and that his brother had heard rumours of his marriage. Hervey refused to speak on the subject and amused himself with a pair of opera singers while he waited for

Elizabeth to appear in London. They quarrelled, then made up. He visited her frequently at night, borrowed money against future prizes to pay her debts and left to take up his appointment as master and commander of the *Porcupine* sloop. He had finally got promotion. During two months in command he destroyed one French privateer and captured another. Then John Byng, now a rear admiral, offered to make Hervey the captain of his flagship, giving him the final push up the ladder. Hervey took command of the beautiful Spanish prize *Princessa* in January 1747, a twenty-three-year-old post captain. He was not quite the youngest captain in the navy, but he was back on the high road to fortune. When *Princessa* was preparing for sea early next year he spent more time with Elizabeth, leaving her pregnant with a child who was possibly his. The boy lived only for a few weeks.

In the Mediterranean, Byng chose to hoist his flag in the *Boyne* and left Hervey with his own ship. Even better, Byng gave his favourite protégé many fine cruises, so that within the two years before the Treaty of Aix-la-Chapelle ended the war in October 1748, Hervey had made an estimated £9,000 from prize money. At Leghorn he also made a name for himself as a hero by personally cutting away a burning ship full of powder that threatened the harbour and everything in it, before towing her into open water where she blew up harmlessly.

Now Hervey, himself a 'follower' of his 'friend' Lord Byng, began to establish his own following. This was how the navy (and all other spheres of life) worked in the eighteenth century. A patron would get jobs for loyal followers. If they were good and they did well, the patron's influence and prestige increased accordingly. When they got commands, the followers would find roles for their patron's more junior protégés. In this way an interest-group of 'friends' was established, united by common loyalty. When a senior patron was in power, all the best patronage flowed to his closest 'friends'. In a ship, a captain's followers also hoped to be rewarded, even if it was only with a slightly better rating. Men might follow a captain for prize money, out of regional loyalty, or merely because they liked him, but it was important to a captain to have a following of trustworthy seamen.

At this time, the most powerful man in the navy was George

Anson, First Lord of the Admiralty. Hervey was one of many who noticed with envious resentment that plum appointments went to men who had sailed with Anson on his famous voyage round the world in 1740 to 1744. These loyal followers included George Saunders (Osborn's second in command) and Augustus Keppel.

George, Lord Anson in 1755 by James McArdell after Joshua Reynolds.

In John Byng, Hervey seemed to have the second best patron, and in his shadow the gallant young captain began to build up his own following – men who followed him from ship to ship. The men came and went, but there were three who later followed Hervey from *Hampton Court* into *Monmouth* who had first met him in 1747. William Parvin and John Burgess had joined *Princessa* in 1744, and William Mallard, a tobacco-chewing Londoner, a year later. Of these three oldest retainers, Burgess became a particular favourite, a 'Sober, Active and Diligent Man' in whom the captain had total confidence.

Along with *Princessa*'s second lieutenant Peter Foulkes, Parvin, Burgess and Mallard were amongst the sixty men that Hervey took with him in 1748 into his next ship, the 24-gun frigate *Phoenix*. With marines and others her total complement was 160 men, so Hervey provided half the sailors. In a frigate with a small crew like *Phoenix*, ordinary men got a decent share of prize money and Hervey's followers did well out of his luck.

From the Mediterranean, Hervey wrote to Elizabeth to tell her of his prizes and new-found affluence. He made no further effort to be faithful. In Leghorn he enjoyed the attentions of the wives of two Italian merchants, and in Lisbon on the way home that of his old flame, the opera singer Elena Paghetti. On one remarkable morning in Lisbon, while he waited to freight the *Phoenix* with Brazilian gold, he, the Spanish Duke de Bagnos and the French Comte de Vergennes 'went in cloaks to upwards of, I verily believe, thirty ladys' houses – ladies of pleasure, I mean'.

However, there was nothing Hervey could do that Chudleigh could not top. By the time he returned to London she was well on the way to the reputation for unscrupulous fortune hunting that caused Edward Thomson to give her a central role in his *Meretriciad*, an epic poem about classy whores. Hervey paid her debts – a mere £1,000 or so – then had an *éclaircissement* with her, a frank exchange of views, as a result of which he 'took a resolution from this afternoon of going abroad and never having any more to do in that affair'. He went first to Newmarket and then to Ickworth. She remained in London for the fireworks and parties held to celebrate the peace, putting in a particularly impressive performance at the Venetian Ambassador's daytime masquerade at Ranelagh. She went

as Iphigenia, sacrificed when the Greek fleet sailed for Troy, but as
Horace Walpole put it, 'so naked that you would have taken her for
Andromeda'. An allusion to Hervey's desertion of her for the sea may
have been intended, but it had the effect of accelerating his plans for
further foreign travel. Indeed, from this time she was for him 'a clog . . .
that would not let me remain in England with any satisfaction to myself'.

Iphigenia *by Charles Mosley, 1749, shows the masquerade costume with which
Elizabeth Chudleigh delighted George II and disgusted her husband.*

The day that a print was published of Elizabeth in her topless costume, her husband set off for Paris. Hervey fell in love with the French capital, and several opera dancers and aristocrats later, he fell for a Frenchwoman, Suzanne-Felix de Caze. It took him some time to win Suzanne's heart, but by April 1750 she was entirely his and in December, when finally he was forced to leave the French metropolis, she was seven months pregnant. It is fairly certain that this child, born in February 1751, was Hervey's son. They kept in touch by letter through George Selwyn, but within a year she had confessed, resolved to be faithful to her husband and wanted Hervey as a friend.

Her dejected lover consoled himself in Lisbon, for after three years ashore, in 1752 Hervey got orders to take *Phoenix* to sea again, and to join George Edgcumbe's peacetime Mediterranean squadron. Three men we shall meet again joined *Phoenix* when she commissioned. John Blake was a capable Irish able seaman from Waterford, then aged twenty-five. Louis d'Amour may well have been Hervey's personal cook, since he already had a steward. He went everywhere with the captain from then on. Sam Blow was an intelligent eighteen-year-old able seaman. With Parvin, Mallard and Burgess they shared in gentle cruises, diplomatic visits and frequent lavish entertainments. The band that Hervey always kept played frequently. These were soft and pleasant times, with passengers often on board. For six weeks in 1754 they even had two leopards and an antelope, presents given to Hervey in Algiers.

Hervey took advantage of every sexual opportunity that offered itself and soon had at least one girl in every port. His diary mentions affairs with more than thirty women between 1749 and 1757. He was never one to refuse a one-night-stand, or even what intercourse could be crammed into a short afternoon, in the case of Princess Ippolita Pignatelli, but he found much to appreciate in many of his lovers and became very fond of several. Mademoiselle Sarrazin was one such. She embarked with her maid in the *Phoenix* in August 1753 and remained in Hervey's keeping as they cruised the Mediterranean until February 1754. The seamen must have known her well by sight, and must have joked about their captain's tastes.

In 1754, during a brief visit to Portugal, Hervey was kidnapped at
gunpoint. Expecting to be murdered at any moment, he was driven
through the night to a *quinta* where he was invited into the bedroom
of a beautiful lady. Even Hervey took some time to recover his poise
before, 'feeling myself in the arms of a very fine and a very luxurious
woman, those sensations soon began to get the better of all others, as
they were ever ready enough to do with me'. His hostess insisted on
total secrecy, and he returned home, entranced, to Mlle Sarrazin, who
immediately demanded an explanation for his nightlong absence from
her bed. After several secret liaisons, he finally identified his mysterious
abductress: she was Henriette-Julie-Gabrièle, Duchess of Cadaval, a
princess of the house of Lorraine on the fringe of the Portuguese royal
family.

In that year Hervey fell in love. He must have glimpsed Pellina
Brignole-Sale in 1748 when he made a diplomatic visit to her
brother-in-law the Doge of Genoa. Genoa had been allied with
France and Spain against Britain, Austria and Savoy. When the
Savoyards overran Liguria in 1746, Gian Francesco Brignole-Sale
had led the popular revolt that expelled them from the city. Hervey
then visited the French commander, the Duc de Richelieu, who
was staying at Pellinetta's house. He met her again in 1752 when he
found her 'very handsome and sensible for an Italian', but it was not
until August 1754 that 'that intimacy began which lasted all the
while I was in the Mediterranean, and which friendship can only
finish with myself'. According to the custom of the Genoese, she
made him her *cicisbeo*, her particular companion and escort. He gave
a party for her and thirty others on board the *Phoenix*, where they
danced almost all night and no doubt admired the 'tygers' from
Algiers. She was 'not perfectly happy with her husband who was a
very sour, niggardly, ill-looking man, and had very little attention
to anything but his money'.

After spending most of August 1754 with her, he returned the
following February for the carnival. This time he got what he wanted,
'one whole night with her, malgré all the difficulties and risks that
would attend it'. She feigned an inflammation of the eye for a couple
of days and kept her room in the Palazzo Rosso darkened. Hervey and

others were with her in the evening. He pretended to leave, she sent the company into another room, and he dodged into her cabinet, back into her bedroom, took off his coat and shoes, and joined her in her bed 'which was covered by one of their great thick sort of down quilts'. The bed had heavy curtains on three sides and the company, now including her husband, returned to sit in dim light on the fourth. This went on for an hour. After supper, Ridolfo Brignole-Sale returned, and 'I was frightened at his d—'d *douceurs*, and especially when he offered to bring a light to the bed-side to show her some India handkerchiefs he had that morning bought for her, but which she put off, and away he went, leaving me in the arms of one of the loveliest women that ever was. I lay till near daylight and performed wonders.'

On 10 March she swore on the cross she wore round her neck 'that she would never make any intimacy with anyone else as long as she lived'. Hervey 'had already experienced that the use of confessions and absolutions with these ladies made all that very easy when the passions cooled, or new ones succeeded'.

Returning to the British Mediterranean headquarters at Minorca in Spring 1755, 'all the conversation was on thoughts of war'. There was great tension on the borders of the British and French colonies in America where war seemed imminent, and also in Silesia between Prussia and Austria. Austria wanted British help, as in the previous war, against Prussia and France. As Elector of Hanover, a Prince of the Empire, George II had a duty to support the Austrian Empress, but Britain did not want to be drawn into a European land war. Austria was beginning to explore an alliance with France, a total upheaval of the traditional pattern of European diplomacy.

Hervey himself 'found I was very much in love with Pellinetta by my being displeased with everything about me'. He wrote to her constantly. He was sent back to Genoa in late July to find out what the Republic would do when war broke out. British colonial forces under Edward Braddock and George Washington had launched an attack on the French Fort Duquesne that barred their path to westward expansion. Admiral Boscawen had been sent to prevent French reinforcements reaching America, arrived too late, but attacked anyway and seized two French warships without provocation. The news 'made a great noise everywhere, as a war was inevitable'. The British consul, Dick, found the King's arms over his door 'with a t—d stuck upon it with a paper, and wrote on it some very scurrilous words on the King'.

Hervey countered with all the diplomatic charm he possessed. He dined about Genoa. On one hot, scented, Italian summer night, he 'had the three sisters Pellinetta, Argentina and Angelina on board to musick' as his men looked on wistfully. He went with Pellinetta to see her brother-in-law, the former Doge, who 'talked of a neutrality, and how much he wished the Court of England should know that was the sentiments of the Genoese, but as I knew this great man was entirely Frenchified I gave very little credit to anything he said, but however took care he should not see my opinion of him'. The secretary of state sent an express 'to read to all the trade to warn them of an approaching war with France'.

Hervey remained in Genoa all August and the following spring he received a letter informing him that Pellinetta had given birth to a girl on 13 April – the dates and the letter both imply that she was Hervey's daughter.

From the newspapers the Phoenixes learned of General Braddock's army's massacre and his death near Fort Duquesne. While escorting a convoy of merchant ships to Turkey, Hervey received orders to seize all French ships and send them to a British port. War had still not been declared. *Phoenix* made so many captures in 1755 that even the private men reckoned on £50 each, while the captain anticipated £14,000. All the prizes they made were taken to the harbour at Port Mahon, Minorca, where Hervey 'got in with' the very pretty daughter of the tavern keeper.

At Minorca they got wind of French plans to seize the island. A visit by *Phoenix* to Nice confirmed the danger, but Governor Blakeney was slow to organise a defence. Hervey went out a second time for intelligence, discovered the French had already sailed and found himself cut off from Port Mahon. He joined Admiral Byng as he approached Minorca with a relieving fleet substantially weaker than the French one. Hervey recommended landing the troops immediately, but with sick crews for his ships Byng decided to retain them to help fight the French fleet. As senior frigate captain, Hervey was responsible for observing and recording what happened during the battle that followed.

Both fleets engaged in line of battle, and the British closed gradually on the French. Then the *Intrépide*, fifth in the British line, was damaged, drove on the ships astern of her, and forced them to back sail. This made a gap in the British line. Byng tried to reform rather than go pell-mell for the French, since Admiral Matthews had been court-martialled for doing that in 1744, but the pause to reform allowed Admiral Galissonnière to draw clear while doing serious damage to the exposed ships in the British van. A council of war following the battle decided the fleet must return to secure Gibraltar and the Strait. Hervey argued in favour of staying off Minorca and waiting for reinforcements, while trying to help the garrison.

Byng transferred Hervey to the badly damaged *Defiance*, whose captain had been killed, and sent him to get the hospital at Gibraltar ready. When Hervey went aboard *Defiance* he found so many sick and wounded that he could only muster 226 out of 400 fit for duty. At Gibraltar he found five fresh ships sent out to reinforce Byng. One was the *Hampton Court*, with orders for him to take command of her, so his followers changed ship with him again. Hervey also discovered at Gibraltar that Lord Edgcumbe had failed to send the prizes away from Minorca before the French arrived so that he and his men had lost their imagined riches. 'Tis hard to have a Fortune thus almost in one's Pocket & yet be as poor as a Rat', he wrote to his sister.

Despite the reinforcement, Byng was hesitant about returning to Minorca. On 2 July Sir Edward Hawke arrived to replace him. Hawke sailed immediately, but when he reached Minorca he found the island had already surrendered. Hervey returned to England for Byng's court martial and did his utmost to defend his patron. He lodged together with his old friend Gardiner at Gosport for the trial at which they both gave evidence.

The government needed a scapegoat for Minorca and the king was determined to see Byng condemned. Moreover, however Hervey and Gardiner presented the facts, Byng had not behaved with the reckless disregard for odds that was expected of the Royal Navy in desperate cases. He had not even shown much energetic determination to take a risk. He had been too conscious of the sickness in his fleet and the poor quality of his ships and seamen, the result of government miscalculation of French intentions.

Admiral Byng's execution by a firing squad of marines on board the Monarque 1757.

The death of a patron was a potential catastrophe for his followers. For that patron to be executed as Admiral Byng was in 1757 was almost as bad as it could get. Hervey had been outspoken in Byng's defence in full knowledge that his stand would not be approved. Fortunately, very few men except King George II believed that Byng deserved to be executed. Dismissed, possibly, but not executed. Moreover, while Admiral Anson's faction was powerful, it did not monopolise all interest. So, as politics would have it, Admiral Osborn, appointed to the Mediterranean Command in Byng's place in 1757, was Byng's brother-in-law. Hervey had suffered a setback, but in the Mediterranean he still had a 'friend' in command even if the second in command, Rear Admiral Charles Saunders, was Admiral Anson's most favoured follower and therefore, from Hervey's point of view, to be treated with caution.

Admiral Osborn sailed for the Mediterranean in May 1757 with a small squadron that included the *Monmouth*. His task was to prevent the French leaving the Mediterranean and to keep the Spanish neutral. Hervey sailed out in Osborn's flagship the *Prince*. He had just parted with his steward William Cradock, who left his service to marry Elizabeth Chudleigh's maid. Cradock was replaced by Daniel Cameron and John Finney, one of whom must have been the new steward, the other probably a valet. Louis D'Amour, probably the cook, and Hervey's Scottish clerk Ninian Dunbar accompanied Hervey and they rejoined *Hampton Court* together. That summer Hervey cruised with *Revenge* and together they destroyed a French frigate and captured several prizes.

Since Hervey knew Genoa so well, Osborn sent him in July to investigate a report that the Genoese were building ships for the French and shipping cannon to Toulon. The diplomatic situation was complex since Austrian Tuscany was at war with Britain's ally Prussia but not with Britain. Hervey realised that Genoa was bound to help France, but diplomacy could place limits on that help. As usual he spent as much time as possible with Pellinetta. He renewed other old acquaintances at Leghorn and cruised alongside Gardiner in *Monmouth*.

The 'murder' of Byng continued to depress Hervey, as it had depressed Gardiner. 'I can never wipe it off my spirits,' he wrote to his sister in 1757, 'it gives a gloominess to everything relating to the Profession I am in, and is such a check on all Sallies of joy'. In March 1758, when he obtained command of the *Monmouth*, he would have been in the highest spirits 'but that I have almost every minute of this day been reflecting, that this very day last year was that Horrid, cruel & unjust execution which deprived me of the most Agreeable as well as usefull Friend that I, or any other Body could ask'. Then he suffered another blow. On the morning of 25 March he was called to the flagship to discover that the sixty-three-year-old admiral had suffered a paralytic stroke. Hervey wrote that he had brought it on himself 'by his constant anxiety and watching the French and the different duties of the fleet, which he carried to too great an excess and minuteness for his time of life'. His speech was faulty, his mouth paralysed on one side, and the surgeons of the fleet in consultation feared for his life. After a few days the admiral began to recover, but it was clear he would have to go home. Hervey reported to the Admiralty, asking for a replacement. With Osborn gone, his influence in the fleet might cease, so Hervey hurriedly got his new command ready for sea.

On 1 April he completed *Monmouth*'s crew with ninety-one men from *Hampton Court*. His switches of personnel were both generous and ruthless. *Monmouth*'s senior lieutenants were promoted, Robert Carkett to post captain, Stephen Hammick into Admiral Osborn's flagship, a shift that normally led to an early promotion to master and commander. The senior surviving mate was also promoted into Saunders' flagship. They got the preferment they wished for, but their promotion enabled Hervey to replace them with men he could trust to back him up. One lesson that Hervey hadn't forgotten was to surround himself with people he trusted.

Into *Monmouth* he brought as senior lieutenants St John Chinnery and Edward Hutchins from *Hampton Court*. They could dominate third and fourth lieutenants James Baron and David Winzar if necessary. To replace the mates, Hervey introduced two of *Hampton Court*'s, John McLaurin, an experienced and highly promising twenty-five-year-old ambitious for a commission, and Henry Reeves, a follower from *Phoenix*. There were three vacancies for midshipmen and Hervey filled these also with followers from *Hampton Court*.

He put the best seamen amongst his most trusted followers into the key petty officer roles. The ship's performance depended on these responsible and, in battle, dangerous roles, and they were better rewarded as a result. Hervey brought in four quartermasters from *Hampton Court* of whom two were old followers – Irishman John Blake, rated quartermaster since 1756, and John Harvey, a mere landsman in *Phoenix* in 1748, promoted from able seaman in *Hampton Court*. The new sailmaker was Thomas Varley, sailmaker's crew and then mate in *Hampton Court*. John Irwin had been able, yeoman and boatswain's mate and Jacob Adam Steffins had been gunner's mate in *Hampton Court*: both became yeomen of the sheets. They were joined by Adam Trumbull, able in *Phoenix* in 1754, then coxwain and yeoman of the sheets in *Hampton Court*. The trusted former Princessa John Burgess retained his position as gunner's mate with a couple of new quarter-gunners. Hervey made Sam Blow his coxwain, commander of his barge.

In this way he achieved two goals. He infiltrated his own people into the command structure and made sure that he had good people in place. It was almost inevitable that Hervey should promote his own men, rather than unknown people from the new ship, but his favouritism had one serious disadvantage. It offended the old Monmouths, who felt that those who had fought in the battle deserved the promotions and therefore resented the incomers.

More than eighty of *Monmouth*'s heroes were in hospital and according to Lieutenant Winzar's log the first fifty-seven of *Monmouth*'s hospital cases at least were wounded. Others may have been feverish. Although Gibraltar had been a British fortress ever since its capture from the Spanish in 1703, it was still an underdeveloped base, though the hospital had recently been improved. In 1742 there had been nothing there but 'two Sheds, or Hutts, capable of receiving about Thirty Men': in 1744 a new building had been completed at a cost of £20,997.

It is not possible to trace the fate of the wounded men in any detail, but only seven died in hospital. Forty-one returned to *Monmouth* before she left Gibraltar, of whom two died at sea during the summer. Nineteen left the ship's books as 'unserviceable' in May: perhaps amputees who were clearly too badly maimed to continue in the navy. Two men who had been wounded on 1 March died at the Haslar Hospital at Gosport in November, two more at Rochester Hospital in March 1759. However, the survival rate suggests that the medical staff in the ship and in the hospital did their job tolerably well.

A final change to the personnel came as a result of the calamity that overtook the flagship of the new commander, Vice Admiral Thomas Broderick, on her way to Gibraltar.

While crossing the Bay of Biscay in thick fog the *Prince George* caught fire. It broke out in the boatswain's storeroom, but by the time they got the fire hose into the water, they could not reach or even see the flames for the dense smoke. Once it became clear that the fire was beyond control, the men panicked. They lowered the admiral's barge to ensure his safety, but when forty people piled in to a boat designed for fifteen, Broderick stripped naked and took to the water. Fog delayed any rescue and then the merchantmen were afraid to come close in case the flagship exploded. After an hour, Admiral Broderick was picked up by a merchantman's boat. Some of the crew remaining on board jumped into the water and drowned, others burned on deck. The loaded guns went off at random, sinking swimmers as the ship rolled. 260 out of 745 people were saved.

Boatswain File Fewin was a witness at the court martial of Captain Peyton for the loss of his ship. Asked when the ship sank, he replied, 'I can't tell for I was so long in the water that I was almost dead.' The fire had not been Fewin's fault, and the man impressed Hervey. The boatswain was an important man in a ship since he had charge of all the 'Rigging, Cables, Cordage, Anchors, Sails, Boats, &c.' and also enforced the smooth working and discipline of the crew, supervising and relieving watches. Fewin had immense experience. Warrant officers progressed from small ships to important ones and Fewin was qualified by experience for the second-rate ninety-gun ship that had just exploded. Having been boatswain of the sixty-gun *Medway* in 1744, he was in his late-fifties. Hervey shared Arthur Gardiner's poor opinion of his present boatswain, James Everitt, and quickly got rid of him. On 24 May he departed and next day Fewin came in. Hervey also took *Prince George*'s purser on a temporary basis, since Samuel Furzer had decided to make the *Foudroyant* his last battle.

By that time the *Monmouth* was back at sea. Broderick, now commanding the squadron, was worried that the French might try to break out of the Mediterranean in pursuit of their original orders to go to Canada. Admiral Saunders, Osborn's second in command, was also ordered home with the damaged ships and prizes, *Montagu, Revenge, Foudroyant* and *Orphée*. Hervey had got orders to reconnoitre

Toulon and secure the trade. On 29 May, Restoration Day, he gave Admiral Saunders a farewell dinner with the commissioner and the Spanish Governor on board. A fine discharge of gunfire saluted both Charles II and Signor Buccarelli.

Once the Spaniard had gone, the Monmouths set off into the night.

5

The Flying Monmouth

You are hereby required and directed to proceed with His Majesty's Ship under your Command off Toulon, and to make what Observations you can of the Enemies Situation at that Place calling afterwards at Villafranca for more minute Informations of the Enemies Intentions . . .

The *Monmouth* was bound for Toulon, the French Mediterranean base, in order to find out whether or not the French had abandoned their attempt to send their Mediterranean squadron across the Atlantic to oppose British efforts to capture New France. The British strategic goal in summer 1758 was to capture Louisbourg, the French fortress guarding the entrance to the St Lawrence River, and then to seize Quebec, and the Toulon squadron must not be allowed to interfere. At the same time war raged in Germany, where George II's Electorate of Hanover was in danger, and north German and Prussian troops fought French, Austrian and Russian armies, but only distant rumours of the land war reached the Mediterranean, where an uneasy neutrality was prevalent.

On the Mediterranean station every captain was a diplomat, and the admiral was something close to a viceroy. The consuls represented British interests locally, mediated in favour of local interests with the British authorities, and supplied what intelligence they could gather. Naval captains sometimes had to make diplomatic decisions on the spur of the moment, and the better informed they were about local conditions, the better their decisions were likely to be. *An Essay on the Duty and Qualifications of a Sea-Officer* (1765) considered 'learning French . . . an indispensible qualification' since French was the international language, and it was helpful if sea officers could converse in other languages as well.

There were all kinds of complexities to master. The Grand Duchy of Tuscany, for instance, was subject to Austria. Although Austria was fighting Britain's ally Prussia, Britain was not herself at war with Austria. What is more, Britain did not wish to disrupt the important trade through Leghorn by offending the Austrians. Hervey's local task was to protect the British merchant fleets trading with Italy through Leghorn (Livorno) in Austrian Tuscany and with Turkey through Smyrna (Izmir) and Aleppo. In his diplomatic role he must ensure that the 'neutral' states that favoured France – Spain, Genoa, Naples and Malta – remained strictly neutral. For a friendly base *Monmouth* could rely on Livorno, or Leghorn, which remained resolutely open to British trade. Hervey could also use the ports of the friendly Kingdom of Sardinia, Villefranche and Nice, useful for their proximity to Toulon.

Monmouth had a rapid voyage down to Minorca and stood in close to the familiar but now hostile harbour of Port Mahon on 3 June 1758. The next day they saw a sail to the northward and chased after it, flying a Dutch flag as a disguise. After an hour and a half their victim hoisted French colours and came towards them, whereupon they changed their Dutch colours to English and the French ship surrendered. McLaurin went on board to command with six men and provisions for three weeks. She was the *Saint Joseph*, a tartan – a little coasting vessel with one large sail – inward bound from Toulon, laden with wood. She was an insignificant prize, but her captain revealed valuable intelligence. He told Hervey that four French warships were at sea. Two were bound for Malta and two more would call at Malta to leave men to crew a captured British privateer that was under repair there, and then attack British shipping in the Levant. Otherwise, one ship and two frigates were at readiness in Toulon Road while the rest of the fleet was disarmed.

After a rough night of strong gales and squalls, *Monmouth* sailed on towards Toulon. Hervey wanted to steer for Marseilles, but the mistral forced him further east. On 6 June he sent Winzar to investigate a ship

French map, published in 1764, of the area in which Monmouth *cruised in summer 1758.*

that seemed to be abandoned. She 'proved to be a tartan, judged to be French, who had met with & been plundered by a Turk, having no living soul on board, & her rigging &c all cut to pieces'. They took out whatever was useful – three small anchors and several hawsers – then they set her on fire.

Monmouth approached the Ile de Levant, to the east of Toulon, under cover of darkness. Hervey reinforced the *St Joseph* with one of the lieutenants, seven petty officers and forty men and sent her close inshore late at night, while *Monmouth* remained four miles out to sea. The idea was that small merchantmen, alarmed by the unidentified warship, would hug the coastline, where they would be snapped up by the apparently innocent tartan. The first prize approached *Monmouth* at midday, two more in the second dog watch, and finally, around midnight, after a signal with flares, the *St Joseph* returned in triumph with a fourth prize containing 10,000 lemons.

Hervey looked into Toulon, nearly snatching up a large merchant. He continued to cruise, but the coast was now thoroughly alarmed against *Monmouth* and her decoy. Hervey steered for Villefranche and put in there on 10 June with his five prizes. From there he sent reports to Broderick and the Admiralty. What he had discovered confirmed that *Monmouth*'s capture of *Foudroyant* had produced a strategic victory: French efforts to reinforce Canada from the Mediterranean were over for the year and their fleet was disarmed. What was more, the general situation of the French at Toulon was most encouragingly dire. The French could not pay their men, who consequently refused to serve, and shortage of money was starving the French navy of supplies, 'as the Merchts. will not undertake the Contracts for the Government on any terms, as all those made for the Minorca expedition as well as the hire of their Transports and Pay of the Seamen remain unsettled to this day'. Meanwhile, British attacks had brought French trade almost to a standstill 'as none will Insure for any Premium whatever'.

Monmouth spent five days on the Côte d'Azur, during which time Hervey dined with his old friend General Paterson, the governor of the province of Nice, and held a dinner on board *Monmouth* for the local Sardinian officers. Sardinia was neutral but had been allied with Britain in the last war, and Hervey was exploring just how far they might extend their hospitality to a British fleet. He took on board the recently married wife of a Sardinian colonel who wanted to join her husband, and sent a messenger to his elder brother George, Earl of Bristol, who was the ambassador to the King of Sardinia at the capital, Turin. Here, they 'sold all the tartans and made a Dividend of ye money, of 6 French livres [5 shillings] per man'. Flush with silver, or flushed with the result of having spent it, *Monmouth*'s boats towed her out of port in a flat calm.

At Leghorn, John Dick, the British consul, gave Hervey the latest news. Hawke had stopped reinforcements for Louisbourg leaving Rochefort, but some French ships had escaped from Brest and the fate of Britain's main effort for 1758 was still in doubt. In the Mediterranean the French objective was the Turkey trade. Dick told him that the French *Triton*, a 64 like *Monmouth*, with three frigates, was sailing to the east of Malta to capture the British merchant fleet returning from Izmir and Aleppo with their cargoes of spices, silk, satin, cotton and carpets. Hervey looked to his own resources. The frigate *Lyme* was in quarantine at Leghorn, the *Ambuscade* was at Genoa, *Rainbow* was returning to Gibraltar and the *Preston* had sailed for the Levant to escort the British Turkey fleet home. *Preston* alone, with only fifty guns, was not strong enough to protect them. Hervey's clear duty was to intervene. He sent a felucca to summon *Ambuscade*, while *Monmouth* and *Lyme* sailed northward to La Spezia. There, Dick told Hervey he would find ninety-eight British seamen who had seized their French cartel.

The British warships arrived in the evening. 'Here we came for, and found in a french cartill the whole Company of ye *Enterprize* Privatr. of Bristol, who was taken off Toulon ye 14 last month,' wrote David Winzar. 'We took 'em all out being 97,' he continued, and 'at 4am got under sail'. The sullen Bristolian privateersmen had helped take three rich French Turkey ships before being captured themselves, and they had risen on their French guards only to be recaptured by the Royal Navy. The rendezvous with *Ambuscade* was off the island of Gorgona, and from there the cruisers tacked slowly towards Sardinia. Hervey revealed his plans to captains Gwyn and Vernon of *Ambuscade* and *Lyme*. The squadron exercised their great guns. If they met the French they would at best be evenly matched and might have a hard fight. On 27 June they met two Sardinian galleys, into which Hervey put his female passenger, and sailed as fast as possible for Maréttimo, off the west coast of Sicily, where Hervey had been told that the French ships might be found.

They got no further information from passing vessels and reached Pantellaria on 29 June without having seen the French. Next day they saw three vessels and cleared for action. They chased so fast that a crack appeared in *Lyme*'s mainmast, but the ships proved to be Dutchmen from Smyrna heading for Amsterdam. *Lyme* needed two days at anchor to repair her mast, so Hervey decided to do it at Malta, where he would consult the British consul as to the latest news.

As they approached Malta on the evening of 1 July, *Monmouth*'s lookout saw a distant sail that looked like a frigate. In very light airs they chased all night and at dawn, as the seamen began the daily routine of scrubbing the decks, they saw a French frigate about four miles away in almost a flat calm, close inshore but no closer than they were to Valetta. Hervey could not cut her off from the land so as to ensure getting her intact, but with *Monmouth*'s speed through the water in the faintest breath of air, he could stop her escaping into Valetta harbour. He set his course to intercept.

Ambuscade and *Lyme* had been caught out by currents in the night and were several gunshots astern of the Frenchman. Hervey signalled to them to chase and sent orders to destroy the French ship even though she was in the neutral waters of Malta, 'as I had my reasons for paying very little regard to the neutrality of the island of Malta, as they regarded it so little towards the subjects of His Majesty whenever they could show a partiality to the French'. Strictly speaking, he should not attack so close to a 'neutral' port, but most of the Knights of Malta were Frenchmen, their bias towards France was ill-concealed, and their power was small enough for Hervey to stage a demonstration of British strength without worrying overmuch about diplomatic repercussions.

Monmouth and the French frigate edged closer to the entrance to Valetta harbour. The French frigate's boats were towing her, oarsmen straining as they raced for the safety of the port and its protective batteries. *Monmouth* glided smoothly in, her own boats trailing behind. Soon after six o'clock the French captain realised he had lost the race. His only chance was that his opponent would not risk coming under Maltese fire. According to Hervey's reports the frigate fired first, giving them a legal right to reply. The frigate was struggling to weather a point just off the Lazaretto when Hervey opened fire: 'The instant I fired at her the batteries on shore, which were crowded with people, began to fire at me, being then about a musket shot from the

The French frigate Rose *burning off Valetta with* Monmouth, Ambuscade *and* Lyme.

shore. The French frigate, finding my fire very quick upon her, began to steer wild and run on shore.'

As the frigate ran aground, *Monmouth* brought to and continued to batter the enemy vessel. The Monmouths could see Frenchmen swarming over the sides and into boats. Monmouth's own boats shot forward. With the ship providing covering fire, they rowed under a lieutenant 'with orders to destroy her under our fire'. But, long before they reached her, the frigate caught fire and was quickly ablaze. The boats turned back. An hour later she blew up. None of the frigate's shots hit *Monmouth* and the fort's all fell well short.

Hervey took his ship close in to the crowded battlements of the stronghold of the Knights of St John. Looking into Valetta harbour, Hervey could see only the captured Bristol privateer, the powerful *Tyger*, of thirty-six guns. Built in St Malo but captured by Bristolians, the *Tyger* was 'famous in the last war' for its rich captures. After two hours a deputation from the Grand Master emerged from the harbour and came aboard. They were hostile and angry, demanding to know 'why I had in this manner broke the neutrality of the port by destroying a French man-of-war under their very walls'. Hervey replied sarcastically in French that having had the honour to see his eminence the Grand Master on his balcony, he could not do otherwise than to give him a salute. He expressed his own displeasure at having been shot at by a neutral state and said that he would appear before the port the next day and that if one single shot was fired he would immediately destroy their galleys, which he knew to be loading corn in Sicily.

He returned next morning with *Ambuscade* and *Lyme* with their colours flying and guns run out and sailed past the town within musket shot of the walls, but no shot was fired. Hervey determined to sail eastwards in search of the two French ships that were still at large. He transferred John Pooley and Robert Reynard from his carpenter's crew to the frigate to help repair her damaged mast. At this point, however, the purser's steward, David Bowman, confessed that the ship did not contain as much food as everybody had thought. Hervey noted 'a deficiency in provisions of 852 gallons wine, 7 gallons oyl, 47 pieces beef, 8 bushels oatmeal, 3 galls flour, 1054 lbs raisins, 1200 lb being owing to an overcharge at the exchange of pursers and not unknown to Davis Bowman, purser's steward, before we sailed from Gibraltar, but not reported until now'. Hervey sacked Bowman, who was immediately disrated to ordinary. Then they returned to Tuscany to stock up.

Sailing into gentle winds, the voyage back to Leghorn took a languorous ten days. Leghorn was Britain's principal commercial base in the Mediterranean. About thirty English families lived there permanently, and in peacetime tourists constantly passed through on their way to Florence and Rome. It was a cosmopolitan place with religious freedom for Greeks, Armenians, Jews, Muslims and the resident English merchants (other Protestants had to worship in private). It was also the only place in Italy where Protestants might be buried. One third of its 45,000 inhabitants were Jews, who had their own ghetto and handled much of Leghorn's trade. The Turks also had their own quarter, as had the prostitutes, an area 'called by the English Sailors Love Lane and Scratch Alley', which they were not allowed to leave without permission. An English mariner wrote that in Leghorn there were 'many kind-hearted courtesans and brothel-houses, where many a man empties his pockets of moneys in keeping company with them, and here are some English men and women who live here which keep the trade going . . . There are such English men and women in most places of any great trade'.

The morning after *Monmouth* anchored, the longboat went ashore for water, and Consul Dick, who was also the navy's victualling correspondent, sent aboard 2,000 pounds of fresh beef for the crew and took orders for further provisions and new clothes where they were wanted. Market boats crowded round the ship, and for a couple of days the Monmouths relaxed; some of them may have mixed with the kind-hearted courtesans.

For several days *Monmouth* prepared busily for sea. Her men heeled the ship, which involved scrubbing her sides and cleaning away four months' accumulation of filth and weed. They reprovisioned with goods provided by Consul Dick – 37,632 pounds of bread, twenty-three barrels of salt beef, seventy-four barrels of salt pork, twenty-eight barrels of flour, forty-nine pipes of wine, eight containers of oil, fifteen of 'calavances' (chickpeas or dried beans), twenty of rice, thirty-six barrels of raisins, and three butts of vinegar. A large quantity of fresh beef and six live oxen also went on board. These were the staples of the naval diet in the Mediterranean, washed down with watered wine. There was no official issue of spirits, though many men brought private supplies of brandy on board.

Captain Hervey was pleased to find the *Glasgow* in port because he still intended to return to the Levant to destroy the *Triton* and *Minerve*. He sent for her lieutenant to give orders to prepare to sail. Then he went ashore to see the governor, picked up mail from England and wrote to his brother to tell him of his intention to sail for Alexandretta. The weather was too poor to entertain on board, so Hervey dined with the governor, and went to a gathering at Mrs Dick's in the evening. The next day he went to Pisa with his friend and agent James Howe, and several officers from the British ships. John Dick, in his fourth year as consul, 'a good agreeable sensible coxcomb', was their guide. The British consul's was the largest private house in Leghorn, and he had wonderful opportunities to make money through agency with so much trade and so many visiting warships. Dick was the leading prize agent in the Mediterranean, handling the accounts of numerous privateers and cruisers.

Returning to Livorno in the evening, they found another British warship in port, the *Tartar's Prize*, Captain Thomas Baillie. When first of the *Tartar* while her captain was ill, Baillie had taken this ship, a powerful French privateer, and had been appointed captain of her as his reward. He brought a letter from Hervey's brother enclosing one from the Admiralty ordering any British ship at Leghorn to transport Lord Bristol from Turin to the east coast of Spain to take up a new appointment as ambassador in Madrid. He very much hoped that his brother might take the job of escorting him to Spain, where he had been promoted to the vital job of trying to keep the Spanish neutral. Spain was the world's third largest naval power and it was much easier fighting Louis XV alone than taking on the combined might of the two related Bourbon rulers.

This order effectively ruined Hervey's plan. One of his squadron would have to go to Spain, and two ships were not sufficient to guard the Turkey convoy and simultaneously hunt down the French. He decided to comply with his brother's wish and sent a message to him to rendezvous at Genoa. He gave Baillie, whose ship was under-manned, thirty of his supernumerary Bristol privateers.

Monmouth weighed anchor and Hervey set out to Genoa and a meeting with his elder brother George, Earl of Bristol. Hervey's attachment to Genoa must have been a standing joke passed from the old Phoenixes to the Hampton Courts who had been there last summer and now to the Monmouths. Some nods and winks must have been exchanged as *Monmouth* anchored off 'Genoa the superb', bringing in with her as a prize a Livornese vessel caught carrying French goods. The town formed a crescent around the harbour with painted houses banked up the steep hill. The houses all had flat roofs 'adorn'd with the finest Variety of Lemon and Orange Trees, Evergreens and Flower-bushes, which grow in vases & Boxes, and add much to the Beauty of the Prospect'.

Certain passages, which seem to have been the most sexually explicit, were cut out of Hervey's journal by a member of his family during the nineteenth century, and since the censor intervened at this point, it is fair to assume that Hervey resumed his affair with Pellinetta in some style. In the passages of his journal that survived the scissors, he spent all his time with her. *Monmouth* was at Genoa for three weeks, and some of the crew probably got the chance to explore the maze of steep, very narrow streets about the harbour, or climb higher up the hill to where broad, open boulevards ran, lined by the marble-fronted palaces of Genoa's noble merchant families. Hervey's 'whole time was passed here in festivals and *conversazione* at different noblemen's houses, who live most splendidly on these occasions'. He also entertained splendidly: the three weeks cost him £450. When his brother arrived he took him to the French theatre to Pellinetta's box. They visited all the palaces and went to a great *conversazione*. George Hervey had hired a Danish merchant vessel for his baggage and fifteen servants, bringing seven more with him into *Monmouth*.

Some of the entertaining took place in the ship. On 8 August the commander-in-chief of the Republic's forces came aboard, and on 18 August there was a second dinner attended by many of the Genoese nobility for Hervey's brother Lord Bristol. On these occasions when *Monmouth* was transformed into an ambassadorial dining room, the marines got out their uniforms. Hervey's personal servants Daniel Cameron, John Finney and Louis d'Amour took leading roles, the candles were lit and Hervey's silver plate came out.

Once the ships put to sea, the captain and his brother dined on deck almost every day. It was a calm crossing until Minorca, where, with his brother and all his diplomatic baggage in train, Hervey feared to run into a French warship. They sighted 'two large ships, one of which appeared so French that we prepared for action as she stood end on to us with all sail'. They chased and exchanged shots and eventually the vessel proved to be Venetian. Hervey was relieved: 'it was the first time, I confess, that I was happy to find the ship did not prove an enemy'.

The Earl of Bristol disembarked at Alicante with due ceremony to pursue his onward journey to Madrid. The Monmouths lined the ship and cheered, saluting his departure with nineteen guns and three flags flying. The royal standard was hoisted in the ambassador's barge, and the town saluted the ambassador with fifteen guns.

With the crew dancing hornpipes to fiddle music through the summer night, while off-duty officers rattled away at backgammon, *Monmouth* sailed on to Barcelona. There Hervey found an order to return to Gibraltar and received news of the progress of the war. Louisbourg had finally fallen to the British, so *Monmouth*'s effort against the *Foudroyant* had not been in vain. Hawke had prevented a relief force leaving Rochefort, although another gallant French squadron had escaped from Brest and beaten the British fleet under Boscawen in a race across the Atlantic. The French reinforcement had been too small to prevent the capture of the stronghold, but sufficient to dissuade the British from mounting an immediate assault. Four French warships had been destroyed and one taken, but their sacrifice had bought another year's grace for New France: by the time Louisbourg fell it was too late for the British to attack Quebec during 1758. Nevertheless, it was a major victory, saluted with mixed feelings by Hervey's hosts: 'I thought the Spaniards seemed to rejoice at the ill-success of the French, and yet not pleased with our triumphs'.

Monmouth moored in Gibraltar Bay on 13 September and Hervey found orders to return to England. The ship needed repairs that could only be carried out in a dockyard, and the people, who had been away for eighteen months, welcomed the prospect.

There were some adjustments to the crew before they sailed home. They unloaded the remaining privateers from La Spezia, and seven old comrades rejoined – men wounded in the battle with the *Foudroyant* who were now sufficiently recovered to have left hospital. John Evans, the master-at-arms, was one of those who returned fully fit, but others were not so fortunate. John Knowland and a shipmate were placed on the supernumerary list and discharged when the ship reached Plymouth; effectively they were given a charitable lift home. Knowland was an 'old Monmouth', a fifty-three-year-old Irishman, bred to the sea. He had a head wound from the fight and also a rupture in his right side, a common ailment among sailors. A widower with two children and fifteen years' naval service behind him, he took immediate refuge in Greenwich Hospital, where he died eleven years later. Two more wounded men fell ill again during 1759 and were discharged at the end of that campaign. Six others remained unfit and were discharged from the ship's books.

This meant the ship needed a new corporal as well as two carpenter's crew to replace men who had remained in the *Lyme*. Suitable candidates were promoted. First lieutenant St John Chinnery moved away and upwards towards an eventual promotion to master and commander in 1761. In consequence all the lieutenants moved up: Edward Hutchins became first, James Baron second and David Winzar third. As a favour to his father Lord Egmont who was Hervey's friend and political patron, the Honourable Philip Tufton Perceval was made acting fourth.

Perceval had joined *Hampton Court* in 1757 from Admiral Saunders' ship, 'but with a very indifferent character from Saunders of him'. A later shipmate, who was rewarded by Egmont for serving with Perceval despite a difficult voyage in 1759, strove for something good to say about him to his father. In his memoirs he noted when he met Perceval again that he 'found him the same gay, eccentric character. He was never fond of his profession', and in later life 'smarted severely from his dissipation'. Perceval always got jobs but never distinguished himself.

The system that gave accelerated promotion to the sons of influential aristocrats could cut both ways. There were some who made excellent officers: amongst Hervey's contemporaries Augustus Keppel, John Byron and Richard Howe are outstanding examples. It is arguable that their wealth and consequence actually made them more effective in the diplomatic role that naval captains had often to perform. In one of his many guises an officer was 'a person who has the honour and safety of his country in his hands, which may suffer . . . through his indiscretion in transacting affairs with foreigners'. An officer of middling class would have to be a hero to impress Italian noblemen. But there were some, like Perceval, who were so outstandingly bad that they gave their captains a problem. Hervey needed somehow to get rid of Perceval without offending his father Lord Egmont.

Monmouth sailed on 24 September, escorting a convoy of thirty merchant ships back to Portsmouth. These were ships bound for London, Bristol, Dublin and Yarmouth, the biggest of 280 tons and thirty-two men, carrying silk from Leghorn, wine from Malaga, fruit from Alicante. Although the convoy moved slowly, at the pace of the most sluggish merchant, things went well at first. They made Cape St Vincent in four days and a week later Cape Finisterre. Between these two, *Monmouth* searched and seized a Spanish snow laden with French goods, shipped by French merchants at Cadiz. A mate, midshipman and six men took charge of the *Nostra Senora de Pillar*.

The Dublin ships bore away on 10 October and next morning, in a strong easterly gale, *Monmouth* struck soundings thirty-five miles south-west of the Scilly Isles. At the point when the officers guessed they might be in the English Channel they hove the ship to. A seaman threw the deep-sea lead in the direction in which the ship was drifting, so that as it reached the bottom of the sea they were above it. When they found bottom they had 'struck soundings' and knew that they were approaching land.

Sailing onward they encountered the *Arc-en-Ciel*, captured off Louisbourg, full of French prisoners and with damaged masts. After Hervey signalled her to join the convoy, the weather got rough. In 'fresh gales and thick weather' they took down their topgallant masts. Next day the wind was storm-force. After a week's battering, Captain Martin hailed Hervey to ask permission to make for Cork, since his people were ill, and a petty officer and six men went to help the *Bacchus* snow, which had sprung a leak. Only thirteen ships were in sight now. 'We had exceedingly bad weather with Easterly Winds, most under my Courses 'till the 25th. the wind came Westerly & we got into the Channel', recalled Hervey. The battle-damaged ship became cold, damp and uncomfortable in the wet weather. Neither the pumps nor the ventilator were working properly. The lion figurehead was so 'loose and decay'd' that it almost fell off in the storm, while the rails round the head actually were washed away. The ship was 'so leaky that the people cannot lye dry in their hammocks'. As the weather cleared, the weary and disgruntled Monmouths found that in a fortnight they had progressed from the Scilly Isles only to the Lizard.

'The Channel has been in the greatest bustle for some days past', wrote Lady Anson on 2 November, 'that I ever remember to have heard of'. Both Boscawen's fleet and the French squadron from Quebec were inbound from America. The stock market plunged to a rumour that the French had captured the homeward-bound West Indies fleet, and a disabled French ship, blown into the Bristol Channel, caused a panic. As Hervey's battered ships struggled homeward, they passed a convoy of forty ships outward-bound with supplies for the British forces at Louisbourg. Hervey sent the Spanish snow into Plymouth, giving her prize crew a few days in their home port. A final blow almost wrecked his fleet on Dunnose point: 'in the Morning of the 28th. we were obliged to crowd all the sail we cd. to weather Dunnose, & made the sigl. for the Trade to do the same – Many bore up for the Needles – it blowing so hard they cd. not carry sail'.

At Portsmouth Hervey reported to a bewildered port admiral. The convoy for an attack on Martinique had been scattered – two ships had just arrived from Louisbourg, having lost contact with Boscawen in a gale on the Newfoundland Banks. In the evening the *Echo* came in, bringing 'a very confused acct. that Mr. Boscawen in the *Namur*, Sir Charles Hardy in the *Royal William* with the *Somerset* & *Bienfaisant* & log-wood ship they were bringing home from Cape Briton, were attacked by 6 French Men of War 12 Lgs. to the Westward of Scilly'. Holmes ordered Hervey and the other two ships to get ready for sea and posted to the Admiralty. No order came back. 'There was no further news of Mr. Boscawen & consequently People made a thousand reports.' Finally, Boscawen, Hardy, and the other ships arrived, 'having retaken one of our India ships from the French Men of War that had attacked them'.

Hervey and Robert Narramore the carpenter compiled a long and detailed account of *Monmouth*'s damage for Admiralty secretary John Clevland and the Navy Board. The ship had serious battle damage needing repair as well as normal wear and tear, and it was certain that she would be in dock for some time. The crew was damp but elated to be home. Everybody had been away from Britain for eighteen months, and in such circumstances leave was normally granted to a crew. These men had also fought in a tough but triumphant engagement that had transformed them into national heroes, famous through the land. They all expected to be granted some time to see their friends and families, tell their tales and get spectacularly drunk ashore.

6

Transported as Slaves

*Have inspected the Monmouth and list her defects and opine it will take two
months to put her in condition for service.*

The Portsmouth Officers inspected the ship and sent their report to
the Navy Board. The Navy Board reported to the Admiralty secretary.
The Admiralty secretary ordered Captain Hervey to take his ship to
Chatham dock.

They waited three weeks at Portsmouth for these orders to come
through. No leave was granted and Hervey had his first serious
problem with discipline. Anthony Stephens, a foremast man of the
starboard watch, one of the 'old Monmouths' who had joined the ship
in March 1755, was punished for 'getting drunk, neglecting his duty,
and being guilty of a mutiny when on duty ashore' with thirty-six
lashes at the gangway. This was a severe sentence – three times the
theoretical maximum a captain could award. It might seem to confirm
the Georgian navy's modern reputation for brutality. However,
Stephens was only the fourth man to be given corporal punishment
in two years, and the first to receive more than twelve lashes. James
Young had been thrashed for 'stealing of cloaths from one of the
French prisoners' against Hervey's express command, Richard Barley,
another marine, had been whipped for sleeping at his post, and Daniel
O'Farrell, seaman, had suffered the cat for neglect of duty. The logs
are all in agreement and there is no reason to suppose that there were
other concealed punishments or that *Monmouth*'s crew was in need of
firmer discipline. Maintaining discipline in port was always harder
than at sea, and Stephens was punished severely as a warning to others.

Hervey was irritable and suffering from gout. Wanting to get back to sea quickly, he asked for the newly-built *Resolution*, but First Lord Anson had already promised her to someone else. To add insult, the Admiralty told him that he had to give back his prize the Spanish snow. He sent the papers and prisoners down to Plymouth where the prize had put in, protesting that 'The Cargoe was acknowledged by the Master to be French & openly shipp'd for the Account & Risk of several French Houses at Cadiz which I know – but . . .'

The timing of its capture was unfortunate. By now French merchant shipping had been swept from the seas. In desperation the French allowed neutral ships to carry goods home from their colonies, a right denied to foreigners in peacetime. To deal with this underhand evasion of the consequences of defeat at sea, Britain had invented the 'Rule of the War of 1756', asserting her right to search and seize vessels suspected of carrying French goods. This reversed a treaty of 1674 by which neutrals had been allowed to carry goods belonging to belligerents, but the extent and importance of seaborne trade had increased dramatically since then. The neutral sea powers, Holland, Spain, Denmark and Sweden, were furious at Britain's unilateral rewrite of the rulebook; they maintained that neutrals had every right to trade freely. Now they were threatening to join the war on the French side, and the British, while defending their right to seize neutral ships, were in practice making every possible concession. The Monmouths were amongst the first to suffer from this new conciliatory stance. To their dismay, a prize that should have brought them good money was instead released to its 'Spanish' owners.

Finally, the Admiralty wanted one of *Monmouth*'s people discharged because someone said he was French. 'Mark Nicola' was another foretopman of the starboard watch who had been sailing with *Monmouth* for more than two years. Hervey replied that he could only 'say that Marco Nicholas, enter'd for the Ship the 1st. of Janry: 1756 is a very good man, and a very stout & serviceable one, he says he is a Greek, tho' he once said he was a Provençal when he wanted to be discharged abroad; I find it is his Brother in London that has applied, the man seems to be very indifferent, but I shall comply with any directions'.

The only bonus was that, as a favour to his father, a ship bound for Canada had taken on the dissolute and lazy Philip Tufton Perceval so that he could remain in active service; the Admiralty confirmed that Hervey should discharge his unwanted acting lieutenant from the *Monmouth*.

She sailed with a convoy for London on 9 December and reached the Downs next day. At Deal they took on a pilot with knowledge of the tricky shifting banks and channels of the Thames Estuary to guide them into the London river. The wind came right to get to Gunfleet on 12 December and they moored in muddy gloom at Blackstakes near Chatham, where they took out the guns and then the stores in preparation for docking. Hervey wrote to the Admiralty requesting leave for the crew:

> As I do not suspect any man will leave the ship I shall not apply to Commodore Boyce [William Boys] for the security of any; I hope their Lordships will be pleased to indulge the officers & ships-Company with some leave of absence whilst the ship is repairing, & empower me to acquaint them therewith.
>
> I hope their Lordships will please to give me leave to go to Town, as the Ship is now in the Harbour, & I hope will be up at Chatham tomorrow

Secretary Clevland replied that 'Commodore Boys is directed to give you leave.' But, he continued, 'I am also commanded to inform you, that your ships company cannot have leave at present, as their assistance will be necessary for a short time to fit out some ships that are immediately wanted to go to sea.' On 17 December they moored off King James's Folly and continued to empty the ship. Hervey put *Monmouth* into the hands of his first lieutenant, who conventionally took control in harbour, and disappeared, leaving his crew of home-coming heroes feeling unappreciated, and cheated of their anticipated shore leave.

As they read the newspapers they might have noticed advertisements for the publication of a large and expensive print of 'the taking of the *Foudroyant* in the Mediterranean'. Tobias Smollett's *Critical Review* found the artist 'has struck out a new beauty, in preserving the main light by the firing of the cannon, notwithstanding the fine effect which the moon also occasions'. The print was dedicated 'To the Memory of Captain Gardiner and to the Gallant Officers and Seamen of His Majesty's Ship *Monmouth* who Attack'd and took the *Foudroyant*'. It was ironic that *Monmouth*'s officers and seamen were denied the opportunity to go ashore and buy it.

Peter Canot's 1759 engraving of Richard Paton's painting of the Monmouth *taking the* Foudroyant, *with* Swiftsure *and* Hampton Court *approaching.*

Hervey spent his first evening ashore in St James's Place with his mother and his sister Lepel. Next day he walked to St James's Palace to be presented to his godfather, the famously rude King George II, who 'rumped' him (turned his back on him) without a word. Hervey's successes at sea had not dispelled the displeasure caused by his support for Byng and for the party of the young Prince of Wales. During the time he was in London, his mother's friend Henry Fox took him to Parliament, where he was introduced as member for St Edmund's Bury just before the House adjourned (it was a family seat, and Hervey had learned of his election when he was at Nice), Lord Egmont took him to Savile House to meet the Prince of Wales, where the reception was much warmer and Prince George talked with him for a long time, and he met the Prince's mother, Augusta, Princess of Wales, at Leicester House. Around Christmas, he 'went down to Rochester to speak to the *Monmouth*'s people and pacify them'.

The Admiralty's plans to use the people of *Monmouth* to 'fit out some ships that are immediately wanted to go to sea' had become known. 150 of them were to be sent to Hull to bring down the *Temple*, a seventy-gun ship that had just been built there, and First Lieutenant Edward Hutchins had given this job almost exclusively to 'old Monmouths'. On Christmas Eve they sent a petition to the Admiralty:

> Most Honourable and worthy Lords
>
> This with Humble Submission Intruding upon your Lordships Hoping our boldness your Lordships Will Excuse for it is Necessity Drives us To it and Almost to Dispair for as we understand that we Are to be Transported as Slaves from one Ship to Another which grieves our Hearts full sore

The Monmouths' principal objection was to leaving their ship – there was nothing an eighteenth-century crew hated more. When they volunteered, they joined a ship rather than the navy and their bond to their ship was stronger than that to any captain. They were most afraid that they were to be transferred permanently to the *Temple*. It was an infringement of Englishmen's liberty to treat them like foreign slaves. Although impressment into the navy was a necessary evil, there were certain limits: there were points at which ordinary English seamen could explain to their superiors that they were pushing them too far.

The Monmouths did not wish to appear mutinous, however; just to express their grievance forcibly. They explained that they were

> Very Willing for to serve our Most Royal Sovereign King and contry for any Lawful Occasion whatsomever as your Lordships thinks proper to command we Will Most willingly and cheerfully Undertake. Let our Task be Ever so Hard

They went on to list the five captains they had served under. Gardiner was their apparent favourite, 'whose Loss we greatly Lament and Not without Reason for he was a Most Worthy Loyal Subject To The

Crown of great Britain'. Their next objection was to Hull in January. Mostly Cornishmen, they had been in the Mediterranean for years and did not have the right clothes.

> We Hope your Lordships thinks that we are But Mortal Any More than Other Men for to Undergo it all and now we take it Very Hard after all that we poor Objects in particular Should be pitch'd upon after all our fatigues for to go to Hull for to bring up His Majesty's Ship the *Temple* which is a very cold contry as any in England and us The Old Ship's Company as Hardly Cloaths for to hide Our Nakedness

Finally, they gave vent to what was evidently a simmering resentment against those who had not fought the *Foudroyant*, and against the favouritism shown to the old Hampton Courts by their new senior officers:

> and them that came in ye Room of them that Depart'd in our Most Bloody Engagement they must take their Pleasure that have Undergone nothing and We poor Objects that have Endur'd all ye Hardships that the Briney Waves is Addict'd To Now Must go Away Again Naked To ye world which is a Very Hard Thing to think of

Although the old Monmouths may not have known it, they were not quite as hard done by as they thought. Another hundred men had to take the *Edgar* round to the Nore and many of them were former Hampton Courts. Nevertheless, it is true that few of Hervey's followers were sent to Hull and a handful even went on leave, despite the Admiralty prohibition.

Very few had got leave to go ashore. The old gunner Henry Jeffreys was retiring at fifty-eight after more than sixteen years' naval service, and his servants were discharged with him, although one of them promptly re-entered the ship as a captain's servant. Luke Scardefield, the armourer, from Sidlesham near Chichester, also left the ship, and his mate, John Sympson, was promoted in his place. The captain of marines, master, carpenter, surgeon and both his mates all went on leave, and Hervey took his servants, Louis d'Amour, John Finney and Daniel Cameron. In addition leave was given to Richard Treadenham, a married Hampton Court, and John Parvin, who always sailed with Hervey and would certainly not desert. (As usual he returned with venereal disease.)

Despite the justice of the old Monmouths' complaint, the Lords of the Admiralty ignored it, merely instructing Hervey to pacify them. They were pacified, though they probably remained surly and resentful. On 27 December the whole crew moved out of the empty *Monmouth* and took up residence in the *Monarque*, a French-built 74, captured in 1747. She had been a flagship but was now so old, worn out and leaky that she had been taken out of service. Part of the pacification must have involved women being allowed to come aboard ship, for at least two dozen of the men required cures for venereal disease within a short time. Most of those affected were men sent to the *Edgar*, but one went to the *Temple* and two were old Hampton Courts who remained at Chatham, so we can guess that some of the partying probably took place on the *Monarque* before the crew split up.

A man of war in harbour with women on board. Sea chests make seats around portable tables with hammocks slung overhead.

A naval surgeon described similar circumstances when his ship *Magnanime* went into dock at Plymouth in 1756:

The moment of victory for *Monmouth* as she smashes *Foudroyant*'s mainmast. The huge French flagship is still returning *Monmouth*'s determined broadsides with three or four guns.

This detail from Swaine's painting gives a vivid impression of the menace of the warship as a fighting machine, bristling with cannon. On *Monmouth*'s forecastle seamen run to repair damaged rigging while small arms men pour fire into *Foudroyant*.

Admiral Henry Osforn,
Vice Admiral of Great Britain,
Born 1697. Died 1771.

Admiral Henry Osborn, shown with a compass, commanded the Mediterranean fleet in 1758. Some feared his 'cold saturnine disposition, ill-habituated to the warmth of sincere friendship', but Hervey reckoned his patron 'the most experienced, most alert, vigilant and zealous officer that ever commanded'.

The Herveys during their visit to Paris in 1750. From left to right: Constantine
Phipps senior; Mary Fitzgerald; Lepel Phipps; George Fitzgerald; Augustus Hervey,
then aged twenty-six; his mother Molly Lepel, or Lady Mary Hervey. In the
background is the young Captain Hervey's first post ship, the *Princessa*.

Towed close to the Majorcan shore by her own boats and *Revenge*'s, *Hampton
Court* fires a broadside into the *Nymphe* to sink her before she blows up. The
French crew has fled ashore and her officers have set fire to the frigate to prevent
the British capturing her intact. This was an incident from 1757, which many men
in *Monmouth* and *Dragon* remembered with pride.

Pictures of tars at sea are remarkably rare – Gabriel Bray drew these seamen on the *Pallas* in 1775. In action sailors' bedding was lashed around the sides of the ship as protection against flying bullets; each hammock was numbered with the sailor's berth.

The man leaning against the frigate's bow chaser wears classic naval dress of trousers and short blue jacket. The man in the rigging is trying to spear fish.

Breaming at a careening wharf. The vessel is hauled onto its side by several cranes and seamen burn the old tar off its bottom together with the weeds, shells and rubbish clinging to it. In order for ships to sail fast this had to be done frequently, as it was to *Monmouth* at Gibraltar in spring 1758.

'Tis hard to have a Fortune thus almost in one's Pocket & yet be as poor as a Rat'. Hervey calculated he lost £14,000 in prize money when the French took Port Mahon. Foulkes, Pinker, Burgess, Blake, Parvin and others who sailed with him in *Phoenix*, seen here seizing French vessels in 1755, lost their own smaller fortunes.

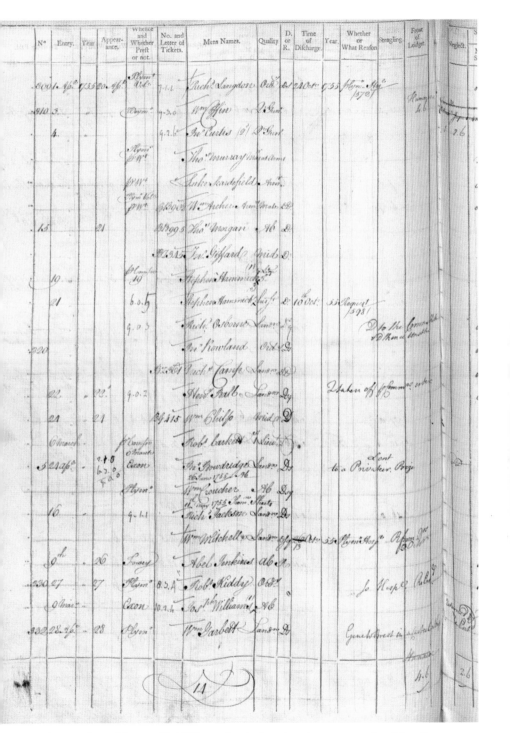

A page from *Monmouth*'s 1755 pay book showing the entry to the ship of
William Coffin, Luke Scardefield, Stephen Hammick and Robert Carkett at
Plymouth in the spring of that year.

'I have been thinking of dear Kitty this whole day'. While *Monmouth* was repaired Captain Hervey spent his time with Kitty Fisher, the eighteen-year-old celebrity sensation of the year. She visited *Monmouth* at Chatham and at Portsmouth, and wanted to sail on to Plymouth.

While this was performing, the whole crew, consisting of 750 men, were put on board the *Canterbury* and another old hulk, and neither officers nor men were permitted to go on shore excepting on some point of duty, and no person suffered to sleep on shore on any account whatever, but the sailors' wives were allowed to come on board. This occasioned a complaint from the secretary, who was likewise purser, of a very extraordinary expenditure of beer, more than the king's allowance, which is a gallon a day to each man, owing to the great number of females on board, who, being mustered by the admiral's order amounted to 492, who all declared themselves married women, and were acknowledged by the sailors as their wives, where or when they were married was never inquired, the simple declaration was considered as sufficient to constitute a nautical and temporary union, and which was authorised by long established custom as practised time immemorial in His Majesty's Navy.

As we have seen, a few Monmouths were genuinely married in relationships as settled as could be expected. Some of these wives possibly travelled to London to meet the ship, having learned from the newspaper or a letter that she was coming in. Other seamen really did have had 'wives' in every major port. There were plenty of women who would marry a sailor, with or without a formal ceremony, for the convenience of relieving him of some of his pay, and would then go on with their normal course of life, in some cases marrying again when convenient. That normal course of life might well involve prostitution, often in combination with some other occupation. Most of the women who came to service the ships in the port of London were pretty rough: quite a number of those desperate or unlucky enough to be hanged at Tyburn claimed to be the wives or widows of seamen. Many had migrated to London from elsewhere, especially from Ireland and the western counties, and were improvising a living there. They were generally pretty young. We know about one group of Hedge Lane prostitutes who were questioned by the magistrate John Fielding in 1758, but it is impossible to know how typical they were. They ranged in age from fifteen to twenty-two, eleven of the twenty-five being eighteen or nineteen. Five said that they had started as prostitutes at fourteen or younger.

On 6 January 1759, Edward Hutchins read out the articles of war, together with the provisions of the new 1758 Navy Act. This required ships to be paid more frequently and provided ways by which men might remit money to their families. A printed abstract of this together with the articles of war were 'constantly hung up & Affixed in the most publick place of the ship' and 'at all times accessible to the Inferior Officers & Seamen on board.'

Two days later James Baron took the designated crew to the *Edgar*, a newly-built sixty-gun ship. He then went to London to ask leave to visit his friends in Cornwall (which their Lordships refused), leaving master's mate Henry Reeves with midshipmen Barnaby Binnock and James Gilbert and two quartermasters in charge of the men. Old Hampton Courts such as John Newins, George Towns and David Seaton were in the party. Next day Lieutenant David Winzar, with midshipmen John Fletcher and Richard Tizard and four quartermasters including John Woods and John Blake, sailed with their men to join the *Chesterfield* at the Nore for their voyage to Hull. The Irishmen Hanlon and Lawler went with them. The marines and about thirty sailors remained in the *Monarque*, several of whom were either ill or elderly. William May, for example, a married Devonian with three children, was fifty-four. He had been a blacksmith before he joined the navy, so he probably helped the armourer with metal-working tasks. William Coffen also stayed in *Monarque*.

Two of the three mates, Samuel Ball and John McLaurin, had leave to go to London to sit their examination to be lieutenants. To pass they had to have six years' experience at sea and to have spent more than two of them in the navy rated midshipman or master's mate. Both twenty-six-year-olds easily had enough experience to qualify, and they both dealt with the ordeal of an oral examination conducted by three naval captains well enough to pass. Within little more than a year McLaurin was recommended to the Admiralty Board 'for diligence, capacity and resolution on every . . . service. His great ambition is to be a lieutenant, for which he has passed, and I believe no man is fitter for the trust.' However, with few vacancies, better-connected people got jobs, and both had to wait twenty years for another war before they were given a commission.

The captain, meanwhile, had gone to his family estate at Ickworth near Bury St Edmunds in order to meet and treat his constituents. He returned to London on 4 January and took a house in Scotland Yard, convenient for the Admiralty and for Parliament, where he attended regularly after sessions resumed on 16 January. His principal concern was to quash a bill that sought to replace pressing with an im-practicably complicated system of conscription by lottery. His evenings were a succession of dinners and visits to the opera, or occasionally the playhouse. Some time was spent with his mother and sisters. His sister told him that her eldest son, Constantine Phipps, had decided that he wanted to go to sea. Hervey entered him immediately on the ship's books, advising him to join the ship when she was about to sail.

After an unconsummated liaison with Isabella Byron, the thirty-seven-year-old Countess of Carlisle, Captain Hervey 'got in' with the vivacious seventeen-year-old Kitty Fisher, that winter's new star in the firmament of London courtesans. During 1759 Catherine Maria Fischer became England's leading celebrity beauty, and later that year, in October, Lady Caroline Fox wrote to her sister of the 'Kitty Fisher style . . . in dress or manner, which all the young women affect now'. Her portrait was published in broadsheets and song books so that she became so well known a national figure that her name got into a nursery rhyme. Pamphleteers agonised that her example, an astonish-ing rags-to-riches leap, was 'enough to debauch half the women in London'.

It was probably Kitty that Captain Hervey took with him when he went to visit the *Monmouth* in late February. They were accompanied by one of her friends, the nineteen-year-old Prince Edward, younger brother of the Prince of Wales, and his 'nymph'. Prince Edward was a midshipman in the navy and keen to see the ship that had defeated the *Foudroyant*. They found her 'in great forwardness'. The foursome then spent the night in Rochester before returning to town next day. As

Kitty Fisher as Cleopatra dissolving pearls in wine by Edward Fisher after Joshua Reynolds, 1759.

soon as he got home, Hervey penned a letter of complaint to the Admiralty, having learned that their Lordships intended to borrow the rest of his crew.

> I now find that the remainder are order'd to carry a ship towards the Bristol Channel and these last are most all of the people that have been with me from Ship to Ship . . . it is cruel upon the People just as they had reason to expect some liberty to enjoy their Money & friends; but that can't be help'd if they can't be spar'd . . .

It is not clear how far Hervey prevailed. Seventy men were loaned to the *Anson* on 7 March, but they came back a week later to help get the *Monmouth* out of the dock.

The captain had not entirely neglected his ship during his holiday in London. On 15 January he wrote to their Lordships requesting them to order the extension of the quarterdeck to match the way most modern ships were built. He explained that this 'will be a great advantage in Time of Action as we work all our head Sails, as well as after-ones on the Quarterdeck, it will be so much more Cover to the People under that Deck, & give more room in Stowing her Men'. Hervey also had another idea for the improvement of his ship's performance. All British two-deckers had rampant lions as figureheads. The *Monmouth*'s was so rotten that it was about to be replaced. Hervey wanted it replaced not with a lion but with a 'a small figure-head, this will be lighter to her Bows, & will be a great Deception to the Enemy in so Snug a ship as the *Monmouth* is'. *Monmouth* was often sent out alone to cruise, and since she was smaller than most British battleships, without the prominent British identification mark he might have even more chance of deceiving the enemy as to his ship's nationality and power. The Admiralty approved both measures, giving orders to 'fix a Scrole to the head with badges instead of ye Lyon'.

Sailors at work on a three-decker at Chatham, with visiting ladies on the stern gallery.

Hervey took Kitty down to Chatham again on 30 March, with a friend called Mrs Squib. Despite very bad weather, Lieutenant Hutchins had finished rigging the ship and they now had all the provisions aboard. They dined on *Monmouth* and Hervey attempted to sail to Blackstakes, but the wind was not right. The next morning Hervey returned with his party to London, leaving Hutchins orders to move the ship as soon as possible. He must also have given orders for a general review of the rating of the crew, because forty-four men, about a sixth of the seamen, were promoted. Twenty-eight of them changed to able seaman from landsman, and sixteen from ordinary. Most of those involved were 'old Monmouths', including such old hands as John Kitchlowe, a thirty-nine-year-old Dubliner, who had joined *Monmouth* as his first ship in 1755. Four had joined the ship as boy servants, became ordinary seamen when old enough, and were now rated able. The Irish recruits who had joined with Peter Hanlon (promoted ten months earlier) all now also became able seamen. Such a review was due: those who were promoted had been on the ship for sufficient time to qualify, assuming their skills were up to it.

This exercise was undoubtedly part of the process of pacifying the crew. Nine of those promoted had recently returned from the *Edgar*, but thirty-three were still away in the *Temple*. Their pay rose from eighteen shillings a lunar month for the landsmen, or nineteen for the ordinary seamen, to twenty-four shillings a month. Another pacifying gesture was the issue of prize money that had just become payable for the privateer *Monmouth* had captured in January 1758 just before the *Foudroyant*. It was 5 April before Hutchins could move to Blackstakes, where the men got the guns back in and loaded the shot and 274 barrels of gunpowder.

Hervey enjoyed a week of intense pleasure before Kitty had to leave London. She had received a letter with an offer of marriage from the forty-nine-year-old Lord Poulett if only she would go to him in Somerset. Hervey paid some debts for which she had been arrested and spent the night with her at Egham, on the road to Hinton St George. He urged her to make sure that she extracted at least a settlement from Poulett since he placed little reliance on the Earl's good faith.

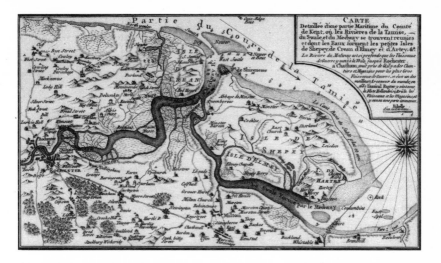

French map of the Thames, Medway and Swale rivers. Chatham dockyard is just below Rochester; Blackstakes, where guns and powder were loaded, is marked 'Blackstack' and the Nore, marked 'Nower', is at the confluence of the Medway and Thames.

Monmouth sailed to the Nore on 11 April and there found the *Hussar* under Captain Carkett, *Monmouth*'s former first lieutenant, made post for beating *Foudroyant*. Carkett had got *Monmouth*'s boatswain's mate, Edward May, a warrant to be his boatswain, and he was supposed to change ship there, but May was yet to return from the *Temple*. Hervey gave him John Broad, one of *Monmouth*'s midshipmen, as a master's mate. Hervey had by now received his orders – to fit out with provisions for Channel service. He had asked for Guinea or Jamaica, but had again been turned down.

The Duke of Newcastle, who liked to control all patronage, was preoccupied with French preparations. The enemy made no secret of their intention to invade Britain, and spies and intercepted letters brought reports of formidable preparations. Forty thousand men had moved to the Channel coast. In early April Newcastle wrote, 'You know, I suppose, that flat-bottomed boats are preparing all along the French coasts.' Good men were needed to defend the British Isles.

The captain finally embarked at the Nore, writing to his sister

Lepel, 'I have got at last to this Cursed Melancholy hole suitable to my present Gloomy Disposition, for dark & sullen it is . . . I have been thinking of Dr. Kitty this whole day'. He was not ashamed of discussing Kitty Fisher with his sister, and the intimacy of the conversation suggests that Lepel Phipps and Kitty had met. Hervey wanted to wait in the Thames for the rest of his men, but a flurry of letters from the Admiralty pressed him to sail for Spithead.

On 17 April commissioner Brett came aboard and paid the ship's company up to June 1758, nine months in arrears. The Royal Navy liked to owe their seamen something to give them less incentive to desert. A few men had deserted while Hervey had been away. He had been correct in his belief that the old Monmouths were reliable, but he had not reckoned with the men he had pressed in Genoa who had deserted as a unit on 14 January from the *Edgar*. The rest of those lent to *Edgar* had rejoined, and so long as he got the old Monmouths back from the *Temple*, Hervey would have a strong crew. He had lost a few hands to the hospital, but a small number of seamen had volunteered, among them a very old acquaintance, William Pinker, who had been Hervey's boatswain in the *Phoenix* and then the *Defiance*. A married Londoner, he was now over fifty, but hearing Hervey was in port had volunteered as an able seaman.

Monmouth took seventeen pressed landsmen from the guardship at the Nore and then sailed down the Swinn towards the Downs. It was quite rare to press people of such poor quality that the captain rated them landsman, and a sign of how desperately difficult it now was to procure good seamen. Seamen with key roles in the merchant service or in fishing normally had 'protections' from the press so that they could not be taken unwillingly from their jobs, but such protections were suspended during the summer of 1759. The difficulty of finding new men of quality made Hervey even more fearful of missing the men from the *Temple* who were supposed to be returning in the *Escort*. Sure enough, they did miss each other, taking opposite routes round the Isle of Sheppey. Being senior officer at the Downs, Hervey sent a cutter racing back after the *Escort* to turn her round. Finally, off Folkstone, he was reunited with the old Monmouths. Since they were much attached to their ship, and since Hervey desperately wanted his experienced crew, there was mutual satisfaction in the reunion and about a quarter of the returning men learned that they had been promoted.

They anchored at Spithead on Monday 23 April. Kitty Fisher arrived by fast coach from London on Thursday and stayed until Friday when, to his great frustration, Hervey got orders to sail immediately for Plymouth. Their Lordships were in a frantic hurry. Hervey sailed, 'taking leave of Kitty who I had great difficulty to prevent going to Plymouth in my ship'. He still had no fourth lieutenant and wrote to tell the Admiralty that he had not heard from George Knight, the follower Hervey had requested for this post who was said to have been 'some time in a Tender at the North of Ireland' pressing men.

On 29 April *Monmouth* anchored in Plymouth Sound and remained off her home port for just a fortnight awaiting further orders. Since they might sail at any time, it is unlikely there was shore leave. They exercised the great guns, got in provisions, and sent their boats to help the *Venus* out of the harbour. Hervey took part in a court martial that resulted in a marine from *Isis* being flogged round the fleet for desertion. A court martial could impose any number of lashes, of which the offender was given an equal number in front of each ship in the fleet. Such exemplary brutal punishments were relatively common in home ports but none of Monmouth's men ever suffered in this way. A few men ran from the boats during this time – some former Hampton Courts as well as new hands. The only old Monmouth to desert was William Vallack. This thirty-year-old foretopman of the starboard watch came from Rame, and the sight of home a few hundred yards away must have proved too much for him.

Monmouth received a final desperate reinforcement of fourteen 'neutral seamen' from Plymouth prison. These prisoners of war had volunteered to serve in the navy in order to escape from captivity in the hulks. In theory, at least, they were not French, and they were Protestants, but it is unlikely that investigations into the backgrounds of volunteers were very thorough. Monmouth picked up such men as Domenico Costa. They were at least able seamen.

97

Before joining *Monmouth*, the recruits were deloused. Doctor Lind's *Essay on Preserving the Health of Seamen*, published in 1757, argued that all recruits should pass through ships with stores of

> slops, shirts, bedding, and all the necessary articles of seamen's apparel; with soap, tubs, and proper conveniences for bathing, and with a room upon deck for fumigating of clothes. Every suspected person, whether imprest at sea, or on shore should be first put on board of her; their stay, however, should be short, as soon as they are stripped of their rags, well washed and cleaned, they should be supplied with new clothes and bedding, and be sent on board the receiving guardships. Such of their apparel as appears tolerably good ought to be cleaned, or, if necessary, fumigated with brimstone and returned to them; but it will be absolutely necessary to destroy all filthy rags, and all such clothes as are brought from Newgate or other prisons.

It took many years for this sensible suggestion to be adopted universally, but it was already compulsory for foreign prisoners and British seamen exchanged out of French gaols to be deloused before boarding naval ships. *Monmouth* also took in five seamen from *Deptford* and a French pilot, Jacques Alexis Renault – a man familiar with navigation on the coast of Brittany.

By May, alarm at the prospect of a French invasion had reached the newspapers. On 13 April Prince Ferdinand had been defeated at Bergen. His subsequent retreat across Hesse freed French troops for the invasion of Britain. The press reported enemy preparations in lurid detail:

> Ten thousand workmen are employed at Havre de Grace, in building 150 flat-bottomed boats, 100 feet long, 24 broad and 10 deep. 100,000 livres are paid to them weekly. These boats are to have a deck, and to carry two pieces of cannon each, and to use either sails or oars, as occasion may require. Some will carry 300 men, with their baggage, and others 150 horses with their riders; 150 more are building at Brest, St. Maloes, Nantes, Port L'Orient, Morlaix and other ports of Britanny.

The great fear was that Holland, Denmark, Sweden or Spain, mistrusting a British monopoly of naval power and outraged at British measures against free trade, would join the war on the French side, and that control of the Channel might be lost. There were very few regulars to defend the coast and so the government called out the militia, which signalled to the people in general that the government believed the threat was real. For all Britain's wealth, she had a population of eight million against France's twenty million.

Lord Lyttelton wrote from London: 'We talk of nothing here but the French invasion; they are certainly making such preparations as have never before been made to invade this Island since the Spanish Armada; but I trust in God and Lord Anson.'

7

The Black Rocks

'I expected when I came to Plymouth to have seen a very Magnificent Place But to my great disappointment found it to be Little Better than Whitby,' wrote Constantine Phipps to his mother, Lepel. 'I had at first a worse opinion of it than it Deserved as I desired my Guide to carry me to the Best inn But I suppose by way of Irony mentioned the Worst Inn in the town & told me that was where almost all gentlemen went I was a good deal surprised when I came to this best inn, & wondered what could be the worst.'

Hervey's nephew arrived in Plymouth with his friend the Hon. Philip Stopford late on a blustery night and some humorous local directed the two fifteen-year-old aristocrats to the least salubrious inn he could think of. Next day, as soon as the wind dropped sufficiently, Hervey sent his barge, white with red trim and oars, to rescue the boys from a town which he too thought 'a C—'d place', largely on account of the constant wind. The first ship-mates the new boys met were Hervey's twenty-four-year-old coxwain, Sam Blow, and other smartly dressed members of the barge's crew such as Joe Pegley and Isaac Pressley, both former Hampton Courts.

Hervey quickly settled the new young gentlemen into a routine of study: 'they get up at six every Morning, Come to Breakfast after having made some little necessary enquiries upon the Deck what People are about & what is going on – then Navigation for two hours then an hour of Latin, which my Chaplain says he understands perfectly – then we dine together at two – afternoon a little Navigation & read French –'. The captain took it upon himself to improve Phipps's fluency in the international language: 'he is to talk

View from the Blockhouse on Devil's Point of a boat rowing to a two-decker anchored off Mount Edgcumbe.

nothing but French ever to me, & keeps it up very well; if I forget myself, I have charged him to answer me in French, & he does, so that it will be well for us both'.

Phipps wrote to his mother that he spent almost all of his time with his uncle, except when he and Stopford were with Edward Chicken, the chaplain, or when they and others were studying with John Wilson, the master, in his cabin in the steerage. For sleeping 'We have a Birth to ourselves But are never in it except when we go to bed; we have a Boy to Clean our Shoes, & call us & make up our Hammocks which I like full as well as a bed . . .'

There were about thirty-five boys aboard, rated 'servant,' aged (theoretically) between eleven and seventeen. Some of them were aboard in the hope that they might one day make officers. Midshipmen could also be young, though *Monmouth*'s youngest was Henry Bryne, aged seventeen, another newcomer to the ship who arrived at the beginning of May. Roughly half the servants had just joined the ship. Boys could leave a ship by request, and the majority chose to do so at the end of any voyage. Some thought better of life at sea before they even left port. A few boys stayed much longer because they were formally apprenticed to one of the officers, or because they took to the life. Some were attached to particular people. Each lieutenant had a servant, and each of the warrant officers had two. The rest were 'captain's servants'. Most had general duties such as fetching food for the messes and cleaning shoes, but they were also trainee seamen who joined the other agile young men in climbing to the highest masts to set and furl the lightest sails.

Glimpses into everyday life in a ship of war of this period are rare, ordinary routine being so unremarkable to most seamen. One outsider who found sealife intriguing was William Todd, an infantry corporal serving temporarily as a marine in the *Thetis* in autumn 1757. Unlike most soldiers, he could write a good copperplate hand and so the gunner, whose log was in arrears, got him excused from other duties in order to serve as his clerk. He copied the missing months from the 'Log Book in the Steeridge from the Quarter-master then upon Duty' and then 'went to the Gunners Cabbin to Book it, & he came in soon after, & sent his Boy into the Hold to fetch up a Can of Beer. And he made some very strong flip, so we Drank freely etc, and he told his Boy that upon Bargue Days I should live with him & the Purser, Carpenter & Boatswain Boys, as their Masters are all in a Mess, & the Boys has the Victuals that comes from them.'

All of the seamen were divided into messes, usually consisting of six friends. On the *Thetis* the gunner, carpenter, boatswain and purser ate together and so did their boys, with whom Todd was to share on 'burgoo days'. These were Mondays, Wednesdays and Fridays, when the men received a pint of oatmeal each and four ounces of cheese as well as bread and butter. The oatmeal made porridge called 'burgoo'. On Sundays and Thursdays each man received a pound of pork, and on Tuesdays and Saturdays two pounds of beef, both usually salted. Warrant officers bought extra food to supplement their rations on the oatmeal days. 'They always has plenty of the Best, as all those 4 Officers has 4 Shillings per day pay, besides the pay of a foremast man, for their Boy which they take Apprentice for 3 or 5 years for only Victuals & Close [clothes] & a great many Other perquisis they have besides.'

As a soldier, Todd was impressed by naval rations. 'I live very well, having Commonly Beef, Pork etc, platter fulls standing besides me & always a Large Rum Bottle, as the Gunner Drinks very hard.' Inventive cooks turned dull ingredients into quite interesting recipes like salmagundi – chopped meat, anchovies, eggs and onions with oil and condiments. Sailors loved to invent cant names for their dishes such as lobscouse, scratch-platter and pandoodle.

Phipps and Stopford fared even better, since the captain had his own more palatable private stores, specially prepared and served to him by his domestics Finney, Cameron and d'Amour. Whenever possible, Hervey invited other captains to dine with him, and sometimes he entertained his own officers. Other captains invited Hervey to dine in return, and on some occasions his young gentlemen accompanied him. He reported home in August that the boys were liked by the 'Captains that are under my Command, who take great notice of them, & will have them frequently to go see them, & I do not dislike now & then carrying them with me'. He felt that dining with other captains taught the boys the manners of men and an officer-like tone that they needed to learn young to be impressive when older.

Gradually the boys became accustomed to the ship's routine. Corporal Todd described how his improvised marines were

> Divided into two Watches the Serjeant took the Starboard & I had the Larboard watch Each of us having 15 Men upon Guard. We planted 5 Centrys, 2 upon the Poop, 2 at the forecastle & one at the Gangway and relived them Every 2 Hours. The Watch stood 4 Hours, but at 4 O Clock in the Morning the Dogwatch, so call'd, only stood to 6 O Clock. From 6 to 8 O Clock this watch had the Decks Every Morning to Wash as it caused the Watchs to do it in their turns etc.

The pattern was the same for *Monmouth*'s marines. Having seventy-five, about twice the complement of *Thetis, Monmouth* had a sergeant and a corporal to govern each watch, Sergeant John Pearson and Isaac Mackrell for one, and Daniel Sullivan and Thomas Fisher for the other. At a guess, *Monmouth* posted ten sentries. The morning dogwatches described by Todd were apparently unique: most ships had evening dogwatches, as is normal today.

After a fortnight at anchor in Plymouth, Hervey finally received orders to join Admiral Hawke at Torbay, and sailed as part of Admiral Hardy's squadron on 15 May, arriving in the empty bay next day. Constantine Phipps seized his last chance to write before leaving England:

> Dear Mama, . . . I obey your orders about my Greek & read twenty or thirty Lines every day just as the stops happen to be besides some odes & a good many Lines in the Satyrs of Horace . . . in French Voltaire's History of the Life of Charles the 12th I took particular care not to forget any of our bagage the Cheese came out just as sound and safe as it set out; Last tuesday morning we sailed from Plymouth here under the command of Sir Charles Hardy in the *Hero* in company with the *Dorsetshire Essex Revenge & Montague* & are to wait for the Grand fleet under Sir Edward Hawke

His first voyage began so smoothly that he did not realise the ship was under way. Hawke's fleet appeared later that day and Phipps soon saw the great man. The marines put on their best uniforms to greet Admirals Hawke and Hardy, and Captains Edgcumbe, Denis, Storr and Geary who were piped aboard to dine in *Monmouth*.

Hervey was wary of Sir Edward Hawke. He had served under him after Byng had been sent home a prisoner in 1756. At that time Hervey had been hostile and critical, finding Hawke irresolute, indifferently intelligent, and ill-informed about the Mediterranean. Nevertheless, even Hervey allowed that Hawke 'certainly had a heart to gain an engagement'. Like many others he detested Hawke's Scottish secretary John Hay, 'a fellow without a grain of under-standing who had been bred up to business in a shop and had the impudence to show his ascendancy over the Admiral to the whole Fleet'.

The admiral was more impressed with the captain than the captain was with the admiral. Admiral Sir Edward Hawke was fifty-four. He had seen his first fleet action at Toulon in 1744, had been promoted rear admiral in 1747 and soon afterwards captured six French ships in the second battle of Finisterre. Since then things had not gone so well. He had directed the naval aspect of the failed Rochefort expedition in 1757, and a misunderstanding had subsequently led him to strike his flag, leading to a severe rebuke from Lord Anson who replaced him in the Channel. With that command restored to him, Hawke was now charged with preventing invasion, a mission upon which the nation's fearful eyes were fixed. Failure would end his career.

Sir Edward Hawke.

On 20 May the fleet weighed. They reached the island of Ouessant, known to Englishmen as Ushant, three days later. The admiral instructed his ships to exercise their great guns to let the French know they were there. Next day Hawke borrowed Jacques Alexis Renault, the French pilot, to guide the *Nottingham* and *Minerva* in a reconnaissance into Brest Water. To everyone's relief, the French fleet was still there.

Hawke had intelligence of four French ships, supposed to be joining the Brest fleet from L'Orient, and he sent his four most daring captains, Augustus Keppel, Richard Howe, John Byron and Hervey with the *Southampton* frigate to intercept them off the Pointe du Raz. To his delight, Hervey found that *Monmouth* outsailed the other ships with ease, so 'that if we met the enemy I should at least have had the satisfaction of leading these noble companions into action'. But the white ensign, flag of Louis XV's Bourbon dynasty, was nowhere to be seen – 'not so much as a White Rag in an open Boat', as a contemptuous Constantine informed his mother. 'As at my setting out from you you expressed a great anxiety for my safety,' he told her, ' I shall begin by letting you know your fears were groundless for at present I almost believe Whitby could furnish out as formidable a fleet as Brest.'

He reported that

> we lay as long as the weather would let us in Hodierne Bay which lays between the Penmarks & Les Saintes. Les Saintes are a chain of Rocks Running out Seven or Eight Leagues from the Land under Water the Reason we were sent there was to intercept four french men of war that were going from L'Orient to Brest to join the Fleet there; as they must come by those Rocks we had a good chance of shewing Mr. de Guebriant their Chef d'Escadre the inside of Sr Edward Hawke's Cabbin, But tho of superior force they did not chuse to shew there faces . . .

Consequently, Constantine boasted cheerfully, he feared to 'loose my French for want of a French Captain to enliven the conversation'. In fact, as Hawke soon discovered, the French ships had already reached Brest before he got his ambush in place.

At the beginning of June the weather turned rough. 'Fresh gales and squally with rain' in the log turned to 'strong gales with showers' and *Monmouth* brought to under her mainsail to ride out the storm. Constantine found it 'much more like January than June' and admitted that he had been seasick. However, he was adamant that 'I like the sea better than ever; when it rains hard & drops into the Cabbin my Uncle asks me if it is not a Charming Life

& better than Mulgrave. All I can say for my self is they have bad weather there too.'

On 5 June the combination of a south-westerly gale and thick fog drove the whole fleet back to Torbay. Hervey passed a day walking on shore with Captain Joseph Austin of his marines and Robert Storr of the *Revenge*, a ship Storr had taken back from Carkett after recovering from the calf wound he had received in beating the *Orphée* the day *Monmouth* beat *Foudroyant*.

After three days the fleet returned to sea, but the bad weather only got worse. On the night of 11 to 12 June in a strong, squally wind with heavy rain, second lieutenant James Baron reported that *Monmouth* had split her fore and maintopsails. They reefed the mainsail and brought to under a balanced mizen. The laconic sea language hides the sheer horror for young topmen like John Trevillick, Richard Damerel and Anthony Stephens, who had to climb violently tossing masts, edge out onto the yards, gather or cut away the topsails and reef the mainsail.

Sailors fortifying themselves with grog and tobacco during a storm.

Dawn revealed only five ships in view. *Monmouth* sailed south and first caught sight of Edgcumbe's *Hero* without masts or bowsprit. Her carpenter had been killed. *Bienfaisant* 'had broke two tillers, and the lower gudgin of her rudder gone', *Temple* had lost her bowsprit and had her foremast sprung, and Keppel's *Torbay* had split all her sails. That day the weather was even worse, with what the toughened Baron described as 'very hard gales with heavy squalls and a great sea'. The damaged ships made for home while *Monmouth* again 'lay to under a balanced mizen from Midnight to 10am'. Then the fleet retired to Torbay with its tail between its legs, without ever having seen France.

Hervey wrote to his sister on 15 June:

> we have had Violent Gales of wind, what we Seamen call Storms indeed, & as bad weather as this Blessed Climate could produce even in the Wrathfull Month of December,
>
> I Dined with Sr. Edw. Hawke to day at three o'-clock, & oblig'd to have Candle-light, thanks to the Darkness & Rain of Heaven:

The storm had cured Constantine of seasickness. Hervey was pleased with his coolness and he was shaping up very well, 'very attentive to everything that passes, much liked by every one; not the least so, by myself you may imagine – and I think he will be just what you both cd. wish him, when we have got over the item of propreté – we want a little Tidyness . . .' Like many fifteen-year-olds Phipps was careless about cleanliness and dress, but time and the example of others would sort that out. Stopford was also promising, 'very smart, well behaved, & as attentive to his learning as he can be, but he has not the same clearness nor quickness of his Comrade, but will do very well – & we are all very happy together excepting your humble Servant, who wishes this very Active Inactivity, all at an end'.

At Torbay the Monmouths heeled the ship and 'boot-topped' her. With no proper place to careen, 'boot-topping' was the best cleaning job that could be done. With the ship forced as far on to her side as was safe, the sailors scraped off all the grass, slime and shells they could reach and recoated the lower sides with tallow and sulphur. Cleaning the ship's bottom of the weeds and accretions that grew on it and slowed her down was a routine art of hard labour, repeated every few weeks.

On the Saturday morning Hervey got the first news of his intended role if the weather ever relented. He went 'to breakfast with Sir Edward, who expressed great concern at being drove in, and told me that he had destined me for a very honourable employment, for I should command his vanguard in at Brest water to watch the fleet's motions, and that on my diligence and skill much must depend, but he was pleased to say he did not doubt of success in my hands.'

On Monday Hervey handed out one of his rare punishments, awarding George York twelve lashes 'for not attending Divine Service and getting in liquor'. The first article of war made Chicken's Sunday services compulsory. The fleet returned to sea in more moderate weather, but arrived off Ushant on 21 June in a thunderstorm. Soon the hard gales set in again. Hervey wrote to his sister complaining of 'the wors't Winter Weather I ever saw, & very little prospect of the enemies being such fools as to come out to be thrash'd by a Superior Force, and they must attack us before they can attack either England or Ireland, therefore you may Sleep quiet in your beds at Yorkshire this year –'

July saw a change and Hervey got his instructions

> to take the *Pallas*, Captain Clements, and two cutters, and to go cruise close in with Brest and to look in on the fleet as frequently as I could, to annoy and distress the enemy every way I could, and to send the Admiral frequent accounts of their situation, and he would soon re-inforce me properly to keep that service on which, he repeated, much depended on my activity and judgement.

Hawke further ordered Hervey 'not to suffer a neutral vessel of any nation whatever to enter that port, but direct them to stand off the coast'.

The task involved danger and concentration, but at least there was the prospect of excitement rather than the dull routine of fleet blockade. Their station was off Saint Matthew's Point, less than ten miles from Brest: they were sailing into the enemy's throat. There was danger on all sides – from the French forts and batteries that lined the windswept cliffs, from the prospect of French attack, but mostly from the danger of being blown on to a lee shore or smashed against one of the innumerable savage rocks that littered the sea like jagged teeth. Navigation close to Brest was extremely dangerous, with hundreds of reefs and half-submerged islets, an Atlantic swell, dramatic tides and strong tidal streams, fierce currents and frequent fog. When the wind opposes the tide there are steep seas with violent overfalls. Between Ushant and the Ile-Molène lay the terrible Passage du Fromveur where the current ran at nine knots, or sixteen kilometres per hour, the fastest in Europe. They still had Renault on board, who knew the coast well. Fortunately, this was also true of the master, John Wilson, who was sufficiently familiar with the approaches to Brest to 'go watch and watch with the pilot'. Hawke appointed Wilson 'extra pilot', with the increase in wages that that duty entailed.

They soon experienced the fog as Hervey went to look into Brest harbour. Renault took them south south-east ½ east from Ushant for about twelve miles until they were running along the Chaussée des Pierres Noires, to the south of the famous Black Rocks that lined the way into Brest like the avenues of standing stones to be found on the Breton shore. Since most of them projected above the water the passage was relatively safe, 'nothing being dangerous besides what is shown by the breakers'. From the Black Rocks they steered east by north ½ north for six miles to pass the seamark monastery of St Matthew's on its lonely point.

From here onwards there was constant danger. Renault pointed out the Parquet Rock to the south, visible with the tide at half ebb, from which a long shoal covered with dangerous rocks stretched towards the fishing harbour of Camaret. They sailed cautiously eastward for another six miles, with Wilson and Renault pointing out to the other officers the pilot marks for avoiding dangerous rocks like the Coq. Finally they reached a point where they could look through the narrow Goulet into the Rade de Brest where the French fleet lay. They hove *Monmouth* to, and Baron counted '20 ships one flag at mizen top, one a broad pennant, all with topsails bent, 8 with foresails'. He also noticed '2 Dutch hoys run in under Ville de Bouteille, where were two bomb batteries, one of six guns and the other of four'.

At five in the evening a curtain of fog descended and the blinded *Monmouth* edged cautiously away, leaving *Pallas* and a cutter inshore. Hervey sent the other cutter back to Hawke with the first of his daily reports:

> Sir,
>
> . . . I think the ships in Brest in general seem but light and are certainly not yet ready for the sea; and though I could discern men in boats alongside of them, I could not see any number about the ships sufficient to think them anything like manned, as they would have appeared on the decks on our standing in, as they did everywhere on shore . . .

Next day they had another look and 'spotted one more chef d'escadre' as well as a single Danish merchantman. Hervey had thought of trying to cut out the Dutch boats he had seen, but Hawke did not want him to risk the *Monmouth*. The admiral sent him two cutters, but Hervey decided that the Dutch were too well protected to be worth the risk. A battery close to the great convent of St Matthew fired two shots at *Monmouth*, and the ship returned fire with three.

During the night Hervey sent a lieutenant, four petty officers and thirty seamen in the pinnace and cutter inshore to the south under the cover of the cutter *Prince Edward*. They returned in the morning with a small French fishing boat, three men and two boys. Hervey sent the master, Jean Musec, ashore with a message for the commander of the battery, keeping Musec's son and another man as hostages. He told the French officer 'if they fired another [shot] I would level the Church'. Musec returned for his son with the commandant's answer to the effect that 'they must fire their signal guns, but that he would take care not to let another ball come out of them'. Hervey tested this by sending the boat and a cutter to bring in a Dutch dogger, and the battery held its fire.

Hervey himself went with Clements in a cutter under cover of darkness to take a look at Conquet, the nearest fishing village to the north. He found that the harbour was dry at low water, the entrance fortified and the place full of troops. On the way there and back they sounded the notorious Passage du Four and found that, despite its tidal race, it 'does not appear at all so difficult as is laid down'.

Hawke sent Hervey a second ship, the *Montagu*, of sixty guns, under Captain John Lendrick. Hervey and Lendrick went on board Michael Clement's frigate *Pallas* and took her 'close to the harbour's mouth; so far in as it is possible even for a frigate to advance'. At the same time Hervey got to know his junior captains. Clement was only twenty-four, a follower of Anson's favourite Piercy Brett, made lieutenant in 1755 and now a post captain in one of the navy's best new 12-pounder, thirty-six-gun frigates. Lendrick, from County Antrim, was thirty-four like Hervey, but did not have his influential friends. Commissioned lieutenant in 1746, he had attracted Hawke's attention the following year when he had fought the *Viper* sloop after her captain was killed in action against the French *Hector*, a powerful whaling vessel. Hawke informed the Admiralty that Lendrick, 'a diligent, careful, good officer and a man of spirit, followed the example of his brave captain and had the good fortune to take her after he had engaged her for about half an hour longer. I have given him an order to act as captain of her till further orders, which I hope will prove fortunate to him, as I think he deserves to be preferred.' However, for some reason their Lordships chose not to confirm Hawke's appointment and Lendrick had waited ten years before becoming master and commander of the *Swallow* sloop. In 1758 he had been made post in a large frigate and was now acting captain of the *Montagu*. Her proper captain, Joshua Rowley, had been captured ashore by the French with the rearguard covering the evacuation of troops at Saint Cas in 1758 after the failed expedition against Saint Malo. Hervey liked diligent men of spirit and Lendrick and he hit it off from the first.

At night the boats went inshore again and the pinnace took and kept a small boat. Next day they sent the captured boat inshore. The Danish merchantman left Brest and Hervey used it to convey his daily message to Hawke:

I send you this with the master of the Danish ship, who is just come out of Brest. I can get nothing out of him more than that they are not half manned and that they have no troops at Brest. Their squadron to appearance remain exactly in the same situation. We are going to stand in again on board the *Pallas*.

On the cloudy, breezy morning of Saturday 14 July came the first genuine alarm. They were set for a quiet day. John Wilson and his mates, McLaurin, Ball and Reeves, had gone off way to the south in the *Hazard* cutter with the masters and mates of *Montagu* and *Pallas* to

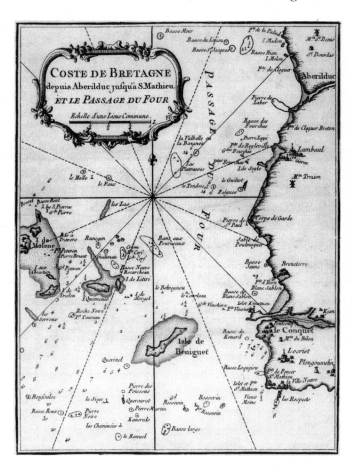

Chart of Conquet and the Passage du Four by Bellin, 1764.

sound and survey the Passage du Raz. This channel between the Pointe du Raz and the Ile-de-Sein, though perilous with its seven-knot tidal race and the Tevennec Rock in the middle, was the shortest route for ships approaching Brest from the south, as most ships did. *Montagu*'s French pilot had gone with them to make sure they did not fall foul of the rocks and shoals that they were charting.

Then, at about eleven o'clock, the lookout caught sight of four other vessels approaching from the north through the Passage du Four. James Baron identified them as a ship, two snows and a dogger.

The wind was a fresh north-easterly, good for getting them up and back again. The tide was still setting to the northward at five or six knots all the way through the Passage du Four between Conquet and the island of Beneguet. As *Monmouth*'s officers watched, the fort at Conquet raised a red flag, a prearranged signal for danger, and the ships put into a small bay just *Monmouth*'s side of the entrance to its little fishing harbour, where the shore was lined with small forts and batteries. The tide and wind combined prevented the merchantmen from entering the harbour. They showed no colours, and from their behaviour Hervey reckoned that they must be an enemy convoy, or at least some ships with supplies for the French. His orders were to allow nothing into Brest harbour, but if the ships got into Conquet with the next tide and unloaded there they might just as well have got to Brest: they only had to carry their cargo a mere dozen easy miles overland.

Hervey wanted to send his boats in to capture the ships before they could unload, but he had to assess the risk. There was very little space in which the *Monmouth* could manoeuvre because of the rocks called Les Mulets off the entrance to Conquet harbour, the shoals that lined the Passage du Four, and those surrounding the island of Beniguet. However, the French pilot assured Hervey that he could place the ship so as to cover the boats without danger from the rocks, and he had already sounded the Passage.

With *Montagu*'s pilot absent in the cutter, she could not come with them, so Hervey ordered Captain Lendrick to 'lay off St. Mathew's Convent & Watch the Motions of the Ships in Brest Harbr'. He signalled Michael Clements in *Pallas* to chase with him and to get her boats manned and armed. With the tide and wind in their favour the ship and the frigate swept in fast under topsails and foresail. In *Monmouth* Baron prepared the lower deck 24-pounders and Winzar the 12-pounders on the deck above. Lieutenants Hutchins and Knight scanned the shore to pinpoint the sources of incoming fire. The young gentlemen, Phipps and Stopford, were on deck as aides. Also with them was the captain's clerk, an experienced seaman named Reynold Thomas, taking careful notes. They identified four forts, each with six to eight guns, one battery of eight and two or three smaller ones with two or three cannon on rocky points.

With all hands anxious to show their prowess in making the perfect turn, *Monmouth* tacked under the southernmost point of Conquet harbour. Seamen ran from the rigging back to their quarters on the guns or in the boats. Keeping just enough sail to balance the effect of the northerly current, *Monmouth* opened fire on the forts. Simultaneously, boatswain Fewin's team lowered her pinnace and cutter into the sea from their sheltered starboard quarter. *Pallas* followed suit. When the suspect ships saw the British boats they hoisted Swedish colours, and as the boats approached they struck them. There was no fighting and Hervey ordered the Swedish colours rehoisted to show that the neutrals were merely in detention. The boarders cut the cables and got the merchantmen under sail. Within little more than an hour, the boats and ships were approaching and Hervey ordered *Pallas* to escort them away.

Monmouth continued to engage the forts for another hour until the prizes were well clear. Her 24-pounders fired 49 roundshot and four grape, while the 12-pounders expended 41 roundshot and 21 grape. They would not all bear on any one target, so they fired slowly and selectively, with grape to frighten the gunners in the exposed batteries. A breathless Phipps reported to his mother, 'our fire was so brisk & the guns so well pointed that they put the french into the greatest confusion we lost not a single man'. The enemy was throwing explosive mortar shells at them but nothing hit. In principle, engaging forts was dangerous and fraught with risk, but in his draft report Hervey was contemptuous of the enemy's efforts: 'their fire was very slow & very bad; soon after we began firing – as we could distinguish their people very plain to run from their guns often –'

At two-thirty *Monmouth* made good her own retreat in the wake of the Swedish vessels. Baron noted that 'the *Pallas* attended them, & brought them to an anchor at the place we came from; while we stood on to reconnoitre the French fleet in Brest'. *Monmouth* returned to examine the Swedish ships and then escorted them some distance before dispatching them with *Pallas* to the admiral with his report:

> Our ships received no damage, and I was glad of an opportunity of shewing these sort of auxiliaries to our Ennemies, what Sanction they are likely to meet with from the French even under the Guns of their Fort in so very intricate a situation, and in sight of 21 Ships of the Line, especially as I had Directions to admit no Vessells whatever into Brest . . .

'I cannot help, Sir, commending to you the bravery of the officers and seamen on this occasion . . .', wrote Hervey to Hawke that evening. Hawke was entirely satisfied with Hervey's conduct and reported to the Admiralty with a robust defence of his dubiously legal total blockade, making it quite clear that Hervey had merely obeyed his orders:

> The four he has now sent to me are furnished with cargoes, according to their own account, which appear to be but too necessary to the enemy in their present equipment. Beside, from their manner of stowage and some other circumstances, there is ground to suspect they have guns and other contraband goods underneath all. As the weather will not permit me to search for them here, I have sent them into Plymouth under care of the *Pallas*, there to be detained till their Lordships' pleasure shall be known, in terms of the latter part of the XI article of the treaty of alliance and commerce between Great Britain and Sweden 21st October 1661 and confirmed by subsequent treaties or otherwise.

Their Lordships received the letter a week later and debated it a week after that, minuting to:

Order the Commissioner at Plymouth to cause these ships to be thoroughly rummaged in the presence of the Customs House officers and some person on behalf of the captors [and] to send if there is any contraband goods on board and report what he finds to the Lords. Let Sir Edward Hawke know the Lords extremely approve of what he has done, and what directions they have given.

The press also approved. The *London Evening Post* first gave a bare announcement that 'HM Frigate *Pallas* is arrived at Plymouth from the Fleet under the command of Sir Edward Hawke, with the four . . . Swedish Vessels, which were cut out from under a French Battery at the Entrance of Brest, by the *Pallas* and *Monmouth*'. It then followed up with a more detailed account in a letter from the fleet, which concluded:

'Tis impossible to tell the great joy this gives our brave Admiral and the whole Fleet:– That Two Ships should take out Four, from under such a Fire, in sight of Twenty Ships of the Line, in their own Port, and Four Flags Flying! We talk of nothing for the present but this brave undertaking, and how well the Captains Hervey and Clements behav'd in so dangerous a Situation, whilst they engaged so warmly. They say, during the Engagement the Hills were cover'd with People. These Prizes are just sent to us from Capt. Hervey, who still keeps his Station, to the great Mortification of the French, who frequently throw Shells at our Ships, standing in to observe their Motions.

The *London Evening Post*'s final contribution was a poem published at the end of the month. It was anonymous, but the poet's knowledge of detail and his echo of Hervey's description of the Swedes as auxiliaries to the French possibly betrays *Monmouth*'s chaplain, Edward Chicken. This latest epic began with a description of the general threat:

> Britannia heard the piercing voice of Fame,
> Thro all her Realms, resound Invasion's Name,
> Proclaim that Gallia's Tyrant-Monarch boasts
> To pour his thousands on her white-cliff Coasts;
> Her free-born Sons in servile Chains to bind . . .

and continued with a rousing account of the combat:

> Full in their Sight two British Ships engage
> Their towring Ramparts, with resistless Rage.
> The *Pallas* frown'd, France shudder'd at her Look:
> The *Monmouth* thunder'd, and the Mountains shook.
> Thy Forts, Conquet! No longer Succours lend,
> Too weak to save, too tim'rous to defend.
> The Ships auxiliar from they Wings are tore,
> And Constans, sorrowing, does their Fate deplore;
> Unable to resist the Show'rs of Fire,
> Thy Guns lie speechless, and thy Troops retire.
> Britons exult! All Gallia trembling stands,
> While HERVEY executes and HAWKE commands.

It was a good beginning to Hervey's career as Hawke's inshore enforcer, and it added yet more lustre to the little *Monmouth*'s glory. 'I don't know whether they will prove prizes,' he wrote to his mother, 'but certainly our taking them was of Great Consequence as they were loaden with Tar, Tar brushes, Timber & Iron'. To have friendly ships bringing military supplies snatched within sight of their principal port was humiliating for the French and a boost to fragile morale at home.

Elsewhere the news was ominous. On 9 July the French had seized Minden and were poised to invade Hanover again. There seemed nothing Prince Ferdinand could do to stop them. The Prussians had suffered a defeat by the Russians and were also in retreat. Intelligence revealed that the Toulon fleet was under orders for Brest and that other French ships had orders for the same port. It looked as if the French were on the move.

8

A Very Honourable Employment

London was tense. In mid-June the Duke of Newcastle had received French invasion plans from a spy in Sweden. Possibilities included an assault on Portsmouth from Le Havre, a landing in Scotland to seize Edinburgh and a landing in Essex from Ostend and Dunkirk for a direct strike at London. The advanced state of French plans and the likelihood of Swedish help with the Scottish enterprise shook him.

All available troops were massing on the coasts and around London. The county militias, raised in 1757, were taking their allotted places for the defence of the realm and the newspapers followed the progress of the Norfolk force to London. 'Great Britain for ever', a song in honour of the militia, was sung every evening by Thomas Lowe at Vauxhall gardens. It was Lowe who had first sung 'Rule Britannia' in 1740. His latest hit was calculated to steady a nervous population:

> Whilst in Array we stand
> What Frenchman dares to land?

Nobody with military experience was under any illusion that the militia could stop a determined force of French regulars, however.

It was likely that the French could not be ready before August, but rumours were flying around. On 7 July the Sussex shopkeeper and diarist Thomas Turner 'received by post the disagreeable news of the French being landed at Dover'. This report caused some frantic selling of stock before it proved unfounded. It was commonly assumed that the French would land: 'We are here in the utmost expectation of invasion', wrote army agent John Calcraft on 8 July. 'I, who could never believe it before, am convinced the French will attempt coming, and sometime next month.'

In order to stop them, Hawke intended to maintain a close and enduring blockade of France's principal naval base at Brest. Nobody before had tried to close off the port of Brest completely for any length of time. Normally the British based their fleet at Torbay with watchers stationed off Brest. Under these circumstances the French found it easy to break out with their fleet, and even easier to bring in supplies. Hawke intended to keep the main fleet off Ushant for months on end with an inshore squadron at the very mouth of the port, which was calculated to force the French to fight if they chose to come out. If they did not, he would deprive them of supplies and humiliate them. Inevitably, westerly gales would force him further out to sea in order to avoid being driven on to their coast, but the same winds would prevent the French leaving port. As soon as the wind allowed, Hervey was to get back on station and Hawke would follow.

What had previously made this strategy unthinkable was not so much the weather as the difficulty of keeping ships and men in fighting condition for long enough. Vessels suffered damage and became covered in weed. Men became ill, scurvy and fever reduced crews to feeble inefficiency and, as they began to die, so ships had to go home.

The chief problem was scurvy, the traditional scourge of naval operations. During his voyage round the world, Anson's men had recovered miraculously after finding turnips, sorrel, watercress, seals and sea lions on the island of Juan Fernández. Ever since then he had been convinced of the antiscorbutic properties of fresh food: the general belief was that salt provisions were bad and fresh meat was good. The link to vitamin C was years in the future, although many sailors knew of the value of fresh lemons, and now there was a growing belief in fresh green vegetables and salads.

Acute scurvy was a hideous affliction. William Hutchinson, a privateer captain who was appointed head dock master at Liverpool harbour in 1759, described his own experience of the ailment on a voyage to India:

> after being about four months in our passage from the Downs, after eating a hearty breakfast of salt beef, I found myself taken with a pain

under my left breast, where I had formerly received a dangerous blow. From this time the sea scurvy increased upon me, as it had done upon many others, a good while before me; and I observed that they soon took to their hammocks below, and became black in their armpits and hams, their limbs being stiff and swelled, with red specks, and soon died; I therefore kept exercising in my duty, and went aloft as long as possible, and till forbidden by the officers, who found it troublesome to get me down with safety, as I frequently lost the use of my hands and feet, for a time, in the same manner as I had done when I received the abovementioned blow.

The opening of old wounds was a commonly observed consequence of scurvy, as were the symptoms he observed in his colleagues. Unable to go aloft, Hutchinson

endeavoured to be useful below, and steered the ship, till I could not climb by the notches of the stanchion at the fore hatchway, upon deck, which I told the Captain; who then ordered the carpenter to make a ladder, that answered the purpose for the sick, who were able to get upon deck for the benefit of exercise, and pure air, as that below being much tainted by so many sick. I thus struggled with the disease 'till it increased so that my armpits and hams grew black but did not swell, and I pined away to a weak, helpless condition, with my teeth all loose, and my upper and lower gums swelled and clotted together like a jelly, and they bled to that degree, that I was obliged to lie with my mouth hanging over the side of my hammock, to let the blood run out, and to keep it from clotting so as to choke me.

He kept himself alive until the ship reached Madras 'where, with fresh provisions and fomentations of herbs I got well, and returned on board in eighteen days'. Hutchinson reckoned, like most seamen, that 'the attack of this destructive disease, appeared evidently to proceed from eating too much salt meat, and a short allowance of water &c'.

This was a disease that afflicted huge numbers of the crew simultaneously, ultimately making it impossible to fight or even sail the ship. Four months was reckoned about the longest a naval fleet could keep the sea with safety, but Hawke intended to beat this record. First he would send his vessels home in rotation to repair and clean and to refresh the crews. Second he would get fresh supplies sent out regularly from Portsmouth.

Inevitably, there were teething troubles with the system. In early July an officer of *Bellerophon* complained in a published letter that 'They send us Beer and Water enough, but no fresh provision nor Greens for our People. If the French don't chuse to come out, we shall have a Four-month Cruize, and consequently the Scurvy will prevail amongst the Seamen.'

Hervey took his own measures to obtain fresh provisions. The Monmouths had noticed that some boats regularly visited the island of Beneguet and so they took a closer look: 'Finding there were twenty-one head of cattle on the island, I sent the boats (wind and weather favouring the descent) and in about four hours brought off twenty of them. I take the liberty of sending you one, Sir, as well as the other admirals, and have divided the others to the *Montagu*'s people and our own for a day's fresh meat for them tomorrow'.

They also captured three Frenchmen of whom two, unfortunately, spoke only Breton. The third was communicative and later that day Hervey sent the report of his interrogation to Hawke:

Novel Arche, belonging and habitant of Conquet, taken by the boats of His Majesty's ship *Monmouth* off the Island of Beneguet July 20th 1759:

Says he has not been off Brest of some time, that he rents the island of the convent of St Matthew and maintains his family by killing rabbits, etc.

That he heard the day before yesterday that the fleet with M. Conflans would be twenty-three sail in all of the line, but it was said would not sail till the 25th of August, but he did not believe it would at all. That the *Tonnant* had but 500 men on board, and few of them so many. That they pressed even farmers' boys of 16 and 17 years of age to go on board them. That what people they had, was made up of such; no troops of any kind on board, all doing duty on shore. He heard they wanted guns for two ships [and] the convoy much wanted, as four garvets went to Bordeaux and Nantes for wine and flour for the fleet.

This was all he knew and which was talked of publicly at Conquet; and that he heard we had bombarded Havre de Grace.

Monmouth's officers had watched the French 'exercising their people at loosing and working their sails – which they do surprisingly bad indeed.' Hervey found this convincing proof of 'the truth of that part of the intelligence in which we have agreed with regard to their want of men'.

The boats' crews enjoyed their hours ashore rustling cattle belonging to the Benedictines of St Mathieu, but before they could feast on fresh beef they had to deal with a further alarm.

They were off St Matthew's Point as usual when at breakfast time they saw seven ships approaching the Passage du Four, escorted by two frigates. 'They loomed large with the wind at east and had French colours out. Boats went out from Conquet to them. A red flag was hoisted in the fort and two guns fired for an alarm to them'. There was no doubt this time that the garrison of Conquet was warning a French convoy to take precautions so that they did not share the fate of the Swedes.

Monmouth's officers continued to study developments through their spyglasses:

> One, which appeared the commanding frigate, came through the Passage du Four with two of the ships that kept close to Conquet Point and anchored in the mouth of the harbour, within the rocks of what they call Les Mulets, the tide not letting them go in. The other four hauled their wind and did not come through the Passage du Four, but plied in that bay which is called Whitesand Bay, just to the northernmost point of Conquet.

This was a good opportunity to damage the enemy, but the pilot, Jacques Renault, refused to take responsibility: it was the height of the flood tide and there was only a light easterly to work with. The smaller, more manoeuvrable *Pallas* was still away escorting the Swedes. They could only watch and wait.

'About 11,' reported Hervey, 'tide of flood beginning to slacken and the wind rather freshening, I persuaded the pilot to take charge of us to run up and let us at least see if it were possible to cut those ships away or destroy them. The *Montagu* I ordered to follow as close as possible.' In the meanwhile, a Spanish snow had come out of Brest harbour bound for Swansea. Hervey stopped her and sent a lieutenant to her in the cutter with a report for the admiral 'under pretence to the Spaniard that I was obliged to send all vessels to the fleet that went into or came out of Brest'.

They saw that the ships were warping into the little harbour of Conquet. One of *Monmouth*'s officers recalled:

> The Tide slackening at Eleven, the Pilot took charge, and we and the *Montague* went in and fired at one of the Frigates, and the Forts and Batteries which covered her. This we continued about half an Hour, till the Wind died away and veered to the Southward. We received little Damage, one Shot in our Bends, and some running Rigging cut; the *Montague* one Shot in her Foremast, and many through her Sails.

The falling wind 'obliged us to get out as fast as we could, this place being very narrow, tides very rapid, surrounded with rocks and shoals, and not above one mile and a half to work in. We got out about three quarters past 2, when the four ships to the northward of the passage got under way and plied still further into Whitesand Bay.'

Hervey then 'plied up to Brest harbour against wind and tide' until he could look through the Goulet, reporting to Hawke:

> Appearance of the French fleet in Brest Road from the *Monmouth*'s quarterdeck, July 21st at 5, 6 and 7 p.m.; Camaret Point S. by E., Haystacks S.S.W, harbour's mouth E. by N. 4 miles:
>
> There appeared twenty-two large ships – all their colours flying and four flags, as before.
>
> One of these that lay the eastmost had only a small jack at the ensign staff and which I take to be the ship that last came out of their basin and I think appears to be not above a 50-gun ship at most. Beyond these were two smaller ships that appeared frigates of the smallest rate with colours flying also. The ships appeared to be in the same position and one was bending his mainsail. There were many boats about them.

Soon afterwards they learned that the French ships they had halted 'came from St. Maloes, ten Sail in all, hired to carry Troops from Brest to retake Goree [in Senegal], with five Men of War, if they could have escaped the Vigilance of our Admiral. The *Thames* and *Swallow* Sloop chased them into that Passage from the Eastward, and took two of the ten, a Ship of 208 Tons and a Snow.'

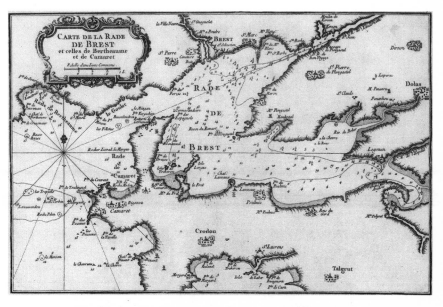

Chart of Brest Road and Berthaume and Camaret Bays by Bellin 1764. To look into Brest Monmouth *would sail just ahead of the compass point.*

Monmouth and *Montagu* anchored in their usual places for the night. Fortunately, their lookouts were alert. At first light they made out four French ships of the line slipping out of Brest harbour in an attempt to take them by surprise. Hervey made a swift decision to fight rather than run. Reynold Thomas, the clerk, recorded that he 'hailed the *Montague* & told them he was determined not to be drove off the station – but to endeavour to draw these ships to the Fleet by coming to Action.' *Monmouth*'s anonymous officer wrote, 'she answered with three loud Cheers. Near five we saw the *Colchester* of 50 Guns, and a Frigate, from the Admiral, to Leeward, and made a Signal for all Cruizers to make Sail.' The French ships were five miles away to the west.

Hervey scribbled a brief note to Hawke:

Monmouth off Brest 22 July 1759 at ½ past 4 a.m.

Sir,

I have but just time to tell you by the cutter that four sail of the enemy's ships are now out of the Road laying to, which is to drive us off (the others not moving) and then get their convoy in from Conquet. The *Colchester* and a frigate is in sight; therefore we will not be drove off easily.

Hervey told the cutter's lieutenant to order the *Colchester* and frigate to 'make more sail up to us'. The four French ships were steering towards the fort at Bertheaume, under easy sail, apparently prepared to fight. *Monmouth* cleared for action. The risk now was that without *Colchester* and the frigate the two ships might be beaten by the four before Hawke's nearest ships came to the rescue. Hervey set the mainsail for extra speed and repeated the signal for the two smaller ships to join him: the clear implication of Thomas's exact minutes is that Hervey thought *Colchester*'s officers either culpably unobservant or unwilling to sacrifice themselves.

As soon as the cutter reached him Hawke signalled *Torbay, Dorsetshire, Magnanime* and *Dunkirk* to chase in to support *Monmouth* and *Montagu*, and then prepared to follow with the whole fleet, hoping against hope that Hervey could provoke the general engagement they so wanted.

If the French had ever had any intention of fighting, the aggressive British response dissuaded them. At six in the morning two of Hawke's ships came into *Monmouth*'s view level with the Black Rocks. On their hilltop lookout post, the French signalled that the British fleet was in sight. Hervey saw the French ships turn. In frustration he hoisted a broad pendant and British colours, to show that he was in command of a squadron and ready for battle, and fired his chaser at the leewardmost of them. 'They would not stay for us', complained the officer who wrote to the papers. 'We chased them with all the Sail we could make, as did the *Montague*.'

An hour later the British fleet was in sight. Hervey tried every trick he knew to squeeze out more speed. He hailed Lendrick again 'to make all sail he could to get up & bring the ships to Action as he would also'. Quarter of an hour later *Monmouth* made her first tack into the Goulet, the bottleneck leading to Brest harbour. At this point, nearly three hours after her signal was first hoisted, the *Colchester* finally made sail.

Monmouth and *Montagu* zigzagged onward, tacking roughly every half an hour. They tacked six times, an operation that required all hands: in this narrow space they could not afford to make a mistake. It was all in vain. In the lee of the land they lost the wind and they now gained significantly only on the last French ship, which was falling behind. Hervey could now make out Richard Howe's *Magnanime*. Being in sight of a senior captain, he took down his broad pendant, the badge of a commodore in temporary command of a squadron. Then, after the sixth tack, he fired as many starboard guns as would bear on the lagging Frenchman, but failed to slow her down.

It was now clear that unless they disabled this ship, they could not catch her before she got under the shelter of the forts guarding the inner entrance to the Goulet. By counting her gun ports they identified her as a seventy-four. Thomas recorded that 'The Captain Order'd the Guns to be fired that would bear to disable them if possible – and explained these reasons on the Deck, as otherwise he would have obey'd his Orders & not fired 'till alongside.' They were under constant fire from mortars and guns in the forts, but most of their shot and shells fell short. The French ship only fired three or four shots at them and missed.

Monmouth's officer wrote that

At half past Ten, perceiving the Enemy would get in, and that some of our Larboard Guns would bear and reach, we fired, and tried to disable them, then tacked several Times. Their Bomb Batteries fired at us, and a large Shell fell very near. We told our Larboard Guns into one of them, and shot away her Mizen-top-mast; she was ashore on a rock for a quarter of an Hour, but the Flood raised her off again. The *Montague* played her Part, but we had got in under their Guns and Bomb

Batteries, and the Pilot of the *Magnanime*, by Signal, made us sensible we were in great Danger.

This signal from Richard Howe, recalling *Monmouth* and *Montagu*, gave Hervey the excuse to call off his pursuit with honour intact. *Monmouth* shortened sail and brought to. Then Hervey hailed Lendrick and ordered him to cease fire, since his shots were falling short of the target. Lendrick agreed that to continue forward involved too great a risk and the two ships began to sail back down the Goulet, still under fire from the forts. Half an hour later, on a signal from the French admiral, nine ships unfurled topsails and steered before the wind to leave Brest. Hervey signalled Hawke that the enemy was coming out of port. *Monmouth*'s officers watched Hawke's response:

> He was some Miles without: He did not run but formed the Fleet into a Line a-head, with their Larboard Tacks on Board, stood towards us, then wore and formed a-breast of the Harbour with the Starboard Tacks, and brought to in full View of the Enemy. Had it not been for their numberless Batteries ashore, he would not have waited for them, but have gone into their road to them.

Just for a moment, an officer with Hawke's fleet reported,

> we concluded they were all coming out to give us Battle; you would have been pleased to see the Spirits every Heart was in, when the Signal was made and repeated for seeing the Enemy coming out: But alas! We soon found our Joys were groundless, for altho' their Sails were hoisted, and their Top-gallant-Sails set they remained fast at Anchor

A quarter of an hour later, on a second signal, the French ships lowered their topsails. Hervey signalled Hawke that they had remained at anchor and sailed to join some boats that were coming towards him.

The officer with Hawke's fleet who wrote to the papers enjoyed the manner in which the French tamely

> submitted to the Indignity of seeing four of their large Ships retire from two of ours, and in Sight of their whole Fleet, and close to their Batteries. This whole Action, and the Manner we heard and saw the

old *Monmouth* behave, has done the greatest Honour to her and her Commander, and is the whole talk of the Fleet, being a most extraordinary Action, and would have ended in taking one of them, had they had three or four Miles more to go.

Hawke was delighted. 'Never did officer show greater conduct and resolution than did Captain Hervey and was bravely seconded by Captain Lendrick', he wrote to Clevland. To Hervey he sent his warmest letter yet:

> Your behaviour yesterday gave me the greatest satisfaction and merits the highest approbation. I had an additional pleasure, too, that of there being so many witnesses of it. I sincerely thank you, Sir, for your conduct and bravery and beg farther that you will, in a public manner in my name, thank your officers and company for their gallantly seconding your endeavour to destroy the enemy.

This public thanks from the admiral went down very well on *Monmouth*. The writer to the newspaper reported:

> By our brave Captain, our Officers and Men have received the Admiral's Thanks for our behaving like Men. If they would but come out, we would trim their Jackets for them. We have had a great deal of Fatigue in watching them; but this thanks from our great Man has lightened our Hearts, made us forget all our Toils, and we'll make him amends when we meet the Enemy.

Phipps told his father:

> you will I dare say be glad to hear that our behaviour was seen & admired by all the fleet on the 22^d & on the 23^d my Uncle receiv'd a Letter from Sir Edward Hawke to thank him & the ships company for their behaviour. I wonder what Madame de Sevigné & the Frater would think of this pretty manner of proceeding were they now au Rochers

Phipps was also excited by the news given them by a Dutch merchant-man leaving Conquet that 'on ye 21st when we cannonaded ye French convoy there, they had ten men killed & wounded in ye ships

& ashore by our Cannon & twelve on shore by the bursting of one of their own guns'. *Monmouth* had suffered no casualties at all.

Hervey added a note on Constantine:

> Your Boy is very happy, & thank God very well; very good & very Brave – we have had three very smart, & sound Trials of him within these three weeks I assure you – when you write touch a little on the point of Spruceness, we are not quite the thing for an officer in that – & that's all, & indeed that's a trifle – when every other merit he has & is by much (witht. flattery) fitter for an officer than many Captains I have the misfortune to be acquainted with

One point that emerges from *Monmouth*'s quarterdeck minutes is that Hawke had given his ships standing orders to open fire on the enemy only from close alongside an enemy ship. When Hervey opened fire from long range in an attempt to disable the slowest of the French ships, the minutes stress that he explained his 'reasons on the Deck, as otherwise he would have obey'd his Orders & not fired 'till alongside'. Hervey was evidently of Hawke's mind, and would not have done battle from long range in normal circumstances. Protégés of Hawke, such as William Locker, cherished this preference for engaging Frenchmen closely, and they trained their pupils to do the same. Thus, after the battle of the Nile in 1797, Horatio Nelson would remind his old patron Locker, 'it is you who always told me, "Lay a Frenchman close, and you will beat him"', referring to Locker's success against a larger French privateer in 1757. In this way Hawke's precepts came to be applied at Trafalgar.

The incident established a new friendship between Hervey and 'Black Dick' Howe. There had been misunderstandings between them in the past, so Hervey was particularly pleased when Howe 'broke out in the greatest praise & Commendations of me to the Adml. in public'. He was also touched by Howe's tact when his pilot 'acquainted him of my Risk & Danger by following the Ships in so farr & being Engaged with them & their Forts'. Thinking that the acutely honour-conscious Hervey might not turn his back on the French unless they could see that he had been told to, Howe 'took upon him, to make a Sigl. to call me in, as if he had repeated one from the Adml.'

Hervey knew that his sister had a soft spot for the handsome Howe and told her, "twas very noble, very handsome, very like himself what few but himself could have thought of, & none but himself would have executed – all together he has charmed me you know I always confess'd he was an admirable officer, for our little Differences never blinded me – in which I believe I was most to blame.'

Contact with the main fleet meant letters from home. Chaplain Edward Chicken's brought heartbreak. On 13 July his wife Elizabeth had drowned with a man from Hull and another from Beverley while boating on Hornsea Mere. How this affected him we cannot know. When he made a will on 2 August 1759, he already knew of his wife's death. His daughter Elizabeth, to whom he left his belongings, was cared for by her grandmother and her aunt Mary Legard.

For some time there was little to distract the chaplain from his private grief. The summer weather was benign. The crew went through routine tasks like splicing and knotting worn rigging and turning old rope into junk wadding for the guns. Men fished over the side.

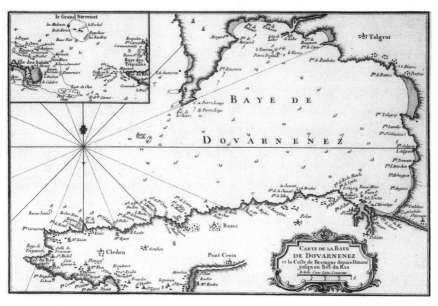

Chart of Douarnenez Bay and the Passage du Raz through the Saints by Bellin 1764.

On the night of 9 August the French tried to slip out six *chasse-marées* heavily laden with powder and musket balls. Hervey may have had some inkling of it, for next morning he sent Captain Clements, who had rejoined with *Pallas*, to look into Douarnenez Bay. Clements had orders to survey the bay, but as he approached he caught the French convoy by surprise. Hearing gunfire, Hervey sent *Monmouth's* cutter in support. The frigate silenced a fort and drove away a body of musketeers who were firing from the beach, and her boats captured five of the six *chasse-marées*. Their crews escaped ashore with nearly all their papers, but the one document Clements recovered showed that the convoy was bound for the mouth of the Loire. 'I expect in about 2 years to receive ye sum of £0 s1 d3 for these Prizes', wrote Constantine Phipps to his mother, more or less tongue in cheek. After sending the prizes to Hawke, Hervey took his little squadron into Douarnenez Bay to take soundings and make a survey, while ensuring that no more French convoys could try to hug the shore and slip by to the south.

Like others the squadron had undertaken, the survey of Douarnenez Bay would be used in future Admiralty operations against Brest. In each ship the master was responsible for buying charts and bringing them aboard. John Wilson was expected to possess a *Neptune François*, the official French marine atlas. Originally produced for Louis XIV's navy in 1693 when it was state of the art, this work had been reissued without significant alteration in 1753 and still placed Brest thirty-five miles out of position. It remained the best atlas available, but British officers were encouraged to carry out more precise local surveys whenever possible.

Admiral Anson was a driving force behind the production by naval officers of empirical, scientifically accurate drawings and surveys wherever and whenever possible. Behind mathematics and French, drawing was regarded as the key ancillary accomplishment for naval officers. Perspective drawing was a skill that had only recently been mastered by most English artists and drawing masters, and this was the first war to be illustrated with convincingly accurate drawings and maps.

It had been raining for five days when news arrived of Prince Ferdinand's great victory at Minden on 4 August, a triumph in which the British infantry earned the lion's share of the glory. Against all expectation, the French advance in Germany was halted and Hanover saved. With the German front stabilised, the French position in America again looked desperate unless they could strike a blow at Britain itself.

Hawke stood in to the Black Rocks with the entire fleet and as soon as the weather cleared enough for the French to see them, each ship fired a twenty-one-gun *feu de joie* to express their exultation to the ships that remained pent up uselessly in port.

The arrival of the admiral provided an opportunity to write home, and Constantine Phipps had exciting news of a royal visit: 'on ye 27th Prince Edward Came on board us to look into Brest but the wind did not prove Favourable so he laid on board that night but next morning it proving westerly he left us.'

Constantine's parents congratulated him on his part in *Monmouth*'s successes. His mother also congratulated her brother the captain. 'I dare say your Health is drunk from the ministers tables to the militia ale houses,' she wrote, 'how glorious it is to be in a situation to make such a figure, to be of real use to ones country, such an Honor to ones family & such a gratification to ones own pride.' She was still convinced the French would try something: 'I do think the french wont have been at all that expence & preparation at home only to be laught at abroad they have certainly some scheme wch I hope ye will all get the better of.'

The day Prince Edward left, Hervey had the captains of his squadron with him. Samuel Barrington of *Achilles*, George Balfour of *Bienfaisant*, John Lendrick of *Nottingham* and Joseph Fraine of *Southampton* were all men with strong fighting records. They were joined by Thomas Gittins, master of the *Prince Edward* cutter, who brought Lieutenant George Knight back from an errand to the admiral. Hervey reprimanded Gittins for cruising at too great a distance from *Monmouth* and failing to respond to signals. Gittins, who was drunk, replied so insolently that Hervey had him locked up and sent him as a prisoner to Hawke.

The incessant strain was beginning to make Hervey even more short-tempered than usual. Summer was ending and the fogs and gales of autumn were already setting in. An officer wrote home reporting *Pallas*'s capture of the *chasse-marées* as further evidence of Hervey's diligence. He was sceptical of the fleet's chances of remaining on station: 'We fear we shall not be able to remain much longer in so dangerous a Situation, for the Season will soon prevent us from safely working our Ships amidst such a Number of Rocks and Islands, and on an Enemy's Coast.' There had already been one serious alarm when they found the ship driving in the night. A sharp rock had cut through the cable close to the anchor. *Revenge* had given them a best bower to replace it, but with rocks close around them on every side, accidents like that could be fatal, especially in bad weather.

The first few days of September were especially bad and Hervey gave his little squadron instructions for unforeseen eventualities: 'In case of separation by any Unavoidable Accident The place of Rendezvous is from three to Eight Lgs due Wt: from St Mathews Point in the Bay of Brest and after looking for me thereabouts for five days, you are to open the Rendezvous you Received from Sr Edw Hawke and endeavour to join him according to that.' The main body of the fleet got well out to sea. An officer wrote home, 'We have had lately very bad Weather, and very hard Gales of Westerly Wind, which put us all in Pain for Commodore Hervey's Squadron, which still continues off Brest, close to the Enemy.'

The difficult period of the operation was beginning. *Monmouth* had now been out for more than ten weeks, and the likelihood of illness rose with every passing day. They were gambling with the elements now too; normally fleets retired from the Breton coast in the face of autumn gales. To stay in the confined, rock-strewn waters just outside the French naval base was to invite trouble. The skills of *Monmouth*'s seamen were about to be given a severe examination.

9

All ye Hardships that the
Briney Waves is Addict'd to

'God knows when we shall see you,' wrote Hervey to his sister, 'the ships are all taking their Turns home for fourteen Days or so, but me – the Adml. says, & writes that he cannot spare me, I must be contented to go when he does only'.

Hervey was tired but he was also proud: 'I find he told the Prince the other day, that no one cd. have perform'd this Critical Service I have been these two months & am still upon, so much to the Honor & Service of my Country, as Myself – c'est bien flateur pour moy – and sweetens the D—'d bitterness, Danger, & fatigue of the Employment . . .'

As time went by, the strain of blockading increased, especially for those stationed close to the rocks off Brest. Hawke sent his ships home in ones and twos to boot-top and to refresh the crews, but thanks to Hawke's faith in Hervey and his men, *Monmouth* remained where she was.

This was possible because of recent improvements to the efficiency of the naval supply system and the quality of food. From its principal depot at the Redhouse, Deptford, the navy now manufactured its own victuals. In 1755 they had built new flourmills at Deptford and Dover. The next year they had added another at Deptford with a kiln to dry peas and a mill to grind oats. In 1758 they had replaced the unpopular Suffolk cheese with more expensive cheese from Cheshire, Warwickshire and Gloucestershire. By this time the Admiralty slaughtered, packed and stored all the meat it purchased in England. A new slaughterhouse had been built at Dover in 1756 and the Plymouth slaughterhouse rebuilt and extended in 1757. They employed top men: brewmaster John Raymond of the Hartshorn brewery at

Deptford had twenty-two years' experience, including seven as chairman of the Brewers' Company. They still had problems: during 1759 the beer brewed at Plymouth rapidly went off, but the installation next year of a new vat removed the problem.

This extraordinarily energetic logistical effort underpinned Hawke's innovative naval blockade. As his ships ran out of food, he had more sent out from England. He demanded fresh beef, mutton and greens, and the victualling board supplied live cattle, sheep and boatloads of vegetables. This sort of thing had never been done before.

Monmouth had been provisioned for three months on 1 April, with a six-week supply of beer. She took in more beer and water at Torbay in early June and some beer and bread at the beginning of July. She was beginning to run very short before ships sent out from England in late July arrived with supplies.

In preparation, the purser, Richard Jones, condemned 160 pounds of butter and 1050 pounds of cheese as unfit for consumption. *Monmouth* had also used 2,264 pounds of gunpowder in her various fights with the enemy. They loaded substantial quantities of standard provisions of every kind, with thirty-five tons of water. Then the crew boot-topped the *Monmouth* where she was off Brest. The sight of British warships calmly restocking and cleaning just outside their principal port must have been depressing for the French. A second victualler visited on 14 August and a third sloop laden with wine arrived 4 days later. Hawke had complained repeatedly that the beer he was sent from Plymouth was bad, so the commissioners supplied wine instead.

Loading the eight pipes of wine cost the first injury that we know of that summer to one of *Monmouth*'s crew – one of the best men, too. John Blake was a thirty-one-year-old from the prosperous Irish city of Waterford, and one of Hervey's most faithful followers, having joined the frigate *Phoenix* when Hervey took her to sea in 1752. As one of the six quartermasters, he would have been assisting whichever of the three mates, Ball, Reeves or McLaurin, took charge of stowing the barrels. Using a yardarm as an improvised crane, the experienced forecastle men lifted these out of the hold of the victualler and into the hold of the *Monmouth*. File Fewin supervised from the gangway, the mechanical use of ropes and pulleys being the boatswain's province. Stowing was the master's department, and his deputies, the quarter-masters, placed the casks so as to maintain the trim of the ship, resting them horizontally on their quarters, 'bung up' against each other so that they did not shift about. Unfortunately, in bunging them up, Blake's hand was trapped by the 'chime' or rim of a barrel, lacerating the thumb and fingers of his right hand, 'whereby he lost ye nail of the fore, & partly the use of the middle finger by a contraction of the tendons'.

Knowledge of the state of health of *Monmouth*'s crew is limited, owing to lack of sources. Surgeon's journals are extremely rare, and Robert Smith's has not survived. We know of Blake's injury from the certificate he produced to those who examined his case for compensation from the Chatham Chest, which all seamen paid money into to form an insurance fund against injury while on His Majesty's Service. They thought Blake's wound worth £4. No other certificates for 1759 exist for Monmouths, but this may be because they have not survived rather than because nobody else was injured. Nevertheless, there are indications that this seasoned crew suffered low levels of accidental injury and sickness.

Deaths at sea were always recorded in the logs and the muster, although the cause was rarely explained unless they were killed in action, making their dependants eligible for a pension. Several Monmouths died in hospital in England during the spring of 1759, but the first to die at sea was the recently promoted marine corporal Thomas Fisher on 26 August. Several of his colleagues, including the other corporal Isaac Mackrell, had been treated for venereal disease during the spring. A couple of other men were sufficiently ill to be sent to Plymouth Hospital at the beginning of September.

From the beginning of August, *Monmouth*'s log gives an exact account of the expenditure of meat. It fits the known pattern for the naval diet – pork on Sunday, beef on Tuesday, pork on Thursday, beef on Saturday. The quantities in the casks suggest that each man received more than a pound of pork and about a pound and a half of beef. One Tuesday they missed their beef because they were taking in 100 tons of beer, but they got it next Monday instead. This pattern continued until 27 August when the whole fleet came to the Black Rocks off Brest. At that point *Monmouth* got the first of the fresh beef that Hawke had arranged to be sent over from home.

Bullocks and sheep had to be lifted on to the ship, also by yardarm crane, than penned, and looked after by a suitable landsman. The ship's butcher slaughtered beasts as they were required. Current research indicates that fresh meat really does have some effect against scurvy, as was believed then. But the Admiralty had also ordered the Victualling Board to send out fresh vegetables. They were already sending cabbages, carrots, turnips, potatoes and onions to the fleet, and from 20 August the *Catwater* sloop was employed exclusively in carrying roots, greens and apples over to Ushant.

The vegetables were used as a side dish for all, but the sick also ate vegetables in portable soup. The Amiralty quickly grasped the value of the recent invention by London businesswoman Mrs Dubois of a method of condensing beef into a solid tablet. They had the raw material in the offal of beef slaughtered at Deptford and soup tablets could easily be carried aboard ship to feed sick seamen. In 1756 they had awarded Mrs Dubois a contract to manufacture portable soup at Deptford, and a few months later contracts were issued at Portsmouth and Plymouth. Surgeons added mutton to the recipe to make the soup more 'light & nourishing to the sick'. In 1757 surgeons had reported favourably on its effects.

The ships with hardened crews and surgeons who believed in the virtue of fresh meat and vegetables came through the long months off Brest almost unscathed by scurvy. *Monmouth* was one of them. The senior doctor at Portsmouth, James Lind, argued that the continued health of most of Hawke's crews was 'entirely owing to this fleet having been well supplied with fresh meat and greens'.

Monmouth was soon back on station after the gales of early September. A cutter arrived with a message from Hervey's brother, the Spanish ambassador, for Hawke, warning that de la Clue's Toulon squadron had escaped from the Mediterranean heading for Brest, but that Boscawen was following them. On 13 September the *Fly* cutter brought news from Hawke of Boscawen's victory over the escaping

French off Cape Lagos, but also of the possible arrival of the French ships that had not been captured. Hawke ordered Hervey to do his 'utmost to destroy the French ships that have escaped in case you should fall in with them'.

An officer of the *Nottingham* wrote to his brother in London:

> we are now Six at Anchor in Sight of the French Fleet at Brest: and though it is a most troublesome and dangerous Situation, we bear those Inconveniences with Pleasure. Three Days ago the Commodore went with his Ship close to the Enemy, leaving us all in a Line of Battle without him. He brought out two very large Vessels that lay under a Fort, laden with Stones of six and seven Hundred Weight each, ready cut for the repairing their Bason.

James Baron went in with two of *Monmouth*'s boats to cut out these large vessels. The taste for fresh food had evidently set in, for Hervey then used the capacious boats to raid another island, Lédénès-de-Molène, at dawn on 15 September. Constantine Phipps gave his mother an account of their latest escapade:

> on ye 15th our boats conquer'd an Island in sight of the fleet in Brest from whence they Brought 35 Bullocks, Cows hogs & 3 horses one of which my Uncle has got. Yesterday my uncle went off the most formidable Island of Molene with ye Cutter & all ye Ships barges to take it & they hung out a flag of truce our Boat went to answer it & the Governor sent off a Capitulation in which he Desired Monr: Le Commandant d'avoir pour agreable to accept 24 Vaches de Mellieur de notre Isle with fowles Greens fruit &c &c Monr: Le Commandant took their Cows Greens & fruit but refused their fowles as what he took was a sufficient insult & that taking ye fowls would only Distress ye Poor inhabitants already miserable enough

Nottingham's officer told his brother, 'Our Captain [Lendrick] tells me that the commodore sent the Governor Word, That he was sorry if what he had done had distressed the Inhabitants; but he meant it only as an Insult to the French Fleet, and to shew them, and all Europe, that they could not protect their own People in their Sight, much less dare to attempt the Invasion of England.' Nevertheless,

Hervey's calculated insult also benefited health and morale in his hard-working squadron: 'This has put our People in great Spirits, it being five or six Days fresh Provisions for all the Ships Crews here, besides much Milk for the Men who have the Scurvy, which we were much in want of, as our People begin to fall down with that Distemper.'

The *Nottingham* was evidently already troubled with scurvy, but it was not until 3 October that *Monmouth*'s butcher killed sheep 'for the sick', rather than for the ship's company as a whole. The crew stayed remarkably healthy, since the captain and surgeon were among the more forward-looking officers of the navy.

The squadron was very much on the alert when, during the evening of 17 September, they saw three French ships slip out of the Goulet and anchor in Cameret Bay just outside Brest harbour but under the protection of 'almost all the Cannons and Mortars that line the entrance to that port'. That night Hervey had *Montagu* and *Nottingham* guard the passage between the Black Rocks and La Parquette, while he went south with *Achilles* and *Bienfaisant* to guard the Passage du Raz. They returned in the morning to find that the French had not moved.

The French ships got under sail but never left the cover of the forts at the mouth of the Goulet. Hervey now 'began to imagine their scheme was to draw our ships in, that with little Wind, a great swell, & flood tide, we might in this season be in danger of getting within the Goulette'. The sky was black and the wind was westerly, all of which spelled danger. He signalled to *Achilles* to cover the approaching victuallers and to *Nottingham* and *Bienfaisant* to get between *Monmouth* and *Achilles*. *Monmouth* and *Montagu* approached within three miles of the French, who were surrounded by about a hundred boats, before they turned back.

The victuallers returned to the fleet with the tale that they had

found that brave Commander, with another Ship, driving before them three very large French ships of War . . . The *Monmouth* fired some Shot at them just as they tack'd about from her, which they were in too great a Hurry to return. The Commodore stood out again to join the rest of his Ships off St. Matthew's. We are told that there were 70 or 80

Fishing Boats, and other smaller Vessels, full of Men, well armed, about these three Ships, intending, had it fallen calm, to have destroyed the *Monmouth*.

In former times Hervey had taken trouble to send his own publicity to the London press. Now he no longer needed to since others did it for him. The fame of Hervey and his ship, the little black *Monmouth*, was spreading rapidly.

That night and next morning, while *Bienfaisant*, *Southampton* and the cutter were on the lookout, the other ships unloaded the victuallers. Hervey's bargemen rowed him to *Bienfaisant* and with the other lookouts they approached the French, who had once again retired to Cameret. As Hervey approached, the three ships at Cameret got under sail, as did another six in the harbour, hoping to trap *Bienfaisant* between them, but the wind died away. The English crews watched scornfully as the French ships got hopelessly tangled up as they attempted to turn round in the narrows.

Overnight, Hervey had *Bienfaisant* and the cutter watching the route south, but he did not expect the French to move. The next day he stood in towards Brest with all his ships, leaving them at first at proper distances to form a line should the French choose to fight. Hervey had noticed that whereas earlier in the year the hillsides around Brest had been crowded with spectators, they were now bare. He drove the ships from Cameret headlong towards their port, and then stopped to insult the French fleet. First he hoisted a French pendant under his own red one, then a Bourbon flag under a Union Jack, then he fired on the sternmost ship. Needless to say, the French did not come out to fight him.

On 25 September Prince Edward visited again, and this time Hervey was able to take him to look at the French fleet in Brest harbour. 'I shew'd him the French Fleet & Coast in perfection,' wrote Hervey to his sister. Edward Hutchins noted that the French forts fired at them from three separate places, with the irritating schooner sending signals. After two days on board, Prince Edward returned to the fleet. Hawke was now convinced they would give up trying to get out: '– indeed these three last days they have had very fine fair winds nothing moves – but Barges with streamers & Ladies going off to Dinner to their Admls. every day.'

Hervey decided to stir the French up by cutting out a small schooner, anchored under the fort at Cameret, whose duty was to watch the motions of Hervey's squadron. The vessel was normally employed as a tender to Admiral Conflans's flagship, so its capture would be particularly insulting. With French guns commanding Camaret harbour, it was very hazardous. On 28 September he sent the cutter to take a close look at the schooner while routinely checking the state of affairs in Brest. The vessel was very well protected. As Constantine Phipps remarked, 'it was a very bold undertaking as she anchored within less than Muskett shot of Camaret Castle in which are 2 48 pounders & 17 36 Pounders'. Nevertheless, Hervey decided to cut her out and to lead the attack in person. David Winzar was his number two, commanding *Monmouth*'s barge. John McLaurin went with them. Each of the other ships sent its barge under command of a lieutenant, and the party gathered aboard *Monmouth* in the afternoon.

They set out at seven o'clock, just after dark, on 29 September and rowed the slim, thirty-foot barges silently towards the French schooner. The lieutenant commanding *Achilles*'s boat reported that 'having row'd till near One in the Morning, we got into a Bay, close to the French Fleet, in order to attack a little Yatcht belonging to the French Admiral. As soon as Commodore Hervey, who led us, got Sight of the Fort, under which the Vessel lay, the Yatcht hail'd the *Monmouth*'s Boat, and fired'.

They had been detected when still a hundred yards away. The schooner fired its two 2-pounders twice but narrowly missed the boats, which were now racing towards it with muskets cracking in return: 'we immediately all fired our Small Arms, and pull'd on board as fast as possible. The Commodore himself and his People were first on board, and carried her thro' all their Fire. We boarded next, to follow their brave Example.'

Winzar, Hervey and McLaurin clambered into the schooner with their select band of bargemen. At first the Frenchmen on board fought fiercely, and a musket ball went through Hervey's coat, but by the time the men from *Achilles* boarded, the Monmouths were already winning a fierce struggle in which a dozen of the thirty-six Frenchmen were wounded. 'We found them with Swords and Pistols in Hand; the French running under the Deck, begging their Lives', wrote their lieutenant. 'Our People cut her Cable, and our Boats brought her out in the Midst of incessant Firing from the Shore.'

British sailors boarding a Frenchman. This illustration from the Naval Chronicle *shows a later action in daylight, but the French vessel is of a similar size and similarly armed with swivels and larger guns.*

Constantine Phipps reported that 'the french men behaved very well & made a Tollerable Resistance but he at Last carried her without the loss of one man the french had 5 or 6 wounded amongst whom was the first Captain and his Brother'. As the prize papers reveal, this was an underestimate. As soon as it was clear that the schooner had been taken, the heavy guns in Cameret castle and the other batteries tried to pick them out, firing wildly into the darkness. 'We found ourselves in great Danger, nevertheless we tow'd and halloo'd all the Way. In the Morning we were met by the rest of the Ships Boats. We got to our Ships not a little tired, nor a little pleased at a Conquest that might have been more dearly bought; but nothing could have been done here so mortifying to the French.'

On the *Monmouth*, Lieutenant Hutchins heard the guns and Constantine waited excitedly for the return of the boats. As a French speaker, he was ordered to record the names and ranks of the French prisoners. He noted that 'they had 36 Hands on board of whom a great part were officers'.

McLaurin took charge of the prize with another petty officer and ten men and sent her to the admiral and then on to Plymouth, where the lucky prize crew got some leave. David Winzar had the honour of carrying Hervey's report to Hawke. Later in the morning seventeen Frenchmen, mostly wounded, were sent ashore under a flag of truce. Conflans wrote to Hervey, thanking him for his treatment of the wounded and apologising for the rude reception of a previous emmissary.

Achilles's lieutenant reported that 'The Commodore, who received no Hurt, a Shot only passing thro' his Coat, has generously given up all his Share of the Prize and Head-Money to the People who went in the Barges with him; and we believe that all the Captains of his Squadron will follow so worthy an Example.' Hawke followed suit with regard to prize money, 'my share of which I give up to the crews of the five barges for their gallant behaviour'. He added that 'HRH is mightily pleased with your taking the Garvette.'

Hervey sent a letter to his sister with Winzar, having just had time to add a postscript announcing 'I am just returned from a furious attack. & have myself with my Barges Carried a King's Vessell with 36 men Sword in hand under several forts.' Lepel affected to be unimpressed when the news reached her a fortnight later: 'My dear Augustus, how can you be so rash to go risk your life for a little foolish vessel? I cou'd scarce believe you were safe even while I read your own letter; think what a trifling space wou'd have directed that Ball fatally, wch pass'd thro' your great coat; how cou'd you have expos'd yourself more if it had been to take the whole fleet?'

The Phippses were in domestic chaos during the rebuilding of Mulgrave Castle 'wch tho' not near finished has almost ruined us', and leaving for London at the end of the month. Lepell sent what news there was: 'no news yet from America, people are in great apprehensions for the success of Quebec, General Wolfe is as desperate as you, so perhaps may fall at some small fort, before he reaches the Citadell.'

British forces under General Wolfe and Admiral Saunders had sailed up the St Lawrence river and were laying siege to the French stronghold of Quebec. On the outcome of that attack, led by the much-admired, dashing young general, the American War would turn. Meanwhile, militia units were still being deployed to contest a French attack on Britain's own shores. 'I don't find that the threatened invasion is so much despised at home, as you seem to do; preparations are making every where for their reception & I regret having no longer chappard [her French cook] to make some fricassees for them, I am afraid they won't be content with your cheese & Beer . . .'

For her part, she could only imagine what it was like in Brest, though it was perfectly possible in England for wives and relatives to trace the course of the war by buying inexpensive maps and plans. Ladies could even buy a 'Geographical Fan Mount of the Seat of War in the Kingdoms of Prussia . . . &c. Designed as an Introduction in Geography, for those Ladies who are not versed in that Science'. At least three good plans of Brest and its surroundings were advertised in the London papers in 1758. One of Jean Rocque's, at 1s. 6d., showed 'the Soundings, and all the Batteries'. Smaller copies appeared in all the monthly magazines. These plans showed clearly how dangerous it was to be close to the shore of Brest, surrounded by rocks and islands, when the autumnal westerly gales set in, driving ships straight on to the coast.

Hervey's previous letter had told her that 'in westerly winds there is much to be feared on our Accounts – for the situation then is terrible, yet (thank God) we have had no sort of Accident to any of my Squadron . . .' Now at Mulgrave, on its exposed hill above Whitby, the wind was tearing leaves from the trees. 'The westerly winds are now very violent,' she wrote on 16 October; 'I cou'd not sleep last night for the noise they made & the fear that your squadron shou'd be still more sensible of them'.

She was right to be alarmed. In that storm the men in *Monmouth* were indeed in danger. Hervey had already shifted *Monmouth*'s normal anchorage between St Matthew's Point and the Parquet shoal to one south of the westernmost of the Black Rocks. This proved to be a particularly rewarding spot for fishing, but its main virtue was that it was much easier to get out to sea in case of a sudden westerly gale. Hervey had looked into Brest on 9 October and warned Hawke that he expected difficulty in keeping up his strict blockade:

> You will give me leave to observe, Sir, that the season comes on fast when I fear, if the enemy is so intent on getting out two or three ships, they must at last find an opportunity of a shore wind and thick weather, when our ships have been obliged to stand off, by which means the greatest vigilance and boldest perseverance to keep this dangerous coast on board may be frustrated.

In a postscript he reiterated that he appreciated the need to stay close in but was 'as thoroughly convinced that this season greatly increases the hazard of it, as you must be sensible. However, Douarnenez [Bay] must be the resource if catched with any sudden gale westerly.' Douarnenez's potential as an emergency shelter from westerlies explains why Hervey and Hawke had been so eager to survey it. Hervey reminded Hawke that *Dunkirk* had no pilot so that he had to keep her close by.

This was the last Hawke heard of Hervey for some time. 'In the evening of the 11th,' Hawke reported to Clevland, 'we had a hard gale at W.S.W. Next morning the *Royal Ann* made the signal of distress and parted company. Yesterday and this day, the gale rather increasing, I thought it better to bear up for Plymouth than run the risk of being scattered and driven farther to the eastward.' The reassuring thing, he reminded Clevland, was that 'while this wind shall continue, it is impossible for the enemy to stir.'

At Plymouth the weather was so bad that Clevland's messenger could not get from the shore to the fleet for ten hours. 'The weather continues to grow worse or I should have been at sea again', Hawke continued. 'As the *Monmouth, Dunkirk, Bienfaisant, Hero, Resolution* and *Defiance* are not come in, I am apprehensive some of them may be got to the eastward.' Rumour magnified these anxieties, and in

London Hervey's mother was shocked to read a newspaper report stating that 'the *Monmouth* was by a storm drove on the coast of Brittany'.

Monmouth's officer of the watch saw the gale coming and stood out to get beyond Ushant, from where they could be blown eastwards into clear water rather than on to rocks. After a day of pouring rain the wind whipped up at night. Gunner Simenton with Burgess and Pattey checked the guns were secure. Fewin reinforced the rigging. Towards midnight the young Irishman Peter Hanlon, now rated able and a topman, followed Stephens, Damerel and Trevillick up the swinging shrouds and along the pitching yard to furl the fore topsail. Then they got the topgallant yards with their soaked sails down on deck, with Fewin's shrill call carrying instructions from the deck up through the howling wind. Rainwater streamed off their dread-noughts and tarred breeches. Others clewed up the weather sheet, partly clewed the lee sheet to save the sails from ripping and took in the mizen topsail.

Two ways of surviving a storm: on the left with balanced mizen and storm staysails; on the right lying to under the main course.

As 12 October dawned the gale continued to increase and the seas became huge. Narramore wedged the masts. Fewin rigged lifelines on the upper decks to give the men something to cling on to. Robert Narramore reported water in the well as the ship's timbers strained. Hanlon and his mates went aloft again, water streaming from their tarred clothes, to get the topgallant masts down on deck. John Blake's team braced the yards to the wind, and William Corrin hung out over the sea to get the studding sail booms from the lower yards down upon deck to be ready to reef the courses, while Coffen helped him rig in the jib boom and get the spritsail yard on to the deck.

All through the next day's storm the little squadron of *Monmouth*, *Nottingham*, *Dunkirk* and *Bienfaisant* kept in sight of each other, under reefed maintopsails, storm staysails and balanced mizen, holding their position not far from Ushant. Most of the crew huddled below decks. The next day was squallier. They lost the log while throwing it to test their speed and split the foretopmast staysail. *Nottingham* had to run for Plymouth, but the rest stayed out. All next day the wind blew, and then, during the night of 15 October, it got calmer. By this time they were less than sixty miles from the Lizard, but little further east. On 17 October the wind swung to the east and Hervey hurried back to Brest, reaching the Black Rocks on Thursday 18 October. It was still pouring with rain and in this 'thick weather' it was not until Saturday that he could look into Brest and assure himself that nothing had changed.

When Hawke arrived off Ushant he sent *Torbay* ahead to find out if Hervey was there and then followed in with the squadron 'till I discovered the *Monmouth, Dunkirk,* and *Bienfaisant* at anchor off the Black Rocks'. Keppel could not get close to Brest, but returned with Hervey's exact report from earlier that morning and his opinion that 'I can only add that I think them exactly as they were, and as I am certain nothing whatever has got out since I have been on this station, so I believe this hard westerly wind has not brought anything in'. Hervey also revealed that just before the storm struck he had been disabled with gout in both feet, 'and though I am much better, I am far from being well, being only able to be carried from gallery to gallery as I want to look out, from whence I took the view of the enemy's ships this morning'.

Hawke promised Hervey that as soon as the reinforcement he was expecting from Portsmouth arrived he would send *Monmouth* in to refresh along with *Bienfaisant*, whose crew was sickly. For the benefit of whoever replaced Hervey, Hawke asked for 'the best remarks you have made of the soundings, dangers, anchoring ground and batteries within the limits of your station, with their bearings, the flowings of the tides their setting, and the heighth they rise with draught thereof, – if you have any artists to draw them; and direct all the Captains under your orders to do the same'.

With this note came the news that 'It is said an express is arrived with the news that Quebeck is taken, and that General Wolfe and another General officer is killed.' It was the news that all England had been waiting for that summer – the stronghold of New France had fallen; but the army's young idol had died. 'I think Wolfe's memory should be forever dear to his country', Phipps wrote home. 'Their joy for the taking Quebec will stop the tears which would flow for the Hero to whom they owe so valuable an acquisition'.

The Monmouths had another narrow escape two nights later, this time in a flat calm when Winzar suddenly realised that a rock had cut through the anchor cable and they were drifting 'in a prodigious rippling of tide and not far from the seams to judge by the noise of the breakers'. From their anchorage off the Black Rocks they were carried rapidly southward towards the waves breaking over the deadly 'Seams' off the Pointe du Raz. Phipps reported cheerfully, 'We were very near being lost t'other night my Uncle (who is still laid up with the gout) was Brought upon deck'. Hervey made an instant decision to anchor, which saved them, with the tide setting at four and a half knots. After midnight a gentle breeze allowed them to get under sail, and they 'sounded very often until daylight'.

Phipps was being given more and more responsibility, standing watches like a junior officer: 'he now watches – & shall soon be a Midshipman – believe me 'tis best to push them on always when one can – I have already been longer at sea than ever a Ship in this world was know to be hereabouts – I fear bad weather is again coming on'.

He was right. On 28 October, in strong gales and driving rain, they again got in the boats, struck the topgallant masts, and headed for the open sea. The topmen again furled the fore and mizen topsails, close-reefed the main one and the ship lay to. They returned to Brest on 1 November and Hervey wrote to his sister, 'this is a Horrid place now long Dark Nights, short foggy Windy Days, & nought but Terror all round which Nature & Art have seem'd to vie with each other which shd. render it most formidable'. He was in a particularly bad mood. Not only was he still in pain and unable to walk, but he had just been told that his pay had been stopped, pending adjustment of a mistake made by Reynold Thomas in the paperwork involved in discharging one of *Monmouth*'s injured men:

> after sacrificing one's Health and keeping six Months (what no ship ever did before) upon such a station – to be applauded, & yet so gratefully repaid – as to have all my Pay stop'd for a mistake in my Clerk, about the form of a twelve Pound Tickett for a Poor man; that should have had his Discharge on <u>wrote</u> Paper & not <u>Printed</u> – which is literally all the Difference, & they have made me to forfeit all my last years pay – so that I am now 19 Months without receiving any – there's a Service your Son has chose – I have told him enough of it, and when all is over, & they want you no more, then you are dismissed with the Honorable maintenance of <u>five Shillings a Day</u> Bravo!

It was a bitter twist to *Monmouth*'s significant part in a year that had seen an astonishing sequence of victories. First had come news of success in West Africa, then India. The richest French sugar island, Guadeloupe, had been seized. Boscawen's victory off Cape Lagos had been followed by Prince Ferdinand's at Minden and the French retreat from Hesse. Finally, a series of small victories in Canada had been capped by the fall of the great French fortress there. Hervey continued:

> What success has the [year] 59 produced, I hope it will not elate us too much, & enduce our Leaders to carry on a very expensive war, which in the End is always doubtfull, – but rather let it incline us to close an honorable and lasting – tho' perhaps less advantageous Peace than Uncertain Victories if obtained might give us – voila justement le but de mon politic – qu'en dites vous? I believe Mr. Phipps wd. subscribe

to that – I want a peace with France, and a War with the Dutch, those
hatefull Interested Dogs . . .

The time had come for peace with France and retribution for the
irritating, opportunistic neutrals.

His own part in the *annus mirabilis* of 1759 was over. *Monmouth* was
leaking badly, as was Lendrick's *Nottingham*. *Foudroyant* and *Anson* had
many men ill and also went home. Hawke wrote:

> Keeping the sea in the last gale of wind has greatly shattered the
> *Monmouth,* as their Lordships will perceive by the accompanying copies
> of letters and reports. Captain Hervey has also suffered much in his
> constitution by the fatigues and watchings of the critical station he has
> been on since the 1st of July. Through the whole he has given such
> proofs of diligence, activity, intrepidity and judgement that it would be
> doing injustice to his merit as an officer not to acknowledge that I part
> with him with the greatest regret.

Monmouth's work had not been in vain. 'Our marine officers',
reported a French journal, 'attribute all the misfortunes of our fleet to
the intrepidity of that little squadron that was so long cruising this year
at the very entrance of Brest'.

Half-mad Jack Addles from the Sea

Monmouth, Foudroyant and *Nottingham* limped past John Smeaton's newly completed, granite-built lighthouse on the Eddystone on 6 November. Using Maker Church as their seamark, they sailed into Plymouth Sound. *Monmouth* was letting in water at a rate of twenty-one inches an hour with the men still pumping in relays, so next day they got the ship into the Hamoaze, the broad part of the Tamar estuary where the dock was situated. They passed through the narrow, turbulent Cremyll passage where the water was 'like a boiling pot, in which a helmsman can scarce command the steerage of his boat from the run of the tide', into this relatively sheltered water. In driving rain they lashed *Monmouth* alongside the *Prince Henry* hulk, and began to unload her.

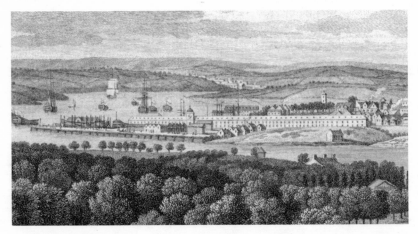

The entrance to the Hamoaze with Plymouth Dock. The Prince Henry *hulk is on the extreme left.*

Constantine Phipps scribbled a few lines to his parents: 'still in Plymouth & getting everything out Ready for ye Dock which is not yet Ready for us . . . I was ashore yesterday & again this morning', before leaping on the coach that splashed up the newly-built Great West Road to London. 'I sent him away at 10 minutes Warning,' explained the captain to Lepel Phipps, 'that there might not be 5 days lost to him, as the Coach goes out but twice a Week, & his Heart was set on getting to you'. Hervey sent instructions for new clothes for him:

> – he carried but three shirts & his uniform which you'll see is in Good Order, but he is outgrown it, therefore we want another Suit of Uniform & a Blue Great Coat – half a Dozn. Shirts with little, little, very little Ruffles: some shoes some good strong stockings and a hat et nous voila – but I wd. not have the Cloaths made 'till about three or four days before he is coming away, & then a little in the Country fashion, too long & too Big rather for present Wear

It rained almost constantly and strong winds lashed the ships in harbour. The 'state' of the ship delivered to the port admirals on 9 November showed that *Monmouth* had only twenty-four sick on board and six ashore, which was remarkable after so long at sea. She had also brought home twenty-eight sick supernumeraries belonging to other ships. Her captain was unable to put either foot on deck and had to be carried off the ship. The document also shows just how good her crew now was, at least on paper. *Monmouth* had only four seamen rated ordinary and nineteen landsmen to 328 rated petty and able. Only *Achilles*, whose men were all rated able, had a crew that was more showily rated – the other ships in port had far more inexperienced men. *Bienfaisant*, for instance, another 'sixty-four', had 104 ordinary and 98 landsmen to 173 petty and able.

The ship herself was described as 'leaky and very foul, last cleaned 15 March 1759', but before she could dock another ship had to be cleaned. This meant that finally there was an opportunity for shore leave. The boys were given two weeks from 13 November, other men one week in batches. It was more meaningful leave than they could have had in London earlier, since many could now visit their families. William Champlyn's wife Mary was in Egg Buckland just beyond Plymouth with their son William, born early in 1758. Edward Salmon went ashore to Cawsand and created a son who was christened John Wickett Salmon the following September. William May's wife Grace came from Chudleigh but probably lived in or near the new town of Dock that was growing up round the royal dockyard. Richard Meager's wife Sarah lived there too.

For those without families near Plymouth there was ample entertainment on shore. A gazetteer published that year in Exeter wrote of Plymouth being most crowded

> in its most flourishing wicked Time of what some call a good red-hot War with France, when indeed 'tis too much over-stock'd with Inhabitants new-come from Ireland, Cornwall, and other Parts, and gather'd Flocks of Females, charitably inclined to solace money'd Sailors in Distress; and, that they may do it honestly, and with a good Conscience, marry them ex tempore, possibly Half a Dozen successively in as many Months; their unfortunate former Husbands dying almost as soon as out of the Sound (in a double Meaning).

The writer blamed the wartime incomers:

> The true Plymothians themselves are in the main allow'd to be as polite, genteel, religious and worthy a People as those enjoy'd by any other place. [But in wartime] thro' the vast Resort of the Necessitous, the Rapacious, the Lewd by land, and of the half-mad Jack Addles from the Sea, the Scene are alter'd much, and very grievous to the best Natives. Then is (tho' but in common with other Sea-port Towns) too much introduced Sharping, Tricking, Debauchery, Pride, Insolence, Prophanness, Impurity with Insolence . . .

How true it was that sailors might marry each time they had leave is difficult to establish. A survey of pensions paid between 1750 and 1770 to sea officers' widows revealed only one widow of two husbands, although there were ten officers with two widows. One of them was George Knight, fourth lieutenant of the *Monmouth*, who had married Elizabeth in 1764 and Janet in 1766.

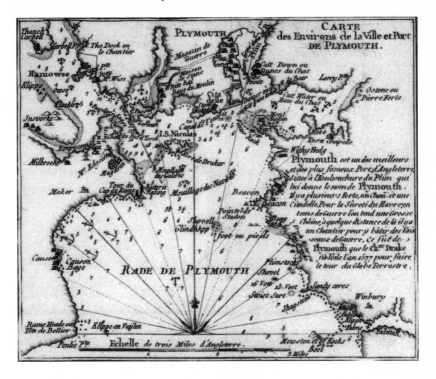

Chart of Plymouth.

The Monmouths had been paid in April and had had little opportunity to spend their money since. Edward Salmon, Richard Treadenham and a few other married men sent home remittances to genuine wives and families in accordance with the 1758 act designed to eliminate the hardships that naval bureaucracy might cause, but most spent their money with profligate generosity. The act had made pay more regular and allowed men to have some or all of it sent to their homes, but most of the crew were young and unmarried. In 1760 one captain chastised his men with the observation that 'whenever ye get any money paid, ye do not act with it like rational creatures, and lay it out on clothes and necessaries, but ye throw it immediately away on dirty whores and in stinking gin'. Such behaviour seems to have been very common. Sailors ashore frequented the theatre, and a whole genre of prints that showed sailors at play was

155

certainly designed with their custom in mind. Plymouth had a new Theatre Royal in George Street, but otherwise its leisure facilities focused on sex and booze.

With these temptations so close at hand, men went ashore without permission and some overstayed their leave. It was sometimes difficult to retrieve these 'ramblers' and 'stragglers', and occasionally the attempt led to violence and a court martial. One took place while *Monmouth* was at Plymouth.

At the hearing it was reported that James Samber, acting lieutenant of the *Defiance*, was dispatched ashore with two midshipmen, Harvey and Buckley, to round up men absent without leave. At four in the afternoon Harvey had spotted one of them, Patrick Wilson. Wilson refused to go aboard and Harvey, afraid to seize him, said he could have until six. At seven Harvey found him again, and this time he had Samber and Buckley with him, armed with staves. Samber 'took him by the collar and desired him to come', whereupon Wilson, according to Samber's evidence, 'immediately took a knife out of his pocket and opening it, made two or three strokes at me, intending to cut me with it'. Buckley said that he and Samber then knocked Wilson down until he dropped the knife. It was dark, Buckley said, and he was not sure whether Wilson used it. He also seemed much in liquor. Harvey said Wilson tried to cut Buckley. A passing seamen 'saw the prisoner with three gentlemen after him, who struck him with their sticks, he ran but they overtook him'. He heard the officer say if he would go quietly he would forgive him. According to Samber 'he refused, saying he would die first' and was very abusive. He was sufficiently sober that he 'knew me and called me by name'. Harvey said Wilson sat down, refused to move and hit Harvey with his fist. He appeared drunk. He recognised them after they knocked his knife away, but possibly not before. Eventually the three of them got Wilson to the guard house by force, but he collared Samber several times on the way and tore his coat. Wilson said that he was drunk and did not remember drawing the knife.

The vagueness with which both midshipmen addressed the question of whether Wilson used the knife against Samber and whether he knew who he was dealing with was a deliberate attempt to help him escape Article 21 of the Articles of War, read out once a month to all crews:

If any officer, mariner, soldier or other person in the fleet, shall strike any of his superior officers, or draw, or offer to draw, or lift up any weapon against him, being in the execution of his office, on any pretence whatsoever, every such person being convicted of any such offense, by the sentence of a court martial, shall suffer death.

But Samber was merciless and so was the court. On 28 November Wilson was hanged from the yardarm of the *Barfleur* and displayed to all the fleet.

While the men enjoyed their leave, the captain settled outstanding business. He was asked whether midshipman James Gilbert, a follower from *Hampton Court*, would make a gunner. He replied that Gilbert was a fine seaman and worthy of promotion, but if the Admiralty wanted a gunner John Burgess was a better choice. 'This Man', he wrote, 'has been Quarter Gunner, & Gunner's Mate, in every ship I have had the Honor to command, and has taken every method to qualifie himself for every Branch of the Gunner's Duty, he is a Sober, Active and Diligent Man'. Neither got immediate promotion.

Others did. First lieutenant Edward Hutchins was promoted into the flagship *St George*. In his place Hervey brought in his old friend, Peter Foulkes, a Cheshire man who had been his first lieutenant for eleven years in *Princessa, Phoenix* and *Hampton Court*. Foulkes had suffered more than most in Byng's disgrace: Byng had promoted him captain of *Phoenix* when Hervey took *Defiance*, but the Admiralty had refused to ratify the disgraced admiral's appointment.

Master's mate John McLaurin had been in Plymouth for a month, attending to the *Mercure*. He had passed for lieutenant in March 1759 and very much wanted a commission, but on 26 November he took the realist's second option by accepting the offer of a warrant as master of the sloop *Hornet*. Her master and commander George Johnstone was a charismatic if controversial figure: one striking eccentricity was that he had *Hornet's* cabin lined with bookshelves. Hervey promoted Edward Salmon to master's mate in McLaurin's place.

On 19 November, news that Conflans had escaped from Brest had reached London, causing consternation and foreboding that, despite all the summer's efforts, the French might yet come. 29 November was set aside as a day of thanksgiving for success in Canada, but nobody was counting his chickens, and at least one preacher took as his text psalm xxvii, verse 3: 'Tho' an host of men were laid against me, yet shall not my heart be afraid'. That very day, however, the fate of the invasion was finally settled – a dispatch arrived with the news of Hawke's destruction of Conflans's fleet at Quiberon. In a full gale Hawke had followed the French into the bay, and, during the battle and the stormy night following, three French ships had sunk with terrible loss of life and two had been captured. Five had escaped into the estuary of the Vilaine but were effectively trapped there. Two British ships had gone aground and were lost.

It was an action that 'very few men would have had the nerve to hazard'. The Duke of York remarked that 'Providence never shew'd us more favor in my poor opinion than in this instance, for it is next to a miracle, that upon such a Coast, with such a wind, many more of our ships did not go ashore.' The second Sunday of December was set aside for another national thanksgiving for the part that Providence had played in removing the threat of invasion, but the consummate seamanship of the officers and men of the British fleet had also played its part in the greatest victory of its kind that the Royal Navy had ever achieved.

It was the victory that completed the work that the Monmouths had done during the summer, but they themselves had missed it. 'Their Lordships will give me leave to have the honour of congratulating them on the success of His Majesty's fleet,' wrote Hervey, 'tho' I shall ever condole with myself for the misfortune of not having had it in my power to contribute towards it.' He went on leave to London to find the capital celebrating the bonfires and illuminations. He was unfit for sea, and less than pleased about the weakness he had inherited from his difficult grandmother: 'I am still with both feet up, – what a horrid situation! physicians here advise against going out – 19 yrs heat with the benefit of an hereditary Gout – thanks be to my Good Lady Bristol of Pious & Immortal Memory! D—n her for a B—!'

However, he never liked cruising in home waters in winter and he may already have known that he might be changing into a brand new ship. He confided to Lepel: 'entre nous – (but this is to be whisper'd between Phipps, you, & I,) should I not go out again this winter, or have another ship I do not propose he shd. go out 'till I do, & his time shall go on equally – but I charge you not a Word of this hint to any whatever'.

Molly Hervey reported to a friend that illness had forced her son to stay indoors until late January. At the beginning of the new year, *Monmouth* set sail for Quiberon Bay with a temporary captain. Soon afterwards Hervey was appointed to the seventy-four-gun *Dragon*, building at Deptford. He had a fine new ship of the latest and most powerful design, but he had to find a new ship's company from scratch. The Admiralty appointed his officers, giving his own views due consideration.

Some of *Dragon*'s new officers almost certainly visited the ship as she stood on the stocks. Tourists wandered freely among these growing ships, and the officers probably joined the crowd that watched her launched in March 1760.

Although Deptford was only three miles below London Bridge, it was a town with open space between it and the city, a large, bustling community with a population of 10,000. In 1756 the royal dockyard alone employed 1,236, but Deptford was also the navy's principal victualling depot as well as a shipbuilding centre. Owing to the silting of the Thames, the *Dragon* was one of the largest ships that could be built there and the river had to be dredged periodically to get such ships out. She stood, as she waited, proud and pristine, supported by wooden props in one of the slips either side of the huge, red-brick storehouse. A Deptford shipwright named John Cleveley, who was a painter in his spare time, recorded many similar launches in precise detail: *Dragon*'s exposed keel gleaming white, then a black stripe, then a band of ochre that became red when the gun ports opened, then another black stripe. Above her flew four huge flags: the Admiralty's anchor, the royal arms, the Union Jack and a red ensign.

Dragon was of the Bellona class, a bold new design by Surveyor of the Navy Thomas Slade that was adopted as the standard for future battleships. Within that class *Dragon* herself, proving an excellent ship, was taken as a model by the Admiralty, 'judging it of great importance that every ship of the same class should be built so nearly to resemble each other that the masts, yards, furniture and other stores provided may serve for every other ship of the same rank'.

On 4 March she slipped gleaming into the river to await her masts and rigging. Three days later the ship's muster book opened with Hervey's name first on the list. He received his commission and went to Deptford, where he found the people of the yard putting the finishing touches to their work on the ship. He met his purser, James Perrott, son of a navy shipwright with a secondary business as a coal merchant, and his master, Henry Middleton. Middleton was a married man, nearing superannuation after at least thirteen years with a warrant. Like other warrant officers, masters started with little vessels and gradually qualified for ships of larger rates. This was Middleton's first third-rate ship.

Four of the lieutenants and the core of the crew were turned over from *Revenge*, although none of the officers had been with *Revenge* long enough to know her men well, and three of them were inexperienced. First lieutenant Joseph Hanby had passed for lieutenant all of four years before, and second lieutenant John Robinson was only thirty-three, two years younger than Captain Hervey. He had gone to sea very late at twenty-six, so he had eight years' experience to Hervey's twenty-four, but he had powerful friends. Having begun the war in *Culloden* under Captain Henry Ward, he had been a midshipman at the battle of Mahon in 1756, had transferred to Henry Osborn's flagship *Prince* and then to Edward Hawke's flagship *Ramillies*. He had qualified for lieutenant the year before, in 1759, and had immediately been appointed to *Revenge*. (He was lucky to have left *Ramillies*. On 14 February 1760 she had been wrecked near Bolt Tail and only twenty-seven men survived out of nearly 800 on board.)

Dragon's third lieutenant was Dandy Kidd, whose father was one of the captains who had started on Admiral Anson's epic voyage round the world of 1740 to 1744. Dandy Kidd senior had died off Brazil in 1741 when his five-year-old son was at boarding school near Stratford, Essex. The boy was motherless and probably illegitimate, but his father's will had provided for his education and training 'in some profession or business'. Like Robinson, Kidd was a new lieutenant, qualified in the last year with only four years' documented service. Fourth lieutenant William Osborn was a different type, more like *Monmouth*'s officers. He was about ten years older than the captain and had qualified for lieutenant at thirty-three after more than nine years in the navy. A shipmate of Robinson's, he had also just escaped the watery grave that would have been his had he remained in Hawke's flagship *Ramillies*.

The seamen trickled in, towing their sea chests, on 11 and 12 March. There should have been three hundred of them, but thirty-seven never turned up at all. They were in a sulky frame of mind. First, they had been turned over, and second, they had been denied leave until they had rigged *Dragon*. Mariners hated being 'turned over' from ship to ship, and the Revenges were no exception. Like the Monmouths they were a hardened, settled crew. They did not have the clear regional identity that the Monmouths had, but they bore a common grudge, having been pressed together in autumn 1755.

For seamen in wartime the press was a regular hazard. At the beginning of any war and on regular occasions thereafter an impress officer set up headquarters in a tavern like the Black Boy and Trumpet at Saint Katherine's Stairs. Here he took in volunteers and collected information. Volunteers received a bounty and had the right to choose their ship. In the evening, his gang of armed seamen would raid the haunts frequented by sailors on shore. Such attempts to gather men were usually resisted with violence – the local authorities were rarely sympathetic to the press. The gangs could usually recognise seaman by their dress, their weatherbeaten faces and rolling gait – they were not interested in pressing landsmen, unless desperate, or short of specialists like barbers, tailors or butchers. Usually there were enough inexperienced volunteers; captains only wanted trainees if proper seamen could not be found.

It was often easier to find real seamen by searching merchant ships as they approached their home port. Men hid, but the gangs knew where to find them. Pressed men were crammed into a tender – more or less imprisoned – then taken to a receiving ship which distributed them to ships needing crews. Pressing at the beginning of a war was an eventuality that seamen expected and some even welcomed, but reformers viewed the press as a violent intrusion on individual rights. The alternative view was that the Royal Navy was a force of citizens in arms, like the ancient Greek navy, and that British seamen had a patriotic duty to serve in time of war. Some sailors were proud to take that view. Most weren't.

Revenge had been crewed at the time of the annual arrival of the East Indies fleet, which coincided fortuitously with the appearance of West Indies ships that had sailed before the hurricane season set in. Many Revenges were therefore fine long-distance seamen from these sources. The *Golden Fleece* tender in the Thames had brought in one haul, the rest had been picked up at the Nore or in the Downs where merchant ships had gathered to wait for a wind to take them up river. Most were Londoners of a sort, but London was just as cosmopolitan a place then as it is now. William Oberg, for instance, pressed into *Revenge*, was a Swede who was taken with several other Scandinavians. Although its share of Britain's trade was declining relative to growing ports like Bristol and Liverpool, London was still by far the country's busiest port: its own trade had doubled in the previous fifty years.

Most of the men who joined *Dragon* had been with *Revenge* for several years. A few were inexperienced recent recruits, but even they had fought a major battle. The day the *Monmouth* had beaten the *Foudroyant*, the *Revenge* had beaten the *Orphée*. *Orphée* was much smaller than *Foudroyant*, but she had fought more effectively. In his determination to prevent the French ship's escape, Captain Storr had attacked at pistol shot from a disadvantageous position for an hour and a half before *Berwick* had come up and *Orphée* had surrendered. Consequently, *Revenge* had taken heavy casualties and shared in the glory of the day. In the immediate past, the swift-sailing *Revenge* had led Hawke's fleet in the November chase into Quiberon Bay. *Revenge* had engaged and delayed the much larger French eighty-gun flagship *Formidable*, and then the seventy-four-gun *Magnifique*, allowing other British ships to catch them. That night the Revenges had fought their way off the rocky lee shore with the ship in a very leaky condition. They had played a full part in Hawke's great victory.

The Revenges considered themselves national heroes, and that increased their sense of ill-usage at being turned over and denied leave. The many Londoners among them were the most disgruntled of all at their imposed forced labour so close to the pleasures of home. The ship's policeman, master-at-arms Alexander Mowet, led them in. Mowet, from Edinburgh, was one of a substantial contingent of Scotsmen who, like him, had been in *Revenge* since mobilisation five years earlier. Quarter-gunner David Belford was another, a married man from Dunbar, and quartermaster's mate William Buchanan, a married man in his late thirties, a third. An officer and forty of *Revenge*'s marines soon joined them.

They finished rigging the ship on 2 April and passed the next day paying the masts and blacking the blocks and yards. That day the Revenges penned a petition to the Admiralty:

> May it please your Lordships, whereas your Lordships were pleased to say that you wou'd give the Revenge's Crew Liberty as soon as they had rigg'd the *Dragon*: We humbly pray leave to lay these lines before your Lordships to let you know that we have perform'd what was demanded and most humbly petition to your Lordships that you will be so generously disposed as to grant us the Liberty aforesaid, and your Lordships may depend on our returning to the Ship at the Time limited, and your Lordships Petitioners shall ever pray, &c

They enclosed it within a covering letter to Hervey:

> Having had recourse a few Days ago to the Lords of the Admiralty for obtaining Liberty, their Lordships Condescended so far to grant it as soon as the *Dragon* would be rigged, which being now performd (we flatter ourselves to your Honour's satisfaction) we humbly Entreat you'l please to sollicit for us the said Liberty according to their Lordships promise and we Solemnly Engage not to abuse the Indulgence but will Every Individual of us return to our Duty at the time prefixed
>
> The whole Ships Company belonging to the *Dragon*, Deptford April 3d 1760

This time, their Lordships responded favourably. Three days later the entire ship's company was on shore with a fortnight's leave until 18 April.

It was a short walk or boat ride from Deptford to London. The south bank of the river was lined with shipyards but thinly populated, and with fields close to the road that ran behind the yards. Continuous housing began first on the north bank at Limehouse with its lime kilns. There the Dragons would have felt their first sensation of being in London. From there the Ratcliff Highway led to East Smithfield and the Tower. Below it, along the river, lay Wapping, essentially a long, narrow street two miles long, handsomely paved, winding along the Thames, inhabited by multitudes of seamen. The Ratcliff highway, Rosemary Land above it and Nightingale Lane, which ran from Wapping to East Smithfield, were much frequented by prostitutes. Opposite Wapping on the south bank was Redriff and then Rotherhithe, communities where more mariners lived. The celebrated cross-dressing former marine Hannah Snell ran a tavern in Wapping at the sign of the Female Warrior, one of many drinking dens frequented by sailors ashore.

This was the seaman's heartland, markedly different in character from the rest of London. 'When one goes into Rotherhithe and Wapping, which places are chiefly inhabited by sailors,' wrote Sir John Fielding, 'a man would be apt to suspect himself in another country. Their manner of living, speaking, acting, dressing, and behaving, are so very peculiar to themselves.' As London's most active magistrate, Fielding had considerable experience of seamen, so he was not altogether subscribing to popular prejudice when he added, 'Yet with all their oddities, they are perhaps the bravest and boldest fellows in the universe.'

Tars entertaining their mistresses at Spring Gardens, Stepney.

To the north of Limehouse was the little village of Stepney, with pubs and market gardens on the very edge of town. *The Treat at Stepney* shows sailors in their best shoregoing rig in Spring Gardens, a downmarket pleasure garden that flourished until 1764: 'At Stepney now, with Cakes and Ale, / Our Tars their Mistresses regale' the verses underneath begin. Kit has married one 'in haste', Frank is under the table looking up the skirts of another. More darkly, the *Public Advertiser* for Sunday 13 April recorded a quarrel over a woman between English and Portuguese seamen in which the Portuguese drew their knives and killed three Englishmen before being taken into custody. At least one of the former Revenges, James Miller, lived round here with his wife Eleanor and three children in the parish of St George in the East, with its modern church designed by Hawksmoor.

A short walk into town north of the Tower lay Goodman's fields with its theatre and the first concentration of prostitutes. Further on beyond the city itself were the main attractions of the theatres of Covent Garden and Drury Lane, with a further concentration of whores and more along the Strand and Piccadilly. With their pockets full of ready money, sailors did not slum it. They were found in the main shopping thoroughfare in the most fashionable part of town, not in the dark alleyways where the parsimonious James Boswell, future biographer of Samuel Johnson, had furtive sex with cheap girls. In 1748 three seamen of HMS *Grafton* reckoned they were robbed in the Star Tavern in the Strand. When they complained, they were ejected, so they went back to Wapping where their shipmates were drinking, returned in force and destroyed the place, trashing the brothel next door for good measure.

Sailors in their shoregoing rig were a well-known hazard on London streets, exuberant, careless, generous, impossible to discipline. Until the 1753 Marriage Act outlawed the practice, they could obtain instant marriages in the 'Rules of the Fleet'. The print *The Sailors Fleet Wedding Entertainment*, published in 1747, shows the aftermath of a Fleet wedding between a sailor (who, like such old Monmouths as David Winzar, had a share in the two victories off Cape Finisterre which yielded substantial prize money) and his landlady's daughter from Redriff:

THE SAILORS FLEET WEDDING ENTERTAINMENT.

Jack, rich in Prizes, now the Knot is ty'd | *The Bawd, now from her Daughters change* | *The Lawyer grins & Pig with wanton Glance* | *The Skimmington Observe, Mirth to provoke*
Sits pleas'd by her he thinks his maiden Bride | *With pleasure smiles to think how he's deceiv'd* | *Seems much delighted by Tom's antic Dance* | *Sam points the Horns, with many a bawdy Joke.*
But tho a modest Look by Molly's shown, | *Experienc'd in the Trade, and void of Shame,* | *He kisses Kate, vows she shall be his Wife* | *For Spouse's Cloaths the Bailiff's Crew are seen*
She only longs for what she oft has known, | *To her the Man in Crape imparts his Flame,* | *While Cat & Dog resemble nuptial Strife.* | *And change, oh sad Mishap! the jovial Scene.*

Publish'd according to Act of Parliament, November ye 10, 1747. Price 6 d. by M. Cooper

Nov. 1747

The Sailors Fleet Wedding Entertainment *published by Mary Cooper in*
1747 shows tars disposing of prize money.

> Jack, rich in Prizes, now the Knot is ty'd
> Sits pleas'd by her he thinks his maiden Bride
> But tho a modest Look by Molly's shown,
> She only longs for what she oft has known.

On the Strand, hawkers tried to sell spendthrift sailors ballads and
broadsheets like *Kitty Fisher's Merry Thought* with her whole-length
portrait. Some of them knew their captain had had her in his ship.
They might have fallen for 'The Inestimable Prolifick elixir . . . the
only true and infallible cure for Impotency in Men at 5s a bottle' sold
near the Tower. Some possibly invested in 'The Grand Anti-
Siphylicon against venereal disease', a measure that might possibly
remove the need for a subsequent embarrassing and even more
expensive visit to the ship's surgeon.

As far as shows went, Mrs Midnight's animal comedians were performing, as was Mr Maddox the rope dancer. True British tars preferred the famously provocative and lascivious dances of the alluring Nancy Dawson. With the successful fleet so much in fashion, she was dancing hornpipes. Saddler's Wells in Islington was showing *The Volunteers or Harlequin Deserter*, but the main show in town was David Garrick's pantomime *Harlequin's Invasion*. This mocked the attempt of Monsieur Harlequin to invade Parnassus, Shakespeare's realm, and culminated in an enduring song, 'Heart of Oak', which celebrated their own recent triumph:

> Come chear up, my lads, 'tis to glory we steer,
> To add something more to this glorious year:
> To honour we call you, not press you like slaves,
> For who are so free as we sons of the waves?
>
> Heart of oak are our ships, heart of oak are our men;
> We always are ready, steady boys, steady,
> We'll fight and we'll conquer again and again.
>
> We ne'er see our foes, but we wish them to stay;
> They never see us, but they wish us away;
> If they run, why we follow, and run them ashore;
> For if they won't fight us we cannot do more . . .

'Heart of Oak' was a certain success with 'money'd sailors' on leave who had just trounced the French fleet, and it immediately became a naval favourite.

Captain Hervey was also enjoying the pleasures of the town. He renewed his acquaintance with Kitty Fisher and joined the Society of Dilettanti, the celebrated club for cultured sophisticates. His wife Elizabeth was notoriously attached to Evelyn Pierrepoint, second duke of Kingston. On 4 June 1760 she gave a splendid ball in honour of the birthday of the Prince of Wales. Her parties were the most fashionable in London, much frequented by the ambassadors of foreign courts.

His wife's antics concentrated Hervey's mind on his ship. On 13 March he asked for the boatswain and gunner of *Monmouth* to be transferred to *Dragon*. *Revenge*'s gunner, fifty-five-year-old Peake Rogers, was about to be pensioned off and too ill to go on board to sign for stores. Without him nothing could be done and nothing was done before May, despite Hervey's frequent complaints. By then the boatswain and carpenter had loaded their stores and the officers had got their extra luxuries on board. *Dragon* had no gunner, but she had two masters-at-arms. Hervey sent back the Admiralty appointee, keeping *Revenge*'s Alexander Mowet.

Being a bigger ship than *Monmouth* with a proper complement of 650 instead of 480, she needed another lieutenant. When James Samber had been acting as a lieutenant in the *Defiance* during the summer the year before, he had not yet undergone his examination. It must have made the court martial in which he was involved even more traumatic, but passed for a lieutenant on 2 April and immediately joined *Dragon* as his first appointment. He was twenty-four and had sailed in East India Company ships for three years before joining *Chichester* late in 1755.

18 April was the day that the people were supposed to return from leave. The following day most of them actually did turn up, and on 20 April they weighed anchor and sailed *Dragon* to Long Reach, near Dartford. Her captain had acknowledged receipt of his orders, but lamented that his horse had fallen on top of him and that he could hardly move in bed. It is difficult to suppress the suspicion that his horse might have been Kitty Fisher. The new Dragons lifted all their powerful guns in – twenty-eight 32-pounders, each nearly ten foot long and weighing nearly three tons, twenty-eight 18-pounders at just over two tons each, and eighteen 9-pounders, each weighing rather more than a ton.

By then the captain had appeared for duty. On 3 May Hervey sent the Admiralty a list of twenty-five men who had still not returned from their leave, hoping that the lords 'will have them advertised'. No 'description book' had been sent from the *Revenge* so he could not describe them. He reminded their lordships that another thirty-seven had never appeared in the first place, so that they were not even on the ship's books. On the document, Clevland noted the resolution to 'post the usual advertisements for the men from *Revenge* to repair to the *Dragon*', and in all the major London papers for 5 May a notice appeared:

Admiralty Office, May 5, 1760

   The Leave of Absence given to the Company of His Majesty's Ship the *Revenge*, who were turned over into the *Dragon*, being expired, and several of the said Men not yet having appeared on board her; my Lords Commissioners of the Admiralty do herby strictly direct them to repair immediately on board the *Dragon* in Long Reach, on pain of forfeiting their wages for the *Revenge*, and being taken up by the Marshal of the Admiralty and tried at a Court Martial as Deserters. J. Clevland

The missing 'half-mad Jack Addles' returned to the ship, having taken an extra three weeks' holiday and incurred £1 fines for 'straggling', – or they hid away in town, were marked 'run', and forfeited their pay. Some were delayed by unforseen accidents. They knew that they would be paid for the previous year's service soon after they returned to the *Dragon*, so there was a significant disincentive to run.

'Rambling', without permission, around the pubs close to a ship in dock was a breach of discipline that was usually ignored. 'Straggling' further from the ship rarely incurred more than a small fine. The case had to be aggravated by something like the violence offered by Patrick Wilson to James Samber before people might really be tried at a court martial as deserters. In this respect naval discipline was usually flexible and the system worked better because its savage penalties were rarely applied.

I I

Monmouths and Dragons

The Revenges provided *Dragon* with about half a crew. The officers now had to find the other half, sufficient to bring her up to her full complement of 540 seamen and 110 marines. This far into the war, there were serious problems getting enough men. All the seamen who were any good had already been brought into the navy, and the supply of willing recruits from the land had also been exhausted. The only seamen available were men who had been turned over from ships that had foundered or needed repair, those who really did not want to be in the navy, or those who were normally exempt from being pressed.

Certain seamen were protected from the press. They included masters and mates of large merchant ships, fishermen, colliers and whalers. The apprentice boys and foreigners who crewed London merchantmen in wartime also enjoyed protection. Protections were often forged. Robert Carkett, when captain of *Revenge* in 1758, complained of Magnus Oren and Hans Johnson, 'that keeps the sign of the Prince of Denmark's Arms, Wapping Old Stairs', that they fraudulently helped their Danish compatriots, several of whom were in his ship. 'Them are the Persons that troubles their Lordships with Petitions of this nature and gets them protections and supply's them'. Occasionally, at times of need, these protections were suspended and men of these classes were picked up during a 'hot press'. Such was the case during the whole summer of 1759, and this went down very badly. In July the newspapers reported the murder of a lieutenant who boarded a Greenland ship to press. The whalers cut his wooden leg to pieces, almost cut his arm off and wounded him in the other leg. He died in hospital.

Desperation led the navy to press in places where press gangs did not usually dare to operate. Pressing was a normal hazard in London and on the southern and eastern coasts, but gangs rarely visited the west. Pressing ashore in Liverpool, for instance, was reckoned next to impossible: 'there's not a seaport in England where a man fights so much uphill to carry on the Impress service as at Liverpool'. Bristol merchants turned to privateering in time of war and the civic authorities strove hard to keep Bristolians out of the navy. They considered themselves immune from pressing:

> Here is our chief encouragement, our ship belongs to Bristol,
> Poor Londoners when coming home they surely will be pressed all,
> We've no such fear when home we steer, with prizes under convoy,
> We'll frolic round all Bristol town, sweet liberty we enjoy.

Sometimes, however, they made the mistake of frolicking elsewhere. In September 1759 a pitched battle took place at the Angel Inn at Cardiff between the seventy privateers of the *Eagle* galley of Bristol and a thirty-two-man press gang, in which the press gang underestimated the number of privateersmen and narrowly escaped massacre. One man was killed and four were dangerously wounded. By 1760, however, there were so few French merchantmen still sailing that Bristol had turned back to trade. Meanwhile in 1759 in a gesture to neutral carriers, the Admiralty had revoked the licenses of the small privateers, which also had the desirable side-effect of releasing privateersmen to the navy.

One of the first jobs of newly warranted master John McLaurin's new ship the *Hornet* was to secure a press tender from Newcastle bound for the Nore. It contained an exceptionally large number of men, 125, 112 of them able seamen pressed in the Tyne. They mutinied, the officer in charge lost his nerve, and Captain Johnstone was obliged to fire on the tender to prevent its escape and to send McLaurin, 'a man whom I could depend on', to restore order. McLaurin foiled a second attempted mutiny and brought the ship safely to Yarmouth, and Johnstone was acquitted of the murder of a man who had been killed by the shooting by a subsequent court martial.

It was in these circumstances that *Dragon* had to complete her crew. Even boys were hard to come by, but here *Dragon* made use of a fresh resource. Just before the Admiralty finally instructed the truant Revenges to return to *Dragon* at Long Reach, fifteen miles below London Bridge, another advertisement was placed in the *Public Advertiser*. On Friday 2 May 1760 the Marine Society announced:

> Wanted to serve on board His Majesty's Ships of War, Thirty or forty stout lads not under fourteen Years of Age, and of the Stature of four feet and four inches, that go with their own and Friends Consent, and are no Apprentices. Such lads by applying to the Marine Society at their office over the Royal Exchange, on Thursday next, at Eleven in the Morning, will be equipped with complete Cloathings and Beddings for the Sea Service and sent on board immediately

For many years parishes had pointed unwanted or unruly boys in the direction of the navy. Apprentices who proved so difficult that they were turned away by their masters also ended up at sea. This was the fate of Hogarth's Idle Apprentice, depicted being rowed out to a frigate at Deptford to join a man of war. Hogarth's night scenes are littered with homeless children sleeping rough on the streets, many of whom lived by thieving, picking pockets and selling sex. The authorities were keen to remove these ragged boys from the streets, and they became one of the more promising answers to the Royal Navy's manning problem.

In 1756 a group of philanthropic merchants led by Jonas Hanway, who appreciated that the only answer to the shortage of naval manpower was to convert landmen into seamen, had set up the Marine Society. At first they tried to help by removing one of the expenses for recruits by supplying them with clothes and bedding. As we have seen, this was a considerable expense, and the society's only problem was that many of their recruits absconded with the clothes they had been given. Soon afterwards they expanded their programme by recruiting boys to start as officer's servants and grow up to be seamen. Their aim here was twofold, as Jonas Hanway explained. Their first object was 'the removing of those who are

The frontispiece to Jonas Hanway, Three Letters *on the subject of the* Marine Society, *1758, shows vagrant children recruited and clothed.*

Vagrants, Pilferers, or by extreme *poverty* and *ignorance*, are pernicious to the community' from the streets. The second was 'to encourage the *industrious poor* to send their children to sea'. By December 1757 the society was boasting that it had 'cleared the land of 500 thieves and robbers'.

The allegorical illustration to Hanway's pamphlet shows these two groups clearly – the urban vagrants in rags, the paupers with tearful but relieved parents. Another print (*see above*) is set in the society's room above the Royal Exchange in Cornhill, with the committee gathered around the table, processing candidates brought in by hopeful, weeping mothers or determined parish officers. To the left stand the new recruits, transformed into smart, promising youths by their brand new naval slops. They wear short coats over jackets, long, loose trousers and hats.

The first two Marine Society boys rowed, like Hogarth's Tom Idle, to join *Dragon*, where the line of windmills marked Millwall and a

In this episode from William Hogarth's 1747 series Industry and Idleness *the unruly apprentice Tom Idle is forced to join the Royal Navy.*

gibbet stood out starkly opposite Deptford dock, were seventeen-year-old Robert Rogers, four foot nine inches tall, an orphan or runaway from Whitechapel who became third lieutenant Dandy Kidd's servant, and Joseph Buckley, aged thirteen, from Deptford, four foot six, equally alone in the world, who became servant to the sailing master. The next batch responded to the 2 May advertisement, appeared at the Royal Exchange a week later, and joined the ship off Erith. Three were 'friendless' waifs: Ben Anderson, thirteen and four foot three inches tall, from Plymouth, fourteen-year-old John Carter from the slum parish of Saint Giles, and William Halliday from York. Two were brought in by impoverished parents: George Martin, whose mother lived in Old Street, and William Rickets, whose father was a weaver from Stroud water.

On 18 May *Dragon* sailed for the familiar, dismal mud of the Nore. A couple of days later the commissioner came aboard to pay the Revenges, and the same day the crew was completed from the receiving ship at the Nore, *Princess Royal*, which in January had been struck by a 'putrid fever' she had not shaken off entirely. *Dragon* also received men turned over from the *Captain* and from the sloop *Experiment*, together with a lot of pressed men of very dubious quality and poor health.

Captain was a ship in which Hervey himself had served when she was brand new. More recently her crew had taken part in Byng's battle off Minorca and had been with Saunders's fleet at Quebec. The Captains were led by midshipman James Fellows, a Londoner from Southwark. His group included James Sutherland, who had a wife in Gosport, John Matthews, an Irishman from Waterford like Hervey's follower John Blake, and Thomas Williams. Williams was a veteran of fifty-two. By trade a Thames waterman from Shadwell, he had served in the navy all this war and most of the last. The Experiments, by contrast, were nearly all young ordinary seamen, and both they and the pressed men needed new clothes. A high proportion of the pressed men came from a sweep of north-eastern Scotland, as their names reveal. William and George Patience, for instance, rated ordinary seamen, were fishermen from Avoch in the Black Isle whose protections were no good in a hot press.

With a full complement and sufficient experienced seamen to avoid disaster, *Dragon* was ready to go to sea. The Admiralty ordered Hervey to join Admiral Boscawen in Quiberon Bay. Admiral the Hon. Edward Boscawen, known as 'Old Dreadnought' to some and 'Wry-necked Dick' to others, was another aggressive leader who appreciated talented subordinates and cared for his men. This re-doubtable, plain-speaking Cornishman had captured Louisbourg at the mouth of the St Lawrence in 1758 and had defeated the French Mediterranean squadron off Portugal in 1759. *Dragon* reached St Helens on 1 June and paused to pick up more marines and a caulker. Duncan McArthur, from the frigate *Liverpool*, built and crewed in that port, had been driven ashore and very nearly wrecked as well as taking at least a couple of prizes in the last two years.

Ten days later, during the night, *Dragon* anchored off the mouth of the Vilaine where the fleet was guarding the ships that Hawke had trapped there. At sunrise the crew filled the deck and the shrouds and saluted the admiral with three cheers.

James McArdell's print of Admiral Edward Boscawen after Joshua Reynolds's painting, published in 1758.

Hervey's main hope for improving his crew was to persuade the excellent men of the *Monmouth* to change ships into the *Dragon*. He got the Admiralty's permission to turn them over, but when the news reached the Monmouths they were far from happy to comply. Two hundred seamen subscribed to a petition to Admiral Boscawen stating that their 'desire is that we may continue on board ye Monmouth'. In a fairly impressive demonstration of British nautical literacy, eighty-eight of them could sign their names. In a second letter, mates Henry Reeves and Edward Salmon, Reynold Thomas the clerk and midshipmen including Samuel Blow protested that a change was 'quite contrary to our inclinations'. Lieutenants Baron and Winzar, sailing master Wilson, chaplain Chicken, and, in his absence in a *chasse-marée* prize, even George

Knight, also explained that 'It is much against our Inclinations to leave the Ship in which we have been all this War and some of us all the last.'

Presented with this situation, Hervey explained that he had no wish to force anybody to do anything, but would be delighted to take anybody who would come willingly. Captain Joseph Austin and Lieutenant George Preston brought over the marines as a body. Fifty-five seamen also changed ship, led by Hervey's old friend first lieutenant Foulkes. For the most part these were valuable men and loyal followers: Simonton the gunner, with his mate John Burgess and Sympson the armourer. Fewin the boatswain came with his mate Pinker, as did Varley the sailmaker and three of his yeomen, Trumbull, Irvine and Steffins, and the French pilot, Renault. Inevitably, old John Parvin followed Hervey too. John Blake changed ship with half the quartermasters and seven of the midshipmen, including Richard Tizard of Weymouth, an 'old Monmouth'. A handful of other 'old Monmouths' also followed Hervey, including the Irishman Peter Hanlon, but none of them was Cornish. If Hervey had ever seriously hoped that the Monmouths would turnover en masse he was disappointed, but he probably only ever banked on picking up his trusted senior people.

It is possible that the Monmouths disliked Hervey as a captain, but it is more likely that loyalty to their ship was their strongest tie, especially for those who had served in *Monmouth* for a long time. The Monmouths were also a settled and happy company. They knew each other, they were good at what they did, and consequently life was satisfying and easy. *Dragon*'s complement was 650, whereas *Monmouth*'s was 490. If they joined *Dragon* they would have to rub along with another 160 people who might not be congenial company, and share prize money with another 160, giving private men a smaller share. Quite a few seamen who had followed Hervey into *Monmouth* chose to stay where they were, one other factor being that *Monmouth* was about to return to England where there was a promise of further leave, whereas *Dragon* was outward bound.

While sailmaker Thomas Varley sewed their new numbers onto their new hammocks, Foulkes devised a general round of promotions to fill the remaining petty officer's ratings, most of which were given to those who changed ship. William Coffen became a midshipman like his fellow citizen of Weymouth, Richard Tizard.

The value of these promotions varied. One key consideration was whether it shifted you a grade in the divisions of the crew for prize money. In general parlance the groups consisted of commissioned officers, warrant officers, petty officers and private men; the real grouping was slightly different. A master's mate ranked with senior warrant officers like the boatswain, as did the lieutenants of marines, which gave you a tenth share of an eighth of prize money in *Monmouth* and a twelfth share in *Dragon*. A quartermaster ranked with a midshipman in the next rank down, sharing roughly a fiftieth share of one eighth of prize money. The senior warrant officers' mates and yeomen also qualified, as did the ship's corporals and the marine sergeants. However, the armourer and cook (even though they had warrants) and the quarter-gunners only qualified for a private seaman's share of prize money – in *Monmouth* 1/420th of a quarter of the fund and in *Dragon* even less.

To complete his company, Boscawen gave Hervey sixteen former prisoners of the French who had been exchanged. To prevent them and his other pressed men escaping, Foulkes posted an officer to row guard round the ship. Desertion was theoretically a capital offence, but

The sail-maker and his mate sewing numbers on hammocks.

extreme penalties were applied only in the presence of an admiral and often only in a home port. About the time that *Dragon* joined his fleet, Admiral Boscawen was somewhat embarrassed when three seamen, Dicker, Brown and Herbert, were caught deserting after stealing a boat and other property from *Swiftsure*. He would have been lenient if he could have found anybody to say a word in their favour, but, as he explained, Brown and Herbert had come to the navy from Newgate prison and Dicker was an old offender. Realising that they were in trouble, Brown and Herbert offered their bodies to *Swiftsure*'s surgeon to be anatomised in exchange for a bottle of brandy. Boscawen resolved the issue by making them play Russian roulette. Herbert drew the short straw and was executed, leaving the surgeon cheated of half his bottle of spirits.

The danger of staying put and the need to work up the crew into an efficient team persuaded Boscawen to give Hervey a cruise. The unusually large number of landsmen had to learn the ropes almost literally. Hervey once heard an anecdote about a Spanish squadron putting to sea with so many raw seamen that 'they put cards to all the different ropes, and so were ordered to "Pull away the Ace of Spades", "Make fast the King of Hearts", and so on'. Whatever the truth of this story, it gives a sense of how confusing the spider's web of rigging must have been to men who had never sailed in such a ship before.

Boscawen had intelligence that the island of Groix, opposite L'Orient just to the north, was sparsely populated and weakly garrisoned. During his cruise Hervey was to test how true this was. *Monmouth* sailed for home on 16 June and next day *Dragon* made sail with *Conqueror* as her consort. The mission provided the ideal opportunity to give the men some practice at working together. First of all Hervey sounded round the island, first at four miles distance then at three-quarters of a mile. Then they checked what was in the port and sailed in close to test the reaction of the forts and batteries. When these opened fire, Hervey used them for target practice for his newly chosen gun crews. Storms provided good training for the men, but with an inexperienced crew accidents were common, and *Dragon* had a fair share that summer: John Robinson, a young volunteer, 'fell from the maintop and expired soon afterwards'.

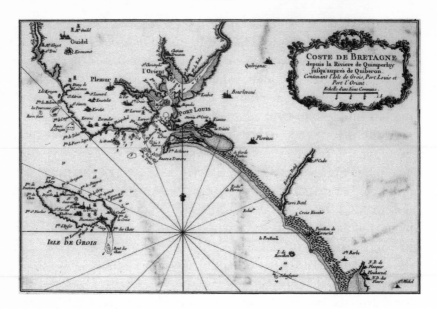

Chart of Lorient and the island of Groix with the Quimperlay river at the top.

They suffered two bad storms, one of which claimed the life of Jacques Alexis Renault, who died at midnight on 29 June. Then, at the beginning of July, they switched their operations to the mouth of the river leading to Quimperlé and a nearby creek. Here, Hervey made a great deal of noise so that his cruise looked more like a raid and less like a reconnaissance of Groix. On 3 July the boats chased two *chasse-marées* into the creek, but Hervey recalled them when they came under fire from a coastal battery. Next day they boarded another pair of vessels that turned out to be privateers from Guernsey. A few days later they exchanged fire with the same battery again as the boats chased another vessel that escaped into the creek, and the day after that Hervey manned and armed the pinnace and barge and sent them to cruise off the river mouth. They returned in the afternoon with a shallop laden with wood.

Hervey had had enough of the battery. That evening he sent in the shallop, manned and armed, to cut out all the fishing boats in the mouth of the creek. The familiar French shallop sailed cheerfully past the battery and then, to the guards' surprise, disgorged English tars who started to cut out the fishing boats. Under cover of this distraction, Hervey 'went on shore with all his Boats, surpris'd the Guard, (a sergeant, corporal and twenty men of Guardes de Costes) broke the four guns of the Battery, threw them over the rocks, carried the Guard off and return'd to his ship without a single man hurt'.

All this good practice in dangerous boat work and accurate firing was designed to foster *esprit de corps* amongst the new ship's company. The following morning he returned the shallops and the thirty-four prisoners, but next day he sent the boats in again to scuttle and burn a vessel that had taken shelter in the creek. This time they were opposed by the militia, and *Dragon* fired ten 18-pounders to scatter this body of troops. Returning to Quiberon Bay, they sailed between Groix and the mainland. Forts both sides fired at them but their shot fell short.

Hervey made his report to Boscawen. While they were off the Morbihan the men exercised constantly with small arms. The boat took the *Saint Anne chasse-marée* loaded, much to the amusement of the captors, with wooden shoes. The English saw the clogs worn by French peasants as one of the badges of their slavery. Then, on 26 July, Hervey was ordered to proceed with *Dragon, Conqueror, Venus, Brilliant, Aeolus* and the *Dorset* cutter to Groix. He was to take the island if it could be done without serious loss.

They sailed the next day with White the carpenter, his mate Phillips, Richard Treadenham and the rest of the carpenter's crew making scaling ladders and the people practising with small arms under James Samber, the junior lieutenant, and Mowet, the master-at-arms. On 28 July, with the batteries both sides firing at them, they anchored in line of battle between Groix and the shore. The following day Hervey sent a flag of truce to the island. That night at '½ past 10 Cap Hervey and Harrison with ye officers marines and seamen belonging to ye ships as many as ye boats coud stow went from ye ships to land on ye island Groix ½ past 2 boats returned not being able to land at ye place appointed'. There was probably too much surf or too many rocks, but the place may also have been defended. They hung around for a day; a vessel from Boscawen came and went with news of failure. Hervey sent the small cutter to sound on the east side of the island, but that night there was a massive thunderstorm and the weather deteriorated. Fresh gales, thick weather and rain turned to strong gales with rain and finally hard gales and squalls before the squadron bore away for Quiberon Bay.

After ten more days at Quiberon, *Dragon* sailed for home with about thirty men sick and needing some repair. They moored at Spithead on 22 August, after a gale in which they lost the main yard, and sent thirteen sick men straight to hospital. Another fifteen were soon sent after them to Haslar Hospital or to the *Blenheim* hospital ship. They entered the port on 1 September. It was usual for the officers to leave unreliable men in the 'guard ship' well away from the shore, and Foulkes put a few he suspected might run into the *Royal Sovereign* with two midshipmen. Hervey immediately asked for leave and left for London.

For the autumn and winter of 1760 several 'surveys of the sick' survive in the papers of the port admiral at Portsmouth. These documents provide a rare insight into the ailments of seamen considered unfit to continue to serve. That October an investigation was conducted on board the *Blenheim* hospital ship, where four Dragons were classed unserviceable. Andrew Bowden, aged thirty-eight, had been pressed into the *Revenge* in 1756 by Lieutenant Hanby at Gibraltar. He was in the *Blenheim* owing to 'loss of sight': he was going or had gone blind. Bryant Kennedy, aged twenty-three, had been pressed into the *Dragon* that summer in Quiberon Bay and was now lame from a fall. The other two – thirty-four-year-old Joseph Clements, enlisted in 1755 at Hull, and John Davis, aged twenty-three, pressed at Lisbon in 1759 – were consumptive. Davis was ill enough to put his mark to a will, leaving everything he had to his 'true and trusty friend Andrew Bowden'. A year later his dim-sighted shipmate inherited what little Davis owned.

In late December, when James Lind, the dedicated physician at the Haslar Hospital ordered another survey, *Dragon* had thirty-four men in her sick bay and three in the hospital. This time the records give fewer details. Some – two consumptive, two suffering from fits – should never have been on the ship at all. Two were dropsical; thirty-six-year-old James Raddle was shaking with palsy. James Bernard's 'incontinence of urine' was clearly a nuisance on board, where cleanliness was crucial to the health of all, while William Snook had a lame shoulder and bad legs. Three had ulcers. The others had typical seaman's injuries – ruptures from lifting things, damage from falls. One of Hervey's most trusty followers fell victim to this survey. John Irvine had been able seaman, yeoman of the sheets and boatswain's mate in *Hampton Court*, then yeoman in *Monmouth* and *Dragon*. They were jobs for an older man, and his rheumatism had finally got the better of him.

The details taken on the *Blenheim* of when a man was recruited and by whom were intended as a means of tracking who it was who was sending unsuitable recruits to the navy – men whose physical condition was such that they should never have been pressed or allowed to volunteer – since caring for such people in hospital or having them sent home was an expensive nuisance.

If *Dragon* lost a fair few men to illness and injury, she lost even more to desertion. Sixty-six men ran away – about a tenth of the crew – causing their lordships to complain to the captain. Hervey wrote back on 23 November:

> I had already made enquiry into the cause of such numbers deserting during my leave of Absence as I was no less surprized, having put every Man onboard the Guardship at Spithead, that cd. be suspected: but I found the Officers had constantly the Watch & Centurions I had order'd, and Petty Officers to pick up the seamen on shore; several of which they had taken up & sent off to the guardships for Neglect of Duty: Indeed very few of those gone will be of any loss to the service, unless they should ever recover the Pay their desertion has forfeited.
>
> I must beg leave to assure their Lordships that had I the least reason to imagine it was owing to any neglect, or want of Discipline in the officers, I should have thought it my Duty to have represented it; but I can only impute it to the Natural Levity in Seamen and the Mixture of which a new Ship's Company is mostly composed of.

In fact he had only put about twenty men into the guard ships – the seamen freed from French prison, a class of men notorious for running as soon as they got the chance, as well as some Revenges who were being punished for overstaying their leave in April. The ship's official reports indicate that about twenty men were ashore with leave in any one week and about the same number were reported absent without leave. The true figure was evidently somewhat higher, with sixty-six 'stragglers' on shore failing to return. The behaviour of the men ashore was so exceptionally bad that in early November the mayor of Portsmouth complained to Admiral Holborne. Such were the 'riots and disorders about the town by seamen' that Holborne banned shore leave and asked the captains to keep their men on board, leaving the citizens of Portsmouth poorer but safer. This probably contributed to the desertion problem.

Portsmouth was not the most salubrious of places, according to the author of the 1759 gazetteer: 'The Streets are not the cleanest, nor Smells most savoury; but the continuous Resort of Seamen &c. makes it always full of People, who seem in a Hurry.' He remarked on the 'rows of houses within the new Works for yard officers' which made the naval station a town in itself, and a town that was constantly growing. For relaxation it was better to visit Gosport, 'a large town, of great Trade, where Sailors Wives live for the most Part, and where

French chart showing Spithead, Portsmouth, the Royal Dockyard, Gosport and Porchester.

The ship is about to sail and Moll gives John a last tender embrace before climbing down into the boat, praying that the bullets will miss him. The sentimental scene etched by Charles Mosley was repeated over and over when the Monmouths left Plymouth.

Admiral Francis Holborne with his midshipman son Francis in 1756. Hervey despised Holborne as 'a commander-in-chief for the Navy whom no-one would have scarce trusted a line of battle ship with'. His punishment for failing to take Louisbourg in 1757 was to be appointed port admiral at Portsmouth where he remained for eight years.

Constantine John Phipps joined *Monmouth* when he was fourteen, considerably older than Holborne's midshipman son. This portrait shows Phipps in 1773 as a captain of twenty-eight, commanding the expedition to the Arctic on which Nelson served as a midshipman.

This detail from Dominic Serres' painting shows *Monmouth* looking into Brest
in September 1759. In the distance is the blockaded French fleet at anchor.
Monmouth is firing a signal gun to the ships of her squadron, as they challenge
the French to come out and fight.

Sailor fishing from a cannon. Tars supplemented their standard rations in a variety of ways. 'Much Fish to be procured there for the Ships Companies', Hervey noted approvingly of *Monmouth*'s anchorage off Brest during autumn 1759.

This view of marines eating pease gives a sense of the sparsely furnished, dimly lit, claustrophobic lower decks; the huge cables are a frequent feature in Gabriel Bray's drawings. The setting is the frigate *Pallas*, *Monmouth*'s consort in the inshore squadron in summer 1759.

The purser's assistant handled day-to-day victualling, making sure the correct measures of food were delivered to each mess. *Monmouth*'s steward Thomas Toddy carried out this task repeatedly during autumn 1759.

A view of the gun wharf at Portsmouth, clean and efficient with modern government buildings in the distance and clean naval figures in the foreground.

'The Streets are not the cleanest, nor Smells most savoury': a sketch by Gabriel Bray of the view from the Navy coffee house window towards the dockyard gates, one of the smarter areas.

A view by John Cleveley of the launch of the *Cambridge* on 21 October 1755 at Deptford Dock, with the Master shipwright's house to the left and the great storeroom on the right. *Dragon*'s launch in 1760 would have looked very similar.

Workmen at Woolwich Arsenal manufacturing, grading and stacking solid iron cannon balls. The gate at the back of the yard leads to the bank of the Thames.

MEN of WAR, BOUND for the PORT of PLEASURE.

Liberty men on their way from Chatham, where their ship has docked, to London, 'the port of pleasure' – each has already picked up a woman and each woman is taking charge of the sailor's purse. Sailors ashore are usually depicted armed with a cudgel like the one leaning on the box.

Travellers generally chuse to lodge, everything being cheaper and more convenient than at Portsmouth'. Travel between the two was easy since 'Boats are continually passing from one to t'other side, it being just as Southwark is to London except there's no Bridge.' The Haslar Hospital was at Gosport. Still under scaffolding but now almost complete, it would be for many years the largest brick building in Europe. Here, too, 'Needy Sailors are entertained here with occasional Wives in brief, as they are at Amsterdam, & in Truth – perhaps in every other large Sea-port Town for Ships of war.'

A number of Dragons had wives at Gosport, though whether they were 'occasional Wives in brief' or the more permanent kind is difficult to determine. James Sutherland probably visited his wife Sarah and James Stuart, marine, his 'dear friend' Rosanna Rice. Rosanna was possibly one of the Gosport girls who went around in gangs singing songs like:

> Don't you see the ships a-coming?
> Don't you see them in full sail?
> Don't you see the ships a-coming?
> With the prizes at their tail?
> Oh my little rolling sailor . . .

On 8 October 1760, Constantine Phipps, in London, scribbled a note to his father at Mulgrave Castle to tell him that he had just heard that there was an 'Expedition fitting out . . . so that I must go on Monday with Captain Austin'. Lepel was 'greatly shocked' but uncle Augustus 'says I cannot properly stay longer than Monday'. In fact departure proved less urgent. Phipps wrote again from the St James's Coffee House on 15 October:

I am now hearing all the different Opinions of Coffee House Politicians concerning the destination of our expedition & am a person of no small consequence as being the only seaman here & give my opinion as wisely as an Oracle. I am asked about Brest, Port Louis, Belle Isle, Rochfort &c for we are destined to all these places besides Minorca, Martinico, Louisiana cum multis aliis . . . I hear many Guard Officers complaining of the Hardship of Going to sea in small

Transports at this time of year & being stuffed in a Cabbin like a stage coach as they Term it others exulting in not being obliged to go . . .

That day *Dragon* completed her stores for four months and a couple of days later she anchored at Spithead. The men were scraping and paying and varnishing. The commissioner paid the former Monmouths and the officers' stores were loaded. A further draft of pressed men from the receiving ship completed the crew.

At government level much wrangling was going on. They could not decide whether to send the expedition to Belle Isle off Brittany or Mauritius in the Indian Ocean. They wanted to seize a French island to exchange for Minorca when peace came, since it was considered vital to have a Mediterranean base and Minorca was ideally situated to counter Toulon. Augustus Keppel, who was to command the expedition, had looked at Belle Isle during the summer and was doubtful of the feasibility of taking it. Hawke was against the project and King George decided it was impossible. William Pitt, prime minister, was furious.

Next morning, quite unexpectedly, the king died. This left the throne to his twenty-two-year-old grandson. George III was wholly under the influence of his handsome tutor, John Stuart, Earl of Bute, who was widely believed to be his mother's lover. Pitt and Bute were on good terms, and within a fortnight the expedition was back on.

On 31 October Portsmouth's guns fired a salute for the proclamation of King George III. Next day *Dragon* fired a nineteen-gun salute. They waited. On 1 December they saluted the arrival of Commodore Keppel. Hervey received the order of battle and order of sailing, and found that he was in a position of honour ahead of the commodore. He received his sealed orders and the instruction as soon as the fleet was in sight of the enemy's coast, 'to get your ship ready for anchoring against the batteries and open the sealed packet as soon as signal is made for anchoring in enemy's port'. The weather was appalling, with hard gales preventing any possibility of sailing. Then they were told that the expedition had been cancelled because it was too late in the year.

By the beginning of January the ship was back in harbour, having taken the precaution of putting all the new pressed men into the guard ship *Pembroke* so that this lot could not run away. The fact that he had volunteered did not save William Watson of Morpeth from sharing this fate. Captain Hervey returned to London with Cameron, Finney and Louis d'Amour, the purser and chaplain went on leave, and so did thirteen of the more well-to-do boys and about twenty of the men, chiefly former Monmouths who had not had leave in September.

Suddenly, in late February, the expedition was back on. Hervey received orders to put himself under Keppel 'to be employed in a particular service'. They had not yet decided where to send him; for most of March Mauritius was the objective. For some reason Hervey could not join the ship. He must either have been ill or his presence must have been necessary in Parliament. Late in March the Admiralty sent an order for Archibald Clevland to command the *Dragon* during Captain Hervey's absence and for John Lendrick to take Clevland's ship *Windsor*. Clevland came aboard immediately with three servants, two midshipmen, his coxwain, corporal and trumpeter, fifteen seamen and John le Brune, his cook.

That day Belle Isle again became the objective. The threat that Spain might join the war, combined with a possibility of peace – something the young king strongly favoured – meant that Pitt wanted a quick conquest. By now Pitt was notorious for madcap demands for amphibious assaults on France, and so far they had all ended in failure. The French coast was strongly fortified. An expedition against Rochefort in 1757 had ended in ignominious farce when, having sailed there, the generals decided not to attack. At St Malo in 1758 the army had at least landed, but it soon re-embarked, and although it then occupied Cherbourg briefly, the campaign ended with the capture of the naval rearguard by the French during a frantic evacuation at St Cas. It was with some scepticism, therefore, that the great fleet sailed from St Helens on 30 March 1761.

12

The Island Fortress

His first sight of Belle Isle appalled General Hodgson: 'the whole Island is a Fortification, the little nature had left undone, had been amply supply'd by art . . .'. The fleet swept round the island at first light. On the seaward side the Atlantic beat against what was known locally as the '*côte sauvage*', an inhospitable shoreline of jagged rocks where it was totally impossible to land. The only harbour that side was so dangerous that 'they who know it best will scarce attempt to enter it, except in desperate cases, when there is no other visible means of avoiding shipwreck'. The side facing the French mainland was little better. The marines stared from the bulwarks at the towering, grey cliffs that rose sheer out of the water for most of its length. Above the cliffs the land was flat or gently rolling pasture divided by drystone walls, with occasional gullies leading steeply down to isolated bays and coves. All of these were guarded by forts and batteries. The one obvious landing beach, Les Grands Sables, was protected along its entire length by a wall with bastions for artillery.

Keppel and Hodgson got into a cutter to take a closer look. Studholme Hodgson was a protegé of the king's uncle, the Duke of Cumberland, and had been a close friend to the Keppel family since serving as aide-de-camp to Augustus Keppel's father at the Battle of Dettingen. As a brigadier in 1757 he had been a member of the council of war that had decided unanimously not to attack Rochefort, and he might have felt that he was being sent on a second mission impossible. Augustus Keppel had been a handsome youth before he had lost most of his teeth and hair during Anson's voyage round the world in the 1740s, but the sacrifice had led to his rapid advancement under Anson's patronage. He was a circumspect courtier, but he was

Map of Belle Isle by Charles Nicholas Bellin, 1761.

also an efficient seaman and an effective officer. He had already pointed out the unlikelihood of success against the island fortress, but he was not prepared to face the dishonour of sailing tamely home without having tried to take it. Nor could Hodgson do that twice.

Their ships sailed on and anchored in the Grande Rade, making an imposing sight, being more than a hundred sail including eleven ships of the line. But opposite them the little town of Palais was dwarfed by the enormous citadel built by Vauban.

Keppel and Hodgson made their choice:

> at one of the bays of Point Locmaria, the General and myself thought a descent might be tried; but as the wind was southerly, it could not possibly be attempted at this time At twelve o'clock the whole fleet anchored in the Great Road, when I immediately went with General Hodgson to the northern part of the island, to be as well informed of the strength of the enemy's works as the time would admit. While we were on this necessary service, the ships of war were preparing the flat-boats.

In the Grande Rade troops and ships prepared for an assault. Peter Foulkes sent sixteen men and two petty officers to the *Grampus* transport to fetch flatboat number 118, which they lowered into the water and rowed to the *Dragon*. The crew of about twenty commanded by a midshipman, and a similar number manning *Dragon*'s own barge, were to take part in the landing planned for next day in the bay just beyond Locmaria Point. *Dragon*'s contribution was minor – the main burden fell on the crews of Keppel's *Valiant*, Rowley's *Superbe* and Barton's *Temeraire*. *Dragon* herself was to support *Achilles* in silencing the six-gun coastal battery that defended the sandy cove called Port d'Andro (on this island every little beach was called a port). Ninety of *Dragon*'s best marines left the ship to serve with the two marine battalions commanded by Lieutenant Colonel John McKenzie. To their disgust, they were allocated to a diversionary threat against Sauzon at the other end of the island, together with the two weakest battalions of soldiers, Stuart's and Grey's.

The flatboats were new. In previous wars, and earlier in this war, Britain had tried to land troops in ships' boats, but they could not carry enough men and in any case it was difficult to get them close enough to the shore for troops to wade to land while keeping their powder dry. This new design had been tried out on the Thames in 1758:

> On Wednesday last two Boats of a new Construction, built for landing his Majesty's Forces in shallow Waters, were launched, and sailed down the Thames. They are designed to carry fifty Soldiers each with their Arms, are rowed by twenty Oars, and go much swifter than any other Vessels on the River.

Some were larger, with twenty-four oars and sixty soldiers. The officer, drummer and corporal sat in the stern with the boat's coxwain, and the oarsmen had positions clear of the soldiers, who sat in threes and twos on the thwarts. Two petty officers sat in the bows to push off and pull in. The flats had been used with success at Quebec: this was to be their second major trial.

During the night the assault force moved to a position off Locmaria Point. *Dragon* led with *Achilles*. Keppel himself sailed in support in *Prince of Orange*, with *Hampton Court* and the *Firedrake, Furnace* and

Infernal bomb ships. The purser of the *Prince of Orange*, Richard Short, an artist, had, for the last two years, been in America at Louisbourg and then at Quebec and had taken the opportunity while he was there to make drawings of the scenery and of the city in its ruined state after the siege. *Prince of Orange* had returned to England at the end of 1760 and Short, being a man of business, saw the opportunity to turn his drawings of the scene of the famous victory to account and had made arrangements to have his drawings engraved and published, employing eight leading landscape engravers on the copper plates. Now he was contemplating another series of prints and, from the deck of *Prince of Orange*, he intended to record the unfolding events.

There was an inauspicious start. *Dragon* was towing her boats, and at ten the pinnace got tangled up with the longboat's hawse, capsized, broke adrift and was swept away 'by which accident John Adams, boatkeeper, was drowned'. Once they had reached a position off the point, they attached a cable to the stream anchor to act as a 'spring'. This was a means of turning a stationary ship so that its guns faced the enemy. With the stream anchor attached by one rope to the bows, a second rope was passed out of the stern and fastened to the first rope some distance from the ship. As the second rope was tightened by turning the capstan, the ship was turned into position to face the chosen target.

The attack had to be made at low tide. When the tide was high the sea beat against the feet of the cliffs, whereas at low tide a wide sand beach was exposed so that boats could land to the side of the bay as well as at its inner extremity. The thirty-six flatboats gathered around the *Temeraire*, whose captain, Barton, was to command the assault.

The French commander Sainte-Croix had all morning to deploy, and guessed his enemy's intention correctly. The force off Locmaria was bound to attack between the Pointe de Kerdonis and the Pointe d'Arsic, and those places were only two miles apart. He placed a battalion of the Regiment de Nice at Port d'Arsic, part of the Battalion de Dinant at Port de Locmaria, the other Battalion de Nice to the west of Port Andro, and the Regiment de Bigorre took post on the heights of the Pointe de Kerdonis. The rest of the island was defended only by coastguards and armed peasants. Saint-Croix even ordered the remaining Dinant units from Sauzan to Locmaria.

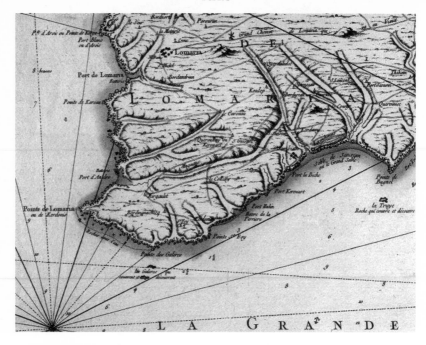

*Detail of Bellin's map showing the area between the Pointe d'Arsic and the
Grand Sable. The first assault was directed at Port d'Andro.*

Achilles and *Dragon* sailed up to the little horseshoe bay at midday,
anchored beneath the battery and silenced its fire. Their signal
midshipmen hoisted the signal that informed Keppel of success. With
Prince of Orange and the transports he advanced towards the shore and
gave the flatboats the order to attack. Thirty-six boats moved forward
in three lines, the first two of nine boats, the last of eighteen. Each boat
carried sixty British grenadiers, the picked assault companies of
Erskine's, Beauclerk's, Morgan's and Craufurd's regiments. Captain
Barton of *Téméraire* was in overall command of three divisions, led by
Pascal, Rowley and James Chads of the *Vesuvius* (Chads had been a
lieutenant in Richard Howe's *Magnanime* and later led the boats to the
foot of the Heights of Abraham at Quebec.) *Dragon*'s boats, carrying
men from Craufurd's, were towards the rear in the centre.

As the boats approached, the watchers on the ships sensed danger.
Dragon, Achilles and *Infernal* opened fire again. The officers had seen 'several

Having silenced the fort, Achilles *hoists a Dutch flag as a signal for the flat boats to attack. Detail of the 1762 engraving by Peter Canot.*

French Regulars pass and repass to a small Block house behind the Battery, We both fired many shot at them & the Infernal fired several shells'.

At two o'clock the boats pulled for the shore. At the entrance to the bay they encountered difficulties – underwater stakes and palisades which obstructed the boats. Some landed, others began confused manoeuvres to avoid the stakes, while the French opened fire from all sides. Brigadier Guy Carleton, the officer commanding the assault force of grenadiers, was wounded. Some boats landed to the left, near the battery as three companies of the Regiment de Nice advanced into prepared trenches on the slope above, from where they kept up a sustained fire on the beach. In the centre, five companies of Bigorre, together with the coastguards, advanced to meet the largest body of British grenadiers, now led by Colonel Thomas and Major McClean. Reconnaissance had not revealed that the ground behind the bay had been prepared. It turned out to be 'a kind of amphitheatre surrounded by strong entrenchments one above the other and guarded by the pieces of cannon covered by a Fraise'. The beach became a killing ground: 'after having several times in vain attempted to form: being exposed to a terrible fire as well from the Enemy's cannon and musquetry, and both col. Thomas and the Major being wounded, they were obliged to take shelter under the Rocks where most of them were taken prisoners.'

The Dragons looked on in horror as 'those that attempted to land was attacked by a strong fire of Musquettry from the Intrenchments on both sides of the Bay by which all that landed were killed wounded or taken prisoners'. General Hodgson's secretary Thomas Pincke 'who was on the poop, on board the *Dragon*, looking through a glass to satisfy his curiosity . . . got a shot in his forehead'.

In one spot there was hope. One boat had landed at the very edge of the cove on the right, unperceived by the French. Sixty of Erskine's grenadiers, led by Major Purcell and Captain Osborn, found a path and scrambled up the rocks. On the ships all eyes followed this little band. They saw 'the people got safe to the top of the Hill'. This one success might swing things, but

> It was to be wished they had halted there till they had made the Signal for landing and had been join'd by some others, when by an attack from so unexpected a Quarter, they might have thrown the Enemy into confusion not easily to have been got the better of: but they rather chose like Britons to march boldly up the summit of the Hill, where they were discovered by the Enemy who attacked them with 200 grenadiers.

Captains Dumont and Grau with the nearest companies of Bigorre marched to meet them, and 'the Major's party after giving their fire charged with their Bayonets'. The French also fired and charged. There was a fierce mêlée in which Dumont and Purcell were killed and Grau wounded, but there were more than twice as many Frenchmen and the British fled back down the rocks. A few 'got down the Rocks again & was taken by our Boats'. The other survivors were taken prisoner. *Dragon* and *Achilles* opened up on the trenches to cover the retreating boats, for which Hodgson was grateful, reporting, 'We came off very well in our retreat, as the fire of the ships prevented the enemy from coming to the brink of the rocks to fire on the boats.'

After only half an hour he had seen enough. Hodgson made a signal

Bow view of Dragon *off Andro showing her figurehead and forecastle with her crew watching the fighting.*

for a parley and the French ceased fire as the British pulled out: 'several of the Boats came on board of us with the wounded soldiers & seamen which we received on board – amongst whom was Major General Carleton'. Once they had taken in what was left of the assault force, the ships weighed and anchored again further out.

The army left behind seventy-six killed and 246 prisoners. Seventy-two soldiers were wounded. Among the seamen there were fifteen killed and thirty wounded, almost all from *Valiant* and *Vesuvius*. Eighteen of the French were killed and seventy-six wounded.

Dragon soon had at least twenty-five seriously wounded men on board. Surgeons James Watt and his mates John Wills and John Wallace were as busy as if the ship had been heavily engaged herself. One of the soldiers they had rescued was also a surgeon and he helped, but they lost two seamen from *Valiant* who died of their wounds that afternoon. Another from *Vesuvius* died during the night.

195

A storm blew up. At eight in the morning a squall hit *Dragon* so hard that she drove from her anchor. They cut the cable and got under sail, but before they could get the ship under control she collided with the *Swallow* transport, smashing away the headrails on the larboard side and breaking the stock of the small anchor. They tried to give *Swallow* an anchor, but lost it in the swell. Elsewhere, several of the transports were blown out to sea. By the time the weather moderated, twenty-two of the remaining flatboats had been lost.

Keppel wrote to Pitt reporting his failure. With very few boats and the cream of his grenadier assault troops gone he did not believe that another attack could be mounted. The weather continued to be stormy. Ten days later, after a thorough reconnaissance of the island, Keppel and Hodgson agreed that no further attack looked worthwhile, but when Keppel summoned the captains of all the ships to the *Valiant* on 18 April, either this council of war or the arrival of reinforcements changed his mind.

On *Dragon*, meanwhile, John Purnell the carpenter and John Phillips his mate repaired the headrails, so that the men could relieve themselves with less danger, and made a new bumpkin, while the medical staff transferred most of the wounded soldiers to the hospital ship.

Then, on 13 April, they had a stroke of luck. The lookout spotted first their signal flying on the *Valiant* to chase a strange sail, and then the strange sail. A little brig came round the south end of Belle Isle and hoisted a French pendant to one of the forts. Belle Isle was the preferred landfall for ships bound for France from America, so there was a chance of a valuable prize. *Dragon* immediately signalled that the strange sail was an enemy and she and the speedy twenty-eight-gun frigate *Aquilon* cut their cables and made sail, *Dragon* cutting away her longboat for good measure. At ten they got within gunshot and opened fire with her bow chasers, as did the faster *Aquilon*. *Dragon* fired eleven shots with her 18-pounders and seventeen with the forecastle 9-pounders before the *Aquilon* caught up with the brig and forced it to surrender. To the delight of Captains Cleveland and Ogle, she proved to be *La Poste*, returning from Saint-Domingue with a cargo of sugar and indigo.

The next day, another squally, stormy one, the fid of the fore-topmast broke and the topmen had to climb up and lash the topmast to the head of the foremast in pouring rain. They recovered the longboat, which had been picked up by a bomb vessel, and sent all the remaining wounded soldiers to the hospital ship. Some of *Dragon*'s seamen, including William Ansley, went into the prize.

A week later Archibald Clevland was again summoned to the *Valiant*, where Keppel gave him his orders for the attack in two days' time. They were going to attack the south part of the island again, but this time several attacks would be made over a broader front. The main assault under Craufurd and Howe was to be on Port de Locmaria, and *Dragon* would be one of the ships covering that attack, where the soldiers would be given the flatboats. Threats were also to be made against Port d'Arsic to the left and Port d'Andro to the right of the main thrust. A second force under Lambert was to attempt to land on the other side of the Pointe de Kerdonis at the the Havre de la Perrière, with a further threat against Samezun. For the first time, the marines would see some action, for the two marine battalions were attached to Lambert's force. They would approach the beach in the ships' longboats to which the marines, at least, were accustomed. The newly arrived squadron that had brought reserves of cavalry and artillery from England would be deployed in a second dummy bluff against Sauzon.

22 April was promising: light winds and misty weather that limited the view of the French scouts, clearing later to a day of sullen grey cloud. Keppel could not have hoped for better. *Dragon* rounded the Pointe de Kerdonis with *Achilles* and *Sandwich*. *Barrington* attacked the same battery that they had silenced before. *Dragon* sailed on and anchored close to the shore within fifty yards of the next battery guarding Port de Locmaria. There was another more heavily fortified affair a little further up the coast, high on Pointe d'Arsic, and both *Sandwich* and *Prince of Orange* positioned themselves to knock that out. On *Prince of Orange*, purser Richard Short once more pinned a sheet of paper to his easel and began to draw.

The battery did *Dragon* some damage, cutting several shrouds and ropes and wounding the maintopsail yard, but they silenced it and dismounted the guns and then directed their fire at the entrenchments which more careful observation had detected covering this cove too. The chase guns were pointing at Pointe d'Arsic, so they kept those firing at that more stubborn target, high enough for the ships to have difficulty hitting it. The troops were in position to make their landing around the middle of the day, but this time they were going to put in a really heavy naval bombardment first. It was not until mid-afternoon that the flats began to gather under *Dragon*'s stern.

A couple of miles to the north, *Dragon*'s marines waited nervously in their longboats for low tide when the beaches would be exposed beneath the cliffs. The old Monmouths and Revenges among them had seen fierce action at sea, and the Monmouths had already taken part in many boat attacks – indeed, Hervey had put all *Dragon*'s marines through their paces the previous summer. But quite a few of the marines had joined since then, and the honour of the new corps was at stake. The marines had been formed for just such occasions as these, and they were supposed to be specialists in amphibious warfare, yet General Hodgson still preferred his grenadiers.

George Preston and Sergeant John Pearson had the former Monmouths in one boat – Thomas Nelcoat, now corporal, Richard Hughes from Glamorgan, the grey-eyed Irishman James Young, Daniel Walkeley from Gloucester and the sandy-haired Cornishman John Hye. All of them had been at sea for at least three years and considered themselves veterans already, even if they had never before taken part in an attack on this scale. In the other boat were the new men under the new captain Robert Kennedy, a Scot from the small smuggling village of Ballantrae on the Ayrshire coast who had replaced Austin in January. They were smaller men than the tall grenadiers – mostly about five foot five or six. Otherwise, they looked similar. For shore duty they were wearing their red coats and breeches, and their mitre hats looked like those worn by grenadiers, but were smaller.

It was the grenadiers of Beauclerk and Craufurd's regiments who led the way, rowed in by seamen from Sir Thomas Stanhope's *Swiftsure*. Stanhope had been knighted for his part in Admiral Boscawen's victory off Cape Lagos the previous summer, and he

Spectators crowd the Swiftsure's *deck bowsprit to watch the marines rowing towards the cliffs at St Foy.*

commanded the naval aspect of this attack which was intended to suck in some of the best French troops before the real assault was launched.

Captain Patterson of Beauclerk's and Captain Gordon of Craufurd's leaped from the two first boats to reach the beach not far from Kerdonis, where the Regiment de Nice was expecting an attack on the sandy coves at Perrière and St Foy. Patterson avoided the coves, but landed between them. He found a stair cut into the rock and led his hundred men up it. Not far from the top was a low stone wall, and the company took shelter behind it. The French immediately attacked. Harrison was wounded and was being carried back to the boat when Gordon's men were driven back down the stair or over the twelve-foot rock face. A French officer offered them quarter from the top of the rocks, and they threw down their guns and surrendered.

Major Skinner landed with another boatload of men at the Pointe des Galeres and reached the clifftop in time to see the prisoners being marched off and white-coated French soldiers advancing on his right. He 'very judiciously inclined to his left', and there found the marines and Lord Pulteney's independent companies scrambling up the cliff face and hurrying up a very narrow path. The marines landed on the least accessible of the beaches between the Pointe des Galeres and the Pointe de Kerdonis at the foot of the tallest and most imposing cliff on the island. There were no easy gullies leading up from this beach, so the French had left it unguarded, thinking it impossible that the British could scale the cliff. Indeed, even the British soldiers admitted that the marines 'climbed up rocks, which at other times woud have been thought inaccessible'. Pulteney's men and the remaining grenadiers followed their example. 'Here they formed and being opposed by only two hundred picquets of the Regt. of Nice they advanced & drove the enemy about six hundred yards directly in front.'

Saint-Croix was using the chapel of St Foy as an observation post. It gave him a great view of the best beach at La Perrière, where his men had defeated the landing, but the marines were hidden from him by the cliff until, to his astonishment, he saw them forming up at the top. He signalled to the Regiment de Bigorre at Port d'Andro to intervene. He intended them to take the British on the flank, but they mistook the order and attacked Pulteney's battalion from in front, driving Lord Pulteney and his men back. But Major Ramsey had landed with two boatloads of Louden's grenadiers where Purcell had made his successful landing on the previous assault, between the Pointe de Kerdonis and the cove at Andro, and they suddenly appeared behind the flank of the French, firing briskly. The French broke and ran.

Hodgson was about to launch the attack on Locmaria when he saw that Lambert had landed successfully and ordered Craufurd's boats to support the landing on the Pointe de Kerdonis instead. By nightfall the entire force had landed and advanced to a position from Fort la Biche to the village of Colletty, with a ravine protecting their front, sealing off the promontory. The British lost about thirty killed. Colonel McKenzie and Captain Murray of the marines were both wounded, but none of *Dragon*'s marines was hurt.

Saint-Croix pulled back to the citadel and the next day Hodgson advanced towards le Palais. Then things began to go wrong again. 'It rained prodigious hard.' The weather was so bad that for days they could not begin to land artillery and supplies. Meanwhile, Saint-Croix threw up six earth redoubts to defend le Palais. The bomb ships tried to interrupt their work by throwing shells, but they could not throw them far enough. Despite frantic work from the carpenters of the various ships repairing flats and adapting them for artillery, it was not until 1 May that Hodgson was able to open up a battery against the enemy redoubts.

The night after the British opened their siege, Saint-Croix, who had respectfully declined a summons to surrender, launched a savage sally against the British trenches. He achieved complete surprise. Several hundred men were killed and Major-General Craufurd was captured with his aides and sixty others. But the setback was not serious – the marine battalions went onshore to make up the loss of manpower. It was much more serious that Hodgson's guns had little effect on the redoubts. He complained that two of his vaunted brass guns burst, one after twenty shots and another after only nine. Hodgson's letters home consisted entirely of a litany of complaints, and although some of them were quite witty, it is hardly surprising that his superiors became irritated with him.

The redoubt on the extreme right of his own line proved particularly troublesome, and Hodgson decided to try to storm it. He got all the mortars and cohorns with the army to open fire on the battery a little before daybreak. Lieutenant Colonel Phillips, who commanded the advanced post nearest the sea, was to have a captain and a hundred men advanced a little before his village, ready to march and attack if they saw the enemy uneasy at the bombardment.

The bombardment was so effective that the French partly evacuated the redoubt until it ended. It was a detachment of marines who led the attack with bayonets fixed, and there were Dragons amongst them. Erskine's grenadiers supported. There was a fierce fight for redoubt number one. Corporal Michael Small, leading his platoon, had both jawbones broken by a musket ball, while another ball broke Irishman

Edward Burke's arm. It took a second charge to carry the position. The second redoubt put up much weaker resistance. Seeing the first two redoubts lost, Saint-Croix ordered a withdrawal to the citadel and the French fled, chased into the houses by the victorious marines and grenadiers. They lost about 150 killed and wounded in the fight, and the British took seventy-five prisoners, seven of whom were sent to *Dragon*. British casualties were fifteen killed and thirty wounded, many of them marines.

Burke, Small and another Dragon named Taylor were carried to the hospital to be treated by the army surgeons. The surgeons debated Burke's case. The traditional answer to a compound fracture such as Burke had suffered was to saw the arm off straight away, but one of the surgeons, a thirty-two-year-old named John Hunter, had other ideas. He advocated minimal intervention with clean bullet wounds like Taylor's, and preferred to try to save arms. Burke's case was a qualified success. He survived and kept the arm, though he could never use it properly again.

Purnell, Phillips and their crew went to work again adapting the flats. This time they had to be strengthened to take *Dragon*'s own lower-deck 32-pounders. On 15 May they landed one, and on 16 May another, together with ammunition. A party of fifty seamen went ashore to haul the guns into position and fire them. *Dragon*'s guns helped make up a battery of twelve 32-pounders from the ships, firing at bastion Dauphin. Another ten 24-pounders battered bastion La Mer. The batteries were completed on 23 May and began to cannonade the citadel. Time was running out for Saint-Croix.

On 21 May Archibald Clevland sailed home in his own ship, the *Windsor*, and John Lendrick, the Ulsterman who had worked with *Monmouth* off Brest, took temporary command of *Dragon*. The prize sugar went back on board the prize. The armourers, John Sympson and his fellow blacksmiths Light and Hall set up their forge on shore and began to repair the ship's ironwork. After only a year it was 'decayed and broke'.

The men continued constantly to land powder and shot and carry it to the batteries, which pounded away at Vauban's fortress. On 6 June

Dragon had her first man killed – Philip Farrell was shot dead while rowing guard in the ship's barge under the citadel. Two days later part of the castle wall collapsed and Saint-Croix surrendered. Finally, on a showery 11 June, 'the French troops marched out from citadel & our troops marched in'. The Union Jack was hoisted above le Palais, and all the ships in the fleet were manned with sailors in the shrouds who all gave three cheers while the batteries on shore saluted. The boats took the French to the transports, and the next day they sailed for L'Orient.

The siege of Belle Isle was over. The island became a vegetable garden for the garrison and the fleet in Quiberon Bay, and as a result, during spring and summer scurvy disappeared.

Belle Isle was a triumph for *Dragon*'s marines. First lieutenant George Preston wrote to Keppel to stake his claim to preferment, explaining that he

> has been at sea during the whole war, was in the *Monmouth* at the taking of the *Foudroyant*, and on every other service that ship was employed on.
>
> That flattering himself his behaviour has always met with the approbation of his senior officers; and being the eldest 1st lieutenant of the battalion of marines employed in the siege of Belleisle, he humbly begs you will be pleased to recommend him . . . for promotion.

It took a while to come through, but by the beginning of December he was a captain, and left *Dragon* to command the marines on board *Modeste*.

For the marine forces as a corps, Belle Isle was the first unqualified success. Initially despised by Hodgson, they had been instrumental in effecting the successful landing by appearing where they were least expected at the top of the highest cliff on the island, had been rewarded with the honour of leading the assault on the French redoubts, and succeeded there too. Marine tradition has it that the laurels around the globe still worn by marines as their cap badge were awarded for conspicuous gallantry at Belle Isle.

TARS

The news reached London on 13 June, and there were bonfires and illuminations once again. Pitt now had his island to barter for Minorca, which was just as well, since the impetus towards peace was growing.

13

The Remote Regions of the Earth

King George III was crowned in September 1761 while still riding a wave of popularity. Unlike his grandfather he spoke English, and the way he referred to Britain as 'this my native country' contrasted favourably with the preference that his antecedents had seemed to show for their native Hanover. National reconciliation and international peace were his keynote ambitions. These were laudable goals, but they quickly brought problems. For nearly fifty years the Whigs who had supported the Hanoverian succession had enjoyed power to the exclusion of high-church Tories, some of whom, especially in Scotland, had sympathised with the exiled Stuart dynasty. Giving influence back to disenchanted Tories meant taking it away from loyal Whigs. Making peace proved equally difficult because the French drove a hard bargain, while continued military success raised public expectations at home. Moreover, the adolescent king and his Scottish favourite, Bute, were startlingly naïve and ill-informed. The Duke of Devonshire, leader of one great Whig clan, 'was surprised to find they knew mankind and the carte de pays so little'.

Peace negotiations had already opened, driven forward by Bute and the king and backed by popular feeling. Most wanted peace as much as Captain Hervey. However, Pitt insisted on maintaining the war effort, and success followed success with a regularity that embarrassed the peacemakers. Their apparent unenthusiasm over British victories soon reached the newspapers, and Bute's unpopularity steadily increased. He was not a great negotiator: the duc de Choiseul, acting for France, was more than a match for him. Choiseul's trump card was the threat that Spain would enter the war on France's side to extend and prolong it. To counter this influence, Pitt made undisguised preparations to seize French West Indian islands, which he intended to attack as soon as the hurricanes ceased in the autumn.

By September 1761 the evidence that France and Spain were reaching agreement in an alliance against Britain was strong. Pitt argued for a pre-emptive strike against Spain, the Cabinet objected, protesting that Britain had already achieved her war aims and that further conquest would only increase resentment of her maritime domination. Denied a Spanish war, and finding his influence with the king outweighed by Bute's, Pitt resigned in October. But the attacks that he had planned against the French went ahead in order to improve the British negotiating position.

Dragon had anchored in Plymouth Sound on 30 August and Lendrick had handed the ship back to Hervey, who came aboard with his attendants Finney and d'Amour. On the way home Lendrick had helped to capture another rich merchantman from Saint-Domingue, leaving the crew with the promise of a little more prize money to add to what the ex-Monmouths received when they reached Plymouth as their share of the prizes taken in 1759 and the head money for the *Rose* frigate burned at Malta. The Monmouths and Revenges also got their payout for the *Foudroyant* and *Orphée*.

First lieutenant Peter Foulkes further raised morale with a general rerating, a year to the day after the previous one. As a result, twenty-nine landsmen and ordinary seamen saw their wages rise by around twenty-five per cent to those of able, seven able seamen became quarter-gunners, and eleven filled other vacancies as petty officers. Assuming that those newly rated able had genuinely become competent seamen – and *Dragon*'s performance suggests that they had – this illustrates how successful the process of training unskilled novices was in increasing the number of seamen in Britain.

To take a couple of examples, among the pressed men who had joined on 1 April 1760 were William and George Patience, the fishermen from Avoch in north-east Scotland, who knew the sea, but not large men-of-war. After seventeen months as 'ordinary' seamen they were now rated 'able'. Edward Dunn had joined *Monmouth* in spring 1757 as an unskilled Dublin landsman, and after two years in *Monmouth* had been rated able. Now, four and a half years after joining the navy, he had shown enough competence and loyalty to join *Dragon*'s elite quarter-gunners. Two former Hampton Courts made quarter-gunner at the same time, but most of the new petty officers were drawn from the Revenges at the core of *Dragon*'s crew.

If promotion was a carrot to prevent desertion, Foulkes also employed the stick. As the ship went into harbour and then into dock, he sent fifty-four men he judged most likely to run into the guard ship. The move was partly successful: only fourteen men ran while the ship was at Plymouth, even though they received six months' pay in mid-September, between celebrations for the new king's wedding to Princess Charlotte of Mecklenburg-Strelitz and the coronation. *Dragon*'s company remained unstable at the fringes – the runners were nearly all men pressed or turned over into the ship in autumn 1760 or spring 1761 – but the older part of the company was now settled in its ship.

The more important changes were to senior personnel. George Fennell replaced James Perrott as purser, and Alexander Howison replaced Henry Middleton as master. Fennell married Alice Yoldon at Stoke Damerel, the Plymouth dockyard church, on 27 October. The couple already had one son, George, born in 1758, and now they regularised their union before *Dragon* sailed again. Howison was a married forty-year-old Londoner. He had progressed through the ranks and had qualified to be a lieutenant in 1757, but, lacking patronage for a commission, had secured a warrant to be a sailing master. He had remarkably little experience as a master to be given such an important ship, but the appointment suggests that he was technically proficient. As a midshipman he was serving in Richard Howe's *Dunkirk* in America when Howe effectively started the war by attacking and capturing the French *Alcide*. Vincent Brown, another Londoner, came aboard as first lieutenant of marines to replace George Preston, who was soon to leave to command the marines in *Modeste*. He had a sweetheart at Plymouth named Mary Fanning, and their parting, when they sailed, was as tender as that of Fennell and his new wife.

There were also some changes in more junior positions. Three midshipmen who had entered the ship with Lendrick in May also left with him. In place of one of them Hervey promoted his follower John Burgess from gunner's mate to midshipman, putting him in line for a warrant or even a commission.

Surgeon James Watt sent forty-three men to hospital, of whom one died and eleven failed to recover before the ship sailed again. With the casualties and the runners, *Dragon* again needed new men, and just before she sailed she got a further draft of forty-five unwilling pressed hands, petty criminals and rough cases from the receiving ship *Duke*, including Miles Cook, an Englishman in his twenties who had never been to sea (unusually tall at five foot ten, he was one of those sent into the navy to clear the streets), and his friend Bryan Donnolly, who was an Irishman of the same kind, utterly inexperienced at sea.

Dragon sailed on 1 November, having delayed her departure until the *Grenado* bomb vessel was ready because of a rumour that there were two big privateers off St Malo. On 4 November, when *Dragon* was the prescribed 'thirty Leagues to the Westward of the Lizard', Hervey opened his sealed orders and discovered that his destination was Carlisle Bay, Barbados, where Admiral Rodney was gathering a force for the conquest of Martinique. In fact, as he noted sarcastically, he already knew this because the *Grenado* was under open orders to proceed there.

As this news spread about the ship, the weather closed in with strong winds and low visibility. Early the following morning the maintopmast snapped and broke the top of the mizentopmast in its fall. This was a serious accident, and for several days they struggled in high winds and driving rain as Parnell, Phillips, Treadenham and the rest of their crew fitted a new maintopmast.

As the weather moderated, news of their destination caused both excitement and dread. This chance to see the other side of the world was the reason many young men went to sea. One lad William Spavens, who had fought at Quiberon Bay, had grown up at Cleethorpes, fascinated by the idea of travel:

> frequently having a view of Ships sailing by on the Humber, I thought sailors must be happy men to have such opportunities of visiting foreign countries, and beholding the wonderful works of the Creator

in the remote regions of the earth; I considered not the perils and hardships they are sometimes exposed to; I thought of nothing but pleasant gales and prosperous voyages

In their voyages with Hervey, Irish quartermaster John Blake and gunner's mate John Burgess had visited Tetuan, cruised off Cap Bon and Malta, and seen the Greek islands. They had walked the streets of Lisbon, Barcelona, Marseilles, Nice, Genoa, Leghorn and Naples. There was little they did not know about the Mediterranean, but that apart they only knew the Breton coast. They were as ignorant of the other side of the Atlantic as the nervous pressed men and excited boys.

For boys from inland villages, like Marine Society boy William Rickets, or from urban slums, like John Carter, maritime life presented an extraordinary opportunity to travel, to glimpse 'the remote regions of the earth'. They might even come home with a parrot or a monkey, if they could afford one. Of the original seven Marine Society boys, five were still aboard and a further seven had joined in October 1760. These lads were now fourteen or fifteen and shooting up, outgrowing their original clothes. All were excited at the prospect of the tropics, but, as older sailors warned them, many visitors to the Caribbean did not come home.

Malaria, yellow fever, dengue fever, dysentery, dropsy, leprosy, yaws and hookworm were all dreaded West Indian maladies. In the seventeenth century seamen sometimes refused to sail to the West Indies for fear of disease. A normal voyage there was not especially dangerous: two to three per cent of seamen died during trading voyages to the West Indies compared with under one per cent on voyages in northern waters, but this compared with a far worse ten per cent on East Indiamen and a horrifying one in four in West Africa slave ships. What was dangerous was remaining in the West Indies for any length of time. The voyage normally took a few weeks each way, but the mortality rate was four times as high on West Indies ships that stayed away more than eight months. These people spent time in the islands, and that was where the risk lay – and it was often fatal. The European winter months were relatively safe, but after April the rain began to fall and the sickly season started. It has been estimated that between twelve and fifteen per cent of all white immigrants to the West Indies died in their first year, but military expeditions there were the stuff of black legend. The well-known ballad of 'Admiral Hosier's Ghost' commemorated the campaign of 1726–7 when 4,750 men went out and 4,000 died.

Those who had been there before feared the place less, for if you had survived the climate once, you would probably survive it again. Hervey was seasoned after two Caribbean campaigns in his youth, but these campaigns had also taught him the danger of staying after April. In 1741 Admiral Vernon had laid siege to Cartagena in present-day Colombia with a huge fleet in which Hervey had served as a midshipman and a force of regular soldiers. In the six summer months General Wentworth lost 6,000 of his 8,000 soldiers to disease before he abandoned the attack.

For the present, the weather settled and there was music and hornpipes on deck as the temperature climbed above seventy degrees Fahrenheit (20°C). They saw Madeira 'like a stupendous hill, extending from east to west; the clouds seem beneath its summit', then followed the currents towards the Canaries, crossed the Tropic of Cancer and let the North Equatorial Current help them across towards the Windward Isles.

When they crossed the Tropic, first voyagers like Cook and Donnolly, and those like the Marine Society boys who had never crossed the Atlantic, paid for the experience, for this was an occasion when it was usual 'to make all the men and boys in the vessel who have not before seen it, pay a bottle of liquor and a pound of sugar to mix into bumbo or toddy for themselves and the rest of the crew', or to choose between the bottle fine and a ducking. This was an enduring tradition. A decade later the naturalist Joseph Banks (a school friend of Phipps) noted that in Captain Cook's *Endeavour* 'Many of the men however chose to be duckd rather than give up four days allowance of wine which was the price fixd upon, and as for the boys they are always duckd of course.' He then looked on as one by one the victims were tied to a wooden harness and dropped from the yardarm into the sea. Banks was amused 'to see the different faces that were made on this occasion, some grinning and exulting in their hardiness whilst others were almost suffocated'.

A day too early, they had a man at the masthead scouring the horizon for a landfall. Hervey and Howison misjudged the distance by about ninety miles, being a little out with their estimate longitude. They had probably not yet learned how to use Mayer's longitudinal tables, the latest method of calculating longitude, which had been published at the Hanoverian University of Göttingen in 1752 and was accurate to within sixty nautical miles. The navy was getting closer and closer to cracking the problem: at the very same time that *Dragon* was making Barbados, the *Deptford* was bound for Jamaica with Harrison's fourth chronometer on board for its first, promising, test.

As *Dragon* approached Barbados they saw the first of the flying fish, so abundant there, which fascinated William Spavens, the boy from Humberside who wanted to see the world. They were 'about the length of a herring,' he wrote, 'but thicker and rounder; and its fins being large and flexible, when they are expanded they serve in some measure the purpose of wings.' Occasionally, they presented themselves as a meal that did not even have to be caught: 'I have sometimes seen them fly on board of a ship when they have been pursued by the dolphins, which prey upon them in the water; and if they fly out of that element, they are frequently caught by the boobies which hover above the water to devour them'. Spavens found them 'excellent food'.

Dragon reached Carlisle Bay on 12 December, and while the longboat went ashore for water, bumboats came out to the ship laden with exotic fruit: pineapples, oranges, lemons, citrons, limes, figs, tamarinds, cocoa-nuts, pomegranates, guavas and mangos. Others sold unfamiliar fish such as 'parrot-fish, cavelloes, snappers' and the Barbadian favourite flying-fish. They also brought copious quantities of the island's rum, by-product of its sugar plantations. Some dockyard people with slave names, Herriford, Tom, Mingo, Dukesberry, Bristol and Stephen, came aboard at Bridgetown along with four caulkers from *Marlborough* to help *Dragon*'s caulker Duncan McArthur make the ship watertight. She had evidently been leaking after the bad weather.

Hervey reported to Admiral Rodney in the *Marlborough*. Rear Admiral George Rodney, a follower of Edward Hawke, was talented and ambitious, but overbearing, pompous, snobbish and haughty. The son of an army officer with no personal fortune, he had married the sister of the Earl of Northampton in 1753. He already had a good fighting record, but also a mounting reputation for avarice, dishonesty and unscrupulous heartlessness, especially when there was any prospect of financial gain. There was some prospect now, for his orders were to attack Martinique, the French naval base and principal stronghold in the West Indies. For this task he had 2,000 of the men who had taken Belle Isle under William Rufane and 7,000 from America, including veterans of Quebec.

Rodney had arrived at Barbados on 22 November and straightaway had sent Sir James Douglas with his four ships to blockade Martinique, while waiting for the rest of his fleet of six of the line and three bomb vessels to arrive, the ships having been scattered by storms. The British knew remarkably little about Martinique. Rodney had sent ships to survey the coast and tried to find people who knew the interior, but unsubstantiated rumours of strong tides, incessant winds and impassable terrain were making him uneasy. The last British expedition in 1758 had been an embarrassing failure – General Hopson had taken one look at the terrain around Fort Royal and sailed away again. Hervey had been contemptuous: 'a sad acct. it was that they had even trumped up for the public – but the private acct of their conduct was such as surely authorised a public enquiry'. Nevertheless, Fort Royal had developed a reputation as an impregnable stronghold.

The troops from Belle Isle arrived on 14 December, those from America on 24 December and the men soon realised what was afoot. On 23 December *Dragon* sailed two weeks in advance of the main fleet to reinforce the ships blockading Martinique. With *Modeste* under command, she took station off the Diamond Rock to prevent vessels of any kind reaching Port Royal from the east, so that no supplies or news of any kind got through to Martinique.

On the other side of the Atlantic, in the book-lined cabin of the fourteen-gun sloop *Hornet*, Captain George Johnstone interrogated the captain of a French privateer that he had just chased and captured. From the Frenchman he learned that the Spanish had issued an order on 10 December for the capture of all British shipping. He took his prize into Lisbon and there got confirmation that Spain had declared war. On his own initiative he victualled and manned the prize, gave her to his master, John McLaurin, *Monmouth*'s former master's mate, and sent him to warn the West Indies fleet. On 27 December McLaurin set off across the Atlantic.

Four days before that the Brest squadron under Charles, comte de Blénac-Courbon, took advantage of bad weather to slip past Commodore Thomas Spry, who was guarding Brest, and sailed for Martinique. Spry sent Chaloner Ogle in the fast frigate *Aquilon* to warn Rodney that French reinforcements were on their way.

Meanwhile the Earl of Bristol, Captain Hervey's brother, was heading for the Portuguese frontier as fast as he could. On 10 December his demand to know the terms of the treaty between France and Spain had been formally refused and he had announced his departure from Spain. He had written reports and warnings immediately, but the Spanish had refused him all facilities and he could not get his warnings out until he reached Portugal. Nevertheless, he got his news to London before Christmas and on Christmas Eve orders were issued to commence hostilities. Britain declared war on 4 January. The Cabinet met to concert plans two days later, and on 7 January the Admiralty instructed the Navy Board to prepare at Spithead ten thousand tons of transports for overseas service.

Although Rodney did not know it, his attempt to take the French island base was already a race against time. That same day, 7 January, he sailed from Barbados for Martinique with sixteen ships of the line, thirteen frigates and three bombs, together with tenders, transports, and hospital ships.

Dragon had patrolled without incident until 6 January when they saw three sail inshore and Hervey sent the boats after a schooner. The ship stood close in, with the marines firing muskets and the guns grape at the people on shore while the boats cut out the schooner. They cleared her and burned her and the following evening saw Rodney approaching.

On 8 January they watched Sir James Douglas's squadron sailing into St Anne's Bay, destroying the batteries of three and four guns as they came. They saw *Raisonnable*, the leading ship, guided by the man reputed to be the best pilot, hit a reef so hard that all her masts went overboard. *Dragon* joined them in the evening and took in as super-numeraries thirty of *Raisonnable*'s crew. It was not a good start.

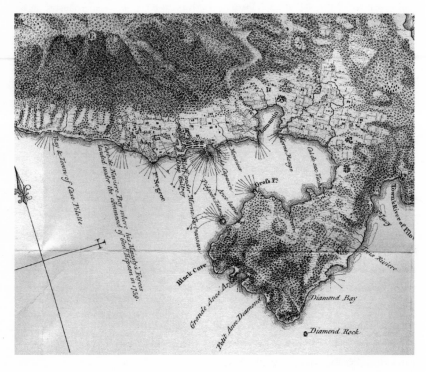

Detail of A View of the Coast of Martinico taken by desire of Rear Adml. Rodney before the attack in Jany. 1762, *engraved by Thomas Kitchin for Mante's* History of the late war in North-America. *The redoubts constructed in 1759 are marked A. The last was on Morne Tartenson. Morne Garnier is marked B.*

General Monckton, commanding the land forces, hoped to send troops overland from Saint Luce to attack the forts at Gros Point, Pigeon Island and Port Royal, but the maps they were using misrepresented the distance, and the engineers, once landed, judged the many ravines and rocky ridges impassable for artillery. They re-embarked to launch an attack from closer to Port Royal Bay, landing again in the Petit Anse d'Arlet. Rodney ordered Hervey to attack the fort in the Grande Anse to secure a retreat for this expedition under Brigadier Haviland.

The Dragons had already enjoyed much target practice with French batteries. They smashed this one within an hour and then landed the marines to occupy the ruins. Captain Kennedy held the ground until relieved by soldiers. Haviland occupied the high ground opposite Pigeon Island, the fortified, sixty-foot vertical rock that guarded the entrance to Port Royal. Once again he judged the approach impossible for artillery and was ordered to re-embark. During the night the French attacked, and light infantryman Donald Ginn of the 17th captured four grenadiers, for which he received four guineas as a reward.

Monckton and Rodney changed plan and decided to land within four miles of Port Royal, on the same beach that Hopson had used in 1759. It had the great advantage of a plentiful and accessible supply of good water, but when Hopson had landed he had despaired at the obstacles between him and his target. Since that time, the French had further fortified the land approaches to the citadel with a series of redoubts and gun positions guarding ravine crossings. The difficult ground, ideal for ambushes by the numerous island irregulars and hired privateersmen, was commanded by fortified batteries and entrenchments on two hills, Morne Tartenson and Morne Garnier. These twin natural barriers guarded the land approach to the citadel from that side. The impressive coastal fortifications, bristling with cannon and mortars, made it far too dangerous to attempt to take ships into the bay beyond the citadel.

On 16 January nine ships of the line bombarded the batteries from Fort Negro westwards along the coast. They silenced them all by noon and the troops raced for the shore in three divisions of flat-bottomed boats. Captain Shuldham led the right and Commodore Swanton commanded the centre. On the left Captain Hervey led the way in *Dragon*'s barge, with his new coxwain, Solomon McCullock, at the tiller. Behind him came the first wave of grenadiers rowed by seamen in the flats. They landed without loss and formed up on the beach before marching to occupy the high ground above it. The light infantry followed and then the battalions. By sunset, two-third of the troops were ashore.

The remaining soldiers landed the next day, together with the marines formed in two battalions of six companies, each 450 strong under the overall command of Major Prosser. *Dragon*'s contingent under Captain Kennedy formed part of the first battalion. They were attached to the 2nd Brigade under William Rufane, who had sailed to Belle Isle in 1761 aboard the *Dragon* and had seen the performance of the marines on that island. They took their post close to the sea on the army's right flank. After the original sergeant major, drawn from *Devonshire*, had committed some breach of discipline, Sergeant John Pearson of *Dragon* had been promoted sergeant major of the marines in his place.

In order to cover the advance of the infantry and light artillery across the difficult ground towards Morne Tartenson, Monckton wanted batteries of heavy artillery to provide covering fire. A large number of seamen were landed to help get the guns into these, and the army engineers began to revise their opinion of the ground across which artillery could move. 'You may fancy you know the sprit of these fellows,' wrote an officer of the light infantry corps, 'but to see them in action exceeds any idea that can be formed of them.' The light infantry were proud of their own innovative style, moving fast across rough terrain, but they could barely believe the determination and mechanical prowess of the tars:

> A hundred or two of them, with ropes and pullies, will do more than all your dray-horses in London. Let but their tackle hold and they will draw you a cannon or mortar on its proper carriage up to any height, though the weight be never so great. It is droll enough to see them tugging along with a good 24 pounder at their heels; on they go huzzaing and hullooing, sometimes up hill, sometimes down hill; now sticking fast in the brakes, presently floundering in the mud and mire; swearing, blasting, damning, sinking and as careless of everything but the matter committed to their charge as if death or danger had nothing

to do with them. We had a thousand of these brave fellows sent to our assistance by the Admiral; and the service they did us, both on shore and on the water, is incredible.

In the midst of this frantic activity John McLaurin, who had made the passage in an amazing twenty-three days, arrived with the news that Spain had declared war. Some days afterwards the commander of a transport vessel confirmed the news, having narrowly escaped capture when visiting a Spanish port. Rodney threw a screen of frigates out to windward of Martinique with orders that Spanish ships were now lawful prize.

The campaign had now become more urgent, but Monckton still had to bring supplies ashore before he could attack. Negro slaves and Barbados volunteers performed crucial work along with the sailors in getting everything in place, and at first light on 24 January the British attacked. Three bodies of grenadiers and the Royal Highlanders advanced to pin down the enemy, driving them from post to post. On the left, the light infantry made an outflanking march. On the right the 2nd Brigade and the marines attacked the redoubts and the two fortified batteries near the sea, helped by a thousand seamen who rowed in to take successive positions from behind. By nine in the morning the French had been driven from Morne Tartenson and the British looked down on the citadel.

The light infantry and Haviland's brigade established positions in plantations on the left, facing the French on Morne Garnier, while the marines transferred from the coast to guard the road between the plantations. Morne Garnier was two kilometres from the sea as the bird flies and 150 metres above sea level. French guns mounted in the batteries dug in on top overlooked everything, and they raked the British with galling fire from above as they attempted to establish their own batteries on Morne Tartenson. It was obvious that they still had to take Morne Garnier before they could take the city.

The seamen dragged the guns forward three miles over ground that even near the sea was broken by ravines. They hauled twenty 24-pounders, each weighting two and a half tons, three thirteen-inch mortars and twenty howitzers. Eventually, 'after a great deal of labour in getting Cannon &c. up places where none but English Tars woud have attempted it', the batteries were ready again. Captain Lucius

O'Bryen commanded the men on shore. He only let them work in the morning and evening, stopping all work between ten and three when the sun was high, at which time they rested in the shade. January is the coolest month in Martinique, but even then the temperature averages seventy-six degrees Fahrenheit (26°C) and the high humidity makes work even thirstier. As if that wasn't enough, on 25 January it rained, turning the rivulets at the bottom of the gullies and ravines into raging torrents and making it even harder for the seamen to drag the guns into their new positions.

The French fire from Morne Garnier was so troublesome that Monckton resolved to attack it immediately. It was liable to be a costly enterprise, and Hervey proposed a naval landing as a diversion while the army stormed the mountain. His offer was accepted gratefully and he drew up and distributed plans. He was going to lead the attack with *Dragon*'s marines and seamen in the centre, *Temeraire* and *Nottingham*'s marines on the left and *Modeste* and *Marlborough*'s on the right. Robert Brice of the *Basilisk* bomb would command the left, and John Botterell of the *Grenado* the right. Other flats and barges full of seamen were to follow. Officers were to obey Midshipmen Philip Stopford, Oliver Templeton and Thomas Underwood who were acting as Hervey's aides-de-camp. On the afternoon of 27 January, the marines of *Dragon* and *Modeste* who were serving ashore received orders to re-embark in preparation for the attack.

They never did so. That afternoon the French left Morne Garnier in full force to attack the light infantry and Haviland's brigade on the left of the British line. The marines, stationed between them, played their part in repelling the French – the attackers were routed, crossed the ravine with their pursuers, and fled to the citadel. The British seized their trenches and guns. The light infantry marched on up the mountain in darkness and seized the cannon and mortars at the summit intact, capturing the few grenadiers who remained there. Morne Garnier had fallen, Hervey's attack was cancelled, and in the morning the French guns were turned on the citadel below.

Monckton built batteries on Morne Garnier and then seized Morne Capuchin and the mouth of the river. Seeing the circle closing, the citadel surrendered on 3 February. Four days later Pigeon Island surrendered. That same day Rodney ordered Hervey to sail to Trinity with the frigates *Penzance, Levant, Lizard* and *Stag* and the *Adventure* and *Providence* tenders. He was to 'endeavour by every means to reduce to His Majts: Obedience, The Forts, Ports, and Domains along the Coast from Trinity to Basse-Point; sending a Flag of Truce first to the Governors or Inhabitants of such places to know if they will accede to the Capitulation already agreed on and Signed by the Collonies of Fort-Royal and the whole Windward part of Martinique'. He was then to 'seize upon and take charge of all such ships and

Detail of Canot's engraving of Dragon *off Trinité with Hervey's returning flag of truce in the distance. The union jack is a signal that Hervey emphasises with a gun.*

vesells as you shall find or hear of on that coast and then return leaving a frigate at Trinity'. As commodore he would 'wear a Broad Pendt at yr Main Top Gallant mast head when not in sight of a superior officer'.

Dragon set out with *Stag* and met the other frigates as they sailed northward. Their boats took 'a privateer sloop that was laying inshore called the *Martinique*', and the following morning 'a small brig called the *Unique*'. On 12 February he sent in a boat under flag of truce to summon Trinity. The boat returned with 'an Inhabitant of Trinity' who informed Hervey that the district had surrendered and gave him a letter from Rodney, which ordered him to seize any privateers and oceangoing vessels but to leave coastal vessels to the inhabitants. He was to leave a frigate at Trinity and another cruising against privateers, and to issue the warning that 'If any attack after this [they] shall be looked upon [as] Pirates [sic]'.

Hervey took possession of a sloop called the *Trinity*, sailed round the island and moored off the commercial capital, St Pierre, with his prizes, *Trinity* and *Martinique*. Saint Pierre had surrendered on 12 February, and the British were now in full possession of the most important French island in the West Indies.

14

The Commodore

In Saint Pierre Bay the Dragons busily loaded provisions and water.
They were not there for long: before two weeks had passed Rodney
ordered Hervey to take *Norwich*, *Penzance* and *Dover* with the frigate
Levant, the *Basilisk* bomb and his sloops *Caesar* and *Trinity* to Saint
Lucia:

> having reconnoitred the Ports of the said Island and made all Ob-
> servations possible, You are at Liberty to make an Attack upon the said
> Island, if you shall judge the Force with you sufficient for that Purpose;
> But in Case you find the enemy stronger than is imagin'd, you are only
> to Block up the said Ports – only offer such terms as leave them entirely
> at our Disposal

If he could secure the surrender of Saint Lucia 'at discretion' – on his
own terms – Hervey was to sail on to Saint Vincent 'where you are to
inform the Chiefs of the Indians that you are not come to molest
them, or to take possession from them, but to rid them of the
Authority the French have usurped over them and to oblige the
French to evacuate that Island'. Once again, when not in sight of a
senior officer he was to hoist the broad swallow-tailed pendant that
showed that he was commodore, a captain commanding a squadron.

The two sloops were both crewed by Dragons. *Trinity* was her
prize, while Hervey had bought *Caesar* to help him take prizes that
tried to evade *Dragon* by running into shallow water. Within two days
the small squadron was at anchor off Castries, the principal port of the
small island.

Hervey was 'entirely at a loss for intelligence concerning the
situation of its French inhabitants, and the troops which defended

As Dragon *and her squadron approach the harbour of Castries a boat with a flag of truce rows out to surrender the island. One of the ship's boats is hoisting her sail.*

it'. The harbour was so shaped that they could not look into it, and the coast was so well defended that a landing was not a possibility. Hervey decided to summon the island to surrender and 'to accompany the officer charged with the summons in person, but dressed as a midshipman, sent, as it were, to serve as an interpreter'. By this stratagem Hervey 'got into the harbour, and had an opportunity of seeing that the water was every where deep; nay, he was carried up to the fortress where the Governor resided.'

The governor refused the surrender, so Hervey prepared to attack the port. However, next morning, as the ships sailed to force the harbour, with the marines and seamen in the boats ready for the assault, the governor sent an offer of capitulation.

> The officer sent on this errand, knowing again the Commodore, whom he had seen the day before in a different character, could not help betraying great surprise; but at the same time, rightly judging of

the real cause of this duplicity, he presently recovered himself; and, without taking any farther notice of it, returned to the Governor, and soon after brought back those articles signed, which the Commodore had sent in by him. The ships then went in and took possession of the harbour, and the whole island immediately submitted

Meanwhile, back in Saint Pierre, Admiral Rodney was receiving disturbing news. First came a warning that the Brest squadron had probably escaped. It was slow arriving and proceeded from a false alarm, but it put Rodney on his guard and he threw out a screen of frigates to windward of the Antilles. On 3 March he sent orders to Hervey 'instantly to dispatch the *Levant* frigate to cruise to windward of the Island of Deseada [La Désirade, esternmost of the Antilles]; in order to look out for the French Squadron which is sail'd from Brest, and hourly expected in these Seas'. He ordered Hervey to abandon his mission to Saint Vincent and return to Martinique.

Next came an express from the new governor of Jamaica. Thanks to Harrison's Number Four chronometer, the *Deptford* had sailed directly to Jamaica, knowing her position to within one and a quarter nautical miles. The governor was greeted with a series of captured letters. These showed that French officers in nearby Saint Domingue (modern Haiti) believed that a French squadron from Brest and a Spanish squadron were about to join forces with them for a combined attack on Jamaica. The new governor reminded Rodney that he had very few ships and very few men and begged for help.

Immediately afterwards Chaloner Ogle arrived in the *Aquilon*, bringing certain news of the escape of the Brest squadron with eight of the line, five frigates and about 3,000 soldiers. Rodney sent *Aquilon* to join the screen of frigates to windward of Martinique. The same day two further frigates arrived with Admiralty orders to commence hostilities against Spain and the same from Admiral Saunders at Gibraltar. Thanks to McLaurin, he had already done so.

Dragon anchored off Saint Pierre on 5 March. On 9 March the *Woolwich* tore in with the *Aquilon*, signalling that they had sighted the enemy. The wind dropped and Rodney could only gather *Woolwich*'s story of having been chased by Blénac's squadron off Trinity. Rodney set off in pursuit, but he lost the French. At first he worried they might have gone to Grenada, besieged by Commodore Swanton. But at Trinity he learned that Blénac had approached cautiously, discovered that the island was in British hands, and disappeared northwards. Rodney decided that Blénac must have gone to Saint Domingue and that the protection of Jamaica was his highest priority. Monckton refused to supply soldiers without positive orders from home, so he set off with ships alone, leaving Douglas in local command.

The Caribbean, from Johann Baptist Hamann's map of New Spain, c. 1720.

At parting, Hervey got some of his followers promoted, among them first lieutenant Peter Foulkes, who went into the admiral's flagship *Marlborough* along with midshipman John Burgess. In the normal way of things, these moves would lead to material advancement when Rodney chose officers for new ships. *Dragon*'s forty-eight-year-old fourth lieutenant, William Osborn, however, could not endure the climate in the West Indies. He had been ill ever since he had arrived at Martinique, and had obtained Rodney's permission to accompany the governor as a guard against privateers on his journey home. Hervey wrote to the Admiralty, adding an endorsement of the officer's competence, which, if logs are anything to go by, was fully justified: 'I beg leave to recommend him to your protection that he may soon be reinstated in some ship at home as he is a very good officer & has long been one.'

This left *Dragon* short of two lieutenants. As first lieutenant Rodney appointed John Henderson from the frigate *Crescent*. Promoted lieutenant early in the war, Henderson had fought while in *Buckingham* in a famous fierce engagement with the larger French *Florissant*. He was now twenty-eight, had been at sea since he was fourteen, and knew the West Indies well. A spell as first lieutenant of a third-rate ship was the last qualification he needed before getting his first command. After getting Hervey to accept an outsider as first lieutenant, Rodney sanctioned the promotion of Constantine Phipps, with Samber moving up a grade. Phipps was not yet eighteen, but although he was obviously promoted because he was Hervey's nephew, he had also shown genuine promise. With the two relatively elderly but highly experienced officers how gone, *Dragon*'s wardroom became a very youthful place. Next in age to the thirty-seven-year-old captain was Robinson, aged thirty-five, then Henderson, twenty-eight, Kidd and Samber, both twenty-six, and Phipps. Even Howison, the master, though older than them all, was only just forty.

These young men had heavy responsibilities. It was no longer sufficient to be a good enough seaman 'to direct the boatswain in strapping of a block, or stowing of an anchor', to 'bustle about, and make work appear to go on briskly in the ship' and to show 'a sort of insensibility amidst fire and smoke'. A modern officer was expected to think of himself as 'a person to whose care his country has committed a considerable number of his fellow subjects, to distribute impartial justice among them, to protect them from injuries, to find out the particular qualifications of each man under him, to put him in that station where he can do the public best service.' His seamanship should be founded on 'a proper foundation in mathematics' and 'the principles of mechanics and geometry'. Professional standards in the Royal Navy were becoming steadily more demanding, even though the formal requirements had not changed. Essentially the system relied on emulation, and where it was not distorted by political and dynastic biases it worked fairly well.

On 18 March Rodney ordered Hervey to sail to St Kitts and wait there for him. On his way from Antigua, Rodney was stunned to receive word that a secret expedition under Sir George Pocock was on its way from England. He was instructed to abandon all enterprises and return to Martinique to give maximum support to Pocock's operation. He must prepare ten ships of the line under Robert Swanton with three or four frigates and all his bomb vessels, and have them ready to reinforce Pocock's fleet. He was very disappointed that someone else was taking operational command.

What Rodney did out of pragmatism and what he did out of pique is sometimes difficult to judge, but he did not exactly obey these orders. He decided to send Douglas to Jamaica with the squadron he had promised for the island's defence, and gave him contradictory orders to defend Jamaica but also to have all his ships ready to join Sir George Pocock, who was expected in mid-April. Less explicably, he sent Swanton to cruise for prizes off the Spanish Main. He wrote to the Admiralty, attempting to convince them that sending ten ships to Jamaica under Douglas was the same as preparing ten ships under Swanton at the Cas Navires rendezvous.

Dragon spent two weeks in Basseterre Road, St Kitts, and many of the men got some time ashore. St Kitts was the wealthiest English island in the sense that it had the highest per capita income in the West Indies – per white capita, presumably. Although black men were not an unusual sight in London or other English ports – it is likely that there were black men in the *Dragon*, though none whose names give them away like Othello Sellours, formerly *Revenge*'s trumpeter, now trumpeter in *Monmouth* – it is unlikely that the Dragons had ever seen so many black people. Spavens was fascinated with the differentiated inhabitants of the islands, 'Creoles, Mustees, Mulattas, and Negroes; the latter of which, though they are chiefly slaves, are by far the most in number'. He explained that

A Creole is a white person born on the island; the Mustees are such as have one white and one mulatta parent; Mulattas are such as have one white and one black parent; and Negroes are such as are entire black, with a sort of short curly hair like wool: Such blacks as have long flank hair are not called Negroes. All blacks are white when born, but presently change their colour.

The town of Basseterre was a smart place, but people dressed in an unfamiliar fashion:

some of the white men wear light thin suits from head to foot, and some do not. Some of the white women too wear full light suits, except stays; whereas some wear neither stays, hat, nor shoes. Some of the women of colour wear only a sconce to hide their nakedness; and some men, particularly the negroes, go as naked as they were born.

The main square, surrounded by the smart town houses of plantation owners, was also the slave market. Spavens had a sound knowledge of the economy of the slave trade:

Many of these are imported from Africa; which country being held by different Princes and Chiefs, they go to war with each other; and if in an engagement between these contending powers, any prisoners are taken unhurt, they are sold to Europeans trading down the coast; and sometimes parents sell their children, and others their nearest relations. These unhappy creatures are bartered for on the coast of Guinea, at the rate of about 5 or 6l. a head, on an average, and carried to the West Indies and America, where they are exposed to sale on board a guineaman as naked as our first parents in Paradise, save only a hippen made of red cloth given to the women to serve in the place of a fig-leaf covering, when the planters go and buy them, as our people in England go to a fair to buy cattle, and give from 50 to 60l. a piece for full-grown slaves.

The Cleethorpes tar had walked about these foreign scenes showing an intelligent and sympathetic interest in the circumstances he witnessed, and some of the less bestial Dragons probably saw St Kitts with the same eyes:

The women slaves desire to be pregnant for more reasons than many of our free-born Englishwomen do, as it procures them milder treatment, and some relaxation from their labour. I have often wondered how their pickininies, i.e. children ever learned to run, as they are frequently left to sprawl about on the sand in or at the doors of the wigwams while the mothers are at work. Some of these people are of as bright a genius as those that rule over them: They suppose they are to return to their native country when they die, and from such a delusion they rejoice at the funerals of their deceased friends, dancing, singing, and playing on such musical instruments as they have, such as the tomtom, i.e. a sort of drum, &c. and using other expressions of joy.

The availability of cheap rum and other temptations of the flesh led, predictably, to a further outbreak of drunkenness and desertion. Thirteen men ran at Saint Kitts, where it was fairly easy to get a well-paid berth home in a West Indiaman, or to slip off in an American ship. Two of Hervey's followers, Joseph Pegley and Isaac Pressley, failed to return to the ship in time when *Dragon* suddenly sailed with Douglas on 2 April. They may have been caught out straggling, as Hervey's followers sometimes were, but it is possible that they had chosen to opt out of a summer campaign in the Caribbean in favour of the very high pay offered to sailors in West Indiamen bound for England. There was a rash of punishments for disobedience, fighting and drunkenness, the two former fuelled by the latter.

Despite a widespread belief to the contrary, there was no official issue of spirits in the navy. All seamen were allowed a gallon of small beer a day until the beer ran out, and after that, as Spavens explained, they got local supplies:

When ships are abroad they cannot get beer, but have an allowance of that sort of liquor which the country produces in lieu thereof, viz. if they are on a long cruise in the home seas and their beer is expended, they have $\frac{1}{2}$ a pint of brandy and $1\frac{1}{2}$ pints of water mixed into grog; if they be in the West Indies, they have an equal quantity of rum-grog; in the East Indies, of arrack-grog; but in the Mediterranean seas or at the Cape of Good Hope, the daily allowance is a pint of white wine mixed with another of water, and served out twice, either at breakfast and dinner or dinner and 4 o'clock in the afternoon.

Dragon does not seem to have issued rum officially until early July, but there was nothing to stop seamen buying their own private supplies, and in the West Indies rum was cheap. Douglas complained to the governor of Antigua that 'not a ship comes into this port whose crew is not made sickly by the quantities of liquor vended to them', and it is unlikely that St Kitts was better. Usually tars mixed spirits with sugar and other ingredients to make punch. 'Flip' was brandy, beer and sugar, 'bumbo' was rum, sugar, water and nutmeg. In the West Indies limes were cheap and made a popular addition to rum punches, with happy anti-scorbutic side effects, since limes contained moderate amounts of vitamin C.

After any run ashore on almost any ship discipline fell apart for a while, and *Dragon* was no exception. The persistently violent former Salamander William Dakers was again punished for fighting, ex-Monmouth marine James Bulboard for drunkenly refusing orders ashore, and more men after the ship sailed. The pattern of discipline in *Dragon* was quite different from that in *Monmouth*, where corporal punishment was exceptional, barely an annual occurrence. In *Dragon*, Hervey and the other temporary captains handed out more frequent punishments. The numbers were not huge – eleven in 1760, seventeen in 1761, twenty-four in 1762 – but there were considerably more in the West Indies than ever before. Either Hervey became unusually short-tempered with his men, or their behaviour was worse. Heat and humidity may have played a part, but a plentiful supply of potent rum was almost certainly the chief problem – it faded away during periods of active service and was at its worst when the ship was in a friendly port.

Dragon sailed ahead of the fleet, exercising the great guns in case of trouble. Douglas sent *Penzance* to reconnoitre Hispaniola and look into Cap François to see if the Spanish had joined the French. If they had, he was to sail to warn Pocock.

Douglas was uncertain whether to wait for Pocock at Jamaica or to try to prevent any junction between French and Spanish squadrons. When he reached Jamaica he learned that the Spanish had not appeared, so there was no immediate danger to the island. However, there was a new factor. An important convoy was expected from

America with troops for the secret expedition, and to reach Jamaica they had to pass close to Cap François. The orders for the senior officer at Jamaica were to wait with all his ships ready for Pocock, but on 12 April Douglas made what turned out to be a crucial decision to send Hervey to stop the French squadron interfering with the convoy, while getting most of his force victualled, watered and cleaned. He gave Hervey *Dragon, Defiance, Temeraire, Stirling Castle, Alcide, Nottingham, Pembroke, Portmahon, Trent, Hussar, Dover, Glasgow* and *Cerberus*, and his orders were:

> whereas Captain Forrest has informed me that a Convoy is soon expected with troops and Provisions from N. America under a weak Escorte, to come down on the North side of Hispaniola, which shou'd it be intercepted by the Enemy's Squadron in Cape François, might be attended with fatal consequences, and frustrate the intended Expedition.
>
> You are . . . [to] . . . cruise to the Eastwd. of the Island of Tortuga and Cape Francois, for the protection of the said Convoy, whom upon falling in with them, you are to see safe to Leeward of Hispaniola or wherever then return to Port Royal for water

Hervey approached his station, once again exercising the great guns, and made a rendezvous with the rest of his squadron at Platform Bay to the south of Cape Nicholas where there was good water to be had. They grouped there on 22 April, the *Caesar* tender towing a sloop that she had captured after *Dragon* had driven it inshore. For some days they cruised off Platform Bay and took and ransomed two French boats loaded with wine. Off Cape St Nicholas Hervey found the *Hussar* under Captain Robert Carkett, with former shipmates master's mates John Broad and William Langman and boatswain Edward May. Midshipman John Samber changed ships out of *Defiance* into *Dragon* to join his elder brother James, the fourth lieutenant, and then was met by the sloop *Bonetta* and her master and commander Lancelot Holmes. He was a former lieutenant of *Hampton Court*, and having been promoted into the flagship when Hervey took over *Monmouth*, he owed his present rank to Hervey.

Holmes was a thirty-six-year-old Cumbrian with some know-ledge of West Indies navigation. In January the Admiralty had sent him to Providence with orders for Governor Shirley to find him reliable pilots for the Old Bahama Channel, the narrow deep-water passage between Cuba and the Bahama bank to the north. Holmes had orders to hurry on to Jamaica, and Shirley complained that he was in too much of a rush, since the best pilots were out on short voyages, but Holmes would not wait for their return. After ten days at Providence, Holmes left with what pilots Shirley could find. There was 'John Kimblin, who is esteem'd to have been the best Pilot for the Navigation of the Old Bahama straights, that ever was in this Place; & tho' old and something Dim-Sighted, is still reputed with the help of his glass to be well Qualified for that Service, and has voluntarily offered himself'. With Kimblin went 'Johonno – a Free Negro Man esteem'd the second best pilot in these Islands' as well as four Americans and three Spaniards of less certain value.

When Douglas reached Jamaica he examined Holmes's pilots and found them totally inadequate. Putting two and two together, he guessed that the pilots were needed to take Pocock's fleet through the Old Bahama Channel to Havana. On 19 April he made an important decision. He sent Captain Elphinstone in the frigate *Richmond* – which had helped chart the St Lawrence during the Quebec campaign – to make a detailed survey of the whole length of the Old Bahama Channel with sketches and bearings from one island to the next, taking with him a sloop from Providence and four of the pilots. Three days later, Douglas had second thoughts on two fronts (second thoughts were char-acteristic of him). He sent Holmes with orders to find Hervey and tell him to return to Port Royal and, should he meet Elphinstone, to swap jobs with him.

Holmes didn't meet Elphinstone, but he did find Hervey, and on 4 May gave him Douglas's orders of 22 April. Hervey decided to ignore them because he reckoned that if he withdrew the French would sail to Havana. He wrote to Douglas:

I have taken two small Vessells from the Cape, with two Intelligent People onboard them; who have acquainted me that the French ships were all to have sailed as the 26th: ultmo.; & had their People and Troops onboard, that tho' some People said they were going to Porto-Prince, yet it was certain they were destined immediately to the Havanna to join the Spaniards, under whose directions this Squadron is said at the Cape to be, and where they have already sent the Calypso Frigate the moment they arrived at the Cape, to acquaint the Spanish Admiral of their Arrival as well as to acquaint him of our Intended Attack; these People inform me that on my Appearing off here, they had an Express at twelve at Night the 25th. from the Platform-Side, and the next Morning their Squadron moor'd again, & will not sail whilst we are off.

Hervey guessed that, given this information, Douglas would want him to stay put:

I imagine you will think it necessary to prevent the French joining with the Spaniards if possible before Sr. George Pocock arrives, as you have been so fortunate by sending these ships so timely to have prevented that Blow already, and which they will infallibly do, if they find I have left the Coast free for them: another Motive is the orders I see the Bonetta is under, by which 'twas probable the rendezvous wd. be about Cape Nicholas.

Hervey sent *Bonetta* to Port Royal with his message and stayed out, somewhat nervous at disobeying orders when Douglas might have been better informed than he was. On this occasion it turned out that Hervey was right. When Douglas received the message on 9 May, he changed his mind again. Two days later he got positive instructions to rendezvous off St Nicholas and changed Hervey's orders again. Unfortunately, however, none of the three ships that Douglas sent to find Hervey ever reached him. On 10 May Hervey decided he must obey his last orders and sailed for Port Royal with *Alcide*, whose crew was sickly, *Temeraire* and *Dover*. He left most of his squadron behind to watch the French, watch for the convoy and watch for Pocock.

James McArdell's engraving of Thomas Hudson's painting of Sir George Pocock.

Admiral Sir George Pocock finally arrived at Barbados on 20 April with five ships of the line, 4,000 soldiers and an enormous fleet of transports and auxiliary vessels. Even though preparations for his expedition had been carried out astonishingly fast, he had got away from England a full month later than he would have wished, and his rough, forty-five day crossing had been no better than average. There was little time left now before the seasons of ill-health and hurricanes threw his great operation into jeopardy. Supplies had been prepared for him at Barbados and they were hurriedly embarked. He now had to pick up Monckton's men, who should be ready in their ships off Fort Royal with the ten ships waiting there, summon the Leeward Island squadron from Jamaica and then rendezvous with a further convoy bringing troops from America before making his great attack.

The astounding objective was known to very few but suspected by far more – Havana, the most powerful Spanish base in the Caribbean, where the treasure fleets assembled for their annual voyage to Cadiz. It had the potential to be the greatest coup of the war. Havana had the largest and most sheltered harbour in the Caribbean, and its fortified dockyard built many of Spain's largest ships. The city was reputed to be enormously rich and full of plunder, but also stoutly fortified, and the Morro Castle that guarded the harbour entrance was said to be the strongest in the New World. If the Spanish were fully prepared and ready to fight, the attack might be a fiasco.

The whole point of the decision, taken two days after Britain's declaration of war against Spain on 4 January to activate a previously existing plan devised by Lord Anson, was to catch Havana by surprise. To this end speed was essential and Pocock, through no fault of his own, was already late.

On 25 April Pocock arrived at Cas Navires and was astonished to find the bay practically empty of ships of war. He was even more incensed when, instead of a visit from Rodney, he received an apologetic message to the effect that Rodney was indisposed with a fever at Saint Pierre. There was no sign of Swanton. Pocock demanded explanations, and finding Rodney's cruising ships were beyond immediate recall, removed Rodney's flagship from him on the grounds that he now needed every decent ship he could get. Leaving Rodney with the little *Rochester* until his other ships returned, Pocock summoned Douglas to Cape St Nicholas and sailed to meet the inbound trading fleet from London at St Kitts. Robert Monckton was also ill and also feeling slighted. Rather than taking a post as third in command of the expedition, he chose to return to New York, leaving Rufane as Governor of Martinique. By the time Albemarle had unloaded and reloaded the transports it was 6 May before they left.

Rodney's latest intelligence was that the Spanish had twenty ships of the line at Havana and the French had seven at Cap François when last heard of. Pocock had picked up the trade at St Kitts and was now sailing with 160 transports, victuallers and hospital ships, forty-six merchant ships and thirteen warships. He met *Hussar* in her cruising ground short of Cap François and learned that Hervey's squadron was in the area. The fleet reached Cape St Nicholas on 17 May and was joined during the next two days by Hervey's ships. He was not pleased to learn that Hervey had sailed back to Jamaica, since foul winds and flat calms had made it difficult to get back again, but he had no choice but to wait for them.

On 20 May John Barry up at the masthead spotted a sail. *Dragon* chased, but unfortunately a block split as they were hoisting the maintopsail and in trying to stop himself falling from the highest point in the ship the lookout broke his little toe. Eventually, Watt had to amputate it. It was an irritating accident and the chase turned out to be just a Carolina merchantman heading for Jamaica. Hervey pressed some colonials to vent his frustration.

It was not until the night of 22 May that *Dragon*, *Dublin*, *Dover* and *Temeraire* joined Pocock's fleet, which was sailing ahead of the slower ships and sluggish bombs, and had brought five pilots from Providence and three from Jamaica. Pocock examined them with Augustus Keppel, his second in command, and found them useless. It was another frustrating setback which put everybody even more on edge – Hervey was already cross that obeying Douglas and returning to Jamaica had made him late for Pocock, and Pocock was increasingly frustrated with the many delays and the inadequate preparations for his arrival. His objective was an awesome responsibility – but success would also make Pocock enormously rich. Indeed, if the gods really smiled and they happened to catch Spanish treasure ships in Havana harbour, he and his colleague General Lord Albemarle might become rich almost beyond imagination. Havana beckoned.

15

The Old Bahama Channel

The Old Bahama Channel, a hundred miles long and fifteen miles wide, was a narrow deep-water route between the rock-strewn north coast of Cuba and the cays, or reefs, that marked the southern edge of the Great Bahama Bank. Once over the bank, the water was too shallow for large ships – at the edge it was twenty-three feet deep and *Dragon*'s draft was more than twenty-two. The channel itself wound its way past a number of rocky obstacles, and was so long and narrow that it gave sailors a feeling of claustrophobia. If bad weather overtook them in the narrows, disaster might ensue. In the hurricane season, violent southerly gales were common, turning the coast of Cuba into a lee shore and bringing sudden heavy squalls of wind, rain and thunder with bright, jagged lightning. In such conditions a fleet was in great peril – might even be destroyed. At present the hurricane season was still distant, but on 23 May, the day that Pocock had to decide whether or not to go on, a terrific electric storm hit the fleet. The *Felicity* transport fired guns of distress 'having her mainmast and topmast shivered by lightning'.

The weather was one gamble, the unknown navigation another. Admiral Anson had given Pocock a Spanish chart of the channel, but nobody knew how accurate it was. That Sunday Pocock examined the five pilots that *Dragon* had brought and found all but one incapable of taking a fleet through to Havana. That one, unfortunately, was John Kimble. For certain he could have done it in his youth, but the fact that he was eighty-six years of age and very dim-sighted was not encouraging. This left Elphinstone and the *Richmond*, but they had not returned, and in Pocock's view it was unlikely that they could possibly return in time, even if they had not met with an accident. He reported to Admiralty Secretary Clevland that Douglas's idea of sending him to sound the channel would have been a good one had there been sufficient time to accomplish the task. Early in May Pocock had hinted to Douglas that he might have to take the southern route round Cuba, and Douglas, in his reply, had betrayed his relief that they might not be taking the fearful risk of the Old Channel.

The decision Pocock had to make now was momentous. He had to ask himself whether it was not just the prospect of plunder that drew him on. If it all went wrong he was answerable for nearly 200 ships and more than 20,000 souls, potential victims of his determination to take an unknown, uncharted, reputedly highly dangerous short cut. In the afternoon Augustus Keppel, who also stood to make a large amount of money, ventured his opinion that 'I think I should determine to continue'. He reasoned that

> I should have been extremely cautious of venturing to give you my opinion for going with so numerous a fleet through the Old Straits of Bahama if the alternative of going to leeward had not the melancholy prospect of defeating the hopes of success against the Havana by the loss of so much time; the advancement of the season, and the increase of sickness among the soldiers are such trying reasons for risking what we may not find so bad as described.

Keppel was being optimistic, perhaps with some reason. The navigation of the St Lawrence to Quebec had been supposed impossible for a hostile fleet, yet there were people present who had seen that done. And under her present captain John Wheelock, the *Pembroke* had led the way up the St Lawrence with the ship's master, James Cook, the future Pacific explorer, navigating. Cook had since been promoted to another ship, but his assistants were still in *Pembroke*; and British navigational skills had improved steadily in recent years. Scientific instruments manufactured in London were widely considered to be the best in the world. The skills of those using them were constantly improving, and there were several accomplished scientific sailors in the fleet. Pocock decided to put his faith in the seamanship of the Royal Navy and hardened his heart to continue. He wrote to Clevland that 'considering the great delay our not going through the straits may occasion, and so much of the proper season being already elapsed, and with the great probability of meeting the *Richmond*, we have determined to proceed so soon as the ships of the line and bombs join us.'

Pocock, however, was still seething about the lack of pilots. He had grilled Lancelot Holmes over hot coals and enclosed to Clevland the correspondence between Holmes and Governor Shirley when Holmes was at Providence, with his 'opinion the Governor did not take the proper method to execute His Majesty's directions'.

In order to pass through the channel as safely as possible, Pocock devised a plan to arrange the fleet in seven divisions, with warships leading and flanking the transports. The frigates and lighter vessels went ahead and to the side to warn the main body of dangers. The dangers were brought vividly home on Tuesday 25 May when Captain John Lindsay joined the *Trent* with the news that the ship watching the French in Cap François, Carkett's *Hussar*, had foundered on a reef in Sunday's thunderstorm. The French had reportedly saved the crew. He also brought news that the departure of the convoy from America had been delayed but it should by now have sailed.

Pocock posted frigates to cruise between Mariguana and West Caicos and off St Nicholas to wait for the convoy, with instructions to send them 'with all possible dispatch' through the channel if they felt it was safe, and round the south side if not.

He then sent Lancelot Holmes ahead in the *Bonetta*, accompanied by Lindsay's *Trent*, a cutter, nine longboats and some smaller vessels, to begin to mark the way. *Dragon*'s longboat was one, commanded by one of the lieutenants, with a petty officer, nine men and provisions for ten days. Holmes had one of the Providence pilots, Captain Thomas Johnson, with him in order to identify the cays to be marked. It started badly – Johnson thought he had found the first island but stationed the *Trent* forty-five leagues eastward of where she should have been. 'This', Pocock wrote angrily to Governor Shirley of Providence, 'occasioned some of the others never to find the cays where they were sent to lie on.' While it was calm, *Dragon* took in two flatboats from the transports, ready for use in the landing.

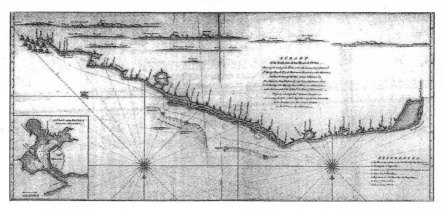

Captain John Elphinstone's chart of the Old Bahama Channel, as presented to the Admiralty after the campaign.

To Pocock's enormous relief, after just one day's sailing up the coast of Cuba, when the fleet was off Puerto de Baracoa, the *Richmond* appeared. Next day the fleet formed into their divisions. *Dragon* was stationed ahead of the first division of the fleet on the larboard side towards the Cuban shore. Ahead of *Dragon* there was only the frigate *Alarm*. Pocock, in his flagship *Namur*, was to starboard of *Dragon*, leading the transports of the first division. That night the fleet continued sailing westward. *Dragon's* longboat was sent out to starboard of the fleet with orders to sound constantly to make sure they did not run into shallow water. The boat returned at five in the morning having found no ground at ninety-five fathoms.

On Sunday afternoon, 30 May, the Dragons saw Cay Romano ahead in the distance. They were currently between Cayo Gonavo and the Macara Bank, at the entrance to the Channel, and just beyond Cay Romano lay the narrowest and most dangerous passage, off Cay Lobos, where the deep-water channel was less than ten miles wide. For the fifty miles beyond that it was only a little wider. At that point the moderate winds they had enjoyed until then fell away to something close to a flat calm. With so little wind, the unknown currents that Pocock was testing constantly for strength and direction came into play. The fleet lay to, while *Mercury*, *Bonetta* and the marker boats

239

went ahead and eventually took up their stations, marking the rocks at the edge of the passage.

On Monday afternoon the boats were in position and the wind was blowing a fresh gale, slightly stronger than they might have wished. The first division edged through the narrows with *Dragon* on the larboard flank nearest the rocky Cay Romano, though the fleet stayed closer to the northern edge of the channel where Cay Lobos was the principal danger. Skipper Archibald Howison remarked on the low, sandy, featureless shore where there were very few seamarks from which to get a bearing.

As it got dark, the boats marking the cays lit fires on them to light the way for succeeding divisions. It took a very long time for all two hundred ships to pass through the danger zone. At ten, three hours after *Namur* and *Dragon* had passed Cay Lobos, Pocock sent a longboat full of tar and junk over to the vessels stationed off that cay to make sure that their fire kept burning brightly until the last divisions of the fleet were past.

At six o'clock that morning Pocock signalled to the fleet to make more sail. They were through. It was a clear day, and from the flagship the officers could see 188 sail. From the *Orford*, on the right of the third division, Lieutenant Philip Orsbridge made drawings of the fleet's progress, which he published on his return to London.

Now Pocock sent the frigates *Alarm* and *Echo* to lie off Cay Sal, the last dangerpoint at the end of the channel, and the fleet exercised its great guns, ready for the battle to come. They sailed along the widening channel in good weather. The *Alarm* spotted five ships and soon identified them as Spaniards. Pocock signalled *Dragon* to follow in chase. The pursuit continued all night and all next morning until Phipps in *Dragon* heard *Alarm*'s guns ahead. *Dragon* cleared for action and the ship's barge set off in pursuit of a schooner to the north-west. *Ripon*'s barge narrowly beat *Dragon*'s to the target, and by the time *Dragon* approached *Alarm* her two opponents had both surrendered. She had captured the small frigate *Thetis* and the *Phoenix*, of eighteen guns. *Mercury* captured a Spanish brig, but two swift schooners escaped towards Havana.

The Spanish captains had left the capital ten days before to cut timber for the dockyard from the forests around the River Sagoa in the Bahama Straits. Nobody had any idea of the presence of a British fleet. An officer of the *Thetis* revealed that there were ten ships of the line at Havana, plus another two that had just been launched but not yet manned. As for soldiers, there were two regiments of regular foot, one of dragoons and one of militia. There were also a regiment of mullatos, one of negroes and several of irregular militia. All of this was profoundly reassuring. The escaping schooners would give the alarm before the British arrived, but they barely had a start on their pursuers. It looked as if no treasure ships were in harbour, but that major disappointment apart, prospects looked good.

As they followed the fleeing Spanish ships, Albemarle and Pocock reached agreement on how they would divide up the booty. The king had given Albemarle two documents relating to divisions of plunder in expeditions of 1694 and 1702, and these antique precedents were helpful since they awarded commanding officers far more than the modern convention of a one-eighth share. The two commanders agreed to split the proceeds evenly between army and navy, but for the time being their mutually agreed personal shares remained strictly secret.

On the morning of Sunday 6 June, as the British fleet approached Havana, the governor of Cuba, Don Juan de Prado, was in church with other Spanish officials, celebrating the feast of the Trinity. They were blithely unaware of the presence of Pocock's fleet in the West Indies. They did not even know officially that war had been declared, since the *aviso* bringing the news had been captured by an English cruiser, although they had learned of the state of war from a Spanish newspaper and had heard various reports of attacks by British ships. They knew that the British had taken Martinique, and they had people watching out for any threat from the normal approach via Jamaica since there would be plenty of time to prepare a defence while the fleet beat up laboriously into the wind. Prado had dismissed the possibility of an approach from the other direction as a total impossibility. It was not until the visiting fleet he had spotted offshore began to lower flatboats into the water that the governor admitted that it might be hostile.

Thunderstruck, Prado summoned the military, naval and civilian authorities to a council of war on 7 June. All was not yet lost. The harbour and city of Havana was so big that it was almost impossible to cut it off from supply, which meant it could easily resist a long siege. The fortress of El Morro, built on a long, towering cliff of solid rock, was impregnable, and the vast harbour was full of ships of war whose guns could be turned against troops that attacked the castle from the east or the city from the west, while El Morro's guns commanded the harbour entrance and the north-western approaches to the city. The regular forces in Cuba were not strong, although two regular regiments had reinforced the local garrison, but the naval crews contained expert gunners and several thousand doughty fighters. A regiment of dragoons and large numbers of mounted militia gave the Spanish a significant advantage in the open country, while irregular hunters could harry and ambush the British in the forests and swamps.

In the long run, the defenders held the advantage. Huge cisterns for gathering rainwater (which fell in torrents when it fell) and storing it away from the heat of the sun were incorporated into the design of the fort and all the houses in the Havana. Other supplies of drinking water were unreliable, although in emergency they had the vast harbour, while the British had only the rivers, one of which had dried to a brackish trickle. Moreover, the season was advanced and British armies were notoriously vulnerable to disease in the West Indian summer. On the Spanish Main, yellow fever was known as *fièbre patriotica* for its value in removing unwanted strangers. In this region, delay could be a decisive weapon.

It was the prospect of a sudden assault that terrified the Cubans. The city wall had been allowed to decay so that there were large fissures in it. The most vulnerable point in the defence was the ridge of La Cabaña, which extended from El Morro along the harbour edge. It commanded the city and, although it had long been recognised as a defensive weakness, practically no progress had been made towards the projected fortifications to secure it against assault. Orders had arrived from Spain for a fortress to be built at the landward end of the ridge, together with a small contribution towards the cost, but

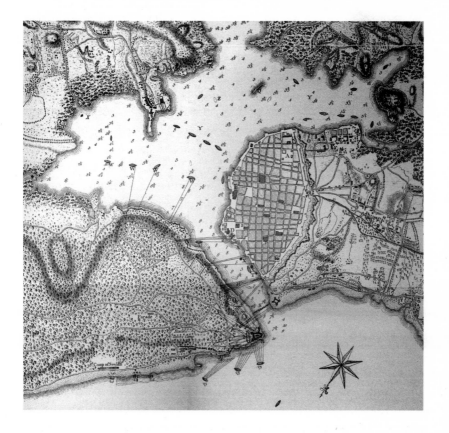

Detail of Kitchin's map for Mante's History. *The Morro is B; the Punta C; E and F are batteries; X marks floating batteries; Y marks Spanish ships.*

construction had ceased when the Mexican diggers had gone down with yellow fever soon after their arrival. To compensate, guns from the ships had been hoisted on to the ridge and a rudimentary battery constructed. Meanwhile, the most dynamic naval officer present, don Luis de Velasco, took command of El Morro. Hervey had met Velasco during a visit to Cadiz in 1752, where the Spanish officers had impressed him. He had remarked then that 'this Marine corps in Spain only wanted practice; they had all the theory of the service requisite'.

The Spanish decided to sink three of the least seaworthy ships to block the narrow bottleneck entrance to the harbour, across which they also constructed a boom. The other ships were disposed about the bay so that their guns swept approaches to city and fort. Armed boats patrolled the creeks leading to the harbour, natural swamps prevented other approaches to the harbour itself. Meanwhile, women, children and other citizens streamed out of the land gates of the city in a panic-stricken jumble, struggling along muddy roads turned into quagmires by frequent torrential downpours of warm rain.

As the Spanish began to concert measures for their defence, the British fleet brought to five leagues off the Cuban coast. Colonel William Howe and Major-General William Keppel went to reconnoitre the shore in the *Alarm*. To the west there was a mixture of thick forest and mangrove swamp as far as the entrance to the River Chorera, which was guarded by a fort. Thinner woods gave way to cleared fields and an open view of the great walled city. The long, narrow, bottle-neck entrance to the harbour was guarded by a fort to the west and to the east by the massive castle of El Morro perched on huge cliffs on a rocky spit of land. Ships could only enter the harbour one by one, and it was immediately evident that it would be suicidal to do so in the face of crossfire from the forts and raking broadsides from the ships within. A sudden naval attack on the harbour was out of the question.

Beyond the castle was a continuous belt of forest. Two small forts guarded the rivers Bacuranao and Coximar, which were four miles apart. Coximar, the nearest to Havana, was about two miles from El Morro. The beach between them looked good for landing, but the developing surf on it portended an approaching storm.

Pocock sent *Richmond* and *Cygnet* to keep an eye on the ships at Havana, which might yet come out to fight. Then he signalled all the captains and masters of the fleet to come aboard *Namur* and they received their orders for the landing. Commodore Keppel was in overall command, with Captain Hervey directing the boats. Each large ship manned three flats and sent a lieutenant to command them. A midshipman commanded each boat, with a petty officer steering, sixteen men rowing and two experienced boatmen in the bows.

Dragon lowered her three flats into the water and sent them to the transports to embark troops. Howe and Keppel returned and reported the beach fine, but in the afternoon came the electric storm they had foreseen. Thunder, lightning and wild winds bent the trees in the woods that lined the shore and stirred up a violent surf on the beach. There was no landing boats in those conditions, so Pocock postponed the attack until next morning.

Dragon retained one company of grenadiers that had already come aboard. Pocock bore away with thirteen of the line, the victuallers and the store ships to make a feint the far side of Havana and to be ready to oppose the Spanish fleet should it choose to emerge from the harbour. He left Keppel with six ships, some smaller vessels and the transports together with the flatboats. Pocock's departure also helped clear the way for the landing. With the store ships out of the way, there was much less room for confusion when unloading the transports.

In the early morning, Generals George Augustus Eliott and William Keppel went on board the *Dragon*, and Keppel's squadron tacked towards the shore. At six o'clock Keppel hoisted the half red, half white flag at the foretopmasthead that instructed the troops to embark in the flatboats, and sent the frigate *Mercury* with Holmes's *Bonetta* and the *Basilisk* bomb to silence the tower at Bacuranao. He sent the frigates *Richmond* and *Trent* close inshore to give covering fire to the troops landing on the beaches, and rowed himself across to the *Richmond*. All along the shore the forest was uncomfortably close to the beach, and Spanish irregulars were seen amongst the trees. Broadsides of grapeshot from the frigates cleared the way for the boats to land.

This was the signal for Hervey to lead the troops ashore, and Keppel hoisted a chequered red and white flag to confirm it. The flats were grouped behind the warships. *Dragon* herself, in the centre, led in the 2nd battalion of grenadiers and the Royal Scots. *Ripon* covered the 35th regiment, *Orford* the 56th. *Valiant* took charge of the 1st battalion of grenadiers, *Temeraire* the light infantry and *Dover* the 3rd Royal Americans. *Pembroke* covered the reserve and Keppel's ship *Valiant* became the Earl of Albemarle's headquarters. *Dragon*'s bargemen had the honour of landing the two generals.

The picked troops making the landing were of high quality. Each British foot regiment had flank companies of grenadiers and light infantry, for which the tallest and speediest recruits were selected. In action these elite companies were grouped together. The battalions of

Detail of James Mason's engraving of the troops reinforcing the initial landing beyond Coximar.

grenadiers were assault units, while the light infantry were trained to move fast in loose order. The Royal Americans were specialists in forest fighting. Some of them were armed with rifles, and the unit developed into the first rifle regiment.

The seamen plied their red-painted oars in silence, forbidden the 'huzzaing' they liked on boat service. Just before they reached the breakers, the midshipman commanding dropped the boat's grapnel so that he could haul it back into deep water. Then the bowmen leapt into the waves to drag the boat in, and the red-coated 'lobsters' leapt ashore as soon as they could.

The landing went perfectly: there was no opposition and there were no casualties. Then, as it began to pour with warm rain again and lightning flashed across the sky, the grenadiers formed up, while the light infantry and Americans pushed into the woods. The whole assault force was on the beach by midday, and still the flats returned to the transports again and again for more men and guns. By three in the afternoon, most of the army was ashore.

Meanwhile, the generals had identified an obstacle to their advance. About six hundred Cubans with about fifteen cannon held the square stone fort at Coximar and an adjacent breastwork that defended the line of the river. Albemarle asked Keppel for help, and Keppel sent *Dragon* to destroy the fort.

Detail of James Mason's engraving showing Dragon *and the Grenado bomb vessel engaging the castle of Coximar.*

Dragon anchored in front of the castle at half past two. Hauling on the spring on the anchor, the crew brought the ship broadside on, while the castle fired at them without reply. Then *Dragon* opened up. The *Thunder* bomb anchored ahead and began to lob explosive shells into the woods. *Mercury*, *Bonetta* and *Basilisk* fired from astern. After a little more than an hour, the Dragons stopped firing: the Cubans had fled leaving smashed guns behind them. Kennedy and fifty marines clambered into one of the flats, the bluejackets rowed them ashore and they took over the castle, hoisting a Union Jack above it.

At this, the army moved on. The advanced guard, commanded by Colonel Carleton, forded the river and relieved the marines, who returned to the ship. 'On being informed of Captain Hervey's success', the Earl of Albemarle 'liberally rewarded the crew of his ship'. The grenadiers and light infantry crossed the river, while the remainder slept on the east bank, 'the army lying upon their arms along the shore, with the pickets advanced into the woods'.

The navy had delivered the most tremendous tactical surprise. Now it was up to the generals to exploit the advantage the admirals had delivered.

British intelligence on Havana was very poor. A hurried assessment had been cobbled together by the chief engineer, Patrick Mackellar, following the sudden decision to go ahead with the expedition, which relied on the reports of several non-military eyewitnesses. It did not even make use of the most recent published accounts, which hinted correctly at the dilapidated state of the city walls. Even the 1759 *Grand Gazetteer* had devoted much of its article on Havana to schemes for seizing the place. It had concluded: 'Tis thought if a Descent was to be made on the W. Side of the City, where it lies open, soon after their Fleets have passed out of the Indies, this Port and City might possibly by reduced by only two Regiments of good Soldiers, carrying with them 2 or 3 Shallops for landing Men, provided with good Arms and Necessaries; and that when the City is master'd, it would be easy to reduce the Castle of Morro.'

As a military man, Mackellar might have discounted this as populist hearsay even if he had read it. He reckoned that if the city was defended by a ditch (as it was, albeit a poor one), it should be stronger than the Morro, which was said to have only masonry defences on the land side. An attack on the city was additionally vulnerable to crossfire from either the Morro, or ships anchored at the bottom of the harbour. It should be easier to bring supplies to the east side where the batteries would be closer to the shore, it should be healthier to camp there and it should be easier to defend the camp and works against sorties. On these grounds Mackellar recommended an attack on the east side of the harbour, but his assessment was hedged around with many uncertainties.

Next morning the army pushed inland along both banks of the Coximar, Albemarle to the East and Carleton's vanguard to the west. William Howe took his American grenadiers through the woods to reconnoitre the ground towards El Morro. As they emerged from the forest, Albemarle and his men got their first view of the great city and of the flat, fertile fields around it. The Spanish dragoons and mounted irregulars attacked Carleton's light infantry but sheered off at their determined fire. This was fortunate, since the infantry had left their bayonets on board ship and could not have withstood a charge. The British marched on and occupied the village of Guanabacoa, securing the Coximar as a water supply and the surrounding fields for fresh provisions. For a few days there was a supply of such local delicacies as pig and 'salted tortoise [turtle], eaten by seamen boiled with garlic', with good, cheap Cuban wine.

While the navy landed guns, ammunition and supplies, seamen cut paths through the woods and the soldiers made camps, the general staff took stock of their position. Now various patrols were sent out to reassess the best method of attack. A new, pressing factor was the lateness of the season. Contemporary critics of the conduct of the expedition remarked (with hindsight) that 'experience in former expeditions might have taught them that whatever is to be effected in the West Indies must be done as expeditiously as possible'. Some of the troops had been sick before they arrived in Cuba. Since then they had been alternately drenched, steamed and roasted. The sickly season was upon them, and those who feared the West Indies stressed the need for a quick resolution. Captain Hervey had been at Cartagena and favoured any gambit that might shorten the siege.

One suggestion that Hervey either originated or supported was an attack on the fortress from the sea. It was possible that rapid fire from naval guns at close range might make a breach for an amphibious assault. At worst they might draw enough fire to enable the guns on the landward side to gain a decisive advantage. On the morning of 9 June Hervey approached the castle in the *Caesar* sloop. Spanish fire prevented him going close enough to take soundings, but he reported that if ships could anchor they could batter the castle without being exposed to any guns other than those on the northern salient and adjacent curtain wall. He reckoned ships should be able to do significant damage to these.

The following night the masters of the *Marlborough*, *Cambridge* and *Culloden* went in silently to take soundings close to El Morro. *Culloden*'s master went 'so nigh that I heard the sentinels speak'. He got his first sounding three-quarters of a mile from shore and was at three and a half fathoms when he heard the sentries and turned back. The master of the

Cambridge, too, went close inshore, where he found four fathoms depth and ten fathoms about a ship's length away. *Marlborough*'s boat sounded in a long line half a mile out. Unfortunately, and crucially, the night was so dark that none of them could judge how high the castle was above them and whether elevated guns could damage it.

Willing as he was to try the effect of ships' guns on the castle, Hervey used his report to Albemarle, and especially his letter to Pocock, to recommend an attack on the town from the western side of the harbour in preference to an attack on the fort. According to him, General Eliott and the engineers with him had reached the same conclusion from their own survey that morning. Keppel's report to Pocock also indicates that someone had suggested changing the point of attack to the western side of the harbour: 'The observations made by the gentlemen of the army this day occasions Lord Albemarle to incline to an alteration in the operation, and therefore [he] wishes you to delay sending the marines hither, as it may be they will be better employed on the western side. . .'.

Edward Fisher's mezzotint of George Keppel, 3rd Earl of Albemarle after Joshua Reynolds's painting.

Lieutenant General George Keppel, third Earl of Albemarle, was a young man in his prime, but unfortunately he was vastly less experienced than his even younger subordinates. At thirty-eight he had no distinguished military record and had never held a major military command, but he had been a member of the household of the king's favourite uncle and military advisor since he was sixteen. As a very young man he had served on the Duke of Cumberland's staff at Culloden and Fontenoy, but had left his role as Lord of the Bedchamber to the Duke to seize his first opportunity of leadership. With one younger brother, William, as a divisional major-general, and another, the precocious Augustus, second in command of the naval forces, the Earl had powerful support, but he himself was out of his depth and insecure.

This was far from true of his subordinates. Second in command was Lieutenant General George Augustus Eliott, later famous for his defence of Gibraltar but already with a high military reputation. The quartermaster general was Colonel Guy Carleton, who had been chosen by Wolfe to be quartermaster general at Quebec and had done well commanding a brigade at Belle Isle. Richard Howe's younger brother William had commanded Wolfe's light infantry at Quebec. Most of the troops at Havana were experienced and some were first class, especially the seasoned veterans from America. But the veterans displeased Albemarle at first sight. He wrote a remarkable account of his first impressions to General Sir Jeffrey Amherst, the commanding officer in America:

> Your officers are all generals, with a thorough contempt for everybody that has not served under Mr. Wolfe; they either suffer, or cannot prevent, the soldiers doing what they please, which is the cause of the great loss by sickness and the numbers falling down daily. I dare not find fault yet; I am greatly afraid they will oblige me to tell them my mind when we are better acquainted. They have conquered in a few days the strongest country you ever saw, in the American [way] – running or with the Indian hoop. That manner of fighting will not always succeed, and I dread their meeting of troops that will stand their ground. They are certainly brave and will be cut to pieces.

Albemarle saw it as his mission to restore Cumberland-style discipline and method to this insubordinate, overconfident, rum-swilling rabble. The remark that 'all your officers are generals' suggests that Albemarle did not altogether welcome advice from subordinates. If he was advised that a sudden amphibious assault on the town with the troops running and whooping might be a good idea, he did not welcome it with open arms.

On 11 June, Guy Carleton seized 'the Spanish redoubt', the battery the enemy had been fortifying on the Cabaña Heights. Spanish possession of this battery had threatened any attack on the Morro; now Albemarle controlled the heights that commanded the castle, the harbour and the city. He had also just discovered that the parapets of the Morro were thin and made of masonry. He settled down to batter it methodically.

On 13 June construction began on two batteries. One was as close to the Morro as the concealing woods allowed – only 190 yards from it. The other was a mortar battery designed to drive the Spanish ships further away – their random volleys of grapeshot into the woods were causing casualties and delays.

For the first few days rain was a nuisance, turning the tracks to mud. Working parties from the ships laboured flat out, cutting roads and hauling cannon up them. The surface of the ground where the batteries were supposed to be dug in proved little better than bare rock, and there was no soil to fill sandbags to protect guns. Instead, some use was made of thorny bush and wooden fascines. Before leaving Martinique, Albemarle had thoughtfully arranged the purchase of several hundred slaves: 'These poor fellows had arrived the day before, and proved extremely useful in carrying ammunition to the several batteries.' But hacking through the woods proved slow and thirsty work, and thirst soon proved to be the biggest problem – the extreme humidity made labour in heat much, much harder, and caused even greater thirst.

The last rain fell on 16 June. Within a week Keppel wrote:

Since the rains have ceased, the water in the Coximar is become so brackish that it is not fit for use, and there being no water in any part where the army are carrying on their works or near any of their encampments, they depend entirely upon the fleet for that article, which the Admiral keeps constantly supplying them with from the Chorera, that being the only water that is tolerable good . . .

Even the puddles on the rocks from which men had been drinking dried up. The seamen replenished their supply by rowing through the mosquito-infested mangrove swamps to the watering place on the more dependable Chorera, but the troops camped on the swampy low ground around Guanabacoa sickened at an alarming rate and their ability to collect supplies diminished. It was a dangerous business anyway, since parties of enemy cavalry roamed the open ground. Foraging in the woods and other forms of straggling to which seamen were addicted proved even more risky. Three Dragons were captured near the river while straggling in this way. Two days later Keppel wrote to Pocock, 'I believe there has not been less than sixty or seventy people caught by the hunters, and they murder many of them and leave them in the woods mangled to pieces.'

Nevertheless, on 20 June the mortar opened fire with one shell every three minutes directed at the fort, while further mortar positions were constructed. The battery near the limekiln forced the Spanish ships to fall back. A Spanish sortie of 29 June intended to destroy this and recapture the Cabaña Heights was repulsed with interest, and the next day the Grand Battery was ready to open fire. Lord Albemarle decided that the simultaneous naval operation against El Morro should go ahead, and Captain Hervey was selected to lead it.

16

The Twelfth Article of War

10. *Every flag officer, captain and commander in the fleet, who, upon signal or order of fight, or sight of any ship or ships which it may be his duty to engage, or who, upon likelihood of engagement, shall not make the necessary preparations for fight, and shall not in his own person, and according to his place, encourage the inferior officers and men to fight courageously, shall suffer death, or such other punishment, as from the nature and degree of the offence a court martial shall deem him to deserve; and if any person in the fleet shall treacherously or cowardly yield or cry for quarter, every person so offending, and being convicted thereof by the sentence of a court martial, shall suffer death.*

11. Every person in the fleet, who shall not duly observe the orders of the admiral, flag officer, commander of any squadron or division, or other his superior officer, for assailing, joining battle with, or making defense against any fleet, squadron, or ship, or shall not obey the orders of his superior officer as aforesaid in the time of action, to the best of his power, or shall not use all possible endeavours to put the same effectually into execution, every person so offending, and being convicted thereof by the sentence of the court martial, shall suffer death, or such other punishment, as from the nature and degree of the offence a court martial shall deem him to deserve.

12. Every person in the fleet, who through cowardice, negligence, or disaffection, shall in time of action withdraw or keep back, or not come into the fight or engagement, or shall not do his utmost to take or destroy every ship which it shall be his duty to engage, and to assist and relieve all and every of His Majesty's ships, or those of his allies, which it shall be his duty to assist and relieve, every such person so offending, and being convicted thereof by the sentence of a court martial, shall suffer death.

Articles of War, 1757

The Articles of War were the rules by which seamen lived. At least once a month the captain read them to the assembled ship's company. Regulations stated that they must also be 'constantly hung up & Affixed in the most publick place of the ship, & that the same are at all times accessible to the Inferior Officers & Seamen on board'. The articles consisted of an apparently random list of warnings and strictures, often repetitious, with crimes very vaguely defined. They had been updated twice recently, in 1749 and again in 1757. The words 'shall be punished by death' recurred frequently, punctuating the paragraphs read out by the captain. Almost as frequently, however, there was a qualification – 'or such other punishment . . .' – which gave scope for exoneration.

The Articles applied to men and officers alike. Few crimes carried a mandatory death sentence. Those that did were intriguing with the enemy, handing a ship to the enemy, setting fire to a ship or magazine, using a weapon against a superior while he was on duty, buggery, murder, and failing through cowardice or carelessness to fight and pursue the enemy or help friends. Cowardice had only become a capital offence in 1749 when Anson had altered the twelfth article so that 'or such other punishment' was removed, leaving death as the only sanction. Once Hervey and the other captains had accepted their orders to make the attack, the Articles of War came into play.

Everybody knew that a naval attack on the Morro was potentially a suicidal operation, and the decision to attempt the attack was taken after much hesitation and discussion. On 22 June Keppel wrote to Pocock that 'I stated all yours and my doubts to Captain Hervey, who is fond of the project, and he proposed by way of clearing the matter to proceed with a fresh breeze in the *Dragon*, take the soundings and survey the batteries without anchoring, and if he finds the ships' guns likely to do service, he will make his report . . .' There is no evidence that *Dragon* made this final check before Keppel delivered his order to Hervey on 26 June:

> Whereas it is judged necessary to make an attack upon the Moro Castle by Sea at the same time that the King's Army open their Batteries by Land against it;

You are hereby required and directed to prepare the Ship you command accordingly, to proceed upon this Service; taking also under your direction his Majesty's Ships *Cambridge* and *Marlborough*, whose Captains have directions to obey all Orders relative to this Service, that you think proper to give them: You will very particularly consider in placing the Ships under you Command, that the Line of their fire be not liable to interrupt the Works and Batteries of the Kings Troops, and as it is intended the *Sterling Castle* shou'd proceed just before you, and fire her Guns without Anchoring, to take off the fire of the Castle, you will give the Captain of her such information and directions, as may enable him to answer the purpose intended by it: The remaining Execution of this attack must be left to your Prudence and Judgement as Circumstances shall at this time require.

This would be a true test of courage. Hervey had taken on forts many times and whould have had a shrewd idea of the odds. *Dragon* had silenced the fort at Coximar with ease, and he may have hoped that El Morro's gunnery would prove equally harmless and wild. It was as yet untested, although with so many naval ships in Havana harbour it was likely that the guns would be manned by naval gunners. Hervey also knew that Captain Luis de Velasco was in command, an officer he had met and respected.

Attacking forts was particularly dangerous for ships because the fort's guns could be exactly aimed, whereas a ship's rose and fell on the wave. The fort's gunners were defended by stone rather than wood, and they could lob explosive shells at the ships, whereas to have any effect on the walls the ships had to come within range of grapeshot. This made it exceptionally dangerous to be on the routinely vulnerable quarterdeck because the guns could fire downwards on to it, so that the parapets offered no protection against them, while musketeers and riflemen hidden behind from stone embrasures could pick off officers at leisure.

To take on what was reputedly the strongest fortress in the Caribbean was an act of courage, bravado or foolhardiness, depending on how you looked at it. What Hervey had undertaken was beyond the call of duty. Considered dispassionately, there was a strong possibility that it would be not only an act of self-sacrifice, but an ineffectual one. Reconnaissance of the angle of fire between castle and ship was obviously flawed and inadequate. Hervey volunteered for the mission, but his subordinates might very reasonably have thought that he had misjudged the situation or that his ambitious gallantry was endangering the crews of the four ships he carried with him.

The plan he devised was designed to spread and minimise the risk. *Stirling Castle* was to sail ahead, leading *Cambridge, Dragon* and *Marlborough* in. She would draw the fire of the fort during the approach phase and then withdraw. This should allow the other ships to get into position and open fire before they received much damage. The old and expendable three-decker *Cambridge* would anchor in the most exposed place opposite the curtain, where eight of the Morro's 24-pounders could scour her decks from above. *Dragon*, behind her, would take on the projecting bastion, while *Marlborough*, further back, provided supporting fire. *Cambridge* could return fire with thirteen 32-pounders, thirteen 18-pounders and the 9-pounders on her upper deck and quarterdeck. *Dragon*, though only a two-decker, could bring to bear one more gun of each type. *Marlborough* was a venerable three-decker of 1706 vintage now mounting only sixty-eight guns.

Hervey's own orders were reassuringly optimistic. They convey the hope that if Spanish morale was shaky, the ships might be able to end the siege at a stroke. The series of signals that he devised for the operation allowed for various contingencies, including a landing to storm the fort under the fire of the ships: 'That we do visibly affect the fort', 'That El Morro slackens in her fire', 'That the works which are towards us seem to be abandoned', 'That I am of opinion they have deserted the upper works of the fort', 'That I am going to land men'. He was, however, sensible enough also to be able to tell Keppel 'If any captain has the misfortune of being disabled from carrying on his command' and to request boats to tow or provide anchors for damaged ships. His orders to Captain James Campbell of *Stirling Castle*, as her first lieutenant remembered them, 'were to keep a cables length ahead of the *Cambridge*, and when we open'd a white building or convent, for to haul off'.

Captain Campbell sought assurance that the attack would only take place if there was a fresh breeze to get the ships in and out again. For this reason, when clearing his ship for action after he and the lieutenants and master read their orders, he left his studding sail booms ashore.

The scene on the evening of 30 June with Dragon, Cambridge *and* Marlborough (nearest), *lying to with their heads to the northward, to allow* Stirling Castle *to get to the westward of them. Detail of James Mason's engraving.*

At four in the afternoon on 30 June *Dragon* weighed anchor and sailed towards El Morro, giving orders to *Cambridge, Marlborough* and *Stirling Castle* to stay close but astern. Around midnight, when the castle was four or five miles south, they brought to for the night. They moved forward again at four the next morning. According to *Dragon*'s log the breeze was moderate, although in *Namur* they recorded 'light winds'. The lack of breeze made the attack more dangerous. If it fell away entirely they might be immobilised in front of the castle.

In the *Stirling Castle* second lieutenant John Barrow had the morning watch. She was then third of the four ships although her proper station was at the front. Barrow had the topsails set in imitation of the *Dragon*. At five, Captain Campbell came on board. *Dragon* hoisted topgallants. Barrow informed Campbell and they followed suit. Reassured by the lack of wind, Campbell was confident the attack would be called off. According to Barrow, he 'told us on the quarterdeck that morning that Commodore Keppel told him we were not to go in, except with a fresh breeze of wind'. However, Hervey's orders said nothing about the wind.

Half an hour later, acting fourth lieutenant Arthur Phillip came on board. He was twenty-three, the son of a German immigrant language teacher who had gone to sea as an apprentice. (In later life he would be the first governor of New South Wales.) To his surprise he saw that his ship was about a mile behind the *Dragon*, that *Marlborough* was about to pass them and that it would be difficult to catch up. He asked the master, William Holman, why they were not using the mainsail and everything else they could set. Holman replied that Campbell had told him to wait for Hervey's signal for line of battle before trying to overtake to get into their station in it. Phillip said that if they did not make a move now, they wouldn't be able to reach their station later. The captain announced that he was waiting for Hervey's signal since, given the meagre wind, 'he did not know whether his ship would be wanted'.

Soon after that the breeze strengthened a little. The sun was already strong, the water bright blue, the beach white, the castle gleaming white against the green forest – a blissful tropical morning. Hervey remarked to Archibald Howison that he was surprised the *Stirling Castle* was not making more sail. Howison backed the mizen topsail and lowered the topgallant sails to let her come up. She showed no sign of hurry, though, and Howison said, 'If we do not get on we shall lose the breeze.' Hervey put out a signal for the *Stirling Castle*. Instead of making more sail, Campbell climbed into his barge to come across. Hervey sent Lieutenant Dandy Kidd to meet him. 'I told him Captain

Hervey was surpriz'd that he had not set more sails and desired he would set steering sails'. He told Campbell Hervey 'did not want him on board, but wanted his ship in his station'. Campbell replied that 'he would have set steering sails but had no yards and no man was more desirous of getting into station than he was'.

Campbell rowed back to his ship and Hervey made the signal to form line of battle. Phillip was on the forecastle of *Stirling Castle* watching for it and reported it immediately. Campbell and his first lieutenant were now in the midst of an angry altercation about how and why the steering sails had been left ashore. *Stirling Castle*, with loose sheathing and her bottom covered with weeds, towing boats, and with the current now working strongly against her, was only making two knots, and could not keep up with the other ships, never mind overtake them.

When *Dragon* was about a mile from El Morro, Captain William Goostrey of the *Cambridge* asked Hervey 'whether he shou'd proceed on as the *Stirling Castle* was so far astern'. Goostrey was a young man in his third year as a post captain. Hervey told him to go ahead, 'and not to lose a moment's time' – they were already behind schedule. The army had opened its bombardment without them. More importantly, for the best chance of damaging the Spanish guns they needed to be fighting at high water, and the tide was already beginning to ebb.

The fort began to fire ranging shots at the *Dragon* as she furled her maintopsail and brought to in order to let *Cambridge* go past. Seeing that *Stirling Castle* still had her mainsail and spritsail furled, Hervey again signalled to her to make more sail. The ships glided forward painfully slowly as the fort's guns found their range and made holes in the sails. *Stirling Castle* should have been protecting them from this. Hervey was furious.

At fifteen minutes past nine Goostrey anchored *Cambridge* a cable's length from the shore and her guns began to fire. After a very short time *Dragon*'s officers saw her hoist the English ensign in the mizentopmast shrouds that signalled her captain was disabled. *Dragon* anchored twenty minutes later in four and a half fathoms of water about a cable's length from the shore. In *Stirling Castle* lieutenants Phillip, Barrow and the master 'observed a convenient place for anchoring between *Dragon* and *Cambridge*' and proposed asking Hervey if they might join the attack. Campbell sent Phillip to ask Hervey what he wanted *Stirling Castle* to do. When he came aboard *Dragon* he was dismissed coldly with the curt response: 'Since your Captain wou'd not lead the *Cambridge* he might lay off to the Northward'.

The forecastlemen let the cable run out, then dropped the best bower. In order to steady *Dragon* still further for accurate gunnery, Hervey sent a boat to drop a kedge anchor to the north. The sun beat down, the seamen stripped to the waist and finally got the order to fire.

Cambridge, Dragon *and* Marlborough *attack the Morro. Captain Lindsey is going on board* Cambridge. *The very top of the castle can just be seen top left through the dense smoke. Detail of Peter Canot's engraving.*

The noise was immense – the Spanish fire was far more energetic and accurate than Hervey had hoped. With so little wind the thick smoke cleared slowly and Hervey could see very little. The tide ebbed and with a sudden shudder *Dragon* touched bottom 'rather abaft the main chains'. They cut the best bower anchor cable to heave on the other, but it was too late – they were immobilised in front of the castle and in deep trouble.

Hervey scribbled a pencil note to Keppel on the back of a set of signals:

> Sir, I have the misfortune to be aground. Pray send a frigate to drop a bower off and send one end of the cable on board here. We luckily are in a good line for our fire at the fort, but the smoke is so great and that makes it impossible to see the effect we have had, or likely to have; nor can we tell when the army will advance. Three shells fell very near us; we cannot tell our damage. Often duller & Ever Yours, A. Hervey

From his distant vantage point off the mouth of the Coximar, Keppel had seen *Cambridge*'s jack at the mizen and had sent the ever dependable Captain John Lindsay in a boat to take command of the ship in Goostrey's place. The next boat to *Dragon* brought a lieutenant from *Cambridge* who scrambled aboard with a graphic account of conditions in his ship. Shouting over the gunfire, he explained that Captain Goostrey and several others were dead, many were wounded, and a number of guns were already dismounted. A shell had just scored a direct hit, exploding in the waist with terrible carnage.

As they spoke, a shot scattered a crew of old Revenges. An oak splinter embedded itself in John Bailey's leg, and his old friend William Buchanan was knocked flying by another as the ball that shattered the wood whizzed across the deck and killed midshipman James Fellows. As the strengthening breeze cleared the smoke, it became obvious that the ships were too low down to reach the guns on the parapet.

Both *Cambridge* and *Dragon* were suffering terribly. Their own guns were having no effect and the fort was smashing them to pieces. Hervey sent the officer on to Keppel with a second note.

> Sir, I have but just time to send the lieutenant of the Cambridge to you with this report and to desire your orders about it. I am unluckily aground, but my guns bear. I cannot perceive their fire to slacken; I hope the shells from the shore will silence them a little. I am afraid they

are too high to do the execution we wished. I have many men out of combat now, and officers wounded; my mast and rigging much cut and only one anchor. I shall stay here as long as I can and wait your orders. *Dragon*, 1 July, 20 minutes past eleven a.m.

Hervey hoisted a blue pendant on the mizen topmast to request a longboat with anchors and hawsers. In *Stirling Castle* Campbell saw his signal and, according to the master, his only response was to remark that if they went to help 'the shot flew very thick and that he stood a bad chance'.

Another boat came alongside the commodore bringing John Lindsay of the *Trent* with Keppel's instructions to take command of the *Cambridge*. Hervey ordered him first to tell Campbell to 'drop an Anchor, two Cables length without the *Dragon*'s Buoy and a little to the Westward to haul the *Dragon* off as she was then on shore'.

Lindsay met Campbell in his barge and gave him his orders, but Campbell wanted them in writing. 'I told him I wish'd he wou'd not insist upon it for I was in haste at that time to go on board and take command of the *Cambridge*, as Captain Goostrey was kill'd.' Lindsay was about to pull away, but Campbell insisted on writing down his orders. He lay on his oars and 'took out his pocket book and wrote them down as I repeated them to him'. Campbell remarked that 'as it blew pretty fresh he wou'd have some difficulty getting the end of the cable on board the *Dragon*'. Lindsay suggested getting a hawser – a thick towing rope – on board first. Campbell then asked 'if Captain Hervey had order'd that he shou'd drop one of his Bower anchors'. Lindsay had already asked for a bower, but recalled that Hervey had not actually specified what anchor and 'told him that he had not mentioned particularly what anchor, but that I imagined it was his intention he shou'd let go his Bower.' He was becoming increasingly irritated with the unnecessary delay that was stopping him getting to the *Cambridge*.

Campbell now said he had a stream anchor in a boat alongside, and would get the cable into another, and send them to haul the *Dragon* off, but Lindsay replied that it was Captain Hervey's orders he should drop the anchor from the ship. Campbell retorted that he would need to be clear for firing. Lindsay said he was not to fire. As Campbell

pulled for the *Stirling Castle*, Lindsay warned him to get ready to attack
the Morro, as he believed Hervey wanted him to anchor ahead of the
Cambridge, Campbell remarked that in that case he couldn't drop the
anchor. Lindsay, furious by now, told him to drop the anchor first –
'Immediately on your getting on board to steer hard a weather and
bear up for the *Dragon*'. Telling his coxwain to remember what had
been said, Lindsay rowed back to *Dragon* and reported to Hervey that
Campbell 'made several difficultys in regard to dropping the Anchor'.

Hervey decided the Dragons had better not rely on Campbell.
They loaded the stream anchor, which was the only one they had left
now, into the longboat, rowed off under fire, and dropped it some
distance to the north. The enemy fire continued 'very quick and
heavy'. By now first lieutenant John Henderson and Lieutenant
Samber's younger brother John were dead, and Dandy Kidd and
Constantine Phipps were both wounded, though Phipps was not
badly hurt. They needed every man they had and bitterly regretted the
absence of the marines serving ashore. Minimal crews manned the
guns while they tried desperately to get the ship afloat – they attached
a hawser to the capstan and the men 'hove a great strain' but the ship
would not move. Others stove barrels of water, wine and spirits abaft,
where they were aground, while more men unloaded stores into
flatboats. Meanwhile shot splashed around them.

Into this maelstrom rowed the frigate *Echo*'s bargemen carrying
Dragon's former acting captain John Lendrick. He 'came to *Dragon*
with orders from Keppel to send on board *Cambridge* and if he found
her in so much trouble and suffering as not to perform, to order her to
cut and get out'. Hervey did not need to send a messenger to know
that *Cambridge* needed to withdraw and sent an officer to order
Lindsay to cut and get out as quickly as possible. He told Lendrick
Dragon was aground and had been for some time and asked the
Ulsterman to lay an anchor for *Dragon* to heave off by. Seeing that
Stirling Castle was at last bearing down, Hervey then told Lendrick to
tell Campbell to go to the assistance of the *Cambridge*, since the *Echo*
was too light for the job.

While Hervey and Lendrick were talking, Captain Edward Jekyll of
the *Rippon* was cruising on the battlefield in one of his boats. Nearing

Stirling Castle 'out of mere curiosity', he noted that they were getting
hawsers into boats. He sailed to Keppel to tell him that *Dragon* was
aground and returned an hour later with orders to tell Campbell to
drop a bower anchor and run a cable on board *Dragon*. They were still
busy with the boats. Jekyll shouted the message to Campbell personally in the larboard gangway. Campbell said he couldn't do it without
going aground himself, but Jekyll pointed out that *Echo* had come and
gone. Campbell said hawsers and a stream cable should be sufficient.

Commodore Keppel commanded the operation from the Orford, *shown in this
detail of James Mason's engraving, with men aloft watching for signals.
Lieutenant Philip Orsbridge, who made the drawings for this set of twelve
prints, belonged to the* Orford.

Lendrick was on board *Echo* by now, got her under way towards *Stirling Castle*, ordered the longboat hoisted out, and was paying out the stream cable to put upon the bower cables when *Stirling Castle* came within hail. Lendrick shouted through his trumpet, 'Captain Campbell, sir, I have been on board Captain Hervey by the Commodore's orders, who has order'd the *Cambridge* to cut, and get out. She has lost her Captain, and a great number of her Men. The Ship is cut to pieces. You must go to her assistance either by taking her in tow or covering of her or she must perish inevitably.' Someone – he assumed it was Campbell – shouted back that they had nothing to take her in tow with because all their hawsers were in the flatboats. 'Warmed a little with the answer from the apparent distress of the *Cambridge*, with a rather more Elevated tone of Voice', Lendrick replied: 'Captain Campbell, sir, this is not a time to make Difficultys. If you don't assist the *Cambridge* she must perish.' He waited for an answer but got none, though the ship was now closer. He took up the trumpet again and said, 'For God's sake, Captain Campbell, make sail to the *Cambridge*'s assistance or she must perish.'

The current had carried *Cambridge* away from El Morro, but in drifting to leeward she was now exposed to fire from the Punta fort at the opposite side of the harbour mouth and from the town. *Stirling Castle* cast off the boats she had astern and continued under the same sail – top and topgallants – towards El Morro, firing her lower-deck guns at long range. Lendrick watched her, but she made no apparent attempt to tow *Cambridge* or to get in her wake to protect her.

Lieutenant Phillip, who was commanding the cutter towing the longboat and stream anchor and one flatboat towing another flat containing hawsers for *Dragon*, emerged from *Stirling Castle*'s stern as Cambell gave the order to go down to the *Cambridge* and the master ordered the topsail dropped.

As *Stirling Castle* approached the danger area, her master noted that 'at almost every shot that went over us Captain Campbell bobb'd, and sometimes fell down upon his hands and knees'. Campbell sent John Buchannan, one of the midshipmen, off the quarterdeck 'to ask the lower deck why they did not fire brisker'. Buchannan said afterwards that 'when I came upon deck again I observed Captain

Campbell leaning his hands upon his knees, under the Breastwork or Barricado. On seeing me he drew out and about two or three feet from the side'.

Cambridge's first lieutenant 'was just come from cutting the head cable' when he saw the *Stirling Castle* 'close upon the weather quarter, banging up alongside'. *Cambridge* was now beyond point blank range of the Morro. 'They hailed and said they were come to take us in tow. As they were to windward and took the wind from us I desir'd her to get out of our way, that we wanted no assistance from them.' He noted with disgust that *Stirling Castle* had steered so that *Cambridge* stood between her and the Morro and as they slanted away *Cambridge* protected *Stirling Castle* from the Punta fort.

Five or six minutes after clearing *Cambridge*, said *Stirling Castle*'s master, 'we went out of range of the enemy's shot, then Captain Campbell said to me with a smiling countenance, "I will be damned if my knees are not tired with stooping"'. They made sail to the northward, turned to windward and dropped anchor.

Dragon and *Marlborough* were now alone in front of the castle, with *Dragon* taking most of the fire. There was now a good breeze to clear the smoke so it must have been obvious to the triumphant Spanish gunners that the British commodore could not move. 'Still engaging the Moro Castle with a constant fire, but we found their Cannon very heavy and their shells fell very near us; we heaving with both capstans', reported the ship's log. They had lightened her as much as they could without throwing the guns overboard, which in un-known shallow water might have done more harm than good, since ships had been known to hole themselves on their own abandoned artillery.

Between them, Lendrick and Phillip had placed a bower anchor where *Dragon* could use it to heave off. *Dragon* had a double capstan, and two hundred men or more were now pushing with all their strength to make the ship respond to the strain on the anchor rope. After a quarter of an hour of constant effort, suddenly 'we felt the ship to float'. There must have been the most enormous cheer and a burst of urgent orders and activity as sails were set to get the ship out. *Dragon* pulled out slowly, firing as she went to cover the more badly damaged *Cambridge*, which began to move away just ahead of them.

Then they were clear and out of range. The steady counter-battery fire continued between the fort and the shore batteries, but on the ship it was a sunny tropical afternoon again. They counted the dead and the maimed and assessed the ship's injuries. The first lieutenant, two midshipmen, twelve seamen and one marine were dead. Two lieutenants and twenty-nine men were wounded, 'the ship much shattered, main and foremasts, main and foretopmast and foreyard much wounded, much rigging cut'. *Cambridge* had fared far worse with twenty-three dead, including her captain, master and one lieutenant, and ninety-five wounded. *Marlborough* and *Stirling Castle* had each lost two killed and eight wounded. Their fire had done practically no damage to the fort.

Dragon and *Marlborough* sailed first to report to Keppel off Coximar. Hervey was still boiling with rage over Campbell's behaviour. Keppel tried to persuade him to be merciful, but after speaking to *Stirling Castle*'s officers, he realised that if he didn't make an issue of it, they would – she had not been a happy ship for some time and there was a history of complaint and counter-complaint aboard her.

Hervey wrote a letter to Pocock and Pocock ordered a court martial. Hervey's cold fury was unmistakable. He must have felt that Campbell was far more culpable under the twelfth article than Admiral Byng had ever been. Nevertheless, he left a loophole for mercy by citing also the tenth and eleventh articles of war.

The court met in August when the fighting was over. The testimony shows that *Stirling Castle*'s officers were divided, but that Lindsay and Lendrick felt at least as strongly as Hervey that Campbell was guilty of cowardice. Although Campbell had the faintest of excuses in the state of the wind, the cumulative evidence against him was irresistible. The most vindictive evidence of personal cowardice came from his own master and midshipman, who both evidently despised their captain and mocked his ducking and diving when the balls flew over at long range.

Campbell escaped with his life, but lost his honour. The court of twelve captains and the president, John Barker, Keppel's second in command, found him guilty under the tenth and eleventh articles. Pretending that his guilt under the fatal twelfth was unproven, they dismissed him from the service.

If Campbell had behaved properly, the attack would have begun earlier and *Cambridge* would not have been damaged before she opened fire. An earlier attack meant higher water and with a better angle of fire it is possible that *Cambridge* and *Dragon* might have damaged El Morro. It is unlikely, however, that they would have done much more damage. Campbell's real crime was that his cowardice emperilled the men on the other ships. The court martial made it plain that there was no room in the Royal Navy for such selfish reluctance to engage, whatever the circumstances.

17

The Exhaling Surface of the Earth

At least one army officer enjoyed a moment of *schadenfreude* at the discomfiture of Captain Hervey and the navy's supposed belief that 'singly they were equal to the undertaking' of reducing the fort. The Earl of Albemarle tactfully sent Hervey a note of thanks, saying that by drawing the fort's fire he had contributed greatly in enabling the army's guns to obtain dominance on their front. Certainly, on that single day the soldiers silenced the opposing guns and destroyed the fragile parapets.

Lobsterly smugness survived less than forty-eight hours, however. After two weeks of hot, dry weather and two days' bombardment, the 'grand battery' of eight guns and two mortars caught fire and was utterly destroyed. 'No rain having fallen for the last fourteen days, the intense heat and unremitting cannonade had dried the fascines to such a degree, that the utmost efforts could not prevent the flames from spreading', wrote Thomas Mante, a marine officer acting as an engineer at Havana. 'The conflagration continued with such violence, as to insinuate itself where neither water could follow to extinguish, or earth to stifle it. The battery was almost wholly consumed. The labour of six hundred men for seventeen days, was almost destroyed in a few hours'.

The Spaniards repaired their works, moved their guns to pinpoint the battery and made it impossible to repair it.

> The Spaniards had two guns only left on the polygon of the attack; all the rest were demolished. To compensate the want of them, they now placed some men upon their ramparts, and kept a hot fire upon the English, who, by cutting down the coppice wood, to unmask their

batteries, found themselves without any cover for the purpose of repairing that which had been burned. But what was still more mortifying, they had no materials for that work.

Spanish fire from the ships, floating batteries, La Punta and the town proved a constant menace. If it had not been for the fact that the Cabaña forced the Spanish to fire high, British engineers reckoned their position would have been untenable. It was a bitter blow:

> This stroke was felt the more severely, as the other hardships of the siege were become, by this time, almost insupportable: Sickness and severe labour had reduced the army to almost half its number. Five thousand soldiers, and three thousand seamen were laid up with various distempers. A want of fresh provisions exasperated the evil, and retarded their recovery. The deficiency of water was, of all their grievances, the most intolerable, and extremely aggravated all the rest of their sufferings. The great distance they were obliged to go to procure a scanty supply of water, was alone sufficient to exhaust all their strength, but joined to the anguish of a dreadful thirst, put an end to their wretched existence.

Some of the soldiers had been ill before they reached Cuba, but in the first half of July the sickness spread alarmingly, although as yet few people died. At first the disaster was attributed to the heat and hard work, although it was soon apparent that the men up on the rock attacking El Morro were suffering less than the relatively idle troops near Guanabacoa and on the west side of the harbour. They put this down to the healthier air and drier conditions on the heights, though really the absence of mosquitoes was the main factor. The seamen, as usual, were healthier than the troops, but the marines and those seamen who came ashore and worked hard under the burning sun soon suffered. At Martinique Captain Lucius O'Bryen had kept the tars on shore duty out of the sun during the heat of the day, but here, with time pressing, the men paid less attention to their own wellbeing.

By 17 July the sickness among the soldiers was so severe that Eliott at Guanabacoa had only 400 of his original 2,500 men fit and had to withdraw. Any possibility of obtaining fresh provisions went with them. Hard work in the sun combined with a scarcity of bad water and the woollen uniforms designed for cooler climates that the soldiers and marines had to wear. The very high humidity made their thirst far worse and yet each night the heavy dew soaked them. A private soldier complained that 'The fatigues on shore were excessive. The bad water brought on disorders that were mortal. You could see the men's tongues hanging out like a mad dog's; a dollar was frequently given for a quart of water', and the commander of the artillery lamented that 'The scanty supply of water exhausted their strength, and joined to the anguish of dreadful thirst, put an end to the existence of many. Five thousand soldiers and three thousand sailors were laid up with various distempers.'

The effects were appalling. An army major wrote home:

> I think myself extremely happy in being among the number of the living, considering the deplorable condition we are now in. You will hardly believe me when I tell you that I have only 33 of my company alive, out of 100 which I landed. Our regiment has lost 8 officers and 500 men. They mostly died of fluxes and intermitting fevers, the general diseases here. The other regiments have lost in proportion. We are now very sickly, when out of 17 battalions here we cannot muster 600 men fit for duty. The appearance of the country is most beautiful; yet a man's life in it is extremely uncertain, as many are in health one morning, and dead before the next.

The 'fluxes' that many suffered – forms of dysentery – were attributable to the bad water. All those who described the illnesses experienced at Havana spoke of fluxes, which were known to be prevalent in the West Indies. David Dundas, aid to the ailing General Eliott, recalled that 'flux, fever and ague were the prevailing disorders, and immediate despondency and apprehension when taken ill were most common and sure signs of a speedy dissolution'. 'Ague' was malarial fever with paroxysms, consisting of a cold, a hot and a sweating stage. All fevers were imprecisely described, chiefly because 'Fevers . . . seldom appear in any two instances exactly alike', as an army medic wrote some years later. The other debilitating illness, typhus, borne by body lice and common in camps, gaols and naval press tenders, had apparently been present among the troops before they reached Cuba.

> The skin acquires a dry and parched feel, the tongue becomes hard and furred, and the secretion of saliva as it were suspended. The confusion of head and tendency to stupor, increase, accompanied with more or less delirium which, being at first transient, becomes gradually more continued. The state of the bowels and urine is irregular, but as the disease proceeds, diarrhoea comes on. Symptoms of putrescency now make their appearance, consisting in small livid spots, like flea-bites, dispersed over the skin. The stupor of the head becomes more permanent; great anxiety prevails about the precordia, and frequent sighing takes place; haemorrhage also arises from different parts, especially from the gums and intestines, being in the latter case conjoined with diarrhoea; and hiccup soon succeeds, to terminate in death.

Doctors blamed foul air for transmitting disease, but in order to keep the air sweet the Royal Navy was obsessed with cleaning decks and clothes. Experience brought awareness of 'filthiness being a chief source of infection and cleanliness an excellent preservative'. Consequently, outbreaks on board ship tended only to occur when ships entertained large numbers of newly-pressed men of poor quality, foreign prisoners or poor soldiers.

Tropical fevers remained a mystery – the mosquito had not yet been identified as the villainous agent, although both it and the swamps in which it bred were suspected. However, as with typhus, foul air – marsh miasma, 'the exhaling surface of the earth', rather than insects was usually blamed. The term 'Yellow Fever' had first been used in 1750, but the disease was still better known as the 'Black Vomit', a name invented in 1729. There was confusion between the black vomit (consisting of blood discoloured by gastric juice) of yellow fever and the dark bilious vomit of the bilious remittent varieties of malaria. Malaria, derived from parasites introduced by the *Anopheles* mosquitoes that luxuriated in the mangrove swamps around Havana, could kill quickly or slowly. People died suddenly of the acute fever in the second phase or equally suddenly from a build-up of parasites in the third phase. They might also waste away through repeated, exhausting attacks that killed them slowly but surely months later.

Yellow fever was spread by a different kind of mosquito, *Aedes aegypti*, which bred in clean water – cisterns and water butts were favourite locations. This mosquito, which has the courtesy to bite humans only during daylight hours, introduces the viruses resulting in both yellow fever and dengue fever. People with the yellow fever virus either succumbed to its vomiting, haemorrhaging, putrescence and coma within a fortnight or they recovered and became immune thereafter.

There may have been cases of yellow fever at Havana, but the yellow element is absent from the brief lists of ailments which stress 'intermitting' or 'remitting' fevers. The recurrence suggests either malaria or dengue fever, which produced painful relapses that could keep victims down for months. In any case the surgeons had difficulty distinguishing one form of fever from another. Mante, the marine turned engineer and then historian, gave a graphic account of the hideous consequences:

> A great number fell victims to a putrid fever. From the appearance of perfect health, three or four short hours robbed them of existence. Many there were who endured a loathesome disease for days, nay, weeks together, living in a state of putrefaction, their bodies full of vermin, and almost eaten away before the spark of life was extinguished. The carrion crows of the country kept constantly hovering over the graves, which rather hid than buried the dead, and frequently scratched away the scanty earth, leaving in every mangled corpse a spectacle of unspeakable loathsomeness and terror to those who, by being engaged in the same enterprise, were exposed to the same fate. Hundreds of carcases were seen floating in the ocean.

To face this horror, *Dragon* had a surgeon, John Watt, and two mates, John Wills from Somerset and John Wallace. Watt and Wallace have names that suggest they may have been Scots, like many other surgeons. Watt had begun his career as a mate in the *Weazle* sloop in 1752, rising to first mate in 1755. He had two boy servants, Thomas Vineyard and James Rawlings. Other ships also had a proportionate staff of surgeons and medicines that they bought for the voyage. Naval surgeons had slightly higher status and prospects than military surgeons. If they were any good at all they had fine opportunities to improve their knowledge through practical experience, just as seamen did. There were incompetents and drunkards among them, but quite a lot were well-meaning, practical men whose cumulative experience led to major improvements in medical science.

In 1760 tropical fever was a major weak point, and it remained so for at least three generations. James Lind, recently appointed physician to the newly built Haslar Hospital, had great belief in the virtue of Peruvian or Jesuit's bark. Bark was effective against malaria because it contained quinine, but it was not until after 1820 that the quinine was isolated. Doses of bark contained variable quantities of quinine and had variable effects – they were no use against yellow fever. Lind later argued that at Havana the physicians were prejudiced against bark because it might produce dropsy and jaundice; their favourite treatment was James's Powder. Lind envied the success of this patent panacea, resented the secrecy surrounding its recipe and distrusted it because it could not possibly be universally effective. In fact it was based on antimony and had some effect against typhus, though none against malaria. Against yellow fever Dr John Hume, surgeon at Jamaica in 1740, recommended bleeding, a clyster of oil as a laxative, and inducing perspiration by wrapping the patient in blankets. (The last method had saved the author Tobias Smollett's life when, as a naval surgeon's mate, he had succumbed at Cartagena.) Hume had also come to believe in bark, and, like many others at the time, noted that people in ships anchored off swampy places were less badly affected than people camped in the swamps.

The day before the attack on El Morro, *Dragon*'s surgeons had cleared the sick bay by sending the sick ashore to a tent erected for the purpose. Three men died there over the next ten days. After the engagement, *Dragon* sailed to the west of the harbour to join Pocock's ships off Chorera. The first task was to get more water to replace what had been jettisoned in order to get the ship afloat. They erected a tent ashore for the coopers, who began to repair damaged barrels, and the crew got the masts down to repair them and set to work knotting and splicing to make good the damaged rigging. John Purnell the carpenter, with Richard Treadenham and the rest of his crew repaired the foreyard, while the caulker Duncan McArthur helped them stop the shot-holes in the side. On 5 July the men heeled the ship so that the carpenters could repair the shot-holes between wind and water. Meanwhile, the armourers set up their forge on shore and began to repair the ironwork. By 20 July the sailors were finishing the renovation of the ship by scraping and paying the sides. They burned off the old layer of tar together with all the weed and other accumulated accretions, scraped the wood bare and then put on a new layer of tar and wax.

Each boat carries two gun barrels. These are rolled to the tripod, where they are lifted onto a carriage and dragged by parties of seamen up to the batteries facing the Morro. The seamen are camping in the shade of the trees.

As the soldiers dropped, more and more work fell to the seamen. 300 seamen from Pocock's ships brought the sea contingent serving with the army to 800 men. The first battalion of marines, including *Dragon's* company under Kennedy, crossed to Coximar to help build new batteries. The existing William's battery was extended to take seven guns, and Captain Dixon's, designed for four mortars, was converted to take five guns by 9 July. Lieutenant Hunter of the *Sutherland* recalled:

> I was sent on shore with a party of Men to assist the operations going on against the Morro; and this was the most fatiguing duty I ever underwent. The ground was our only resting place in the woods; and even that was reduced to a bed of torture by multitudes of Scorpions, Centipedes and Tarantulas. Our wretched beverage was brackish water, and though our Men were dreadfully afflicted with both the flux and scurvy, their only food was Salt Beef.

The sailors escaped the very worst drudgery of carrying 32- and 24-pound cannonballs to the guns. 1,500 slaves, generously supplied at only a third of the normal price for labour by their Jamaican owners, undertook this. Unfortunately, they proved no more immune to disease than anyone else and their numbers shrank day by day.

The worst problem for the besiegers was that they were working on practically bare rock. It was impossible to dig trenches, so the protection for the men as they edged towards the castle had to be built above ground. There was no earth for sandbags, so Albemarle bought up the cotton crop from the homeward-bound Jamaica merchant fleet and stuffed fascines with cotton wool instead of earth as protective padding for the batteries and approaches. The sailors made theirs out of junk, turning the old rope from the damaged shrouds of *Cambridge* and *Dragon* to good use. The engineers wanted 20,000 sandbags, so every stretch of old canvas and every biscuit bag was stuffed with cotton or junk. Simultaneously, the ships' longboats were constantly employed filling water barrels at Chorera and ferrying them to the camp near Coximar. The army needed 500 butts of water a day.

At first the British on La Cabaña were outgunned by El Morro alone and suffered crossfire from the town, ships and floating batteries. The Spanish were determined, courageous and effective, and whatever damage the British did by day was repaired at night. The garrison of El Morro was constantly relieved with fresh soldiers and seamen from the town. Colonel Howe, commanding a force on the west side

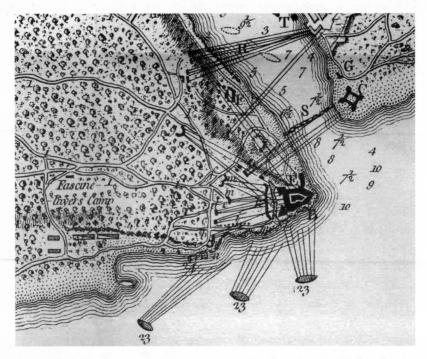

*Detail of Mante's plan of the area around the Morro. b: Fuzer's battery; c:
Valiant's; d: Namur's; e: Grand; f: Dixon's; g: William's; i: the sap; k:
parallel on the glacis; l: breach; m: mortar batteries; 1: roads made by the seamen;
B: Morro; C: Punta; E: Apostles battery; F: Shepherds battery; G: battery
raised by the Spanish; T: frigate sunk by a shell from Dixon's battery.*

of the harbour, built a battery to try to prevent the Spanish crossing
the harbour neck so easily.

British efforts were constantly interrupted. A four-gun emplace-
ment named 'Fuser's battery' was completed on 11 July but demol-
ished by Spanish artillery before it even opened fire. It was repaired,
but two of its guns were dismounted again a day or two later. On 13
July the battery known as 'Namur's' or 'Valiant's' was finished. It
employed the *Temple*'s lower-deck 32-pounder guns (as did Fuser's)
and seamen from *Namur* under Lieutenant Gally and *Valiant* under
Lieutenant Bourmaster. On 15 July the Spanish hit this battery too,
killing three men, wounding others and destroying one gun. Never-

theless, the seamen raised morale all round with their vigorous approach to the task in hand:

> Our sea folks began a new kind of fire, unknown, or at all events, unpractised by artillery people. The greatest fire from one piece of cannon is reckoned by them from eighty to ninety times in twenty-four hours; but our people went on the sea system, firing extremely quick, and with the best direction ever seen, and in sixteen hours fired their guns one hundred and forty-five times.

Commodore Keppel noted with pride that the sea battery fired 144 rounds one day and 146 the next. But he soon began to appreciate the disadvantages. First, rapid fire increased the danger that the guns might overheat and burst or set fire to the inflammable battery walls (which in the case of the sea battery were built of cubes of junk wadding). Second, the guns of all the batteries combined soon required 1,000 cartridges a day, together with shot and shells to match.

Nevertheless, more batteries were added. Lieutenant Philip Orsbridge, who had been making drawings for a visual record of the siege, was placed in charge of fifty men and two 32-pounders from *Orford* mounted with the mortars high on La Cabaña against the ships. A fourth battery was prepared for use on 17 July – Albemarle had written to Pocock on 15 July begging for more seamen to man the new battery and relieve the exhausted Namurs and Valiants, and in response *Dragon* provided a lieutenant, three midshipmen and fifty seamen, plus cartridges and 32-pounder wadding. Military supplies of powder and shot were also running out. Keppel made up the deficiency from his squadron until his ships were down to forty rounds each, at which point desperate demands were sent to Jamaica, and to England to replenish Jamaica after all the Jamaican powder had been sent to Havana. 'The greatest part of those who remained on board the men of war were employed in making junks, blinds, and mantelets; and the 40th regiment, in preparing the gabions that would be wanted to carry on a sap.'

The Spanish sortied from the city against Colonel Howe's outposts, and spiked the guns of the battery that was obstructing the relief of the fort. Next day *Dragon* sent a mate and fourteen men to effect repairs, and Archibald Simonton succeeded in unspiking two of the guns to get them back in use next day.

Things began to look desperate for the Spanish. The guns of the fort were finally silent and, with only determined small arms fire to stop them, the British pushed forward a line of gabions – wicker baskets intended to be stuffed with earth – some stuffed with cotton, most empty, right up the glacis, which allowed the first Englishmen to make it to the covered way on the Spanish side of the glacis. 'This favourable event gave double life to the operations of the English; but it was somewhat damped by a full discovery of what their fears had hitherto made them barely suspect, a new and almost insurmountable difficulty. This was the extraordinary breadth and depth of the ditch'.

The engineers had believed there was no ditch between the glacis and the castle wall. Never in their worst nightmares had they suspected that there would be a ditch sixty feet deep and up to thirty yards wide, cut out of the solid rock. By bringing guns to the edge of the glacis they could try to breach the main walls of the fort, but even then there would be a sheer wall of rock to scale in order to reach the breach. There was no material with which to fill the huge ditch in order to cross it. After all this effort it looked like the castle was impregnable. They were back to square one.

There was one vulnerable point, however. In order to close the ditch to the sea and prevent ships firing along it, the Spanish had left a thin wall of rock. At the top it was rugged and uneven, only two to three feet wide and there was a big drop either side, but a single file of men could cross it and get down from it. Furthermore, at its base they would be concealed and secure from fire from the fort.

On 20 July a call went out for forty miners. Keppel thought that Pocock's flagship *Namur* might yield a few since it had originally been crewed by Boscawen with Cornishmen, and *Dragon* sent four. The seamen dragged four 32-pounders to the crest of the glacis to join the corps of marksmen already stationed there, and under cover of their fire the first miner crossed over the ledge of rock to the foot of the wall. Only three or four men were killed going over.

The miners were soon at work on two tunnels: one beneath the

A combined operation: the detail shows the variety of troops employed against Belle Isle, Martinique and Havana. Sailors in blue and white are drinking with a grenadier (in the tall mitre hat) and fusiliers, while an officer of a highland regiment stands nearby. The British won the Seven Years' War by mastering the art of amphibious operations.

Dominic Serres' painting shows the final attack on Fort Royal, Martinique (right).
The British in the foreground are on Morne Tartenson, but they are
also firing down on the city from the much higher Morne Garnier (left).
General Monckton (centre) is directing operations.

A somewhat unsympathetic
copy of Reynolds's 1761
portrait of Admiral George
Bridges Rodney. Rodney,
who commanded the naval
expedition against Martinique,
was widely detested although
undoubtedly talented and
highly regarded by his crews.

This detail of Dominic Serres's painting shows *Dragon* approaching the town
of Trinité on the north coast of Martinique with her tenders, manned
by Dragons, to the right. She flies a commodore's broad pennant and fires
a signal gun to the ships following.

Dominic Serres's painting of *Dragon* leading Hervey's squadron to attack the port of Castries in St Lucia. A French boat with a flag of truce is approaching in order to surrender the island.

Thomas Hearne's drawing of the *Deal Castle* in the West Indies in 1775. Awnings have been spread over the deck to shade the crew from the sun; the frigate has a goat for milk and poultry for eggs; midshipmen with sextants are taking a noon observation; the officers pace past a ½-pounder swivel.

Augustus Keppel painted by Joshua Reynolds about 1752 – Keppel commanded
the naval forces at Belle Isle and was deputy to Pocock at Havana. Although
they cooperated at Havana, Keppel and Hervey were lifelong enemies
until Hervey's outspoken defence of Keppel during his court martial in
1778 finally united them in friendship.

A British battery manned chiefly by Royal Artillery gunners directs its leisurely fire at the Morro Castle at the end of the promontory guarding the entrance to Havana harbour. The tower of Havana cathedral (left) indicates the position of the town.

Augustus Hervey portrayed by Reynolds after *Dragon*'s return in 1762. 'His failings were those of a warm temper and unguarded disposition; his virtues were those of a heart formed for every thing amiable in private, every thing great in public life', wrote Constantine Phipps of his uncle. He holds a plan of the attack on the Morro, which is also depicted in the distance.

Dragon (left) and *Cambridge* attack the Morro Castle from the sea. The detail of
Richard Paton's painting gives a sense of the size and power of battleships,
though on this occasion the castle beat them. The British have thrown their
dead overboard so the boat rows past floating corpses.

A former sailor whose leg stopped a shot while he served in a frigate stands on the bank opposite Greenwich Hospital where he now resides. A number of Monmouths and Dragons retired to the hospital when they left the sea.

seafront of the sea bastion, the other into the glacis in the hope of blowing part of it into the ditch.

By two o'clock on the night of 22 July they had tunnelled about eighteen feet under the sea bastion of El Morro. Colonel Carleton, brigadier of the night, discussed the proper direction of the sap, or tunnel, on the glacis with the duty engineer, Captain Dixon, and towards dawn they sent a sergeant and twelve men to look into a spur running from El Morro towards the sea. No sooner had the first men got in than a party of Spaniards set upon them, shouting. El Morro's alarm bell rang out, drums beat the reveille in the town, though it was not yet light, and firing broke out all across the land-face of El Morro and from towards the sea.

The men repairing the batteries ran for their arms as a noise of skirmishing broke out from Dixon's and William's batteries towards the town. Each of these was covered by a party of about thirty men who found themselves faced by a force of around 2,000 Spaniards advancing up the slope from the water. They had crossed, from the town in absolute silence in the dark of the night, and had been waiting for dawn to attack. The accidental alarm from the British raid had betrayed them prematurely.

Major Farmer had 150 men under arms in the burned-out Grand Battery and rushed a hundred of them towards the noise of muskets. Carleton gathered the other fifty and followed. Lieutenant Forbes with the Royals guarding the sap on the glacis was quickly joined by the fit remainder of the regiment who were camped under the cliff just below the British batteries. Lieutenant Ashe leading them was mortally wounded as they charged, but they and Farmer's men took the Spanish in the flank and caused them to retreat. The situation remained dangerous for some time, with the British frightened to expose themselves to grapeshot from the floating batteries once it got light, but Keppel's advance with the Royal Americans finally drove the Spanish back to their boats before the sun rose.

The inexperienced Spanish troops, largely militia, were beaten by bluff and prompt action by bold officers and disciplined troops, but as dawn rose the British realised that they had had a very narrow and fortunate escape. Had the attack not been discovered by accident just before it was launched, it was likely that it would have succeeded. The destruction of the British positions at that critical moment when ammunition, morale and manpower were all so low would almost certainly have led to the abandonment of the siege. As it was, the victory encouraged the British to push on.

Further encouragement came a few days later with the long-awaited arrival of part of the convoy of reinforcements from America. They had not done quite as well as Pocock in navigating the Old Bahama Channel – the *Chesterfield* and four of the transports had run on to the cays at the entrance in the dark, and the *Juno* had run aground before leaving the Channel – but the crews and soldiers were safe and Pocock sent frigates to pick them up. This brought a much-needed boost of

Troops move in single file into the narrow breach created by the explosion of the mine on 30 July. Detail of Peter Canot's engraving.

3,000 fresh men to the siege at a crucial turning point. In El Morro, however, Velasco continued to hold out 'with a sullen resolution'.

On the afternoon of 30 July a huge artillery bombardment was directed at El Morro. The sea folks were allowed to fire as fast as they wished (in the excitement the gun operated by *Dragon*'s marines ran out of control and Michael Carney, a twenty-two-year-old from Ellistown in Leicestershire, had his leg crushed by the carriage), then the British sprung the mines with a huge explosion. The one under the glacis failed to achieve much, but the one under the bastion brought down a large part of it, making a breach that was just sufficiently accessible to storm. The troops picked to assault the breach went one by one over the ridge of rock, then scrambled up the rubble and into the fort. A few of them reached the ramparts before the Spanish, who were sheltering in their casements from the artillery bombardment that preceded the assault, and as he led his men up the ramp Velasco was mortally wounded. The British seized the ramparts and slaughtered until the garrison ran for the boats or tried to swim across to the city. Many drowned.

From *Dragon* and the other ships of Pocock's division the remaining seamen looked on anxiously until they saw the Spanish flag fall and a Union Jack rise over the castle. Then, in the naval way, they climbed the shrouds and yards and gave three resounding cheers.

18

The Key to the Riches of Mexico

They lost no time after the castle had surrendered. That evening, during a truce, they struck the sick tent near Coximar and *Dragon* received her sick back on board. Don Luis de Velasco was taken to Havana, where he died the next day.

The firing started up again, coinciding with a thunderstorm that brought the first rain for a fortnight. El Morro's guns were now turned against the city and the Spanish returned fire furiously, seeking to hit the cisterns that were even then refilling with fresh rainwater, providing the British with a good water supply on the eastern hill. The seamen and soldiers combined efforts to build new batteries on La Cabaña and drag more guns up there to hit La Punta and the city.

For nearly a month now George Grumbley, the cook, had been serving out salt rations exclusively. At first the wild cabbage plants had provided a source of greens, but they had all been eaten. They had tried to catch turtles and fish, but men were going down with scurvy now, in addition to their other ailments, and many were beginning to die. Sixteen Dragons had been killed in action on 1 July. Only eleven more had died during the month, and of them some may have been wounded, but during August they began to drop at a rate that soon exceeded one a day. The marines who had served with the army suffered worst, together with those seamen who had been ashore. After six years in the marines, former Hertfordshire labourer Richard Damon found a grave in a Cuban swamp on 4 August, and old Monmouth Daniel Walkeley, who had fought the *Foudroyant*, succumbed ten days later.

Those that were fit kept working. By 10 August Albemarle had forty-nine guns, ten mortars and five howitzers in El Morro and La Cabaña, and *Dragon* contributed two lieutenants and fifty men towards manning them. That day Albemarle summoned the city to surrender, but the governor refused. Next day the guns opened fire. The exchanges were furious at first, but the British silenced the Punta, and soon after nine in the morning the Spanish abandoned it. They then asked for a truce, and after two days' argument over terms, the city surrendered. The survivors were elated, entertaining high hopes of enormous booty.

The Morro in British hands with the Bonetta *and* Cygnet *clearing the boom across the entrance to the harbour. The masts of the Spanish ships sunk to further block the harbour entrance are in the background.*

On 11 August, while things were quiet, eighty-four marines returned from the camp, 'all sick'. The Dragons erected a sick tent on shore for them and the other sick. Five days later they struck the tent and brought their own men back on board. *Dragon* was to go home with the dispatches bearing the news of victory. Hervey got his orders and dispatch on 19 August and sailed two days later.

> Whereas the Packet you will here with recieve [*sic*] directed to the Secretary of the Admiralty is of importance to His Majesty's Service.
>
> You are hereby required and directed to proceed with His Majesty's Ship *Dragon* under your Command, and make the best of your way for England, making Spithead the first Port of your arrival, if the wind favor you for it; where (or at any other Port) immediately on your arrival you are to set out Post yourself for London, and deliver my Packet to the Right Honorable the Lords Commissioners of the Admiralty. Given under my Hand onboard His Majesty's Ship *Namur* off Chorera River near the Havana, the 20th. Augst: 1762.
>
> G: Pocock

Victory had been achieved and it was a hugely impressive conquest. Eyewitness historian Thomas Mante considered it the greatest single victory of the whole Seven Years War:

> Thus did this conquest prove the heaviest blow, in itself, and in its consequences the most decisive, of any that had been given since the commencement of the present hostilities between so many great powers. In the acquisition of Havana were combined all the advantages that could be procured in war. It was a military victory of the first magnitude; it was equal to the greatest naval victory by its effects on the marine of the Spaniards, who lost on that occasion a whole fleet.

Havana had always been the key to the Spanish Main, mainland Spanish America, its importance encapsulated in its coat of arms – three white castles guarding a golden key on a field of sea-blue. The British did not yet know how far Havana had developed as a sugar colony, just how rich and promising the island now was. Moreover, as Pocock's dispatch stated, the capture of Spain's naval base together with her New World fleet left 'all their settlements in this part of the world exposed to any attempts that may be thought proper to be made on them'.

It is impossible to know whether or not the same result might have been achieved far more quickly and at far lower cost in human life by

View of Havana after the surrender. Two barges lead flat boats full of British troops to occupy the Punto fort and the north gate of the city.

the sudden, immediate assault on the city that Captain Hervey and others had wanted. The Spanish would have fought just as bravely, but their defenders would have been spread much more thinly in the city, and the British troops, who were unusually good, might well have made a succeessful assault – these veteran troops had succeeded against the French in Martinique. An all-out assault would definitely have been worth trying at Havana, and had it failed, they could still have fallen back on the slower method. If Havana had fallen faster, it is likely that the next target, Vera Cruz, would have been taken as well.

But a sudden attack was a risk that Lord Albemarle was not capable of taking. His patient, ponderous generalship ruined, through disease, a highly competent veteran army and did serious damage to a similarly skilled fleet. According to the official return, between 7 June and 18 October 5,366 died in the land forces, eighty-eight per cent from disease, and 1,300 seamen died, ninety-five per cent from disease – and these losses do not include those suffered by the ships that left Cuba early, such as *Dragon* and *Cambridge*. Nor do they include the losses suffered after they left Cuba by sick regiments that were sent to America, or the losses of Israel Putnam's company of ninety-eight men of the Connecticut regiment who arrived in Havana at the end of

July, just in time for the climax of the campaign. They were never under fire, but only twenty-two returned home. Brilliant regiments, veterans of the campaigns in America, were totally destroyed. The true figure for losses among the land forces was probably well in excess of fifty per cent, and the toll in lives cut short in the navy was only slightly less appalling.

Dragon was lucky to a degree in that she went home early, loaded with seventeen live bullocks for the use of the sick and a number of passengers. Robert Carkett, the former Monmouth whose *Hussar* had been wrecked off Cap François, had been freed on condition that he did not fight until exchanged for a French prisoner, and took a passage home in the *Dragon* with some of his officers. John Broad, who had left *Monmouth* to be a master's mate in *Hussar*, joined *Dragon*'s crew, and there were also some army officers with a talented physician, Richard Huck, a valuable and badly needed addition to the medical staff, together with twelve Spanish prisoners. They took the normal, more northerly return route, making Cape Florida on 24 August. The voyage was fast and would have been almost uneventful had not most of the crew been ill. Eighteen men died in the first week at sea, fifty-three during the whole five-week voyage.

On 21 September, when they were in the western approaches to the English Channel early in the morning, James Barry at the mast-head spotted a sail to the south-east, at no great distance. It was typical late September weather, blowing a gale, pouring with rain, and visibility was bad. Despite his urgent dispatch, Hervey decided to chase; they wore round and increased sail. Perhaps the other ship did not see them until far too late, perhaps its people could not handle their ship so well in a strong wind. *Dragon* hoisted an ensign and opened fire with her chase guns at eight o'clock in the morning, and the chase hoisted a White French flag and replied with her stern chasers.

Hervey ordered the main topgallant sails set. Andrew Epsley was at the maintopmast head and Edward Brannon just below him in the shrouds, both getting the topgallant yard across, when the main-topmast broke. Epsley fell from the highest point on the ship, lacerated his left arm as he scrabbled desperately for a rope, hit the mainyard and clung on. Brannon fell all the way to the quarterdeck but survived. At almost the same moment the French ship surrendered.

She proved to be the *François Louis*, a 325-ton privateer frigate mounting twenty-four brass 18-pounders, from St Malo bound for Newfoundland with a cargo of military stores. She had a crew of sixty-three with ninety-three officers, soldiers and passengers, each of them worth £5 in head money, and was carrying six hogsheads of tobacco, Dutch snuff, sailcloth, woollen stockings, cloth, ivory buttons, shoe buckles, combs, six hundred pairs of shoes, eight hogsheads of brandy, and sixty-four of wine. She was a good prize, valued by the newspapers at £20,000, and even more valuable to her captors in that *Dragon* had captured her intact and unaided – there were no other ships or admirals to claim a share, and the depleted crew could look forward to higher individual shares than usual.

Dragon struck soundings five days later, about ninety miles short of the Lizard. Three days after that she anchored at Spithead. Captain Hervey rushed ashore and posted to London, arriving at the Admiralty in Whitehall in the early evening. He delivered his dispatch, probably knowing that in it Pocock had recommended him as 'a brave and deserving officer'. He then went to wait on Lord Bute and found him at supper with the duc de Nivernois, the French ambassador. Hervey supped at White's Club in St James's and spread the good news to the assembled nobility. The guns of the Tower woke the city at one o'clock the next morning. On both sides of the Atlantic the British nation celebrated. 'Brighton illuminated his thatched church and all Egham was on fire, and even Bishipgate had its bum-fires and illuminations', reported the *Boston News Letter*, as thrilled as London was at the blow to their Catholic Spanish enemy and the new prospects for trade.

The next day Hervey visited George Marsh and appointed him his prize agent for the *François Louis*. Captains and crews each had separate agents to look after their interests, an arrangement that anticipated potential conflicts, and the ship employed James Dixon, who had also acted for Samuel Furzer, purser of the *Monmouth*. Like most London naval agents he was based close to the Navy Office at the foot of Tower Hill. Dixon lived in Gold's Square off Crutched Friars. George Marsh's house was a hundred yards away in Savage Gardens.

Marsh came from a family of naval administrators. His father was a Chatham yard officer, and one of his brothers had run the yard at Port Mahon, just before the war. Now forty, he himself had started as a clerk at Deptford and set up as a naval agent in 1750 after his marriage to Anne Long. In 1762 he worked in the department of seamen's wages, whilst also undertaking business on his own account. He had handled Hervey's business since March 1759, when Hervey had appointed him following the death of his previous agent, James Henshaw. He passed Hervey's accounts, saw his prizes through the courts and loaned him money when needed, administering his financial affairs at home while the captain was at sea. He thought of Hervey as 'my hearty good friend' – (friend) chiefly in the sense of patron.

George Marsh; detail of a pastel by Johann Gerhard Huck.

Back at Spithead meanwhile, the admiral commanding at Portsmouth, Francis Holbourne, reported to Clevland that 'the *Dragon* being very sickly I have order'd her into the Harbour, where I propose she shall lie quiet some days to rest the people.' The fit Dragons rowed 'a great number of marines and seamen to hospital' and sent all their French and Spanish prisoners to Porchester Castle. *Dragon* sailed into harbour on the first day of October and the men got out the guns and stores. She had 121 men sick on shore, as well as Howison, the master, who was 'supposed to be dying', Watt the surgeon and Lieutenant Holyoak of the marines. The death rate continued in the Haslar Hospital. By November *Dragon* had lost 119 men to disease, more than a sixth of her complement.

Hervey returned to Portsmouth with George Marsh, who took possession of the *François Louis* and paid the men *Dragon*'s share of prizes taken in 1760 and 1761. On 6 October the interrogation of the officers of the *François Louis* took place at the Fountain. This was the first stage in the formal legal progress of condemning a prize. In the presence of a public notary, James Bucknall, Mayor of Portsmouth, put a series of standard questions, the 'Standing Interrogatories', to the captain and two other officers of the captured ship. The Standard Interrogatories were carefully formulated to determine ownership of the captured vessel, the nature of her cargo and the purpose of her voyage.

At first sight the case was cut and dried. Her captain, forty-eight-year-old Thomas Blondelas from St Malo, had a commission as a *lieutenant de frégate*. The ship was owned by Grandclos Meslé of St Malo, but he had hired her to the King of France. She was sailing to Newfoundland on the king's business with stores and reinforcements for the French military expedition that had seized Newfoundland in June. The first hint that things might not progress smoothly came when Blondelas said that when he first saw the *François Louis* in August, he had heard that she was built at Bayonne and, ominously, had once been called the *Queen of England*.

If the *François Louis* proved to be a recaptured British ship, the Dragons were only entitled to salvage, normally set at one-eighth of her value. The valuation of £20,000 might have been inflated, but if it was true, Hervey's share was £7,500. If she was merely salvage he could divide that by eight. Undeterred, he wrote to the Admiralty to offer her for sale to the Royal Navy, as was the custom:

The French Privateer Frigate His Majts Ship *Dragon* took in our Passage home, called the *Francois Louis*, & in the French King's Service, is pierc'd for 26 Guns, has 18 pounders mounted, & is abt. 350 Tons, has a spar Deck, and is not above 3 years old, a very prime sailor & full of very good sails, all newly fitted and is in every respect fit to proceed to sea – I therefore take the Liberty to offer her to their Lordships for Hs: Mts: Service together with all her Furniture &c, if they please to purchase her

On the corner of the letter, secretary Clevland noted their lordships' response: 'To be inspected for possible purchase.'

On 22 October Marsh got the ship's papers translated for the court, but then came the blow. On Wednesday 3 November Peter Trapaud appeared at Doctor's Commons, the Admiralty Court in London, and laid claim to the ship and her goods. He said he was part-owner of the *François Louis*, formerly called the *British Queen*, and named Alexander Cristall as its master. The other owners were Elias Benjamin de la Fontaine, John Isaac Bazin, John Guilt Jnr, Daniel Vialars and Gilbert Heathcote. *Dragon*'s officers must have read the names with a degree of cynicism. Heathcote was, presumably, Sir Gilbert Heathcote, son of a lord mayor, but nearly all the others were French. Indeed, the French-built *British Queen* and her owners had only became British when Guadeloupe was conquered in 1759. The irony was that, with peace looming, they were about to become French again.

The following Monday Alexander Cristall of St Botolph, Aldgate, appeared in court. He described how, during his voyage from Guadaloupe to London, the *British Queen* had been captured on 17 April 1762 by a French privateer and carried to St Malo. He believed her to be the *François Louis*. The main hearing took place on 13 November, and that Saturday morning Marsh argued Hervey's case that when she was captured, *François Louis* belonged to the French navy. The Admiralty Court judge, Sir Thomas Salusbury, condemned her as lawful prize, awarding half the value of the hull and the whole value of the cargo to the captors. It was not the perfect outcome, but it was better than one-eighth.

In the meantime, anxious relatives haunted the streets around Tower Hill, visiting offices and agents to learn the fates of their loved ones. Others travelled to Portsmouth. Elizabeth Treadenham, the wife of Richard, one of Hervey's old Hampton Courts and carpenter's crew in *Dragon*, lived in Blandford Forum, so she probably learned of his death, on the voyage home, in Portsmouth before travelling on to London to settle his affairs. She proved the will that he had made in her favour on 9 November and collected his earnings ten days later – £20 1s. 7d., nearly two years' net pay – then made arrangements to receive his prize money as it became due. Eleanor Miller, who lived in the parish of St George's in the East, near the Ratcliff Highway above Wapping, was married to James, a former *Revenge* who had fought the *Orphée* in 1758 but who had been killed in action against EL Morro on 1 July. She must have learned of his death very quickly, for she proved his will on 26 October, was given his net pay in November – £15 8s. 10d. – and then applied for the bounty available to relatives of men killed in action. She received £15 12s. 10d. in April 1763, and £5 4s. 3d. in trust for her son Richard and £10 8s. 6d. in trust for her daughters Agnes and Eleanor in December. Susanna Henderson, mother of the first lieutenant killed on 1 July, received £74 bounty through her son William, a London apothecary who was his brother's executor and proved his will in October.

These sums would not sustain widows and mothers for long, but they were better than nothing at all, which was what French and Spanish seamen could expect from their bankrupt naval administrations. The Royal Navy did not offer huge salaries, but it did at least pay what it promised reasonably promptly and efficiently and offered some meagre compensation in the cases of bereavement that involved enemy action. The drawback was that far more seamen died from disease than in action with the enemy, in which cases the Royal Navy was not obliged to pay a penny.

Navy officials made a genuine effort to reach widows and orphans. In May 1763 they advertised to poor widows of commission and warrant officers to come or apply by post for the pension for which they might be eligible, but when, in June, they posted a notice of the costs of administration and probate of wills of seamen dying on service or in foreign parts, it was because many beneficiaries had previously believed they were so high that it was not worth trying to claim the money. The charge depended on whether you travelled to prove the will in person or paid a commission to have it done for you. The cost for a will worth less than £5 was 6s., or 12s. with a commission. It rose to 9s. for a will valued up to £20, £1 3s. for one up to £40, and £1 4s. up to £60. After this the commission increased little beyond 12s., becoming a smaller proportion of larger wills. Since most seamen were owed around £20 in pay, together with some prize money and the value of their clothes, it generally was worth claiming.

On 15 December the commissioner came aboard to pay off the ship's company, the pendant that identified *Dragon* as a royal warship was struck and she was put out of commission. The preliminaries of peace had been signed, the war was effectively over, and the Royal Navy had no further use for the crew. They were at last free to go. Having received their pay, the officers and men dispersed, but for the present most gravitated to the capital, where they cruised the streets, eager for pleasure and waiting for their prize money to come through.

Although the navy had finished with them, many crewmen still had naval business to clear up. All of them had prize money to collect. Some were eligible for compensation from the Chatham Chest for injuries suffered in the course of duty. Those who had been injured in the course of duty and had the right to make a claim on the fund had to produce a 'smart ticket' signed by the ship's officers and present themselves for examination. One batch of examinations took place in early January and various Dragons presented themselves.

Andrew Epsley, the little dark-haired twenty-eight-year-old from Sandwich who had fallen from the maintopmasthead during the chase of the *François Louis*, an accident 'occasioning a lameness in his walking ever since', was awarded £4 and a pension of £4 per annum. Four pounds was rather less than a third of what he earned at sea, but it helped him to survive. Michael Carney, the Leicestershire marine, discharged after his leg was crushed by the gun he was serving during the assault on El Morro, also got a £4 pension as well as a £4 payment for his permanent wound. Forty-year-old William Buchanan got £3 for his splinter wound of 1 July, as did his younger friend John Bailey. William Campbell got the same after a 'fall from the ForeYard Arm down on the Fore Castle while Lashing the Jeer Block to the Foreyard Arm' that September. John Chandler similarly suffered 'A Violent Fracture of the Bone of his Nose betwixt the Ship's side & Sheet Anchor that Renderd him unserviceable . . . Getting the Sheat Anchor over the Side at Spithead' on 30 September. For this he received £5. The rash of accidents that autumn was probably the result of the sickness, either because the men working were unwell, or because they were doing the unfamiliar jobs of the sick or dead.

The other insurance or pension policy to which seamen contributed monthly sixpences was the fund that since 1694 had allowed old or injured tars to find refuge at Greenwich Hospital. This also invited applicants. On 17 February 1763 the Admiralty advertised

> that the Lords Commissioners of the Admiralty will, on the first Thursday of every Month, at Eleven of the Clock in the Morning, examine all Seamen and Seafaring Men, who, by Age or Infirmities, are rendered unfit for further Service at Sea, in order to be minuted for the Royal Hospital at Greenwich; at which time they are to attend, with Certificates from the Navy Office of the Time of their Service at Sea

Several Dragons applied in the months after the ship's company disbanded. Thomas Williams became a pensioner in July 1763. He was fifty-five, a childless widower, born in Shadwell and a former Thames waterman, though he had served in the navy for twelve years. Thomas Snibson joined him in 1764, from Guy's Hospital. He was forty-eight, a widower with one daughter, born in Warwickshire, but a seaman by profession. He had been wounded in the left shoulder and died shortly afterwards, in August. Old William Pinker, Hervey's boatswain, with twenty-eight years' naval service, came in February 1764. He died two years later at the age of fifty-eight. More of them took refuge in the hospital over the years.

The Treaty of Paris that formally ended the war was signed on 10 February 1763. Along with many others, the Dragons were dismayed to discover that Havana was to be handed back to Spain. Britain did receive Florida in compensation, but the terms of peace must have seemed a betrayal of all the shipmates who had given their lives to conquer the great fortified naval base. Their disgust was compounded when they learned how the Havana prize money was to be divided. Instead of the normal eighth allowed to commanding officers, the senior officers at Havana had claimed three times that amount – six-fifteenths. The Earl of Albemarle and Admiral Pocock took a third, amounting to a cool £124,697 each. Commodore Keppel received £24,539. The navy's half of the remaining nine-fifteenths was divided up in the conventional manner.

What this meant was that while the capture had been the 'key to the riches of Mexico' for the two commanding officers and their seconds, nobody else did particularly well. Captain Hervey had no great reason to complain over his £1,600 – more than six times his salary – except that it should have been more had the senior officers not been so greedy, but the private seamen received a mere £3 18s. 9d. Petty officers like midshipmen Richard Tizard and William Coffen or quartermaster John Blake got £19.10s. 6d. while boatswain File Fewin and gunner Archibald Simonton got £69 11s. 9d. They would not have got much more even if Albemarle and Pocock had not been so greedy, but that was not the point.

That said, most seamen made the effort to collect their prize money. The Havana money came in four distributions, two by 1763, a third in 1764, and a last, which was not very significant, in 1766. 115 Dragons failed to collect all of their money, but most of these only rejected the final payment. About forty collected none at all – but almost all of these men had either deserted or died in Cuba.

Fortunately the Havana money was roughly matched in value by the proceeds of the *François Louis*. The merchant owners paid up remarkably quickly, and at the beginning of February Marsh placed the notice that the rules obliged him to place in the official *London Gazette*:

> Notice is hereby given, the Prize Money due to the Officers and Company of His Majesty's Ship *Dragon*, the Honourable Augustus John Hervey, Esq; Commander, who were actually on board at the

Taking the *Francois Louis*, a French Ship of War, on the 21st of September 1762, will be paid their respective Shares at the French Horn in Crutched Fryars, on Monday the 21st of February Instant; and will be recalled there the first Monday in every Month for three Years to come, by George Marsh of Savage Gardens, Agent to the Captors.

The custom was to pay on a particular day and then, for those who missed the first day, to hold a monthly recall for the next three years. Any prize money unclaimed after three years was presented to Greenwich Hospital as part of the general pension fund.

The distribution of the first part of *Dragon*'s Havana prize money took place on 1 March 1763 at the King's Head tavern in Fenchurch Street. *Cambridge, Sutherland, Dover* and the *Cygnet* and *Porcupine* sloops were paid on succeeding days in the same week. The King's Head was one of a small number of venues that were employed repeatedly for paying off seamen. Chiefly famous as the place where Elizabeth I had her first drink after being released from the Tower, the ancient tavern stood on the corner of Star Alley, across the paved and cobbled street from Ironmonger's Hall. It was a three-storey building with a modern façade and large doors in the corner opening on to both street and alley.

Dragon and the other ships that returned early from the Havana were recalled together on the first Tuesday of every month. On one of these occasions, on Tuesday 7 July, disorderly queues of seamen and their attorneys stretched down the street for the fourth recall for prize money. A man presented himself before Mr Robinson, clerk to James Dixon, and demanded the prize money due to him in the name of John Campbell. 'I looked on the list, and found John Campbell rated an able seaman. The first payment was 2 *l*.' The claimant looked very young for an able seaman. 'I asked him how long he had belonged to that ship? He said, a year and a half. I asked him the name of his captain; he said, Captain Harvey, I asked him if any of the lieutenants were slain at the Havanna, and their names; he did not know either of their names; he could not answer any other question that was asked him. I told him he was come to receive money falsely, and that I would send for the constable, and take him up.'

At this, the boy confessed that he had been persuaded to pretend to be Campbell by another Dragon named Rearden who was waiting outside. Robinson asked how he was dressed but 'there were two or three hundred seamen at the door, it was impossible to find him out'. Impersonating a seaman in order to claim his wages was treated very seriously and was usually a capital offence. On 5 May 'when we were paying a great many ships, at the King's-head, Fenchurch-street,' Albert Innes, agent for the *Burford*, had caught out Richard Potter of the *African* pretending to be Andrew M'Gee in order to claim £1 15s. due to M'Gee for a French Indiaman taken by *Burford* and other ships on their voyage to Havana. A messmate established that the real M'Gee had returned to Ireland. Potter had been hanged. In this case, however, the court decided the boy had been imposed upon and let him off.

The incident provides a glimpse into these rowdy occasions when the seamen came to claim their money. Fenchurch Street and Crutched Friars probably saw the last major gatherings of the surviving Dragons. 138 out of 650 of them had died since their arrival at the Havana, but nearly all the remainder who were not still in hospital queued to collect their prize money or deputed someone to do it for them. One further payout to them on 7 March was advertised for 'when a Sloop, name unknown, was drove Onshore and taken by the *Dragon*'s Tender in the West Indies' in April 1762.

Just what this prize money amounted to is difficult to calculate, since precise figures survive only for the Havana, and even those vary from account to account. Ordinary men did much better in a small ship, where fewer of them shared the proceeds, than in a huge one like *Dragon*. For the higher grades this was less true: there were almost as many warrant officers in a sloop as in a ship of the line. For an officer, prize money might provide much better rewards than pay. Lieutenant Robinson's net annual pay was just over £142. His Havana prize money was about £140. If the *François Louis* was worth £6,000 he should have received about £150, although his share might have diminished thanks to the officers travelling as passengers. His share of the plunder seized at Martinique, distributed in summer 1764, was worth nearly £13 to him. Then there were smaller sums for smaller prizes like the sloop, or shares in bigger ones. The *Monmouth*'s officers, who shared in several large prizes, must have improved their fortunes substantially during the war. Indeed, *Monmouth*, with her combination of speed, power and frequent cruises, was an ideal ship in which to serve in any of the senior grades.

With all these rough young men hanging around the capital, making up for lost time with sex and periodically collecting handouts of ready cash, some inevitably got into trouble. Miles Cook was one of the rabble of pressed landsmen who had been drafted into the ship in October 1761. About a month after joining *Dragon*, before he knew one rope from another, he had been helping to put the ship about when he carelessly got the slack of the main sheet twisted round his leg. He suffered a 'Violent Contusion on his Left Leg which Turning to an Obstinate Ulcer Render'd him Unfit for Service for several Months'. He was examined in March and given £6.

Cook was then lodging at the Drum in St Thomas Street at the St Giles end of Drury Lane, the most disreputable district in Westminster. On Tuesday 6 April his landlord missed 'two silver watches, value 5l. twelve silver coat-buttons, value 10s. one silver seal, val. 12d. one seal set in silver, value 6d. one gilt band for a hat, value 12d. one gold ring, value 7s. one silver hat-buckle set with stones, value 12d. one piece of silver gilt, one ducat, sixteen guineas, six quarter guineas, eight half guineas, and 6l. in money'. He found Cook's friend Donnolly's 'wife' in bed at their lodgings in Parker's Lane, a favourite street with prostitutes, and Cook and Donnelly were tracked down in the Bull's Head near Piccadilly with some of the missing items in their pockets. Despite Donnolly's protestations of innocence, they were both found guilty at the Old Bailey and sentenced to seven years' transportation.

Thus, in May 1763, the messmates found themselves on their way back across the Atlantic to Maryland. Here they parted company, for while Donnelly settled down to penal servitude in the tobacco plantations, the resourceful Cook had other ideas. In August he was advertised in the *Maryland Gazette* as an escaped convict in Baltimore County, English, aged about thirty, and five foot ten inches tall.

All the other Dragons were temporarily free of the fetters of British society and they went their separate ways. Only the standing officers, purser Fennell, boatswain Fewin, gunner Simonton and carpenter Purnell, remained with the stripped-down *Dragon*, theoretically secure in a job so long as the ship lasted. The officers sought new commissions or went on half pay. Those without a commission were left to their own devices. Some married men went home to their families for the first sustained spell in seven years. Young men who had seen enough of the world left the sea for their villages. Watermen, fishermen, colliers, whalers and merchant seamen went back to their previous occupations and back to their home towns until the next war. The few who preferred always to serve in the navy looked for new ships that remained active in the much smaller peacetime establishment.

In May 1763 Hervey was appointed captain of the famous old *Centurion*, the ship in which Anson had circumnavigated the globe, heading for the Mediterranean where he was to be peacetime commodore. He could not have invented a more congenial job. John Robinson was first lieutenant and William Howdell chaplain. John Blake, William Parvin and William Coffen immediately volunteered to join her crew.

If, like most Monmouths and Dragons, you were born in the 1720s war was more normal than peace during your adult life – between 1739 and 1783 there were twenty-seven years of war and eighteen of peace. Most seamen spent more time in the navy than out of it, and most naval service was active service. In these circumstances you either died young or became very experienced at your job. The navy as a whole gained vast operational experience, logistical systems were honed to a high degree of practical efficiency, and constant practice made ship's crews good at what they did.

In all these departments Britain's navy was well ahead of its rivals. For centuries dominion of the waves – the route to national wealth and power – had been a British national myth. Until now efforts to demonstrate that power had proved all too vulnerable to disease, navigational catastrophe, storms and sheer logistics, but during these years a much more professional navy had gone a long way towards turning the boast that Britannia ruled the waves into a practical reality. With the men, systems and ships that she had, Britain had proved she could exert her naval power just as far as she wished. Never before had she crushed her maritime rivals as she had in the Seven Years War. The generation of experienced seamen that served in *Monmouth* and *Dragon* was the one that conquered the seas and brought Britain global supremacy.

Epilogue

Captain Hervey never took the *Centurion* to the Mediterranean. His friend and patron George Grenville had become First Lord of the Treasury, taking the reins of government from the Earl of Bute, but Grenville rapidly found himself embroiled in a bitter political battle for survival in which he needed his friends about him. Hervey took a lucrative court sinecure as Groom of the Bedchamber and a seat in the House of Commons for Saltash, a borough controlled by the Admiralty. He had already been appointed Colonel of the Plymouth Division of Marines and these posts removed any remaining financial worries.

The famous Venetian libertine Casanova claimed that he compared notes with Hervey during his visit to London in 1764, finding him amusing, urbane and cynical. At that time Hervey was involved, as usual, with the beauty of the moment. Kitty Hunter had recently eloped with Hervey's old friend the Earl of Pembroke, who was already married. After having Pembroke's child she put herself into Hervey's protection. They also produced a child, named Augustus. Hervey loved him dearly and brought him up to the navy.

Hervey's ambitions in the navy and in politics were severely hampered by his health. 'He has never had tolerable health since he was at the Havana', his mother wrote in 1767. Hervey himself lamented to Grenville 'the half-year's tax that my detestable constitution (as it has become) pays every spring and fall for its continuance in this delightful world'. His health limited his ability to undertake any sustained work.

Being appointed Colonel of Marines was not at first a sinecure: Hervey had to go to Plymouth to supervise a new establishment of the corps. There were to be seventy companies in total, twenty-six based at Plymouth, twenty-six at Portsmouth and eighteen at Chatham. All those aged over forty were discharged, along with the infirm. Hervey had to report on those Plymouth officers that had distinguished or disgraced themselves during the war.

His greatest personal achievement in Parliament was his successful campaign to improve the lot of half-pay officers, a subject about which he felt strongly. If they could not secure a commission in a ship in the much smaller peacetime navy, officers received a pension of half their normal pay. A lieutenant got only 2s. a day or a miserly £36 10s. a year, without the free food and lodging they enjoyed in time of war. In 1765 Hervey wrote a series of anonymous letters to the *Public Advertiser*, highlighting their plight. According to his research, nearly five hundred half-pay officers from the army and navy combined were in debtor's prisons by 1764. He presented a petition to the House in 1767 and the Commons voted an extra shilling a day – a 50 per cent increase to a half-pay lieutenant's income. Hervey received a string of letters of thanks.

Another factor that kept Hervey from public life was the notoriety of his wife and marriage. She remained mistress of the Duke of Kingston and a famous hostess, but she had taken to drinking heavily. Frederick the Great, reporting the wedding of his nephew, wrote that 'nothing particular happened save the appearance of an English lady, Madame Chudleigh, who emptied two bottles of wine and staggered as she danced and nearly fell on the floor'. In 1769 she went to law against Hervey, accusing him of claiming falsely that he was married to her. His answer was so weak as to suggest that he colluded in a process that declared her a spinster. She promptly married the Duke. Kingston died in 1773, leaving her his substantial fortune, but his nephew caused a bill of indictment for bigamy to be drawn up against her. While Hervey visited Nice, she was tried by the House of Lords. They found her guilty and she spent the rest of her life abroad, much of it in Russia.

By time of his wife's discomfiture Hervey had settled down with another beauty in distress, Mary Nesbitt, whose husband had gone insane after his bank broke. She remained with Hervey for the rest of his life. In 1775 his elder brother died and he became Earl of Bristol and suddenly enormously rich. He resigned his place at the Admiralty, his colonelcy of marines and his role in the Bedchamber and was promoted rear admiral. War with the American colonies broke out in 1775, and when in 1778 France joined in on the American side, Hervey was invited to be second in command of Keppel's squadron, but he decided that he was too ill to go to sea. Possibly he did not want to serve in the cold Channel waters; possibly he was unwilling to play second fiddle to Keppel; possibly he really was too ill. He was promoted vice admiral in 1778 and was very nearly tempted to sea again, but his health was seriously failing now and he died in 1779 at the age of fifty-five.

Constantine Phipps, by then a key figure in Admiralty politics, wrote to Hervey's followers with the sad news of his uncle's death and a promise of his own support. In particular he wrote to Captain John Robinson, giving him an account of Hervey's death at '20 past 2 without any pain' so that he could break the news to young Augustus, Hervey's child with Kitty Hunter, who was serving in Robinson's ship *Queen*. Robinson had made master and commander in 1765, post captain in 1774, and retired in 1794 as a rear admiral. He never married and died in 1807.

Young Augustus was killed in action during the relief of Gibraltar in 1782.

Of the others who joined the famous old *Centurion* in 1763, chaplain William Howdell showed no apparent ill effects from his time in Havana. He became vicar of West Hythe, Kent and was briefly second master of King's School Canterbury, residing in that city until his death in 1804. The Honourable Philip Stopford was appointed a lieutenant in 1765 and died in that rank in 1793. William Coffen and John Blake sailed the Mediterranean in *Centurion* until the ship paid off in 1769. Hervey's most obstinate follower, John Parvin, saw no reason to stay after his captain left her books on 14 September 1763. He ran a week later.

For naval officers peace was a mixed blessing. Careers stagnated until war broke out, or almost broke out. Peter Foulkes was first lieutenant of *Hero*, armed for Hervey in 1764 for the threatened war against Spain, and first lieutenant of Hervey's *Queen* in 1776 at the beginning of the American war. Foulkes was finally promoted master and commander in 1777 as a result of Hervey's repeated requests. He died in 1782 while in charge of pressing seamen at Dartmouth.

Samuel Ball, midshipman in *Monmouth*, joined *Queen* as a forty-four-year-old master's mate in July 1777. He left in May 1778 for *Prince George* and was promoted lieutenant. As second lieutenant of *Hero* at Plymouth in 1781 he sailed to defend British interests in India with Admiral Hughes's squadron. Ball died during the next year, possibly killed in one of the four battles fought in 1782 between Hughes and the French admiral Suffren.

James Samber, like Phipps, became a lieutenant of the *Deal Castle* in May 1763. He was second lieutenant in *Queen*, and with the patronage of Phipps behind him was promoted master and commander in February 1780, made post in 1782 and retired as a captain in 1804. He lived to see the downfall of Napoleon, dying at eighty-one in 1816.

Dandy Kidd was not so lucky. He was wounded at Havana, went on half pay and probably never recovered his health: he died an unmarried lieutenant in 1772.

Of Hervey's other followers, his onetime coxwain Samuel Blow, midshipman in *Monmouth*, was examined for lieutenant in December 1760 and given a commission in 1777. He remained in continuous employment as a lieutenant, serving in the American war and commanding His Majesty's Gun Boat *Defiance* after the French revolution. He died in 1802 at the age of sixty-eight.

Henry Bryne, midshipman in *Monmouth* and a gentleman with better patronage, was appointed lieutenant in September 1762, commander of *Pomona* in 1771 and post captain in 1775. Unfortunately he did not have luck to match. He died in his frigate *Andromeda* when she went down with all hands during the deadliest of all hurricanes which struck the West Indies in October 1780.

St John Chinnery, who left *Monmouth* late in 1758, was promoted commander in 1761. He got leave to visit Antigua on private business between 1766 and 1769, was made post in 1773 and died affluent but unmarried in 1787, leaving his property to his brother.

John McLaurin, master's mate in *Monmouth*, was not rewarded immediately for his twenty-three-day crossing to Martinique to warn Rodney of the war with Spain, but when Rodney remembered him during the next war his promotion was rapid. Early in 1779 he received a commission as a lieutenant under his old captain, George Johnstone. Later that year he was promoted master and commander of the *Rattlesnake*, and then in June 1780 Rodney made him post as flag captain of his *Princess Royal*. He commanded the frigate *Triton* in the campaigns against de Grasse in 1782 under Samuel Hood and Rodney and died at his home in Greenwich in 1792.

The Hon Philip Tufton Perceval, dissipated son of the intelligent Earl of Egmont and briefly acting lieutenant of *Monmouth*, became a captain, but never captain of a fighting ship. From 1766 until his death in 1795 he commanded royal yachts 'not having been given a flag when his seniority entitled him to one'.

The fast-track promotion that Hervey gave to his nephew Constantine was fully justified by Phipps's later career. After a spell in *Deal Castle*, he was given command of the sloop *Diligence*, though he had been a lieutenant for little more than a year. He was made post in 1765. In 1766 he sailed on a scientific expedition to Newfoundland in the *Niger* with his school friend Joseph Banks, and in 1773 led the expedition towards the North Pole in which the young Horace Nelson took part in the *Carcass*. Phipps became the first European to describe the polar bear and the ivory gull, and his charts were sought after for their accuracy. He was very much involved in the scientific projects undertaken by the navy. In 1775 his father died and he became Lord Mulgrave. In that year he took Banks and the visiting south sea islander Omai to Mulgrave Castle and neighbouring Whitby, and supported Captain Cook's nomination for the Royal Society. He had wide interests, followed Hervey as a member of the Society of Dilettanti, was a member of the Bath Philosophical Society from 1779 to 1787 and a drinking companion of Thomas Gainsborough. A supporter of Sandwich, he became principal spokesman for the Admiralty in the Commons. He was a great expert on his subject, and became a very influential and, on the whole, discerning patron. He married Ann Elizabeth Cholmeley in 1787, but she died bearing a daughter the following year. Phipps died in 1792 while travelling in an attempt to recover his health.

Three of *Dragon*'s warrant officers fared badly after their exertions in Cuba. Archibald Howison, the master, clung to life for a short while after his return to his home in Stepney. He made a will on 23 January 1763 leaving everything to his wife Ann and died soon after that. Boatswain File Fewin witnessed his will, but he lasted little longer, being dead by May 1764. George Grumbley, the cook, made his will in the Haslar Hospital where James Creichton, one of the surgeons, witnessed it. He died in January 1764, leaving his worldly goods to his friend Joseph West of Gosport, Alverstoke, carpenter of HM frigate *Vestal*. He was buried at Gosport.

The others did better. Purser George Fennell returned to his wife Alice and his young son George at their home in Portsmouth. Three daughters were christened there in the next years. He remained purser of the *Dragon*, occasionally exchanging into other ships, until *Dragon* was sold off in 1784. He was connected to and possibly founder of a dynasty of naval businessmen. A George Fennell was 'of the Navy Office' in 1793; another died as purser of the *Thunderer* in 1795; another was a lieutenant and a fourth, his cousin, was accountant to the Treasurer of the Navy from 1780 to his death in 1839.

Gunner Archibald Simonton was promoted to the *Barfleur*, a second-rate. From 1771 until his death in 1779 he was acting gunner of the *Bellona*, a guard ship at Portsmouth where he lived with his wife and two daughters.

John Burgess, gunner's mate in *Monmouth* and *Dragon*, followed Rodney into the *Rochester* and was still alive in 1769 when he received his pay for his time in *Marlborough* in 1762. He may have been the gunner appointed to the *Endeavour* when she was fitted out to view the transit of Venus under Captain Cook. If so, he did not ultimately sail in her – that John Burgess was subsequently gunner to a number of other ships. John Phillips, *Dragon*'s carpenter's mate, enjoyed a short career as a carpenter after Hervey got him promoted into Chaloner Ogle's *Dover* in May 1762. After the war he settled in Portsmouth with his wife Eleanor and died as carpenter of the *Portland* in 1773.

Midshipman Richard Tizard died in 1764.

Monmouth paid off her men in February 1763. Since 1760 they had served with the Western Squadron, blockading the French, with their base at Plymouth. They had continued to take prizes, and although their prize money was often shared with other ships, it added up to a decent total. Their latest earnings – a small share of the frigate *Leverette* and a very small share of the privateer *Zephyr* – were paid to them on their ship or at the Exeter Inn at Plymouth in 1763.

William Corrin, the quarter-gunner in *Monmouth*, had suffered a disabling injury in autumn 1760 when then 'the Surge of the Cable going over His right Wrist . . . renderd him incapable of using it'. In July 1763, aged forty, he entered Greenwich Hospital, where he died in 1776. Greenwich Hospital has changed relatively little since Corrin's time, and it is not too difficult when visiting now to imagine this tough Manxman in retirement, dining in the painted hall, walking in the grounds and watching the tall ships passing on the river.

Most of the Monmouths outlived their beloved ship – the old vessel was broken up finally in 1767. The newspapers paid her the tribute that 'there was no ship she ever chased that she did not overtake: there was no enemy she ever fought that she did not capture'.

Master's mate Edward Salmon had finally left her in March 1762 for preferment into Stephen Hammick's *Baltimore* sloop. He lived to return to Cawsand and to see his children baptised at the lonely landmark church at Maker. John Wicket, conceived during the short visit before Monmouth left for Brest, was followed by Mary, Edward, Robert, Susannah, William, Ann and Elizabeth. Their father died in 1780.

Monmouth's standing officers were old – Gunner Jeffreys had retired and Samuel Furzer the purser resigned his post. He only enjoyed his comfortable house in Woolwich for a short time, since he died in 1762, but he was able to leave substantial legacies to each of his four children. Carpenter Robert Narramore applied for a job in 1772, explaining that he was qualified for a first- or second-rate ship, had been a carpenter for twenty-eight years and was in the *Monmouth* when she took the *Foudroyant*. The official record noted that he was 'old and infirm'. Chaplain Chicken died in 1764, leaving his worldly goods to his daughter Elizabeth.

Robert Carkett was exonerated for the loss of the *Hussar*, which had been the fault of her master and pilot, who promptly deserted to the French. Carkett returned to the Caribbean in the *Active* and then the *Lowestoffe* frigates, based at Pensacola, Florida. In 1778 he was appointed to command the *Stirling Castle* and in 1780 he led the line in an action under Rodney off Martinique. Rodney blamed Carkett for the failure of his plan, but recent scholarship argues that in order to follow Rodney's plan Carkett would have had to disobey one of Rodney's signals, and Rodney was already notorious for destroying disobedient subordinates. Before Carkett had any chance to defend himself, *Stirling Castle* went down with all hands in the same violent hurricane that killed Henry Bryne. He was able to leave his daughter Mary £3,000, while his son Robert received the remainder of his wealth.

Stephen Hammick left *Monmouth* for the flagship in 1758 and was promoted master and commander in 1761. As soon as he could he took Edward Salmon into his new command, the *Baltimore* sloop. By the time of his death in 1781 he owned two houses in the centre of Plymouth and his son, Stephen Hammick junior, was mayor of Plymouth 1791–92.

David Winzar went home to his wife Mary and his children Mary and David at Weymouth. After two and a half years as a half-pay lieutenant, he applied for a year's leave to undertake a voyage to Jamaica in the merchant service. He applied again in 1767, 1768, 1769 and 1770. Between voyages he was based chiefly at the Jamaica Coffee House in London. In 1771 he retired to Weymouth and died there in 1776 at the age of fifty-four. His wife died soon after, suggesting that they may have succumbed to an epidemic, which would have been ironic. Despite his early death, he had raised the fortunes of his family to a steady middling status. Quite a few later Winzars were surgeons, as were the Hammicks.

James Baron returned briefly to Lostwithiel, the county town of Cornwall, where his father was vicar. He remained on half pay until

May and then got a new commission as lieutenant of the seventy-four gun *Fame* in the Hamoaze. In 1764 he married Catherine Spiller, daughter of one of Lostwithiel's leading citizens. In 1769 he was given command of the *Fly* cutter and subsequently commanded his own sloop, the *Catherine*, based in Fowey harbour. By 1788 he had six daughters and two sons. He retired from the navy as master and commander in 1796 and was mayor of Lostwithiel in that year and again in 1801.

By that time Lostwithiel boasted an inn named the Monmouth. It is said to have been named soon after the battle with the *Foudroyant* in tribute to the greatest achievement by local Jack Tars. For many years the action remained famous as the most remarkable of all British victories in single ship combats. The sign showed a small British ship locked in combat with a larger French one in the light of the moon. Beneath was the legend 'The Memorable battle of the Monmouth and Foudroyant'.

Dramatis Personae: Ships' Companies

(grouped by divisions for prize money)

Monmouth

Captain: Arthur Gardiner killed 28 February 1758, then Augustus John Hervey

First Lieutenant: Robert Carkett until 11 March 1758, then St John Chinnery until 13 September 1758, then Edward Hutchins until 7 January 1760, then Peter Foulkes

Second Lieutenant: Stephen Hammick until 11 March 1758, then Edward Hutchins, then James Baron

Third Lieutenant: James Baron until 14 September 1758, then David Winzar

Fourth Lieutenant: David Winzar until 14 September 1758, then Hon. Philip Tufton Percival (acting), then none, then George Knight

Master (navigation and operation of the ship): John Wilson

Captain of marines: Joseph Austin

Lieutenant of marines: George Preston

Boatswain (boats, sails, rigging, colours, anchors, cables and summoning the crew to their duty): James Everitt until 24 May 1758, then File Fewin

Gunner (guns and ammunition): Henry Jeffreys until 20 January 1759, then Archibald Simonton

Carpenter (the ship's frame, masts and yards and all woodwork): Robert Narramore

Purser (finance and supply): Samuel Furzer until 12 May 1758, then Robert Hardy until 15 July 1758, then Richard Jones

Chaplain (spiritual health): Edward Chicken

Surgeon (physical health): Robert Smith

Master's Mates (3 understudies to the master); James Powell died of wounds 3 March 1758; Francis Gall until 7 May 1758; Samuel Ball; John McLaurin from 2 April 1758 to 26 November 1759; Henry Reeves from 8 May 1758; Edward Salmon from 27 November 1759

Midshipman (16 understudies to the lieutenants): Edward Lund until died of wounds 27 April 1758; Richard Tizard; John Fletcher; William Southcote until 2 December 1759; Edward Salmon until 27 November 1759; Robert Fox killed 28 February 1758; Thomas Dixon until 8 June 1759; George White until 11 May 1758; James Reeves; William Langman until 26 February 1760; Roger Snowden until 18 Apr 1758; Thomas Richmond; John Broad until 16 April 1759; Michael McDonough until 26 April 1759; Barnaby Binnock; William Crabb; George Pressick from 2 April 1758; James Gilbert from 19 April 1758; Moses Kennedy from 28 April 1758; Henry Bryne from 5 May 1759

Sailmaker (sails): John Ayres killed 28 February 1758, then Thomas Varley

Captain's Clerk (secretary to captain): George Bernier until 23 September 1758, then Reynold Thomas

Carpenter's mate: David Edwards

Boatswain's mate (2): Edward May until 8 July 1759, John Framingham until 26 April 1758; John Trim from 27 April 1758; William Pinker from 19 July 1759

Gunner's mate (2): William Pattey; David Scott until 11 May 1758; John Burgess from 12 May 1758

Master-at-Arms (small arms, discipline and policing): John Evans

Yeoman of the sheets (4, boatswain's department) William Croucher killed 28 February 1758; Richard Caswell; James Palmer until 10 April 1758; Adam Trumbull from 2 April 1758; John Irvine from 2 April 1758; Jacob Adam Steffins from 11 April 1758

Coxwain (commands captain's barge): Thomas Brown until 13 May 1758, then Samuel Blow

Quartermaster (6, master's department, steering, logs, stowage) Philip Hardy until 26 November 1758; Marmaduke Johns killed 28 February 1758; John Woods; Roger Bowhannon killed 28 February 1758; Robert

Spencer killed 28 February 1758; Joseph Holmes; John Blake from 2 April 1758; Edward Minister from 2 April 1758; John Pray from 2 April 1758; John Harvey from 27 April 1758

Quartermaster's mate (4) Robert Stafford; John Sloper; Nicholas Peake; William Thompson

Yeoman of the Powder Room (2, gunner's department, magazines: John Lee; Richard Vinney

Corporal (2, assistants to master-at-arms) James Pomroy; John Hill until 17 September 1758; Samuel Hill from 18 September 1758

Surgeon's mate (3): Nathaniel Herring first until 22 January 1759, then William Creighton; Mark Cade second until 5 February 1759; William Sharp third until 6 February 1759, then second; Francis O'Connor joined 1759

Sergeant of marines: John Harris, killed 28 February 1758; John Pearson; Daniel Sullivan

Cook (a disabled seaman, preparing food): Thomas Cook

Armourer (gunner's department, blacksmith work): Luke Scardefield until 8 February 1759, then John Sympson

Armourer's mate: John Sympson; Benjamin Halbut from 6 May 1759

Sailmaker's mate: John Sloper

Quartergunner (16, gunner's department but usually elite seamen, each responsible for keeping four guns in prime condition): Joseph Moore; Henry Legassick; Peter Mathews; Richard Green; William Dorey; John Crawford; Thos Gibbons; Robert Ball died 28 November 1758; Richard Cummings; Josepho Pein; Peter Peard; Richard King; Archibald Smith; William Still; John Caskey; William Corrin; William Ballantine; John Moore

Purser's Steward: David Bowman until 15 September 1758, then Thomas Toddy

Sailmaker's crew (2): John Islander; John Tinian

Carpenter's crew (8): John Pooley until September 1758; Thomas Williams; Charles Pond; William Richards; Thomas Whitting; David Thomas; Robert Raynard until September 1758; Robert Marks until 19 January 1759; Charles Davis and William Woody from September 1758; Robert Wallis from January 1759

Cook's mate: Richard Osborn

Corporal of marines: Thomas Fisher, died 26 August 1759; Isaac Mackrell;

Drummer of marines: Caleb Gill

278 seamen and landsmen including Louis d'Amour, Daniel Cameron, William Champlyn, Domenico Costa, William Crossman, Richard Damerel, Edward Dunn, John Eaton, John Finney, Peter Hanlon, John Kitchlowe, John Knowland, Thomas Lawler, Daniel McColl, Walter McFarlane, Archibald Macmillan, William Mallard, William May, Richard Meager, John Newins, Marco Nicholas, Daniel O'Farrell, John Parvin, Joe Pegley, Simon Pengelly, Amos Pitcher, Isaac Pressley, John Radford, Jacques Alexis Renault, Philip Rowden, James Scott, David Seaton, Anthony Stephens, James Strange, James Taylor, George Towns, Richard Treadenham, John Trevillick, William Vallack, Robert Webb, Jabus Yelverton

69 marines including Richard Barley, John Hye, Thomas Nelcoat, James Young

34 servants, including Robert Axworthy, Constantine Phipps, Philip Stopford, William Vine

Total complement 480

Dragon

Captain: Augustus Hervey

First Lieutenant: Joseph Hanby until 11 June 1760, then Peter Foulkes until 17 April 1762, then John Henderson until killed 1 July 1762 then John Robinson

Second Lieutenant: John Robinson until 1 July 1762 then Dandy Kidd

Third Lieutenant: Dandy Kidd until 1 July 1762 then James Samber

Fourth Lieutenant: William Osborn until 14 March 1762, then James Samber until 1 July 1762, then Constantine Phipps

Fifth Lieutenant: James Samber until 16 March 1762, then Constantine Phipps until 1 July 1762, then Edward Waple

Captain of marines: Joseph Austin until 1 January 1761, then Robert Kennedy

Master: Henry Middleton until 4 October 1761, then Archibald Howison

First Lieutenant of marines: George Preston until 3 December 1761, then Vincent Brown

Second Lieutenant of marines: Eusabius Sylvester until 25 November 1760, then Francis Holyoak

Boatswain: File Fewin

Gunner: Archibald Simonton

Carpenter: John White until 17 February 1761 then John Purnell

Chaplain: William Howdell

Surgeon: James Watt

Purser: James Perrott until 1 October 1761, then George Fennell

Master's Mate (3): George Pressick; Richard How until 13 March 1761; Christopher Hudson

Midshipman (16): William Coffen; Richard Tizard; James Reeves; Francis Newton; Thomas Underwood; Constantine Phipps; Philip Stopford; Moses Kennedy; James Fellowes; Jacob Adam Steffins from 14 March 1761; George Towers from 30 June 1761; John Holliday run 17 September 1760; Anthony Surtees run 30 October 1760; John Colpoys until 20 March 1761; William Brozett until 21 March 1761; John Ellis; William Wood from 6 October 1761; John Burgess from 6 October 1761; Oliver Templeton from 6 June 1761 until 16 August 1762; Thomas Saul from 6 June 1761; Jeremiah Elliott from 17 October 1761; Hugh Boyd, John Samuel, Robert Dunkin May to October 1761; John Faulkner from 30 April 1762; Robert Leaver from 1 July 1762; George Young from 1 July 1762; John Samber from 6 May 1762, killed 1 July 1762

Sailmaker: Thomas Varley

Carpenter's mate: John Phillips

Boatswain's mate (2): John Woods, disrated 24 December 1761; William Pinker; William Alexander from April 1762

Gunner's mate (2): William McNeilly; John Burgess until 6 October 1761; John Hawkins from 6 October 1761

Master-at-Arms: Alexander Mowet

Yeoman of the sheets (4): Adam Trumbull; John Irvine until 27 December 1760; Jacob Adam Steffins until 14 March 1761; David Seaton; Philip Burrell from 31 August 1761; James Taylor from 31 August 1761

Coxwain: Ben Hart, then Solomon McCullock from November 1761 to July 1762, then Richard Anderson

Quartermaster (6): John Blake; John Harvey until 27 March 1761 when

left ashore; William Buchanan; James Nottingham; William Pilian; John
Suffolk; John Bell from August 1761 until disrated 20 March 1762; from
30 April 1762 Edward Callett

Quartermaster's mate (4): Walter Calvin; William Stubbs; John Neal;
John Saver run 17 September 1760; from 31 August 1761 John Gibbs

Yeoman of the Powder Room (2): George Barker; William Inglis until 18
February 1761; William Randall from 31 August 1761

Corporal (2) Alexander Norris; Joseph Mass

Surgeon's mate (3): John Wills first; John Slade second; John Wallace third

Sergeant of Marines (2): John Pearson; Samuel Pollock, died 29 June 1761;
Thomas Nelcoat, promoted 29 June 1761

Cook: George Grumbley

Armourer: John Sympson

Armourer's mate (2): Adam Hall (disrated July 1760–August 1761); John
Light;

Sailmaker's mate: Edmund Ryan

Quartergunner (18): Thomas Davies, run 9 January 1761; David Belford;
John Adams; David Nichols, run 15 October 1760; William Randall until
31 August 1761; James Rattenbury; Andrew Mackay, run 4 February
1761; John Ure, until 18 February 1761; Jonathan Thompson, run 3
October 1760; James Sutherland; Henry Davie; John Oliver left ashore 26
March 1761; John Townbull until 27 December 1760; John Russell; Isaac
Pressley; William Ballantine until 4 September 1760; from 31 August
1761 John Phillips, Robert Rice, John Ritchie, Edward Dunn, William
Rippon, Thomas Redshaw, Thomas Martin

Purser's Steward: Robert Buchanan until 6 October 1761, then James
Dorrington

Cooper: John Taylor

Sailmaker's crew (2): unknown, from 31 August 1761 Robert Carter

Carpenter's Crew (8): Thomas Salisbury; William Jones; Richard Pelson;
William Ford; William Robinson, until 10 November 1761; Samuel
Thomas; Richard Treadenham; from 31 August 1761 Robert Cockburn;
Richard Gyle; Richard Hughes; John Perry

Caulker: Duncan McArthur

Barber: William Monroe

Corporal of marines (3): Michael Small until 14 August 1761 (wounded);
William Russell; Thomas Topliss, demoted 19 January 1761; George

Bridgford, promoted 19 January 1761; Thomas Nelcoat, promoted 1 November 1760

Drummer of marines (2): Caleb Gill until 26 October 1761; Jacob Whittingham until 19 February 1761; William Reed from February 1761; Richard Hopkins from October 1761

420 seamen and landsmen, including John Adams, Louis d'Amour, William Ansley, John Bailey, James Barry, James Bernard, Andrew Bowden, Edward Brannon, John Broad, John Campbell, William Campbell, John Chandler, Daniel Cameron, Joseph Clements, Miles Cook, Domenico Costa, William Dakers, John Davis, Bryan Donnolly, Andrew Epsley, Philip Farrell, John Finney, Peter Hanlon, Bryant Kennedy, John Mathews, James Miller, John Newins, William Oberg, George Patience, William Patience, John Parvin, Joe Pegley, James Raddle, Bartholomew Rearden, Jacques Alexis Renault, John Robinson, Thomas Snibson, William Snook, William Watson, Thomas Williams

100 marines, including Richard Barley, James Bulboard, Michael Carney, Richard Damon, Richard Hughes, John Hye, Thomas Nelcoat, James Stuart, Daniel Walkeley, James Young

40 servants, including Ben Anderson, Joseph Buckley, John Carter, William Halliday, George Martin, James Rawlings, William Rickets, Robert Rogers, Thomas Vineyard

Total complement 650

Glossary

aft, towards the stern or back of the ship.

balanced mizen, to **balance** a sail is to contract it by rolling it up at one corner; the mizen sail is balanced by lowering the yard a little, and rolling up a small portion of the sail at the upper corner.

barge, long, slight and narrow boat with at least ten oars, used to carry the captain.

blacking, cover with a mixture of tar and lamp black as protection against sun, wind and water.

board, boarder, to attack the enemy by climbing into his ship and fighting hand to hand, a member of the ship's company appointed to do this.

booms, a light spar, a spare spar, or a floating barrier protecting a harbour mouth; **boom irons**, shaped like a figure 8, attached a boom extension to a yard.

boot top, clean the upper part of a ship's bottom of weed, slime and shells, by leaning it on one side where there is no dock or opportunity to careen, and daubing it with a mixture of tallow, sulphur and resin.

bow, the bows are either side of the foremost part of the ship's hull or the front of the ship; **bow chasers** are guns mounted there, facing forward to fire at ships being chased.

bower, the **best bower** and small bower anchors were the principal anchors of the ship, kept ready for use in the bows.

braces, bracing, rope fastened to the extremities of the yard employed to turn the sails on the mast in order to catch the wind.

bring to, to check the course of an advancing ship by arranging the sails so that they counter each other; she will then lie-to with the sails that are aback balancing the effect of those that are full.

broadside, the simultaneous discharge of all the artillery on one side of a ship.

bum-boats, boats from shore that sell vegetables or other goods to a ship at anchor.

bumpkin, bumkin, a short boom extending from each bow to extend the lower edge of the foresail to windward; it has a large block at its outer end, through which the tack, tied to the corner of the sail, is passed; when this is drawn tight it brings the corner of the sail close to the block and the tack is said to be aboard.

cable, 1. a large, strong rope, usually used to retain a ship at anchor; 2. the standard length of an anchor cable, 120 fathoms (720 feet or 240 yards).

capstan, a mechanical device for hauling in cables, consisting of a vertical revolving drum, into which bars are inserted so that it can be turned by many men.

careen, heave the ship down on one side by hauling on her strengthened masts, so that the bottom of the ship is exposed sufficiently to clean off the weed, filth and shells that gather there after a period at sea and obstruct the ship's progress. The cleaning process, 'breaming', involved burning off the old coating of pitch, with the weeds, scraping, and then recoating with a new mixture of pitch and sulphur.

cartridge, a cloth or paper bag containing the charge of powder for a gun; **cartridge pricker**, the large needle (also a **priming iron** or **wire**) used to clear the touch-hole and expose the powder in the cartridge, once inserted into the cannon.

chains, strong links of iron, bolted to the ship's sides, used to contain the blocks called 'dead-eyes' by which the shrouds supporting the masts are extended.

chase, a vessel pursued by some other (normally 'chace' at this time, the act of pursuing)

chase guns, guns mounted in the bows to fire forward during a pursuit, also known as 'chasers'.

chasse-marée, A French coastal vessel capable of operating in shallow waters, often originally intended to transport fish from a fishing ground to a town, sometimes adapted for use as a small privateer.

cohorn, a small mortar for throwing grenades.

conn, con, give instructions to the helmsmen on the course of the ship from moment to moment, according to the set of the sails, the state of the waves or in order to avoid dangers in confined waters.

course, 1. the direction in which a ship moves; 2. name for the lowest square sails, either foresail or mainsail.

cutter, 1. a small vessel rigged for and aft on a single mast; 2. a type of ship's boat broader, deeper and shorter than the barge and pinnace, more suitable for sailing (when rigged like the larger vessels called cutters) and used chiefly to carry passengers and stores to and from the ship.

dogger, a Dutch two-masted sailing vessel, generally employed in the herring fishery.

fascine, a long, cylindrical bundle of bound sticks used to fill ditches, protect batteries etc.

fid, a square bar of iron with a shoulder at one end, used to support the weight of the top mast when erected at the head of the lower mast, and the topgallant mast similarly.

figurehead, emblematic figure carved at the very front of a ship – *Monmouth* had the conventional lion rampant, replaced in 1759 by a scroll; engravings of *Dragon* appear to show a dragon.

forecastle, a deck built over the forward end of the upper deck.

foresail, the lowest sail hung from the foremast; above it come the foretopsail and foretopgallant.

frigate, a light, nimble ship, built for speed, carrying between twenty and thirty-eight guns, usually employed cruising against the enemy.

gabion, a wicker basket, intended to be filled with earth to provide protection for the besiegers during a siege.

glacis, the parapet of the covered way, beyond the ditch which it conceals from view, extended in a long, sloping bank that can be swept with fire from the ramparts within.

hawser, a large rope, thinner than a cable, but wider than a tow-line.

head, the foremost part of the ship; **heads**, the toilets used by the seamen situated over the bows of the ship.

heel, 1. to incline or be made to incline to either side; 2. the bottom of a mast, rudder, etc.

hot press, a forcible recruiting drive for seamen during which the protections that exempted certain categories of seamen from naval service were suspended and not respected.

hoy, a small coasting vessel carrying goods or passengers, often to or from a ship.

jib, foremost sail of a ship, being a staysail extended from the outer end of the bowsprit, prolonged by the **jib boom**, a boom extending the bowsprit forward, like a topmast.

junk, pieces of chopped up old cable, used for a number of purposes including making wadding.

jury mast, a temporary mast, erected to replace one broken in a storm or battle.

kedge, a small anchor used to keep a ship steady, especially at the turn of the tide, and sometimes to move her from place to place.

larboard, eighteenth-century word meaning the left side of the ship when facing forward; the modern term 'port' was sometimes used already.

launch, a boat longer, lower and flatter-bottomed than a longboat, calculated for rowing and approaching a flat shore, used chiefly in the Mediterranean.

leeward, the direction towards which the wind is blowing.

linstock, a staff about three feet long to which the match is attached, enabling a gun captain to discharge a cannon, whilst standing far enough away to avoid its recoil.

longboat, the largest and strongest of the ship's boats, employed to carry anchors, cables, barrels of water etc.; has a mast and sail and can be decked and armed for cruising short distances against enemy merchant ships or to impress seamen.

make sail, to set sail, increase the quantity of sails, or let out reefs.

mainmast, the tallest, second mast.

mizenmast, the smallest, aftermost mast.

oakum, a substance made from old ropes, driven into the seams or gaps between planks to prevent water from entering.

orlop deck, platform of planks over the hold for the officers' store rooms and the cables.

pay, to daub or anoint a surface to protect it from wind or weather. The bottom is paid with a mixture of tallow, sulphur and resin; the sides are paid with tar, turpentine or resin; rigging with tar; masts along which sails are hoisted are paid with hog's lard, butter or tallow.

pennant, pendant, a long, narrow banner displayed from the mast-head of a ship of war, distinguishing it from other vessels; **broad pendant**, wider, swallow tailed flag flown by a commodore.

petty officer, minor officers corresponding to non-commissioned officers in the army.

pilot, a person with special local knowledge charged with the direction of the ship's course near the coast and while entering rivers or harbours in his district.

pinnace, 1. a small vessel with oars and sails, having two masts rigged like a schooner; 2. as a ship's boat, a small barge rowed by no more than eight oars and used by lieutenants etc.

poop, the highest and aftermost deck of a ship, built over the after end of the quarterdeck.

privateer, a privately owned warship licensed by the admiralty by letter of marque to capture enemy shipping for profit.

protection, a certificate of exemption from impressment, normally granted to certain classes of seamen.

quarterdeck, a deck above the main deck over the after part of the ship.

redoubt, an outwork of a fortress, usually square or polygonal in shape, beyond the glacis but within musket shot of the covered way, or a similarly shaped detached fieldwork.

reef, 1. a tuck taken in a sail to reduce its area; 2. to shorten sail by bundling part of the sail against the yard; 3. a chain of submerged rocks.

sheet anchor, the principal large anchor, stored in reserve with a cable attached ready for use.

shrouds, a range of large ropes extending from the mast-head to the left and right of the ship, to support the masts.

sloop, a small vessel with one mast; **sloop of war**, the smallest warship except a cutter, rigged either as a ship or snow and commanded by a master and commander.

slops, clothes issued by the navy.

snow, the largest of European two-masted vessels.

sound, the operation of finding the depth of the water.

spring, 1. a crack in, or to crack a mast or yard; 2. a rope passed out of one extremity of a ship and attached to a cable extending from the other, when she lies at anchor, used to bring the ship's broadside to bear on some distant object.

starboard, the right side of the ship when facing forward.

stay, a large strong rope supporting a mast forward; **staysail**, a triangular sail extended on a stay.

stern, the after end (back) of a ship; **stern chaser**, a chase gun facing aft (backward) at a pursuer.

stream anchor, a small anchor, like the kedge, for use in rivers, or for moving the ship from place to place in a harbour.

strike, lower: ships strike their ensigns to surrender; an admiral strikes his flag to resign or retire.

studding sails, light sails extended only in moderate and steady breezes on booms beyond the principal sails for extra width of sail.

swivel, a small gun mounted on the side of a ship, usually firing a half-pound shot.

taffrail, taffarel, the upper part of a ship's stern, usually ornamented with sculpture.

tar, 1. liquid, blackish gum from pine or fir trees, boiled and used to pay the sides and rigging of ships and to make canvas waterproof; 2. a figurative expression for a sailor of any kind.

tartan, tartane, a small Mediterranean coasting vessel with one mast and a bowsprit, the very large principal sail extended by a lateen yard.

tompion, a bung or cork used to stop the mouth of a cannon; at sea it is carefully sealed with tallow or putty to prevent water penetrating into the bore and dampening the powder in the chamber.

topgallant mast, slender mast above the topmast, struck down in bad weather; **sail**, the sail above the main course and topsail.

train-tackles, ropes hooked to the rear of a gun carriage to prevent the cannon rolling forward until it is loaded; the **gun-tackles**, attached to bolts on the ship's side, are used to draw it forward; **breechings** restrain the recoil.

vent reamer, a gimlet to clear the touch-hole of a cannon.

wad, wadding, ball of old rope stuffed into the breech of a gun to keep cannon balls in place.

warrant officer, officers with a warrant rather than a commission, divided into warrant sea officers – the master, the surgeon, the purser, the gunner, the boatswain, the carpenter – and inferior officers with warrants, such as the armourer, the cook, the surgeon's mates and the master-at-arms.

yard, a spar hung horizontally from a mast to extend the head or foot of a square sail, yard arm, the extreme end of a yard.

yawl, a ship's boat similar to a cutter but smaller and rowed by six oars.

Acknowledgements

This account was compiled from details discovered by scouring numerous documents in the National Archives. It would not have been possible without the increasingly magnificent computer system and helpful, efficient staff of that exemplary establishment. I would like to thank the people there once again for their patience and hard work. After one special appeal Alistair Hanson gave me some basic guidance on High Court of Admiralty Records.

A second crucially important source for me was the archive at Mulgrave Castle and I am extremely grateful to the Marquis of Normanby and his archivist Joy Moorhead for allowing me access to this previously unseen material and for generous help during a brief, very intensive and highly enjoyable visit. My other principal sources were documents in the Caird Library at the National Maritime Museum (notably lieutenants' logs) and newspapers as well as published documents and secondary sources at Cambridge University Library and I am grateful to their staff for their help. The staff of the Wellcome Institute Library, the British Library and New York Public Library also suffered from my obsession with *Monmouth* and *Dragon*.

At a local level I received guidance and help from various record offices, notably from Gwyn Thomas and the staff of the record offices at Ipswich and Bury, and Kim Cooper, Library Officer at the Cornish Studies Library, Redruth. In Lostwithiel local historian Derek Taylor and Pat Gregory and the staff of Lostwithiel Museum were warmly cooperative and Gillian Kempster and Jim Sheppard gave generous help with genealogical research on the Rame Peninsula. I am grateful to Matthew Little, archivist of Royal Marines Museum and to Peter Duckers of Shropshire Regimental Museum. Tony Barrow and

Nicholas Rodger answered impossible questions with cheerful forbearance.

Through the internet I made contact with a handful of descendants of Monmouths and Dragons who all did their best to help me. I am grateful to Pete Hammett and Tony and Mike Cole-Hamilton for information about David Winzar, Linda Monk and Pat Blandford for information about Luke Scardefield and to J. J. .Heath-Caldwell for a series of revelations about George Marsh. His was one of a number of highly informative websites that greatly facilitated some aspects of my research.

When it came to pictures Sheila O'Connell and the staff of the British Museum print room went very far beyond the call of duty in providing assistance and making it possible to include black and white illustrations. Nigel Talbot and the staff of Grosvenor Prints allowed me to ransack their premises once again. In many cases it continues to be cheaper to buy antique prints from them than to hire scans of them from picture libraries. The staff of the National Maritime Museum did their best to cope with many complicated demands and the National Trust was most generous in accommodating last minute requests to take photographs at Anglesey Abbey and at Ickworth.

To Hugh Belsey, Kate Johnson, Phil and Frances Craig, Steve Mobbs and Pauline Thomas, David Bradshaw, James Campbell, Charles, Lars, Peter and Clive, I owe thanks for their skills, good cheer, or hospitality in foreign ports. So far, with balanced mizen and storm staysails set, I have weathered the occasional demands from Juliette, William and Lily that I should go out and get a proper job. I am very grateful that they haven't yet deserted the ship. Indeed, Juliette was kind enough to take photographs of paintings at Ickworth and Anglesey Abbey.

Rupert Lancaster, Hugo Wilkinson, Juliet Van Oss, Josine Meijer and Kerry Hood have all proved trusty quartermasters in conning this frail bark through blustery weather and sudden violent squalls.

Picture credits

Black and white

p. 2 Bibliothèque nationale, Paris; p. 12 private collection; p. 25 National Maritime Museum PU5250; p. 29 ©British Museum Ee, 2.94 (detail); p. 30 ©British Museum Ee, 2.94 (detail); p. 52 ©British Museum 1902-10-11-3175; p. 54 ©British Museum 1868-8-8-3894; p. 60 private collection; p. 68 Bibliothèque nationale, Paris; p. 85 ©British Museum Ee, 2.94; p. 88 NMM between decks; p. 92 ©British Museum Aa, 9.43; p. 93 ©British Museum 1872-06-08-117; p. 95 Bibliothèque nationale, Paris; p. 101 ©British Museum 1869-04-10-1451 (detail); p. 105 National Maritime Museum PW3452; p. 107 National Maritime Museum PW4047; p. 113 Bibliothèque nationale, Paris; p. 125 Bibliothèque nationale, Paris; p. 131 Bibliothèque nationale, Paris; p. 143 private collection; p. 147 private collection; p. 152 ©British Museum 1869-04-10-1452 (detail); p. 155 Bibliothèque nationale, Paris; p. 164 ©British Museum 1880-11-13-5104; p. 166 ©British Museum 1868-8-8-3837; p. 173 ©British Museum 1872-10-12-5145; p. 174 ©British Museum 1896-07-10-13; p. 176 ©British Museum 1992-10-11-3213; p. 179 Bibliothèque nationale, Paris; p. 184 Bibliothèque nationale, Paris; p. 189 Bibliothèque nationale, Paris; p. 192 Bibliothèque nationale, Paris; p. 193 National Maritime Museum (detail); p. 195 National Maritime Museum (detail); p. 199 National Maritime Museum (detail); p. 214 private collection; p. 219 ©British Museum 1854-10-20-51 (detail); p. 222 ©British Museum 1854-10-20-50 (detail); p. 224 Bibliothèque nationale, Paris; p. 232 National Maritime Museum PW3470; p. 243 private collection; p. 246 National Maritime Museum (detail) or BM 1849-10-03-14; p. 247 National

Maritime museum (detail) or BM 1849-10-03-14; p. 250 National
Portrait Gallery MW37564; p. 258 ©British Museum 1849-10-03-
16 (detail); p. 261 ©British Museum 1849-10-03-17 (detail); p. 265
©British Museum 1849-10-03-16 (detail); p. 276 ©British Museum
1849-10-03-16 (detail); p. 278 private collection; p. 282 ©British
Museum 1849-10-03-18 (detail); p. 285 ©British Museum 1849-10-
03-20 (detail); p. 287 ©British Museum 1849-10-03-20 (detail); p.
290 private collection.

Notes on Sources

Full publication details of the works mentioned below are provided in the bibliography. The narrative is based on the various logs, muster and pay books, together with Augustus Hervey's journal (Erskine) and a wide variety of other manuscript sources. The archive at Mulgrave Castle contains the surviving portion of Augustus Hervey's naval papers. These are used here for the first time since until now it was thought that they had been lost. The rich correspondence of the Hervey and Phipps families at Mulgrave Castle is also completely new. The manuscript sources are listed in the bibliography. Only direct quotations from them are cited in the notes.

The following abreviations are used in the notes:

DNB   *Dictionary of National Biography*
MCA   Mulgrave Castle Archive
NA   National Archives
NMM   National Maritime Museum
SROB   Suffolk Record Office, Bury St Edmunds
SROI   Suffolk Record Office, Ipswich

Author's Note

vii. 'that remarkable superiority', Hutchinson, p. iii.

1 A Question of Honour

1. 'we gave chace steering for the headmost', Baron's log, NMM Adm/L/M/247.
2. 'she was not to be taken:' Entick, III, p. 58.
2. 'had every sail set and were getting up fast', and the quotations following Erskine, p. 271.
4. 'coming up wth: the chase very fast', Wilson's log NA, Adm 52/657.
4. 'Whatever becomes of you and I', Entick, III, p. 57.
5. 'he advised the admiral to bear down, but that he objected thereto' Charnock, V, p. 384.
5. 'Captain Gardiner, two days before he left this port', Entick III, p. 58.
6. 'The British officers knew': my figures for *Monmouth*'s weight of broadside are based on the account of expenditure of shot in Wilson's log NA, Adm 52/657. Rodger was mistaken to revise in *The Command of the Ocean*, p. 274, the figures that he gave in *The Wooden World*, p. 58. Lyon's description of *Monmouth*'s armament in *The Sailing Navy List*, on which Rodger based his revision, is incorrect if the master's log is to be believed.
11. 'not only requires alertness but courage', Thursfield, p. 245.
14. 'we saw the *Revenge*', Wilson's log NA, Adm 52/657.
14. 'called the Twin Sisters', letter from a lieutenant of the *Revenge* dated 2 April 1758, *Universal Magazine*, May 1758. He continued, 'we cruise in concert, and share prize-monies, whether in company, or not; and the gratest harmony subsists between us'.
15. 'before the wind with everything out', Erskine, p. 271.
16. 'This ship', he said, 'must be taken', Entick, III, pp. 58–9.

2 The Music of Great-Guns

18. 'his office in time of battle', Falconer, p. 176.
20. 'carry her masts away', Wilson's log NA, Adm 52/657.
20. 'lashed upon the Grating', O'Loghlen, p. 115.
20. 'Two or three expert Men', O'Loghlen, p. 114.
21. 'principally used by the French', Falconer, p. 266.
21. 'nothing can gall an Enemy so much as a constant Fire', MacIntire, p. 117.

22. 'all the grap & Duble Headd: shott that is Allowed', Wilson's log NA, Adm 52/657.
22. 'balls cut into two equal parts', Falconer, p. 265.
23. 'ran a very great risk', Olaudah Equiano quoted in McLynn, pp. 251–2.
24. 'at first the enemy's fire was much the quickest', Entick, III, p. 57.
25. 'while in the act of encouraging his people', Charnock, V, p. 384.
25. 'Capt Gardiner Recd a Mortal Wound', Carkett's log, NMM Adm/L/ M/247
26. 'Before he expired, he sent for his first lieutenant', Entick, III, pp. 58–9.
26. 'having lain speechless from the minute he was wounded', Winzar's log NMM Adm/L/M/247.
26. 'Don't give up the ship': consciously or unconsciously, the wounded Commander Lawrence of the *Chesapeake* echoed Gardiner's expression, having almost certainly read of the *Monmouth* and *Foudroyant*, and Lawrence's words were adopted by the American fleet. See Ian W. Toll, *Six Frigates*, London, 2006, p. 414.
27. 'The whole cockpit deck, cabins,' surgeon's journal for HMS *Ardent* 1797–8, NA, Adm 101/85/7 printed in Lloyd and Coulter, pp. 59–60.
28. 'In an hour it slackened,' Entick, III, p. 57.
28. 'Broadside, and Broadside,' Winzar's log NMM Adm/L/M/247.
28. 'the Music of Great-Guns', recruiting advertisement for a privateer, *Exeter Flying Post*, 18 February 1780, reproduced in Starkey, plate 6.
29. 'was thrown overboard', Winzar's log NMM Adm/L/M/247.
30. 'imagining the enemy had struck', Baron's log, NMM Adm/L/M/247.
30. 'We had no Tackle' and the quotation following, Winzar's log NMM Adm/L/M/247.
31. 'I got near enough to see by the light of the moon' and the quotation following, Erskine, p. 271.

3 Dead Men's Clothes

32. 'Account of Cloaths sold at the mast', loose paper in NA, Adm 32/113.
33. 'a solid, modern brick house in Woolwich', NA, PROB 31/598/489.
34. 'above their wear', Lavery, *Shipboard Life*, p. 23.
34. 'blue and white checked linen', slop contracts for 1757, NA, Adm 49/ 35.

35. 'appear properly as a quarter deck officer', quoted in Rodger, *Wooden World*, p. 25.
36. 'Tabitha was also awarded a small "bounty" ', NA, Adm 106/3017 and 106/3019 262 and 263; I am grateful to Jim Sheppard for help with the Antony church registers.
38. 'A Sea-Chaplain's Petition', reprinted in Roger Lonsdale ed., *The New Oxford Book of Eighteenth-Century Verse* (Oxford University Press, 1984), pp. 480–2.
42. 'I have treated all my Prisoners en Prince', Hervey to Lepel Phipps, 14 March 1758, MCA, IV, 17/7.
43. 'We were Divided into two Watches,' Cormack and Jones, p. 22.
43. James Young details from NA, Adm 158/283 24th company.
43. 'stealing of cloaths', Wilson's log NA, Adm 52/657.
43. 'Carefull, Sober Man', Gardiner to Clevland, 8 April 57 Spithead, NA Adm 1/1833
44. 'the very ship the French Admiral Galissoniere', and the quotation following Entick, III, p. 58.
45. 'an officer in Osborn's squadron', *London Evening Post*, 15–18 April 1758. Erskine 275; Hervey's rough drafts of Osborn's dispatches and orders are at MCA, VI, 1/187–92.
45. 'a high Encomium on the Bravery', *London Evening Post*, 15–18 April 1758.

4 The New Captain

47. 'Capt Gardiner of the Monmouth was killed', Hervey to Lepel Phipps, 14 March 1758, MCA, IV, 17/7.
47. 'I knew nothing of this gentleman,' Erskine, p. 274.
48. 'Austere in his disposition,' Charnock, IV, p. 181.
53. 'Sober, Active and Diligent Man', Hervey to Clevland, 18 November 1759, NA Adm 1/1894.
53. 'went in cloaks', Erskine, p. 76.
53. 'Took a resolution from this afternoon', Erskine, p. 77.
54. 'So naked that you would have taken her for Andromeda', H. Walpole, Letters, ii. 153, in Old *DNB*.
54. 'a clog . . . that would not let me remain in England', Erskine, p. 93.
56. 'Feeling myself in the arms', Erskine, p. 151.

56. 'very handsome and sensible for an Italian', Erskine, p. 132.
56. 'that intimacy began which lasted', Erskine, p. 171.
56. 'not perfectly happy with her husband', Erskine, p. 172.
56. 'one whole night with her,' and the following quotations, Erskine, p. 177.
57. 'that she would never make any intimacy', and the following quotations, Erskine, p. 178.
58. 'made a great noise everywhere', and the following quotations, Erskine, p. 183.
59. 'Tis hard to have a Fortune thus almost in one's Pocket', Hervey to Lepel Phipps, 29 February 1756, MCA, IV, 8/25.
61. 'I can never wipe it off my spirits,' Hervey to Lepel Phipps, 8 July 1757, MCA, IV, 17/6.
61. 'but that I have almost every minute of this day', Hervey to Lepel Phipps, 14 March 1758, MCA, IV, 17/6.
61. 'by his constant anxiety and watching the French', Erskine, p. 277.
63. 'two Sheds, or Huts,' Baugh, p. 221.
64. 'I can't tell', NA Adm 1/5297

5 The Flying Monmouth

66. 'You are hereby required and directed', MCA, VI, 1/196.
66. 'learning French . . . an indispensible qualification', Knowles. Edward Thompson (p.153) also advised the young officer to 'apply yourself first to French; it is universally spoke and understood, and will give you a superiority wherever you go'.
68. 'proved to be a tartan,' Winzar's log NMM Adm/L/M/247.
69. 'as the Merchts. will not undertake', Hervey to Clevland, 11 June 1758, NA, Adm 1/1893
69. 'sold all the tartans', Winzar's log NMM Adm/L/M/247.
70. 'Here we came for, and found', Winzar's log NMM Adm/L/M/247.
71. 'as I had my reasons for paying very little regard', and the following quotations, Erskine, p. 286.
72. 'Famous in the last war', Powell, p. 235.
72. 'why I had in this manner broke the neutrality', Erskine, p. 286.
73. 'a deficiency in provisions of 852 gallons wine,' Hervey's log, NA Adm 51/3912.

73. 'called by the English Sailors Love Lane', Powell, p. 210.
73. 'many kind-hearted courtesans and brothel-houses', Earle, p. 102.
74. 'a good agreeable sensible coxcomb', Erskine, p. 255.
75. 'adorn'd with the finest Variety of Lemon', Brice, p. 613.
76. 'whole time was passed here in festivals', Erskine, p. 289.
76. 'two large ships, one of which appeared so French', Erskine, p. 290.
77. 'I thought the Spaniards seemed to rejoice', Erskine, p. 291.
78. 'but with a very indifferent character', Erskine, p. 252.
78. 'found him the same gay', Hunter.
78. 'a person who has the honour', Knowles.
79. 'till the 25th the wind came Westerly', manuscript of Hervey's journal, SROB, 941/50/3 (not in Erskine).
79. 'loose and decay'd', Defects of His Majesty's Ship *Monmouth* in NA, Adm 1/1893.
80. 'The Channel has been in the greatest bustle', Corbett, p. 251
80. 'in the Morning of the 28th, and the following quotation, manuscript of Hervey's journal SROB, 941/50/3 (not in Erskine).

6 *Transported as Slaves*

82. 'Have inspected the *Monmouth* and list her defects', Adm 354/60/264 in NMM.
82. 'getting drunk, neglecting his duty', Hervey's log, NA Adm 51/3912.
83. 'The Cargoe was acknowledged', Hervey to Clevland, 11 November 1758, Adm 1/1893.
83. 'say that Marco Nicholas, enter'd for the Ship', Hervey to Clevland, 22 November 1758, Adm 1/1893.
84. 'As I do not suspect any man will leave the ship', Hervey to Clevland, 14 December 1758, Adm 1/1893.
84. 'Commodore Boys is directed', MCA, VI, 1/254.
84. 'The taking of *Foudroyant*', *Public Advertiser*, 13 December 1758.
84. 'has struck out a new beauty', *Critical Review, VII* (1759), p. 171.
86. 'went down to Rochester', Erskine, p. 294.
86. 'Most Honourable and worthy Lords' and the quotations following, *Monmouth*'s ship's company to Clevland 24 December 1758, Adm 354/ 161/67 in NMM.
89. 'While this was performing, the whole crew', Renney, p.63.

89. 'unlucky enough to be hanged at Tyburn', Linebaugh, p. 140.
89. 'one group of Hedge Lane prostitutes', Henderson, p. 18–23.
90. 'constantly hung up & Affixed', regulation noted in *Monmouth*'s muster book, NA Adm 36/6100.
90. 'for diligence, capacity and resolution', Rodger 'The Mutiny in the *James & Thomas*', p. 296.
91. 'Kitty Fisher style . . . in dress or manner' and the quotation following, *DNB*.
91. 'in great forwardness', Erskine, p. 298.
92. 'I now find that the remainder are order'd', Hervey to Clevland 26 February 1759, NA, Adm 1/1894.
92. 'will be a great advantage in Time of Action', and the following quotations, Hervey to Clevland 15 January 1759, NA, Adm 1/1894.
95. 'You know, I suppose, that flat-bottomed boats', quoted in Corbett, p. 366.
96. 'I have got at last to this Cursed Melancholy hole', Hervey to Lepel Phipps, 15 April 1759, MCA, IV, 17/8.
97. 'taking leave of Kitty', Erskine, p. 300.
97. 'some time in a Tender', Hervey to Clevland 26 April 1759, NA, Adm 1/1894.
98. 'slops, shirts, bedding, and all the necessary articles', Lind, *Essay*, pp. 29–30 in Gradish, p. 173.
98. 'Ten thousand workmen are employed', quoted in Marcus, pp. 25–6.
99. 'We talk of nothing here but the French invasion', quoted in Marcus, p. 26.

7 The Black Rocks

100. 'I expected when I came to Plymouth', Constantine to Lepel Phipps, undated, MCA, IV, 17/21.
100. 'a C—'d place', and the quotations following, Hervey to Lepel Phipps, 5 May 1759, MCA, IV, 17/10.
101. 'We have a Birth to ourselves But are never in it', Constantine to Lepel Phipps, undated, MCA, IV, 17/21.
102. 'Log Book in the Steeridge from the Quartermaster', and the quotations following, Cormack and Jones, p. 24.

103. 'Captains that are under my Command,' Hervey to Lepel Phipps, 25 August 1759, MCA, IV, 17/14.
103. 'Divided into two Watches', Cormack and Jones, p. 22.
104. 'Dear Mama, . . . I obey your orders', Constantine to Lepel Phipps, 17 May 1759, MCA, IV, 17/22.
104. 'certainly had a heart to gain an engagement', Erskine, p. 262.
104. 'a fellow without a grain of understanding', Erskine, p. 220.
106. 'that if we met the enemy I should at least', Erskine, p. 302.
106. 'not so much as a White Rag in an open Boat', and the quotations following, Constantine to Lepel Phipps, 17 May 1759, MCA, IV, 17/23.
107. 'had broke two tillers, and the lower gudgin', Erskine, p. 303.
107. 'very hard gales with heavy squalls and a great sea', Baron's log, NMM Adm/L/M/248.
107. 'we have had Violent Gales of wind', and the quotation following, Hervey to Lepel Phipps 15 June 1759, MCA, IV, 17/12.
108. 'to breakfast with Sir Edward,' Erskine, p. 303.
108. 'for not attending Divine Service', Hutchins's log, NMM Adm/L/M/248.
108. 'the wors't Winter Weather I ever saw', Hervey to Lepel Phipps 29 June 1759, MCA, IV, 17/13.
109. 'to take the Pallas, Captain Clements,' Erskine, p. 304.
109. 'not to suffer a neutral vessel', Hawke to Clevland 16 July 1759, Mackay, Hawke Papers, p. 243.
109. 'go watch and watch with the pilot', Hawke to Hervey, 3 July 1759, MCA, VI, 1/200.
110. 'nothing being dangerous besides what is shown', Remarks on the approach to Brest within Ushant made in the Monmouth in the year 1759, NMM AGC 1/28.
110. '20 ships one flag at mizen top', Baron's log, Adm/L/M/248.
110. Sir, . . . I think the ships in Brest', Hervey to Hawke 4 July 1759, Mackay, Hawke Papers, p. 239.
111. 'if they fired another [shot] I would level the Church', and the quotations following, Hervey to Hawke 8 July 1759, NA, Adm 1/91.
111. 'close to the harbour's mouth', Marcus, p. 91.
111. 'a diligent, careful, good officer', Mackay, Hawke Papers, p.32.
112. 'I send you this', Hervey to Hawke 13 July 1755, Mackay, Hawke Papers, p. 242

114. 'lay off St. Mathew's Convent & Watch the Motions', Transactions 14th July, MCA, VI, 1/257.
115. 'our fire was so brisk & the guns so well pointed', Constantine to Lepel Phipps, MCA, IV, 17/24.
115. 'their fire was very slow & very bad;' Transactions 14th July, MCA, VI, 1/257.
115. 'the *Pallas* attended them,' Baron's log, Adm/L/M/248.
115. 'Our ships received no damage,' Transactions 14th July, MCA, VI, 1/257.
115. 'I cannot help, Sir, commending to you the bravery', Hervey to Hawke 15 July 1759, Mackay, *Hawke Papers*, p. 245.
115. 'The four he has now sent to me are furnished with cargoes,' Hawke to Clevland 16 July 1759, Mackay, *Hawke Papers*, p. 243.
116. 'Order the Commissioner at Plymouth', Mackay, *Hawke Papers*, p. 243.
116. 'HM Frigate *Pallas* is arrived at Plymouth', *London Evening Post*, 21–24 July 1759.
116. ' 'Tis impossible to tell the great joy', *London Evening Post*, 24–26 July 1759.
117. 'Britannia heard the piercing voice of Fame,' *London Evening Post*, 31 July–2 Aug 1759.
117. 'I don't know whether', Constantine to Lepel Phipps, MCA, IV, 17/24.

8 A Very Honourable Employment

119. 'Great Britain for ever', *London Evening Post*, 12–14 July 1759.
119. 'received by post the disagreeable news', in Marcus, p. 73.
119. 'We are here in the utmost expectation', Mackay, *Admiral Hawke*, p. 213
120. 'after being about four months', Hutchinson, *Naval Architecture*, pp. 287–8.
122. 'They send us Beer and Water enough,' *London Evening Post*, 7–10 July 1959 (quoted in Marcus, p. 63).
122. 'Finding there were twenty-one head of cattle', Hervey to Hawke 20 July 1759, Mackay, *Hawke Papers*, p. 246.
122. Novel Arche, belonging and habitant of Conquet', enclosure to Hawke 20 July 1759, Mackay, *Hawke Papers*, pp. 246–7.
123. 'exercising their people at loosing and working their sails', Hervey to Hawke 15 July 1759, Mackay, *Hawke Papers*, p. 245.

123. 'They loomed large with the wind at east,' and the quotation following Hervey to Hawke, 21 July 1759, Mackay, *Hawke Papers*, p. 247.

124. 'The Tide slackening at Eleven, the Pilot took charge,' Letter from on board the *Monmouth* dated 22 July, *London Evening Post*, 2–4 August 1759.

124. 'obliged us to get out as fast as we could', and the quotation following Hervey to Hawke, 21 July 1759, Mackay, *Hawke Papers*, pp. 247–8.

125. 'came from St. Maloes, ten Sail in all,' Letter from on board the *Monmouth* dated 22 July, *London Evening Post*, 2–4 August 1759.

125. 'hailed the *Montague* & told them', A Copy of the Minutes Taken from the *Monmouth*'s Quarter Deck July 22nd 1759, MCA, VI, 1/260.

125. 'she answered with three loud Cheers.' Letter from on board the *Monmouth* dated 22 July, *London Evening Post*, 2–4 August 1759.

126. '*Monmouth* off Brest 22 July 1759', Hervey to Hawke, Mackay, *Hawke Papers*, p. 248.

126. 'make more sail up to us', A Copy of the Minutes Taken from the *Monmouth*'s Quarter Deck July 22nd 1759, MCA, VI, 1/260.

126. 'They would not stay for us', Letter from on board the *Monmouth* dated 22 July, *London Evening Post*, 2–4 August 1759.

127. 'to make all sail he could to get up', A Copy of the Minutes Taken from the *Monmouth*'s Quarter Deck July 22nd 1759, MCA, VI, 1/260.

127. 'The Captain Order'd the Guns to be fired that would bear', A Copy of the Minutes Taken from the *Monmouth*'s Quarter Deck July 22nd 1759, MCA, VI, 1/260.

127. 'At half past Ten, perceiving the Enemy would get in,' and the quotation following, Letter from on board the *Monmouth* dated 22 July, *London Evening Post*, 2–4 August 1759.

128. 'we concluded they were all coming out', Extract from officer on board Hawke's fleet 23 July, *London Evening Post*, 2–4 August 1759.

128. 'submitted to the Indignity', Letter from Hawke's fleet dated 22 July 1759, *London Evening Post*, 31 July–2 Aug 1759.

129. 'Never did officer show greater conduct', Hawke to Clevland 23 July 1759, Mackay, *Hawke Papers*, p. 250.

129. Your behaviour yesterday gave me the greatest satisfaction', Hawke to Hervey, 23 July 1759, Mackay, *Hawke Papers*, p. 252.

129. 'By our brave Captain, our Officers and Men', Letter from on board the *Monmouth* dated 22 July, *London Evening Post*, 2–4 August 1759.

129. 'you will I dare say be glad to hear', and the quotation following, Constantine Phipps to his father, undated, MCA, IV, 17/24.
130. 'it is you who always told me,' see John Sugden, *Nelson: A Dream of Glory* (London, 2004) pp. 121–2; Roger Knight, *The Pursuit of Victory* (London, 2005), pp. 43–4.
130. 'broke out in the greatest praise', and the quotation following, Hervey to Lepel Phipps, 25 August 1759, MCA, IV, 17/14.
132. 'I expect in about 2 years to receive ye sum of £0 s1 d3', Constantine to Lepel Phipps 11 August 1759, MCA, IV, 17/27.
133. 'on ye 27th Prince Edward Came on board', Constantine to Lepel Phipps 29 August 1759, MCA, IV, 17/29.
133. 'I dare say your Health is drunk', Lepel Phipps to Hervey 7 August 1759, MCA, IV, 8/65.
134. 'We fear we shall not be able to remain', letter from Hawke's fleet dated 11 August 1759, *London Evening Post*, 21–23 August 1759.
134. 'In case of separation by any Unavoidable Accident', plans for rendezvous From 2d Sept, MCA, VI, 1/209.
134. 'We have had lately very bad Weather,' letter from Hawke's fleet dated 6 September 1759, *London Evening Post*, 21–23 August 1759.

9 All ye Hardships that the Briney Waves is Addict'd to

135. 'God knows when we shall see you,' Hervey to Lepel Phipps 25 August 1759, MCA, IV, 17/14.
137. 'whereby he lost ye nail of the fore,' NA, Adm 82/126.
138. 'light & nourishing to the sick', Gradish, p. 159.
138. 'entirely owing to this fleet having been well supplied', Lind, *Essay*, p.121, quoted Gradish p. 168.
139. 'utmost to destroy the French ships', Hawke to Hervey 13 September 1759, MCA, VI, 1/210.
139. 'we are now Six at Anchor', letter from an officer of the Nottingham off Brest harbour to his brother in London, *London Evening Post*, 25–27 September 1759.
139. 'on ye 15th our boats conquer'd an Island', Constantine to Lepel Phipps 19 September 1759, MCA, IV, 17/30.
139. Our Captain [Lendrick] tells me that the commodore', and the quotation following, letter from an officer of the Nottingham off

Brest harbour to his brother in London, *London Evening Post*, 25–27 September 1759.

140. 'almost all the Cannons and Mortars', and the quotation following, Transactions of His Majesty's squadron stationed off Brest Harbour from the 17th: Septr: to the 20th: followg. 1759, MCA, VI, 1/212.

140. 'found that brave Commander,' letter from an officer off Brest dated 22 September 1759, *London Evening Post*, 2–4 October 1759.

141. 'I shew'd him the French Fleet', and the quotation following, Hervey to Lepel Phipps 27 August 1759, MCA, IV, 17/15.

141. 'it was a very bold undertaking', Constantine to Lepel Phipps, undated, MCA, IV, 17/32.

142. 'having row'd till near one', and the quotations following, A Letter from on board the *Achilles* Man of War, off Brest, dated October 5, *London Evening Post*, 9–11 October 1759.

143. 'the french men behaved very well', Constantine to Lepel Phipps 29 September 1759, MCA, IV, 17/33.

143. 'We found ourselves in great Danger,' and the quotation following, A Letter from on board the *Achilles* Man of War, off Brest, dated October 5, *London Evening Post*, 9–11 October 1759.

144. 'my share of which I give up', Hawke to Hervey 30 September 1759, MCA, VI, 1/213 and NMM HWK/14. £180 head money plus the value of the ship and its contents would be divided between the five ships of the squadron. The captains, however, had a quarter share between them and the Admiral another eighth which they resigned in favour of the men who took part in the raid. Fifty or so men, therefore, split three eighths of the prize money, giving them some decent token reward for their bravery. However, *Mercure* turned out to be a captured Guernsey privateer, so the captors received only half its value.

144. 'I am just returned from a furious attack', Hervey to Lepel Phipps 27 September 1759, MCA, IV, 17/15.

144. 'My dear Augustus, how can you be so rash', Lepel Phipps to Hervey 16 October 1759, MCA, IV, 8/66.

145. 'in westerly winds there is much to be feared', Hervey to Lepel Phipps 27 September 1759, MCA, IV, 17/15.

145. 'The westerly winds are now very violent,' Lepel Phipps to Hervey 16 October 1759, MCA, IV, 8/66.

146. 'You will give me leave to observe, Sir,' Hervey to Hawke 9 October 1759, Mackay, *Hawke Papers*, p. 312.

146. 'In the evening of the 11th,' Hawke to Clevland 13 October 1759, Mackay, *Hawke Papers*, p. 317.

147. 'the *Monmouth* was by a storm', Mary Hervey to Hervey 27 October 1759, Erskine, p. 307.

148. 'till I discovered the *Monmouth*,' Hawke to Clevland 21 October 1759, Mackay, *Hawke Papers*, p. 324.

148. 'I can only add that I think them exactly as they were,' Hervey to Hawke 20 October 1759, Mackay, *Hawke Papers*, p. 322.

149. 'the best remarks you have made of the soundings'. This is presumably Remarks on the approach to Brest within Ushant made in the *Monmouth* in the year 1759, NMM AGC 1/28.

149. 'It is said an express is arrived', Hervey to Hawke 23 October 1759, Mackay, *Hawke Papers*, p. 325.

149. 'I think Wolfe's memory should be forever dear', Constantine to Lepel Phipps 29 October 1759, MCA, IV, 17/35.

149. 'in a prodigious rippling of tide', Winzar's log NMM Adm/L/M/248.

149. 'We were very near being lost t'other night', and the quotation following, Constantine to Lepel Phipps 29 October 1759, MCA, IV, 17/35.

150. 'this is a Horrid place now', and the quotations following, Hervey to Lepel Phipps 1 November 1759, MCA, IV, 17/16.

151. 'Keeping the sea in the last gale of wind', Hawke to Clevland 5 November 1759, Mackay, *Hawke Papers*, p. 333.

151. 'Our marine officers', cited in *London Evening Post*, 13 December 1759.

10 Half-mad Jack Addles from the Sea

152. 'like a boiling pot', Spence, p. 13.

153. 'still in Plymouth & getting everything out Ready for ye Dock', Constantine to Lepel Phipps 8 November 1759, MCA, IV, 17/37.

153. 'I sent him away at 10 minutes Warning,' Hervey to Lepel Phipps 11 November 1759, MCA, IV, 17/18.

153. The 'state' of the ship delivered to the Port Admiral on 9 November, NA, Adm 1/802.

154. 'in its most flourishing wicked Time', Brice, p.1041.

154. 'A survey of pensions paid', NA, Adm 6/332.

155. 'whenever ye get any money paid,' Rodger, *Wooden World*, pp. 79–80.
156. 'took him by the collar and desired him to come', and the quotations following, NA, Adm 1/5298.
157. 'This Man', he wrote, 'has been Quarter Gunner,' Hervey to Clevland 18 November 1759, NA, Adm 1/1894.
158. 'Tho' an host of men were laid against me,' Edward Pickering Rich, *A Sermon Preached on Thursday, Nov. 29, 1759 Being the Day of Public Thanksgiving for the Success of His Majesty's Arms in Canada, and Taking of Quebeck,* London, 1759.
158. 'very few men would have had the nerve to hazard', Marcus, p. 162.
158. 'Providence never shew'd us more favor', Marcus, p. 172.
158. 'Their Lordships will give me leave,' Erskine, p. 310.
158. 'I am still with both feet up,' and the quotation following, Hervey to Lepel Phipps 11 November 1759, MCA, IV, 17/18.
159. 'judging it of great importance that every ship', NA, Adm 95/12, quoted in Lavery, *Ship of the Line*, I, p. 106.
163. 'May it please your Lordships', crew of *Revenge* to the Admiralty, 3 April 1760, NA, Adm 1/1895.
163. 'Having had recourse a few Days ago', ship's company of *Dragon* to Hervey, 3 April 1760, NA, Adm 1/1895.
164. 'When one goes into Rotherhithe and Wapping,' Sir John Fielding, *A Brief Description of the Cities of London and Westminster,* (London, 1776), p. xv.
166. 'The Inestimable Prolifich elixir', and the quotation following, *London Evening Post*, 25–27 September 1759 etc.
168. 'post the usual advertisements', note on turnover recording Admiralty decision on Hervey to Clevland, 3 May 1760, NA, Adm 1/1895.
169. Admiralty Office, May 5, 1760, *Public Advertiser*, 5 May 1760 (repeated on 7 and 9 May).

11 Monmouths and Dragons

170. 'that keeps the sign of the Prince of Denmark's Arms', Carkett to Clevland, 29 October 1758, NA, Adm 1/1606.
171. 'there's not a seaport in England', Rodger, *Wooden World*, p. 169.
171. 'Here is our chief encouragement,' Powell, p. 130.

171. 'In September 1759 a pitched battle', *Bristol Chronicle*, 22 September 1759 repeated in the *London Evening Post*. The account is printed in Powell, p. 206.

171. 'a man whom I could depend on', Rodger 'The Mutiny in the James & Thomas', p. 293.

172. 'the removing of those who are Vagrants', and the quotation following, Pietsch, p. 5.

176. 'Desire is that we may continue', NA, ADM 1/90ff. 257–62.

178. 'Dicker, Brown and Herbert,' NA, Adm 1/90, f.282.

178. 'they put cards to all the different ropes,' Erskine, p. 120.

180. 'fell from the maintop and expired', Hervey's log, NA, Adm 51/270.

181. 'went on shore with all his Boats,' NA, Adm 1/90 f.284.

181. '½ past 10 Cap Hervey and Harrison', NA, Adm 1/90 f.284.

183. 'surveys of the sick', NA, Adm 1/933.

183. 'I had already made enquiry', Hervey to Clevland 23 November 1760, NA, Adm 1/1895.

183. 'riots and disorders about the town', NA, Adm 1/933.

185. 'The Streets are not the cleanest,' Brice, p.1058.

185. 'Don't you see the ships a-coming?' Gardner, quoted in Rodger, *Wooden World*, pp. 135–6.

185. 'Expedition fitting out . . . so that I must go on Monday', Constantine Phipps to his father 8 October 1760, MCA, IV, 17/38.

185. 'I am now hearing all the different Opinions', Constantine Phipps to his father 15 October 1760, MCA, IV, 17/39.

12 The Island Fortress

188. 'the whole Island is a Fortification,' SROI, H.A. 67 894/B/B6.

188. 'they who know it best will scarce attempt to enter it,' Entick, V, p. 117n.

189. 'at one of the bays of Point Locmaria,' Keppel, I, p. 306.

190. On Wednesday last two Boats of a new Construction, *London Evening Post*, 27–29 April 1758.

191. 'by which accident John Adams', and the quotation following, captain's log, Adm 51/270.

193. 'a kind of amphitheatre', and the quotation following, SROI, HA67:894/B/B20.

194. 'those that attempted to land', captain's log, Adm 51/270.
194. 'who was on the poop, on board the *Dragon*', Keppel, I, p. 309.
194. 'the people got safe', captain's log, Adm 51/270.
194. 'It was to be wished they had halted there', and the quotation following, SROI, HA67:894/B/B20.
194. 'got down the Rocks again', captain's log, Adm 51/270.
194. 'We came off very well in our retreat,' Keppel, I, pp. 308–9.
194. 'several of the Boats came on board of us', captain's log, Adm 51/270.
200. 'very judiciously inclined to his left', and the quotations following, SROI, HA67:894/B/B20.
201. 'It rained prodigious hard.' Lieutenant Hamilton's notebook (National Army Museum 6707/11) quoted in Hebbert, p. 87.
202. 'decayed and broke', and the quotations following, captain's log, Adm 51/270.
203. 'has been at sea during the whole war,' NA, Adm 1/91.

13 The Remote Regions of the Earth

205. 'was surprised to find they knew mankind', Langford, p. 345.
208. 'frequently having a view of Ships', Spavens, p. 1.
210. 'I like a stupendous hill', Spavens, p. 6.
210. 'to make all the men and boys in the vessel', Spavens, p. 71.
210. 'Many of the men however chose to be duckd', Earle, p. 97.
211. 'about the length of a herring,' Spavens, p. 7.
212. 'a sad acct. it was that they had even trumped up for the public –', manuscript of Hervey's journal, SROB, 941/50/3 (not in Erskine).
216. 'You may fancy you know' and the quotation following, quoted by Corbett, p. 526.
217. 'after a great deal of labour in getting Cannon &c.' William Paget to Thomas Bennet 10 February 1762, NMM, AGC/P/16.
219. 'endeavour by every means to reduce', Rodney to Hervey, 7 February 1762, MCA VI, 1/227.
220. 'a privateer sloop that was laying inshore', Hervey's log, NA, Adm 51/270.
220. 'If any attack after this', Rodney to Hervey, 'Deliver'd by an Inhabitant of Trinity in my Appearance off there Feb 12th 1762', MCA VI, 1/229.

14 The Commodore

221. 'having reconnoitred the Ports', Rodney to Hervey, 24 February 1762, MCA VI, 1/230.
221. 'entirely at a loss for intelligence', and the quotations following, Mante, pp. 389–90
223. 'instantly to dispatch the *Levant*', Rodney to Hervey, 3 March 1762, MCA VI, 1/231.
224. 'I beg leave for reprimand him', Hervey to Clevland, 15 March 1762, NA Adm 1/1897.
225. 'to direct the boatswain in strapping of a block,' and the quotation following, Knowle.
226. 'Creoles, Mustees, Mulattas, and Negroes;' and the quotations following, Spavens, p. 112–3.
228. 'When ships are abroad they cannot get beer,' Spavens, p. 69.
228. 'not a ship comes into this port', Douglas to George Thomas, Governor of Antigua, 24 November 1760, Rodger, *Douglas Papers*, p. 259.
229. 'whereas Captain Forrest has informed me', Douglas to Hervey, 12 April 1762, MCA VI, 1/234.
230. 'John Kimblin, who is esteem'd', Shirley to Pocock, 29 March 1762, NA, Adm 1/237, printed in Syrett, *Siege and Capture*, p. 79.
231. 'I have taken two small Vessells from the Cape,' Hervey to Douglas 4 May 1762, MCA, VI, 1/237.

15 The Old Bahama Channel

237. 'having her mainmast', Syrett, *Siege and Capture*, p. 125.
237. 'I think I should determine to continue', Syrett, *Siege and Capture*, p. 126.
237. 'considering the great delay our not going', Syrett, *Siege and Capture*, p. 132.
238. 'opinion the Governor did not take', Syrett, *Siege and Capture*, p. 133.
238. ' "This," Pocock wrote angrily', Syrett, *Siege and Capture*, p. 207.
243. 'this Marine corps in Spain only wanted practice', Erskine, p. 129.
243. 'On being informed', Mante, p. 420.
248. ''Tis thought if a Descent was to be made', Brice, p. 689.

249. 'salted tortoise [turtle], eaten by seamen', Brice, p. 688.
249. 'experience in former expeditions', Admiral Charles Knowles, quoted by Corbett, p. 561.
249. 'so nigh that I heard the sentinels speak', Syrett, *Siege and Capture*, p. 185.
250. 'The observations made by the gentlemen', Syrett, *Siege and Capture*, p. 176.
251. 'Your officers are all generals,' Syrett, *Siege and Capture*, pp. 111–12.
252. 'These poor fellows had arrived the day before,' Mante, p. 424.
252. 'Since the rains have ceased,' Syrett, *Siege and Capture*, p. 200.
253. 'I believe there has not been less than sixty or seventy people', Syrett, *Siege and Capture*, p. 191.

16 The Twelfth Article of War

255. 'constantly hung up & Affixed in the most publick place', regulation noted in *Monmouth*'s muster book, NA Adm 36/6100. [repeats chap 6]
255. 'I stated all yours and my doubts', Syrett, *Siege and Capture*, p. 200.
256. 'Whereas it is judged necessary to make an attack', Keppel to Hervey 26 June 1762, MCA, VI, 1/241.
257. 'That we do visibly affect the fort', SROI461/235, Syrett, *Siege and Capture*, p. 211–12.
258. 'were to keep a cables length ahead of the *Cambridge*,' and the quotations following, Court martial of Captain James Campbell, 14–16 August 1762, NA, Adm 1/5301.
262. 'rather abaft the main chains', Hervey's log, NA, Adm 51/270.
262. 'Sir, I have the misfortune to be aground', SROI, Syrett, *Siege and Capture*, p. 213.
262. 'Sir, I have but just time to send the lieutenant of the Cambridge', Syrett, *Siege and Capture*, p. 212.
263. 'the shot flew very thick and that he stood a bad chance', and the quotations following, Court martial of Captain James Campbell, 14–16 August 1762, NA, Adm 1/5301.
264. 'hove a great strain', Hervey's log, NA, Adm 51/270.
264. 'came to *Dragon* with orders from Keppel', and the quotation following, Court martial of Captain James Campbell, 14–16 August 1762, NA, Adm 1/5301.

267. 'we felt the ship to float', and the quotation following, Hervey's log, NA, Adm 51/270.

17 The exhaling surface of the earth

270. 'singly they were equal to the undertaking', Lieutenant-General David Dundas's Memorandum on the Capture of Havana, Syrett, *Siege and Capture*, p. 318n.
270. 'No rain having fallen for the last fourteen days', and the quotations following, Mante, pp. 428–9.
272. 'The scanty supply of water exhausted their strength,' Lieutenant-Colonel Samuel Cleaveland, quoted in Syrett, *Siege and Capture*, p. xxix.
272. 'I think myself extremely happy', quoted in Lloyd and Coulter, p. 120.
272. 'flux, fever and ague were the prevailing disorders,' Lieutenant-General David Dundas's Memorandum on the Capture of Havana, Syrett, *Siege and Capture*, p. 324.
273. 'The skin acquires a dry and parched feel,' Lloyd and Coulter, p. 338.
273. 'filthness being a chief source', James Lind, quoted in Rodger, *Wooden World*, p. 106.
274. 'A great number fell victims', Mante, p. 461.
277. 'I was sent on shore with a party of Men', Hunter.
278. 'Our sea folks began a new kind of fire,' Keppel, I, p. 357.
279. 'The greatest part of those who remained', and the quotation following, Mante, p. 432.
282. 'with a sullen resolution', Mante, p. 440.

18 The Key to the Riches of Mexico

286. 'Whereas the Packet you will here with receive', Pocock to Hervey, 20 August 1762, MCA, VI, 1/242.
286. 'Thus did this conquest prove the heaviest blow', Mante, p. 460.
286. 'all their settlements in this part', Syrett, *Siege and Capture*, p. 294.
290. 'Brighton illuminated his thatched church', *Boston Newsletter*, 16 December 1762, in Russell, p. 304.

290. 'my hearty good friend', George Marsh's memoir, private collection.
290. 'The *Dragon* being very sickly', Holbourne to Clevland, 30 September 1762, NA, Adm 1/938.
291. 'a great number of marines and seamen', Hervey's log, NA, Adm 51/270.
291. 'supposed to be dying', *Dragon's* muster book, NA, Adm 36/5456.
291. interrogation of the officers of the *François Louis*, NA, HCA 32/194.
292. 'The French Privateer Frigate', Hervey to Clevland, 12 October 1762, NA, Adm 1/1897.
292. On Wednesday 3 November Peter Trapaud, NA, HCA 3/284.
293. Elizabeth Treadenham was the wife of Richard, NA, PROB 11/881 (Treadenham); Adm 32/247; PROB 11/880 (Miller); Adm 106/3019, no. 535.
293. In May 1763 they advertised to poor widows, *London Gazette*, 16 May 1763.
294. 'occasioning a lameness in his walking', and the examples following, NA, Adm 82/126.
295. that the Lords Commissioners of the Admiralty will, *London Gazette*, 17 February 1763.
295. Thomas Williams became a pensioner, NA, Adm 73/53.
296. the private seamen received a mere £3 18s. 9d.; these figures are taken from NA, Adm 68/323 which is an account of the prize money that remained unpaid in 1776. Figures for the Havana prize money vary, partly because it was paid in stages, but Adm 68/323 seems to be an authoritative set of accounts.
296. 'Notice is hereby given, the Prize Money due', *London Gazette*, 1–5 February 1763.
297. The distribution of the first part of *Dragon's* Havana prize money, *London Gazette*, 5–8 February 1763.
297. 'I looked on the list, and found John Campbell', Old Bailey Proceedings Online (www.oldbaileyonline.org, 16 April 2007), October 1763, trial of Darby Quin (t17631019–26)
298. 'when we were paying a great many ships,' Old Bailey Proceedings, July 1763, Richard Potter (t17630706–34)
298. 'when a Sloop, name unknown,' *London Gazette*, 17 February 1763.
299. 'Violent confusion on his left leg', NA, Adm 106/3019.
299. 'two silver watches, value 5 1.', Old Bailey Proceedings, April 1763, Miles Cook, Bryan Donnelly and Owen Keney (t17630413–6)

Epilogue

303. 'He has never had tolerable health', Hervey, p. 327
303. 'the half-year's tax that my detestable constitution', Hervey to George Grenville, 17 October 1767, Holmes, p. 211.
304. 'nothing particular happened', old DNB
305. '20 past 2 without any pain', MCA, IV, 8/67.
307. 'not having been given a flag', Charnock, VI, p. 404.
309. 'the Surge of the Cable', NA, Adm 82/126.
310. 'is old and infirm', NA, Adm 6/187.

Bibliography

Bury St Edmunds, Suffolk Record Office

941/50 Hervey papers
1 Letters to Augustus Hervey from Lady Mary Hervey
2 Augustus Hervey correspondence
3 Manuscript of Augustus Hervey's journal
5 Manuscript notes 1746–79
941/ 46/13–14 Diary and expenses of 1st Earl of Bristol

Ipswich, Suffolk Record Office

Keppel papers HA67/461, HA67/ 894/B/1–20

London, British Library

Add. MSS 12129 Hervey's midshipman's logs and account of Cartagena

London, National Maritime Museum

Adm/L/D 191, 192: lieutenants' logs *Dragon*
Adm/L/M/246, 247, 248, 249: lieutenants' logs, *Monmouth*
Adm 354 (in Caird Library): 160/263 request to inspect *Monmouth*'s damage 1758; 160/264 letter from the Portsmouth Officers 1758; 161/67 1758 letter from *Monmouth*'s company; 161/117 Jeffreys' superannuation

AGC/1/28 remarks on the approach to Brest within Ushant made in the *Monmouth* in the year 1759
AGC/P/16 letters from William Paget, chaplain of *Deptford* then *Marlborough*
CLE 1 papers of Captain Michael Clements of *Pallas*
1 HSR/B/8 Proceedings of the *Monmouth* 21 May 1759–20 June 1760
HWK/11 and 14 Hawke's letterbooks
KEP/2, 3 and 7 Keppel's orderbooks
MSY Marine Society; *Fair Minute Book*, MSY/A/1; *Entry Book of Boys* MSY/H/1&2&3
SIG B 8 signal book for Havana

National Archive, Kew

Adm 1
Admirals' correspondence: 90 Boscawen; 91 Keppel; 92 Hawke; 237 Pocock; 384 Osborn
Home ports: 715–8 Chatham and the Nore; 802 Plymouth; 929, 933–4 and 938 Portsmouth
Captains' correspondence: 1606 Carkett 1758; 1608 Clevland 1761; 1833 Gardiner 1756–7; 1893 Hervey 1758; 1894 Hervey 1759; 1895 Hervey 1760; 1896 Hervey 1761; 1897 Hervey 1762; 2050 Lendrick 1761; 2472 Storr 1758
Courts martial: 5297–5301, 1758–62

Adm 6
18 commission and warrant book 1751–58; 87 lieutenants' passing certificates 1753–76; 185 succession books midshipmen, chaplains, masters at arms, schoolmasters 1757–1824; 187 pursers, boatswains, gunners and carpenters applying for employment 1770–1783; 213–9 1774–1800 half pay to flag officers, captains and lieutenants; 332 Minutes of the Commissioners of the Charity for the Relief of Officers' Widows; 427 succession books midshipmen, volunteers, chaplains, masters at arms, schoolmasters 1699–1756

Adm 8
Monthly lists of disposition of ships and officers

Adm 11
39 Warrant officers black book; 65–70 1780–1832 succession books captains, commanders, lieutenants, pursers, boatswains, gunners, carpenters

Adm 12
27B Black book 1741–1793

Adm 18
105 1757–58 warrant officers' superannuation; 106 1758–9
Adm 22
56 pensions to poor widows of sea officers inc warrant offics

Adm 25
1–255 half pay lists

Adm 32
Pay books: 79 *Dragon* 1760–61; 94 *Hampton Court* 1755–8; 97 *James & Thomas* tender 1757–61; 113–15 *Monmouth* 1755–60; 257 *Dragon* 1761–70; 260 *Hussar* 1759–62; 265 *Phoenix* 1752–6; 267 *Revenge* 1755

Adm 33
Pay books: 382 *Princessa* 1742–4; 387 *Monmouth* 1742–4; 404 *Phoenix* 1743–8; 404 *Princessa* Jan 1747–8; 405 *Porcupine* 1746; 406 *Monmouth* 1745–8; 437 *Centurion* 1763–1766; 552 *Defiance* 1756; 614 *Marlborough* 1762; 616 *Monmouth* 1760–61; 636 *Dover* 1762; 661 *Monmouth* 1762–63

Adm 36
Muster books: 2048–2064 *Monmouth* 1742–51; 2641–2 *Porcupine* 1746; 5019 *Baltimore* 1762; 5160–3 *Centurion* 1763–9; 5454–6 *Dragon* 1760–62; 5984 *Ludlow Castle* 1757; 8696 *Queen* 1778; 5528 *Echo* 1762; 5818–5821 *Hampton Court* 1755–8; 6375–6 *Prince* 1757; 6478 *Revenge* 1758; 7162 *James and Thomas* HT 1757–62; 7242 *Fly* cutter 1769; 4997–9 *Royal Ann* 1760–61; 6794–6 *Royal Sovereign* 1759–1761; 5741 *Hornet*; 6064–5; 6094–6104 *Monmouth* 1755–63; 6547–54

Adm 43
Head money vouchers: 14–21, 1757–64

Adm 49
35 Abstracts of Slop contracts 1760–

Adm 51
Captains' logs: 270 *Dragon* 1760–62; 458 *Hornet* 1760; 782 *Revenge* 1758; 3912–6 *Monmouth* 1758–63; 4265 *Monmouth* 1755–7

Adm 52
Masters' logs: 383 *Dragon* 1760–62; 657 *Monmouth* 1757–9; 949 *Monmouth* 1759–63

Adm 68
Unclaimed prize money 322: 1756–70; 323: 1762–6

Adm 73
Greenwich Hospital: 36–39 general entry books; 73/52 rough entry book 1756–79

Adm 82
Chatham chest: 78–82 payments to pensioners 1758–63; 126 and 127 certificates for wounds

Adm 101
Surgeons' journals: 85/7 *Ardent* 1797–8

Adm 102
Hospital musters: 374 Haslar deaths of seamen 1755–65; 399 inventory of drugs 1758

Adm 106
1119/120 copper pots to Robert Smith 1757; 1122/17 carpenter's defects 1763; 1123/42 leave for purser 1763; 1123/156 *Dragon* fitted as guardship; 1130/45 ticket for 909 Robert Billing deceased; 2896–7 succession books 1733–55 masters, surgeons, sailmakers; 2898 1764–84 pursers, boatswains, gunners, carpenters; 2972 list of officers on leave 1762–74; 3017 bounty for seamen slain in fight with the enemy 1742–82; 3019 bounty list of relatives of men killed in action 1751–82

Adm 107

Lieutenants' passing certificates: 3 1712–45; 4 1745–57; 5 1757–62; 6 1762–77 James Baker 107/5 38; Samuel Ball 107/5, 87; Samuel Blow 107/5, James Baron 107/4 379; Henry Bryne 107/5; Robert Carkett 107/3, 501; St John Chinnery 107/4 292; Michael Clement 107/4 334; Peter Foulkes 107/3, 257; Stephen Hammick 107/3, 547; Joseph Hanby 107/4 312; John Henderson 107/4 359; Archibald Hewson 107/4 430; Lancelot Holmes 107/4; George Johnstone 107/4 210; Dandy Kidd 107/5 102; George Knight 107/4 298; John McLaurin 107/5 p.109; William Osborn 107/4 142; John Robinson 107/5 86; James Samber 107/5 222

Adm 118

230–2 marine officers 1757–60

Adm 158

Marine description books

1 Cos 53–80 A–Z 1755–62; 2 Cos 1–46 1755–73; 3 Cos 1–46 1755–82; 4 Cos 71–155 1756–83; 283 Plymouth 18–39 Cos A–Z 1763–83

HCA 3/284

Prize court proceedings: *François Louis*, *Mercure*, five French barks

HCA 32

Prize papers and interrogations: 194 *François Louis*; 219 box 1 *Mercure*; 228 five French barks name unknown

PROB 11

804 William Lee; 833 Robert Fox; 838 Thomas Pattison; 839 John Husbands, John Ayres; 840 Richard Hawkey, Robert Fowler, James Powell, Arthur Gardiner; 841 Marmaduke Johns; 842 William Tozer, Edward Lund, James Crips; 843 Robert Ball, Richard Taylor, John Pidler; 844 Richard Hobb, William Alford, Robert Kiddy, William Crossman(2); 845 Robert Spencer; 846 Richard Treby, Henry Harrison; 848 Robert Row; 849 Thomas Tucker, John Harris; 851 Thomas Fisher; 853 John Davis; 855 John Broadmead, James Nagle; 862 John Davies; 868 Richard Legg; 869 Jean Smith; 871 William Oberg; 877 Edmond Maguire; 880 John Henderson, John Trobridge, Thomas Tapliss, John Cheshire, James

Miller, James Sutherland; 881 Joseph Jover, Richard Treadenham, William Ward, Peter Knight, James Kieff, John Cole, Joseph Handley, Richard Tench; 882 John Matthews, William Cradle, Thomas Whitehall, Samuel Parks, Mathew Hubbard, Vincent Brown, William Arter, Thomas Streaky, John Barker, David Belford; 883 William Watson, John Broad, David Edwards; 884 Walter Caldwell, Archibald Huston otherwise Houison, Alexander Mowet, Obadiah Rigging; 886 Henry Goosewyn, James Lindsey, James Stuart, William Tizzard; 887 John Curtis (2), Richard Wright; 895 Walter Bartlett, George Grumble or Grumbly, John Kayton; 897 File Fewin, Tiede Nichols; 898 Samuel Steele; 899 Edward Chicken; 901 John Evans, William Cook, Ninian Dunbar; 914 Richard Hughes; 920 John Pray; 921 Archibald Clevland, John Connor; 946 John Wills; 949 Daniel Walkely; 976 Dandy Kidd; 991 John Phillips (3); 1051 Richard Meager; 1054 Archibald Simonton; 1073 John Lendrick; 1077 Edward Salmon; 1080 Stephen Hammick; 1081 Robert Carkett; 1093 Peter Foulkes; 1095 Samuel Ball; 1135 Lancelot Holmes; 1151 Saint John Chinnery; 1151 Robert Leaver; 1175 John White; 1240 Hon Philip Stopford; 1244 Robert Kennedy; 1262 George Fennell; 1319 James Perrott; 1376 Samuel Blow; 1382 John Wilson; 1418 Reverend William Howdell; 1469 John Robinson; 1480 James Baron; 1581 James Samber

PROB 31
598/489 Samuel Furzer

T 1/493/272–273 letter from Thomas Mante with memorial of his career 1772

London, Wellcome Institute library

MSS 7628–9 scrapbooks of George Marsh, Commissioner of the Navy and Director of Greenwich Hospital, 1760s–90s

Mulgrave Castle Archive, Lythe near Whitby

IV, 8 letters to Lepel Phipps from Augustus Hervey

IV, 17 letters to Lepel and Constantine Phipps senior from Augustus Hervey and Constantine John Phipps
VI, 1 Augustus Hervey's naval papers (hitherto thought to have been lost)
VI, 10 letters from Constantine John Phipps

Southsea, Royal Marines Museum

7/4/1 Rea, Andrew, *General Orders on the Camp at Belle Isle*
11/13/313 Lt Robert Lloyd's order book as adjutant to one of the two marine battalions at Martinique

Private Collection

Diary of George Marsh

Contemporary Newspapers and Periodicals

London Evening News 1758–9
London Gazette 1761–3
Public Advertiser 1763
Gentleman's Magazine 1758–63
Universal Magazine 1758
Annual Register 5 Oct 1759 (attack on *Mercure*)
Notes and Queries, XI, p. 342 (12 May 1855) explanation of the name of a pub in Lostwithiel, the Memorable Battle of the Monmouth and Foudroyant

Books and Journals

Acerra, Martine, J. Merino and Jean Meyer eds., *Les marines de guerre européennes XVII–XVIIIe siècles*, Paris 1985
Acerra, Martine and André Zysberg, *L'Essor des Marines de Guerres Européennes (vers 1680-vers 1790)*, Paris 1997

Agay, Frédéric d', 'Un episode navale de la guerre de sept ans', Marins et Oceans, II, http://www.statisc.org/pu6_MOZ_DAGAYGUER.html

Anderson, Fred, *Crucible of War*, New York and London 2000

Anon, *A Soldier's Journal*, London 1770

Regulations and instructions relating to His Majesty's Service at sea, 6th edn, London 1746

Atkins, John, *The Navy Surgeon; or, practical System of Surgery*, London 1742

Bares, Albert c. ed., *The two Putnams Israel and Rufus in the Havana expedition 1762 and in the Mississippi River exploration 1772–73 with some account of the company of Military Adventurers*, Hartford 1931

Barrow, Tony, 'The Crewing of Arctic Whalers in the Eighteenth Century: the Evidence of the Shields Muster Rolls', in *Lisbon as a Port Town, the British Seaman and other Maritime Themes*, ed. S. Fisher, Exeter Maritime Studies 2, Exeter 1988

ed., *Pressgangs and Privateers*, Whitley Bay 1993

Baugh, Daniel, *British Naval Administration in the Age of Walpole*, Princeton 1965

Baynham, Henry, *From the Lower Deck*, London 1969

Beatson, Robert, *Naval and Military Memoirs of Great Britain from 1727 to 1783*, 6 vols, London 1804

Black, Jeremy, *Pitt the Elder*, Cambridge 1992

Black, Jeremy and Philip Woodfine eds, *The British Navy and the use of Naval Power in the Eighteenth Century*, Leicester 1988

Boudriot, Jean, *Le Vaisseau de 74 Canons*, 4 vols., Paris 1986–8

Brewer, John, *The Sinews of Power: War, Money and the English State, 1688–1783*, London 1989

Brice, Andrew, *The Grand Gazetteer: or, Topographic Dictionary, both general and special, and ancient as well as modern*, Exeter 1759

Bromley, J. S., *Corsairs and Navies 1660–1760*, London 1987

Brooks, Richard, *The Royal Marines: 1664 to the present*, London 2002

Buchet, Christian, *La Lutte pour l'espace Caraïbe et la façade atlantique de l'Amérique centrale et du sud (1672–1763)*, 2 vols., Paris 1991

Marine, Économie et Société; Un exemple d'interaction: l'avitaillement de la Royal Navy durant la guerre de sept ans, Paris 1999

Carpenter, Kenneth J., *The History of Scurvy and Vitamin C*, Cambridge 1986

Chancellor, E. B., *The Pleasure Haunts of London*, London 1925

Charnock, John, *Biographia Navalis*, 6 vols., London 1794–8

Clowes, William Laird, *The Royal Navy: A History from the Earliest Times to the Present*, 7 vols., London 1897–1903

Coldham, Peter Wilson, *The Complete Book of Emigrants in Bondage, 1614–1775*, Baltimore 1988

Bonded Passengers to America, Baltimore 1983

Emigrants in chains: a social history of forced emigration to the Americas 1607–1776, Stroud 1992

Cole, Richard Cargill, *Thomas Mante: Writer, Soldier, Adventurer*, New York 1993

Collinge, J.M., *Navy Board Officials, 1660–1832*, London 1978

Corbett, Sir Julian, *The Seven Years War: a Study in British Combined Strategy*, London 1907 (Folio Society Edn, ed. Jeremy Black, 2001)

Cormack, Alan and Alan Jones, eds., *The Journal of Corporal William Todd 1745–1762*, Army Records Society vol. 18, Stroud 2001

Creswell, John, *British Admirals of the Eighteenth Century: Tactics in Battle*, London 1972

Crewe, Duncan, *Yellow Jack and the Worm: British Naval administration in the West Indies 1739–1748*, Liverpool 1993

Crouzet, Francois, 'The Second Hundred Years War: Some Reflections', *French History*, X, (1996), pp. 432–50

Cust, Lionel, *History of the Society of Dilettanti: reissued with supplementary chapter, additional list of members*, edited by Sir Sidney Colvin, London 1914

Distad, N. Merrill, 'Jonas Hanway and the Marine Society', *History Today*, XXIII (1973), pp. 434–40

Dobson, Jessie, *John Hunter*, Edinburgh and London 1969

Drummond, J. C. and A Wilbraham, *The Englishman's Food*, London 1939

Duffy, Michael, *Soldiers, Sugar and Seapower*, Oxford 1987

Earle, Peter, *Sailors: English Merchant Seamen 1650–1775*, London 1998

Eder, Markus, *Crime and Punishment in the Royal Navy of the Seven Years' War, 1755–1763*, Aldershot 2004

Ekins, Sir Charles, *Naval Battles from 1744 to the Peace of 1814*, London 1824

Entick, John, *General History of the Late War*, 5 vols, London 1763

Erskine, David ed., *Augustus Hervey's Journal: being the Intimate Account of the Life of a Captain in the Royal Navy Ashore and Afloat 1746–1759*, London 1953

Falconer, William, *An Universal Dictionary of the Marine*, London 1769

Fraser, Edward, *Famous Fighters of the Fleet: Glimpses through the cannon smoke in the days of the Old Navy*, London 1907

Gardner, J. A., *Above and Under Hatches*, ed. C. C. Lloyd, London 1955
Gill, Crispin, *Plymouth: A New History*, Tiverton 1993
Gradish, Stephen F., *The Manning of the British Navy during the Seven Years' War*, London 1980
Harland, John, *Seamanship in the Age of Sail*, London 1984
Hart, Francis Russell, *The Siege of Havana, 1762*, London 1931
Hebbert, F. J., 'The Belle-Isle Expedition of 1761', *Journal of the Society for Army Historical Research*, 64 (1986), pp. 83–92
Henderson, T., *Disorderly Women in Eighteenth-Century London*, London 1999
Hervey, M., *Letters of Mary Lepel*, London 1821
Holmes, Michael R. J., *Augustus Hervey: A Naval Casanova*, Bishop Auckland 1996
Hume, J. A. ed., *Letters and Journals of Lady Mary Coke*, Edinburgh 1889–96
Hunter, William, *The Memoirs of a Veteran Officer*, London 1805
Hutchinson, William, *A Treatise on Practical Seamanship*, Liverpool 1777 (facsimile 1979)
A Treatise on Naval Architecture, Liverpool 1994
Jackson, Robert, *An Outline of the history and Cure of Fever, Endemic and Contagious . . . of the West Indies*, Edinburgh 1798
Jenkins, Ernest Harold, *A History of the French Navy*, London 1973
Kennedy, Paul M., *The Rise and Fall of British Naval Mastery*, London 1976
Keppel, Sonia, *Three Brothers at Havana, 1762*, Salisbury 1981
Keppel, Thomas, *Life of Augustus Viscount Keppel*, 2 vols., London 1842
Knowles, Charles, *An Essay on the Duty and Qualifications of a Sea-Officer*, London 1765; http://www.bruzelius.info/nautica/personnel/knowles (1765).html
Langford, Paul, *A Polite and Commercial People: England 1727–1783*, Oxford 1992
Lavery, Brian, *The Ship of the Line*, 2 vols., London, 1983–4
The Arming and Fitting of English Ships of War 1600–1815, London 1987
Shipboard Life and Organisation 1731–1815, Navy Records Society vol. 138, 1998
Linebaugh, Peter, *The London Hanged: Crime and Civil Society in the Eighteenth Century*, London 1991
Lloyd, C. and J. L. S. Coulter, *Medicine and the Navy, 1200–1900: Vol. Ill, 1715–1815*, Edinburgh 1961
Lloyd, Christopher ed., 'Boscawen's letters to his Wife 1755–56', *The Naval Miscellany* vol 4. Navy Records Society, 1952

Long, W. H., *Naval Yarns*, London 1899

Lyon, David, *The Sailing Navy List: All the Ships of the Royal Navy – Built, Purchased and Captured, 1688–1860*, London 1993

McCreery, Cindy, 'True Blue and Black, Brown and Fair: prints of sailors and their women during the Revolutionary and Napoleonic Wars', *British Journal for Eighteenth-Century Studies*, XXIII (2000), pp. 135–52

MacIntire, John, *A Military Treatise on the Discipline of the Marine Forces, When at Sea, Together with Short Instructions for Detachments to attack on Shore*, 1763

Mackay, Ruddock F., *Admiral Hawke*, Oxford 1965

    ed., *The Hawke Papers: a Selection 1743–1771*, Navy Records Society, 1990

McLynn, Frank, *1759: The Year Britain became Master of the World*, London 2004

Mante, Thomas, *The history of the late war in North-America, and the islands of the West-Indies, including the campaigns of MDCCLXIII and MDCCLXIV against His Majesty's Indian enemies*, London 1772

Marcus, Geoffrey, *Quiberon Bay*, London 1960

Marsden, R.G., *Documents Relating to the Law and Custom of the Sea*, Navy Records Society, vols. 49–50

Marshall, John, *Royal Naval Biography*, 8 vols., London 1823–35

Middleton, Richard, *The Bells of Victory*, Cambridge 1985

Molyneux, Thomas, *Conjunct Expeditions that have been carried on jointly by the Fleet and Army, with a Commentary on Littoral War*, London 1759

Monks, Sarah, 'Our man in Havanna: representation and reputation in Lieutenant Philip Orsbridge's Britannia's Triumph (1765)' in John Bonehill and Geoff, Quilley *Conflicting Visions: War and visual culture in Britain and France c. 1700–1830*, London 2005, pp. 85–114

Moore, Lucy, *Amphibious thing: the life of Lord Hervey*, London 2000

Morriss, Roger, *Guide to British Naval Papers in North America*, London 1994

Mountaine, William, *The Seaman's Vade-Mecum*, London 1767

Mundy, G. B. M., *Life and Correspondence of the late Admiral Lord Rodney*, 2 vols., London 1830

Dann, John C. ed., *The Nagle Journal: a diary of the life of Jacob Nagle, sailor, from the year 1775 to 1841*, London 1988

Nichelson, William, *A Treatise on Practical Navigation and Seamanship*, London 1792

O'Connell, Sheila, *London 1753*, exh. cat., London, British Museum, 2003

O'Loghlan, Lt Terence, *The Marine Volunteer containing the Exercises, Firings and Evolutions of a Battalion of Infantry to which is added Sea Duty and a Supplement* London 1764

Pares, Richard, *War and Trade in the West Indies (1739–1763)*, Oxford 1936

Phillips, Hugh, *The Thames about 1750*, London 1951

Mid-Georgian London: A Topographical and Social Survey of Central and Western London about 1750, London 1954

Pietsch, Roland, 'Urchins for the Sea : The Story of the Marine Society in the Seven Years War', *Journal for Maritime Research*, December 2000

Pocock, Tom, *Battle for Empire: The very First World War 1756–63*, London 2002

Pointon, Marcia, 'The Lives of Kitty Fisher', *British Journal for Eighteenth-Century Studies*, 27 (2004), pp. 77–98

Powell, J. W. Darner, *Bristol Privateers and Ships of War*, Bristol 1930

Pritchard, James, 'The French Navy, 1748–1762; Problems and Perspectives', in Robert William Love ed., *Changing Interpretations and New Sources in Naval History*, New York 1980

Robinson, Charles, N., *The British Tar in Fact and Fiction*, London 1909

Roddis, L. H., *James Lind: Founder of Nautical Medicine*, London 1951

Rodger, N.A.M., *The Wooden World: an Anatomy of the Georgian Navy*, London 1986

'The inner life of the Navy, 1750–1800 change or decay?' in *Guerres et Paix 1600–1815*, Vincennes 1987

'Shipboard Life in the Georgian Navy, 1750–1800; the Decline of the Old Order?' in Lewis R. Fischer et al eds., *The North Sea: Twelve Essays on Social History of Maritime Labour*, Stavanger 1992, pp.29–39

'The Douglas Papers, 1760–62', in *The Naval Miscellany* vol. 5, Navy Records Society

The Insatiable Earl: A Life of John Montagu, Fourth Earl of Sandwich, 1718–1792, London 1993

'The Mutiny in the James & Thomas', *Mariner's Mirror*, LXX, (1984), pp.293–8

'Devon Men and the Navy, 1688–1815', in *The New Maritime History of Devon*, ed. Michael Duffy et al., London 1992, I, pp. 209–15

The Command of the Ocean, London 2004

Russell, Nelson Vance, 'The Reaction in England and America to the Capture of Havana, 1762', *Hispanic American Historical Review*, 9 (1929), pp. 303–316

Smith, William James ed., *The Grenville papers: being the correspondence of Richard Grenville, Earl Temple, K.G., and the Right Hon. George Grenville, their friends and contemporaries*, London 1852–1853

Spavens, William, *The Narrative of William Spavens a Chatham Pensioner*, 1796, reprint London 1998

Spence, Jack, *Nelson's Avenger: The Life of Commander John Pollard RN of Cawsand, Cornwall*, Plymouth 2005

Spinney, D., *Rodney*, London 1969

Stark, Suzanne J., *Female Tars: Women aboard Ship in the Age of Sail*, London 1996

Starkey, David J. *British Privateering Enterprise in the Eighteenth Century*, Exeter 1990

Stuart, Dorothy M., *Molly Lepel*, London 1936

Syrett, David, 'American Provincials and the Havana Campaign of 1762', *New York History*, 49 (1968), pp. 375–390

'The British Landing at Havana: An Example of an Eighteenth-Century Combined Operation', *Mariner's Mirror*, 55 (1969), pp. 325–331

The siege and capture of Havana 1762, Navy Records Society, 114, 1970

The Rodney Papers: Volume I, 1742–1763. Selections from the Correspondence of Admiral Lord Rodney, Navy Records Society, 148, 2005

and R. L. DiNardo eds, *Commissioned Sea Officers of the Royal Navy*, Aldershot 1994

Taillemite, Étienne, *L'Histoire ignorée de la marine française*, Paris 1988

Dictionnaire des marins français, 2nd edn, Paris 2002

Taylor, E.G.R., *The Mathematical Practitioners of Hanoverian England*, Cambridge 1966

Taylor, Gordon, *The Sea Chaplains*, Oxford 1978

Thompson, Edward, *A Sailor's Letters*, 2nd edn, 2 vols., London 1767

Thursfield, H.G. ed., *Five Naval Journals 1789–1817*, Navy Records Society, XCI, 1951

Waddington, Richard, *La Guerre de Sept Ans*, 5 vols., Paris 1899–1914

Wheeler, D., 'A climatic reconstruction of the Battle of Quiberon Bay, 20 November 1759', *Weather*, 50 (1995), pp. 230–239

'The weather vocabulary of an eighteenth-century mariner: the logbooks of Nicholas Pocock, 1740–1821', *Weather*, 50 (1995), pp. 298–304

Williams, Glynn, *The Prize of all the Oceans: the Triumph and Tragedy of Anson's Voyage Round the World*, London 1999

Index

Achilles, the, 133, 140, 142, 143, 144, 153
  Belle Isle and, 190, 192, 193ill, 194, 197
Active, the (frigate), 310
'Admiral Hosier's Ghost' (ballad), 210
Admiralty, the, 62, 90, 96, 116, 157
  Doctor's Commons (Court), 292
  Dragon crew and, 163, 168–9, 225
  Monmouth crew and, 83, 84, 86, 88, 92
  see also Anson, George (First Lord of the Admiralty);
    Clevland, John (Admiralty secretary)
Adventurer, the (tender), 219
Africa, 150
Aix-la-Chapelle, Treaty of (1748), 51
Alarm, the (frigate), 239, 240, 244
Albemarle, General Lord, 234, 245, 247, 250–3,
  250ill
  El Morro siege and, 252, 253, 270, 277, 279
  Havana and, 235, 241, 248, 284–5, 287, 296
Alcide, the, 207, 230, 232
alcohol, 107ill, 122, 135–6, 137, 155, 156
  the Caribbean and, 211, 228–9
Ambuscade, the, 70, 72ill, 73
America, 231, 235, 238, 296, 305, 306
  Franco-British conflict, 1, 5, 57, 133
  troop convoy to Caribbean, 229–30, 232, 234, 238,
    282–3
  troops from, 212, 245, 246, 281, 287–8
Amherst, General Sir Jeffrey, 251
Andromeda, the, 306
animals on board ship, 40, 138, 139–40, 288
Anson, George (First Lord of the Admiralty), 5, 52ill,
  83, 99, 105, 132
  circumnavigation, 52, 120, 160, 188, 300
  followers of, 51–2, 60, 188
  Havana invasion plans, 234, 236
Anson, the, 92, 151
Antigua, 226, 229
Antilles islands, 223
Antony (Cornwall), 7, 36
Aquilon, the (frigate), 196, 213, 223
Arc-en-Ciel, the, 79
aristocracy, British, 7, 78
army, British *see* British army
articles of war, 32, 43, 90, 109, 156–7, 254–5, 268–9
artillery *see* guns
artists, 191, 193ill, 197
Augusta (Princess of Wales), 50, 86
Austin, Joseph (marine captain), 19, 21, 46, 107, 177,
  185, 198
Austria, 57, 61, 66, 67

Austrian Succession, War of the, 50, 51
Ayres, John (master sailmaker), 15, 24, 40

Bacchus, the (snow), 79
Bahama Channel, Old, 231, 236–40, 239ill, 282
Baillie, Captain Thomas, 75
Ball, Samuel (master's mate), 90–1, 113, 306
Baltimore, the (sloop), 309
Banks, Joseph, 210–11, 307
Barbados, 208, 211–12, 233
Barcelona, 77, 209
Barfleur, the (second-rate), 157, 308
Baron, Lieutenant James, 8, 62, 78, 90, 176, 310–11
  blockade of Brest, 107, 110–11, 114, 115, 116, 139
  Foudroyant and, 17, 20, 25, 28, 29–30, 46
Barrington, the, 197
Barrow, Lieutenant John, 259, 260–1
Barton, Captain, 190, 191, 192
Basilisk, the (bomb ship), 218, 221, 245, 247
Beauclerk, George, 198, 199
beer, 122, 135–6, 137, 228
Belle Isle (off Brittany), 186, 187, 188–204, 189ill,
  192ill, 193ill, 216
Bellerophon, the, 122
Bellin, Jacques-Nicolas, 113ill, 125ill, 131ill, 189ill,
  192ill
Bellona class, 159
Bellona, the (guard ship), 308
Beniguet, island of, 113ill, 114, 122
Bergen, battle of (13 April 1759), 98
Bernier, George (captain's clerk), 18–19
Berwick, the, 3, 4, 14, 42, 162
Bienfaisant, the, 80, 149, 153
  in Hervey's squadron, 108, 133, 140, 141, 146, 148
black people
  Caribbean inhabitants, 226–8
  naval crew, 22–3, 226
  slavery and, 217, 227–8, 231
Black Rocks, the (Brest), 110, 126, 133, 138, 140, 146,
  148, 149
Blackstakes (near Chatham), 84, 94, 95ill
Blake, John, 55, 90, 300, 305
  the *Dragon*, 177, 209, 296
  the *Monmouth*, 62, 136–7, 148
Blakeney, Governor (of Minorca), 58
Blénac, Comte de (Charles de Courbon), 213, 223–4
Blenheim, the (hospital ship), 182
Blow, Samuel, 42, 55, 63, 100, 176, 306
bomb ships, 11, 190, 191–2, 197, 201, 208, 218, 238,
  247

367